FIRE FORCE

12

ATSUSH
OHKUB

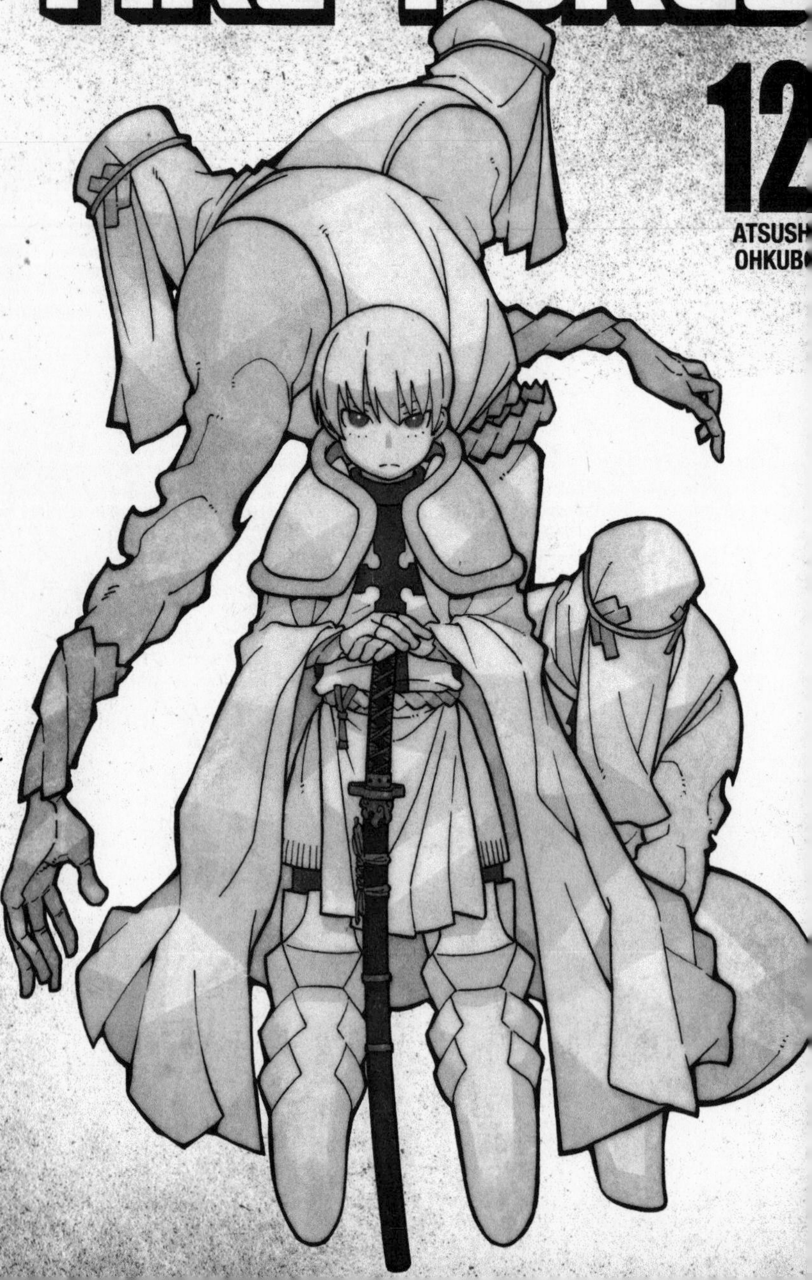

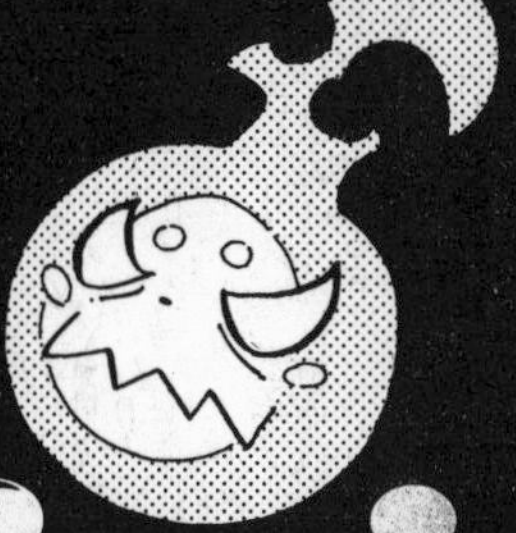

offering to world?

VOL. 12

ATSUSHI OHKUBO

What if you
were
the burn
needed
save the

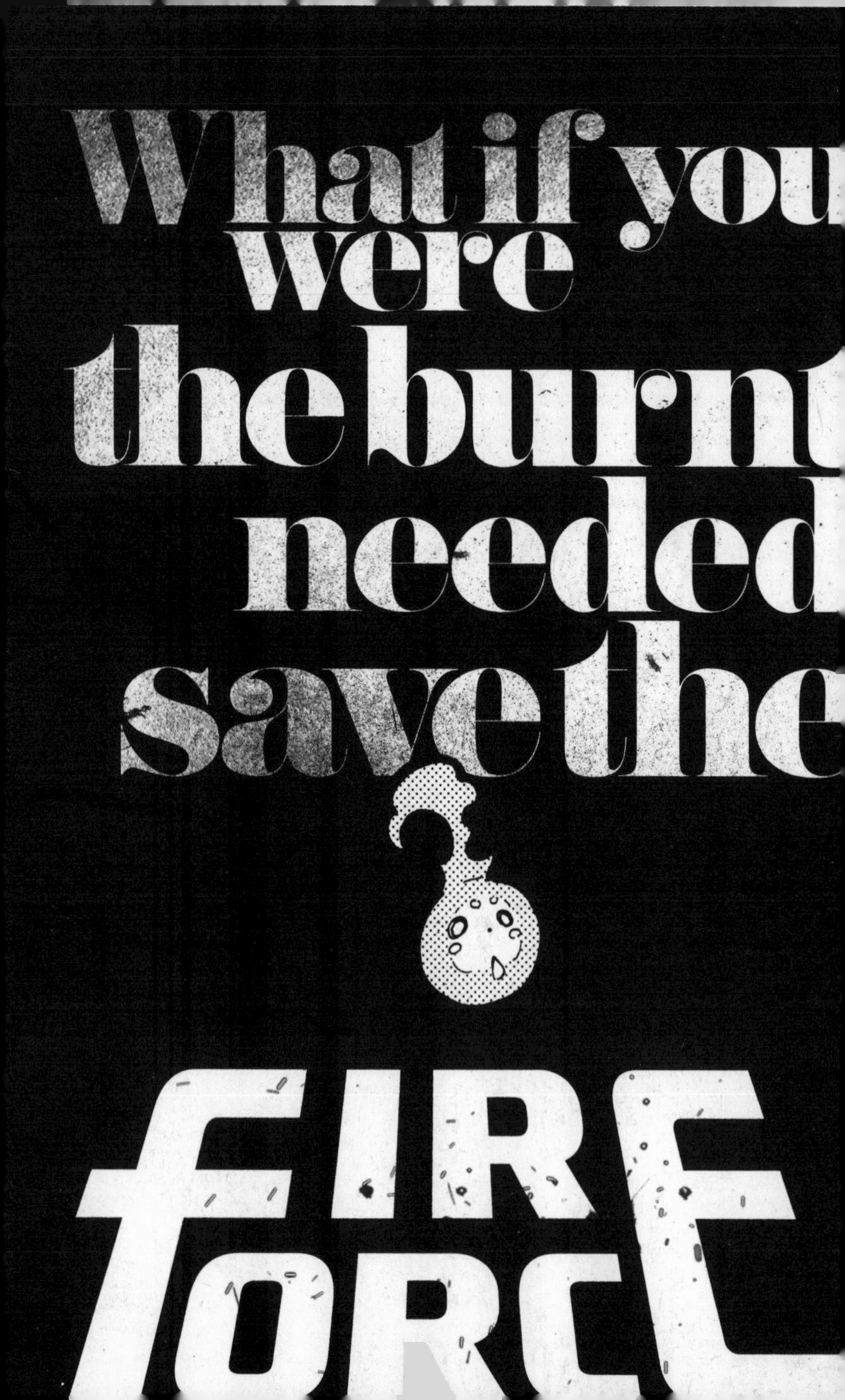

FIRE
FORCE

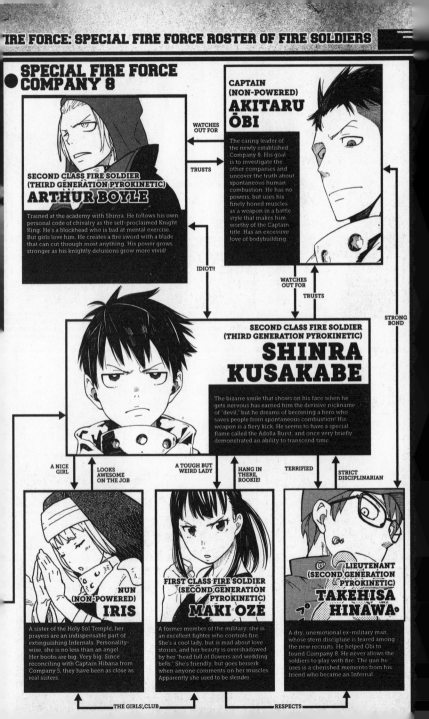

SPECIAL FIRE FORCE COMPANY 8

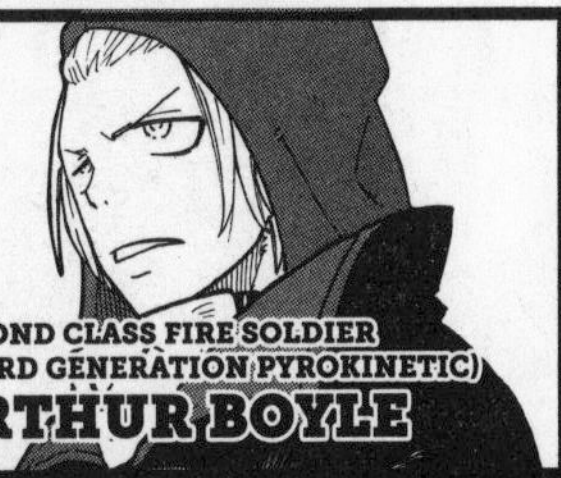

SECOND CLASS FIRE SOLDIER (THIRD GENERATION PYROKINETIC)

ARTHUR BOYLE

Trained at the academy with Shinra. He follows his own personal code of chivalry as the self-proclaimed Knight King. He's a blockhead who is bad at mental exercise. But girls love him. He creates a fire sword with a blade that can cut through most anything. His power grows stronger as his knightly delusions grow more vivid!

WATCHES OUT FOR

TRUSTS

CAPTAIN (NON-POWERED)

AKITARU ŌBI

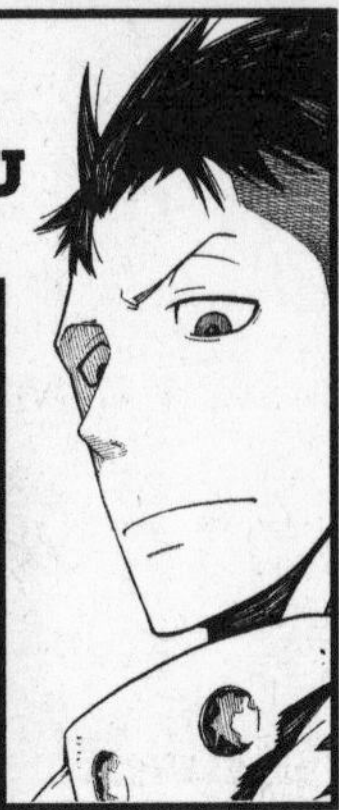

The caring leader of the newly established Company 8. His goal is to investigate the other companies and uncover the truth about spontaneous human combustion. He has no powers, but uses his finely honed muscles as a weapon in a battle style that makes him worthy of the Captain title. Has an excessive love of bodybuilding.

IDIOT!!

WATCHES OUT FOR

TRUSTS

STRONG BOND

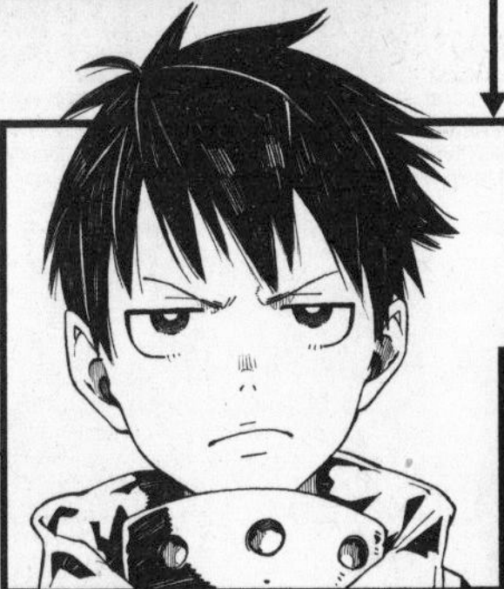

SECOND CLASS FIRE SOLDIER (THIRD GENERATION PYROKINETIC)

SHINRA KUSAKABE

The bizarre smile that shows on his face when he gets nervous has earned him the derisive nickname of "devil," but he dreams of becoming a hero who saves people from spontaneous combustion! His weapon is a fiery kick. He seems to have a special flame called the Adolla Burst, and once very briefly demonstrated an ability to transcend time.

A NICE GIRL

LOOKS AWESOME ON THE JOB

A TOUGH BUT WEIRD LADY

HANG IN THERE, ROOKIE!

TERRIFIED

STRICT DISCIPLINARIAN

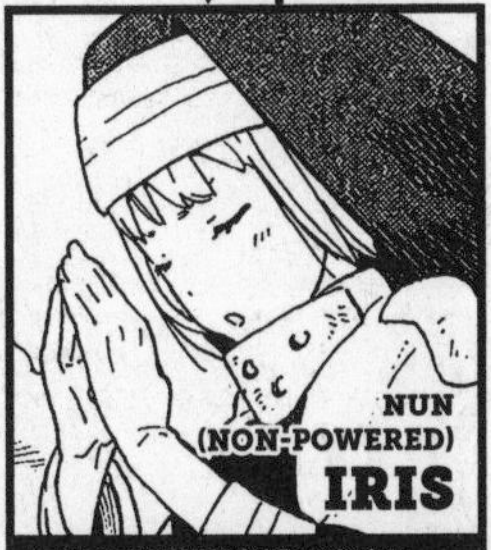

NUN (NON-POWERED)

IRIS

A sister of the Holy Sol Temple, her prayers are an indispensable part of extinguishing Infernals. Personality-wise, she is no less than an angel. Her boobs are big. Very big. Since reconciling with Captain Hibana from Company 5, they have been as close as real sisters.

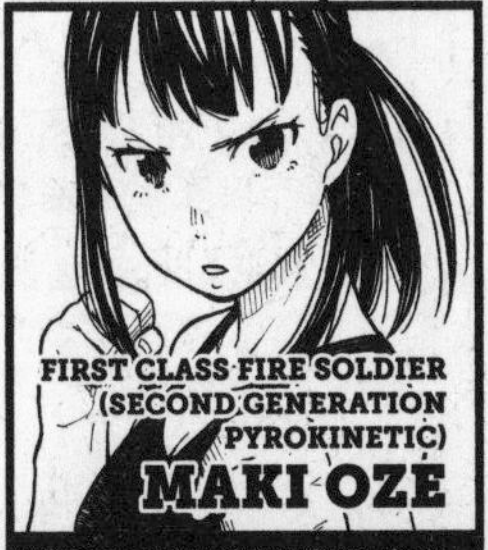

FIRST CLASS FIRE SOLDIER (SECOND GENERATION PYROKINETIC)

MAKI OZE

A former member of the military, she is an excellent fighter who controls fire. She's a cool lady, but is mad about love stories, and her beauty is overshadowed by her "head full of flowers and wedding bells." She's friendly, but goes berserk when anyone comments on her muscles. Apparently she used to be slender.

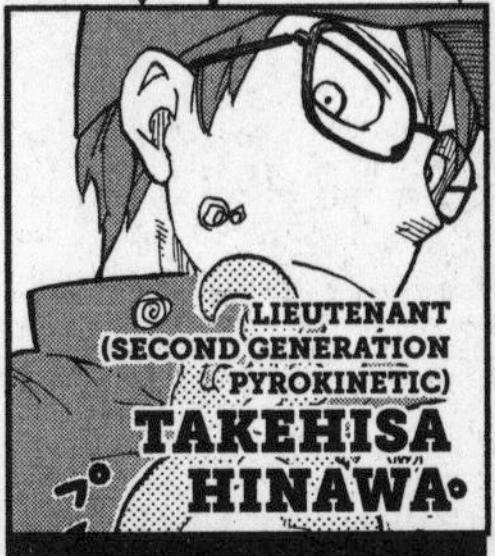

LIEUTENANT (SECOND GENERATION PYROKINETIC)

TAKEHISA HINAWA

A dry, unemotional ex-military man, whose stern discipline is feared among the new recruits. He helped Ōbi to found Company 8. He never allows the soldiers to play with fire. The gun he uses is a cherished memento from his friend who became an Infernal.

THE GIRLS' CLUB

RESPECTS

SPECIAL FIRE FORCE COMPANY 4

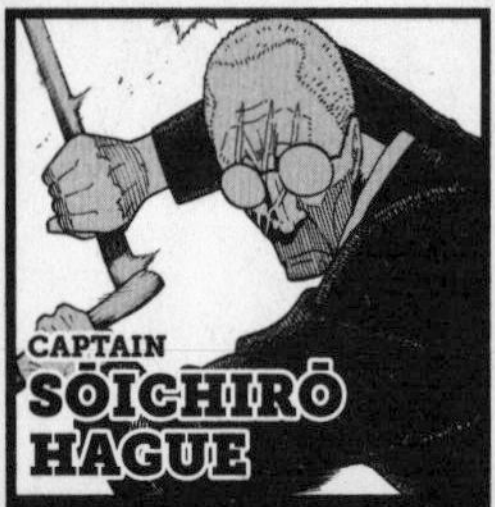

CAPTAIN
SŌICHIRŌ HAGUE

There are rumors that he has changed since his close encounter with an Adolla Burst, but he is normally a lovable old man. He just likes a little bit of pain, that's all.♥ He is loved and respected by his company.

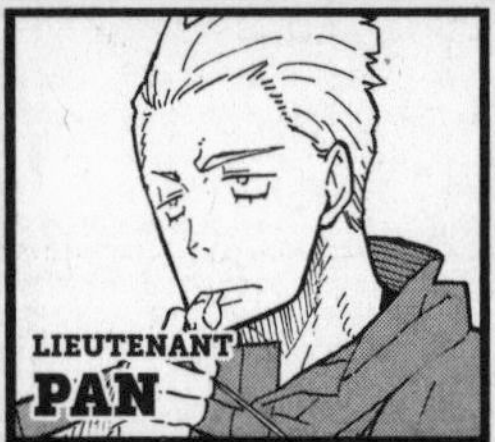

LIEUTENANT
PAN

Served as Shinra and Arthur's instructor at the academy. The Fire Force's greatest master of status enhancements.

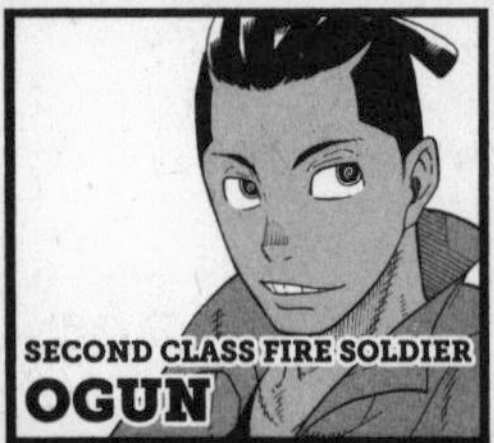

SECOND CLASS FIRE SOLDIER
OGUN

A friend of Shinra and Arthur's from the academy, and top of his class. A good-natured and friendly soldier who controls fire spears.

FOLLOWERS OF THE EVANGELIST

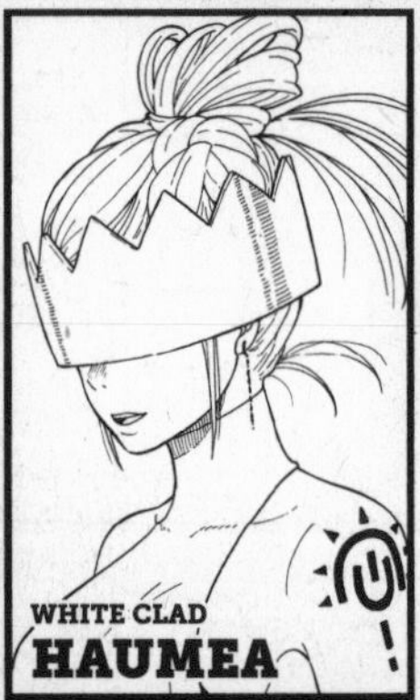

WHITE CLAD
HAUMEA

One of the Evangelist's white-clad combatants. She is a troublesome opponent who can control others with her mind-jacking powers, and she has a foul mouth.

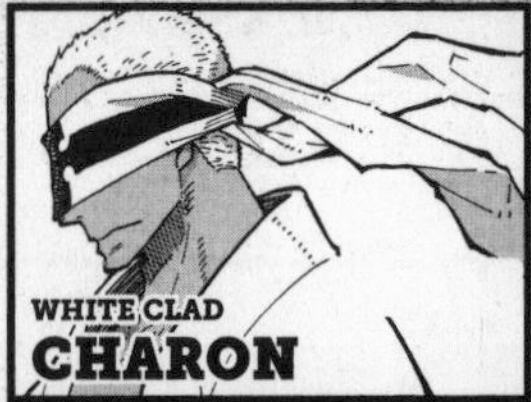

WHITE CLAD
CHARON

A talkative man who won't stop asking questions until he gets an answer. His powers are unknown, but he must be powerful if he's hanging out with Haumea, right?

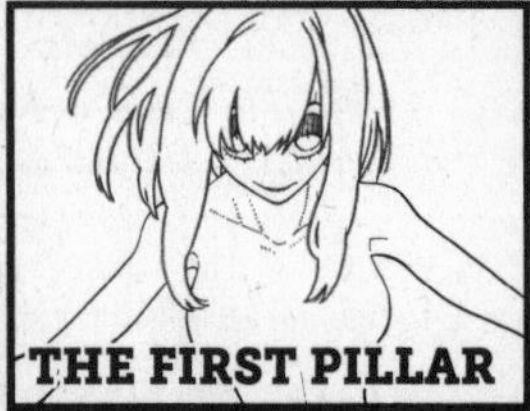

THE FIRST PILLAR

A mysterious woman who has used an Adolla Link to take over Shinra's mind.

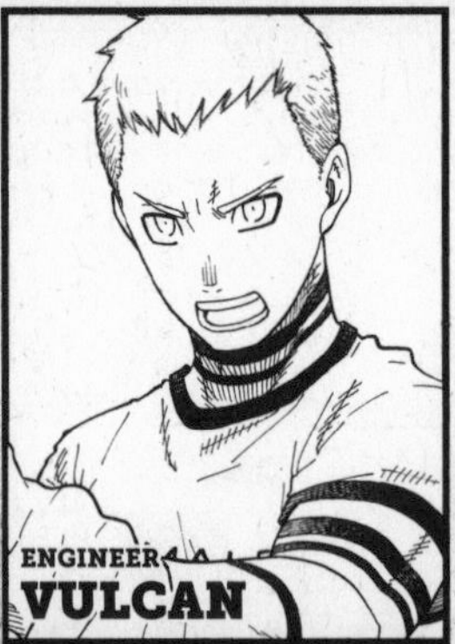

ENGINEER
VULCAN

The greatest engineer of the day, renowned as the God of Fire and the Forge. He sympathized with Ōbi's and Shinra's ideals and agreed to join Company 8 as their engineer.

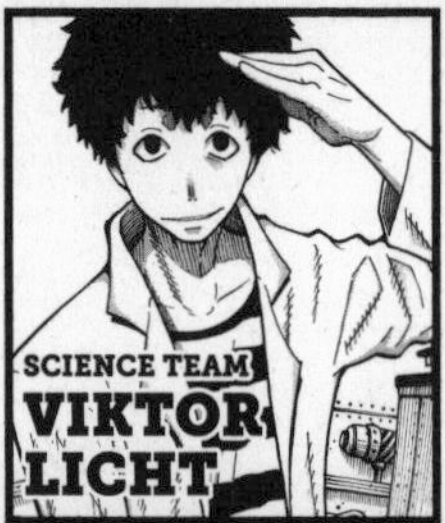

SCIENCE TEAM
VIKTOR LICHT

A morally ambiguous man deployed from Haijima Industries to fill the vacancy in Company 8's science department. Apparently a genius.

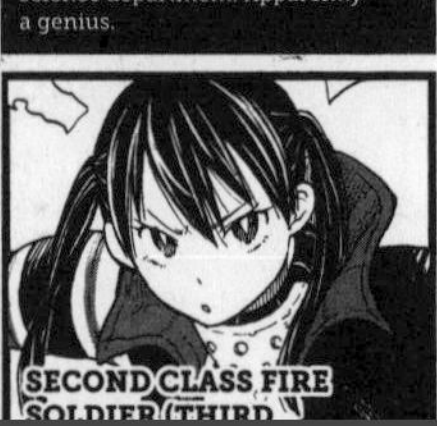

SECOND CLASS FIRE

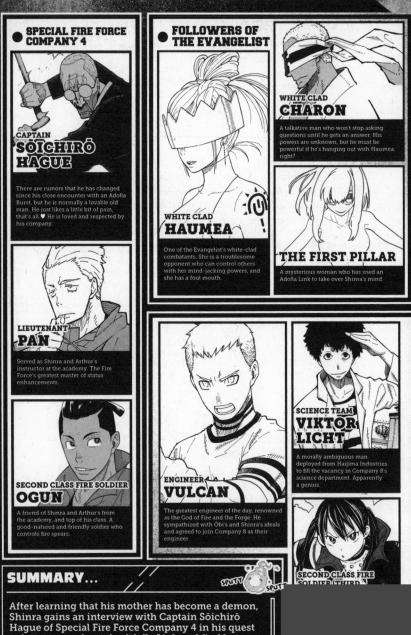

SUMMARY...

After learning that his mother has become a demon, Shinra gains an interview with Captain Sōichirō Hague of Special Fire Force Company 4 in his quest to learn more about the Adolla Link and find her. But in the middle of their meeting, trouble strikes! Someone known as the First Pillar has an Adolla Burst like Shinra's, and is using mental interference to drive Shinra to insanity!! The elite members of Company 4 and Arthur attempt to stop him, but...?!

FIRE FORCE 12

CONTENTS

CHAPTER XCVII:
THE ORIGINS OF THE KNIGHT KING 007

CHAPTER XCVIII:
SHINRA VS. ARTHUR 029

CHAPTER XCIX:
A NEW KINDLING 049

CHAPTER C:
THE SCENT OF THE FLAME 069

CHAPTER CI:
TRAGEDY IN THE FIRE 089

CHAPTER CII:
RAGING FISTS 109

CHAPTER CIII:
GROPING THROUGH THE FLAMES 129

CHAPTER CIV:
BONDS OF THE FIREGROUND 149

CHAPTER CV:
ASSEMBLE! 169

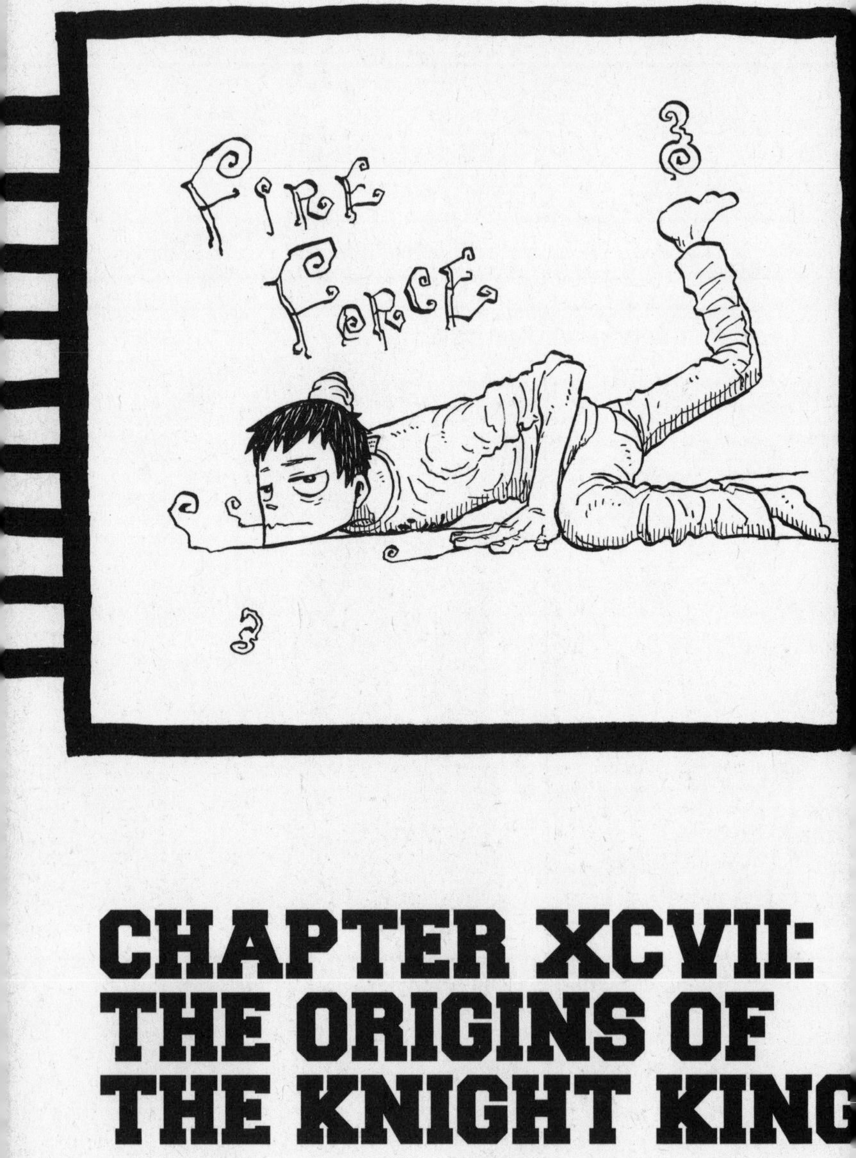
FIRE FORCE

CHAPTER XCVII: THE ORIGINS OF THE KNIGHT KING

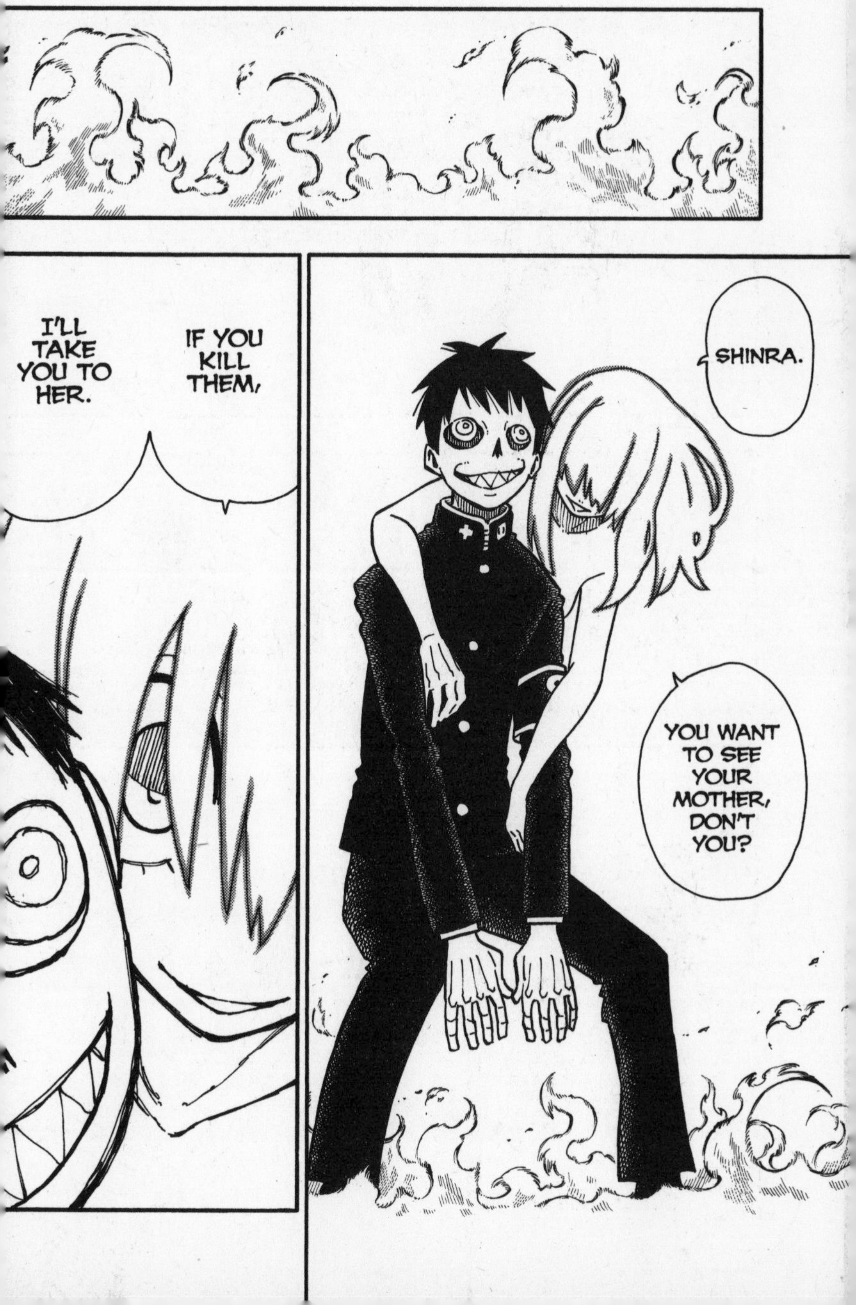
SHINRA.
YOU WANT TO SEE YOUR MOTHER, DON'T YOU?
IF YOU KILL THEM,
I'LL TAKE YOU TO HER.

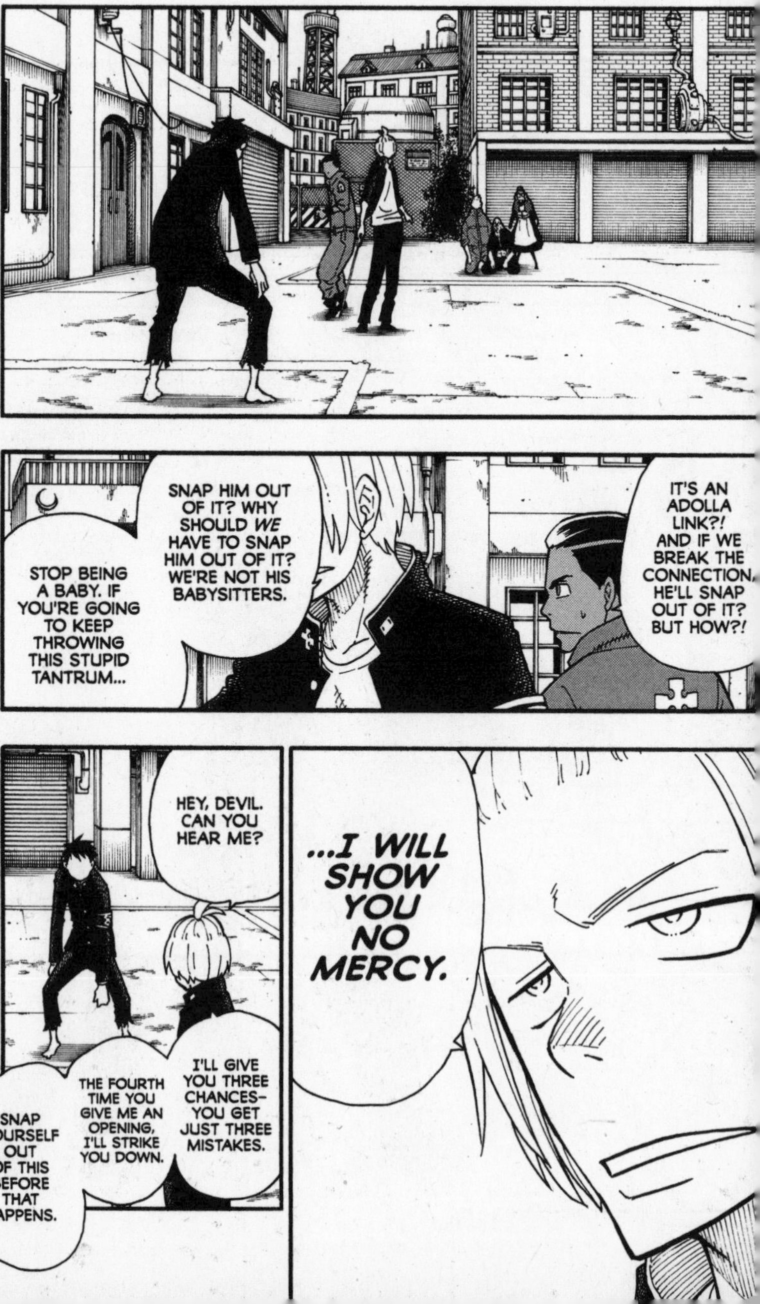
IT'S AN ADOLLA LINK?! AND IF WE BREAK THE CONNECTION, HE'LL SNAP OUT OF IT? BUT HOW?!
SNAP HIM OUT OF IT? WHY SHOULD *WE* HAVE TO SNAP HIM OUT OF IT? WE'RE NOT HIS BABYSITTERS.
STOP BEING A BABY. IF YOU'RE GOING TO KEEP THROWING THIS STUPID TANTRUM...
HEY, DEVIL. CAN YOU HEAR ME?
I'LL GIVE YOU THREE CHANCES–YOU GET JUST THREE MISTAKES.
THE FOURTH TIME YOU GIVE ME AN OPENING, I'LL STRIKE YOU DOWN.
SNAP YOURSELF OUT OF THIS BEFORE THAT HAPPENS.
...I WILL SHOW YOU NO MERCY.

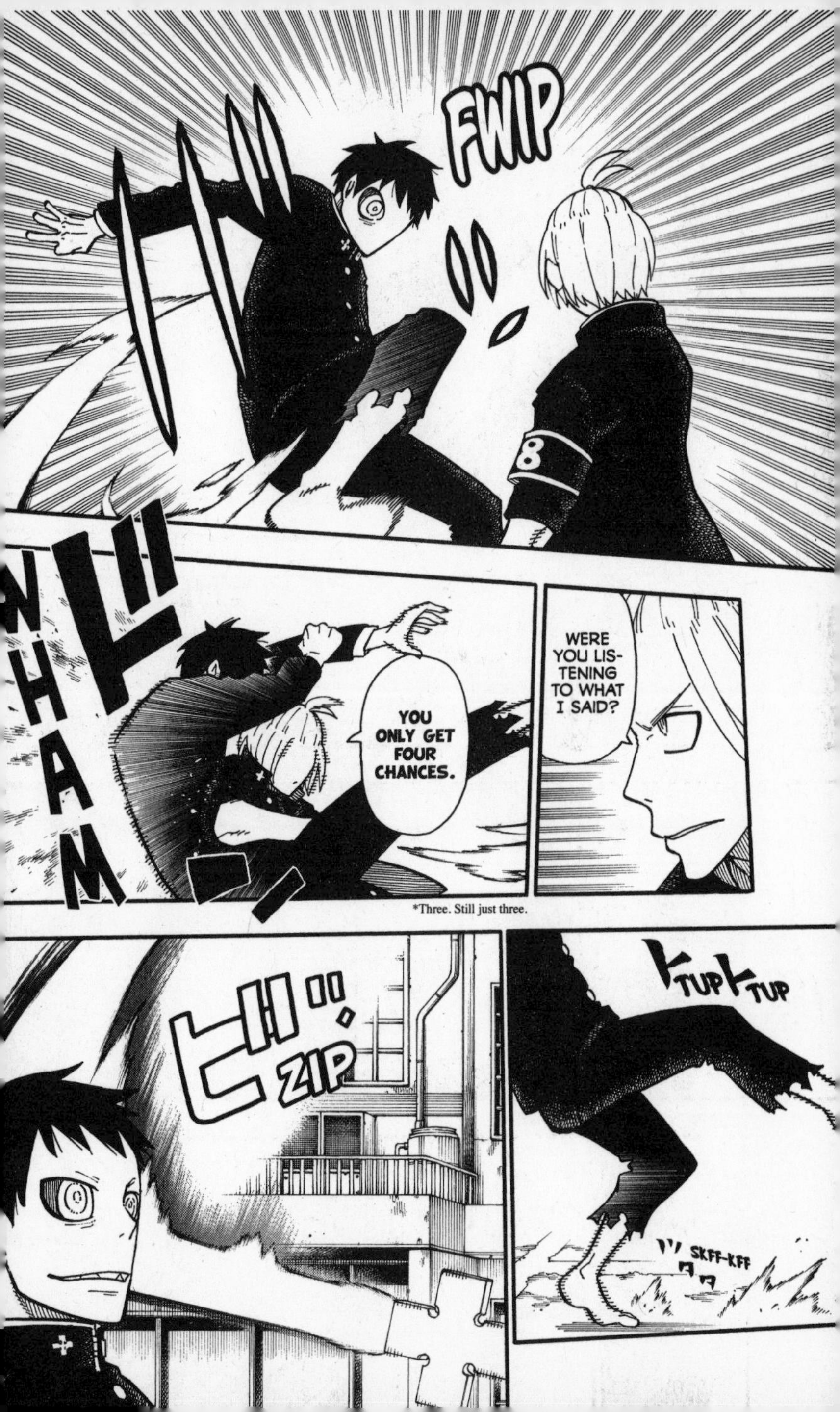
FWIP
WERE YOU LISTENING TO WHAT I SAID?
WHAM
YOU ONLY GET FOUR CHANCES.
TUP TUP
SKFF-KFF
ZIP
*Three. Still just three.

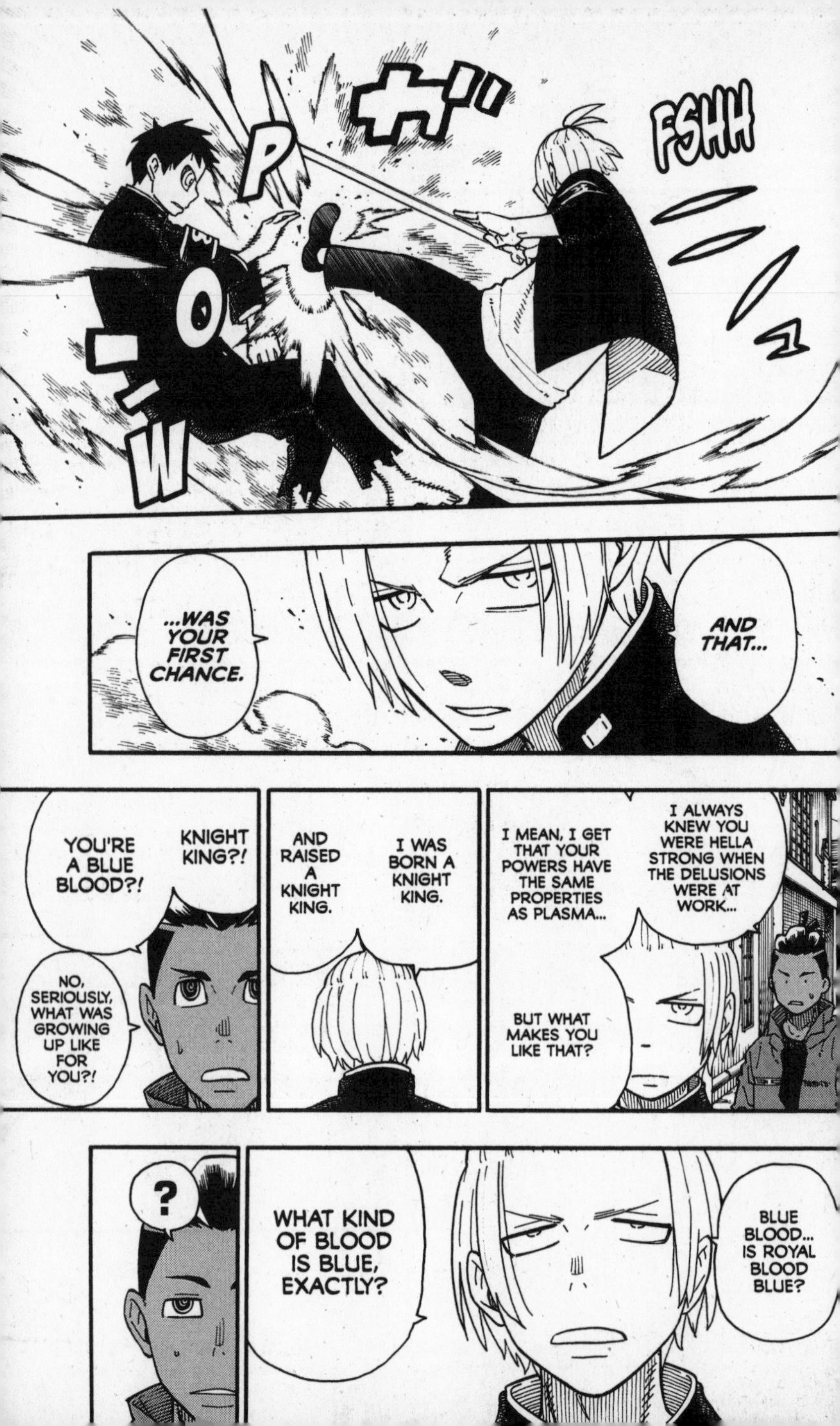
FSHH
POW
AND THAT...
...WAS YOUR FIRST CHANCE.
I ALWAYS KNEW YOU WERE HELLA STRONG WHEN THE DELUSIONS WERE AT WORK...
I MEAN, I GET THAT YOUR POWERS HAVE THE SAME PROPERTIES AS PLASMA...
BUT WHAT MAKES YOU LIKE THAT?
I WAS BORN A KNIGHT KING.
AND RAISED A KNIGHT KING.
KNIGHT KING?!
YOU'RE A BLUE BLOOD?!
NO, SERIOUSLY, WHAT WAS GROWING UP LIKE FOR YOU?!
BLUE BLOOD... IS ROYAL BLOOD BLUE?
WHAT KIND OF BLOOD IS BLUE, EXACTLY?
?

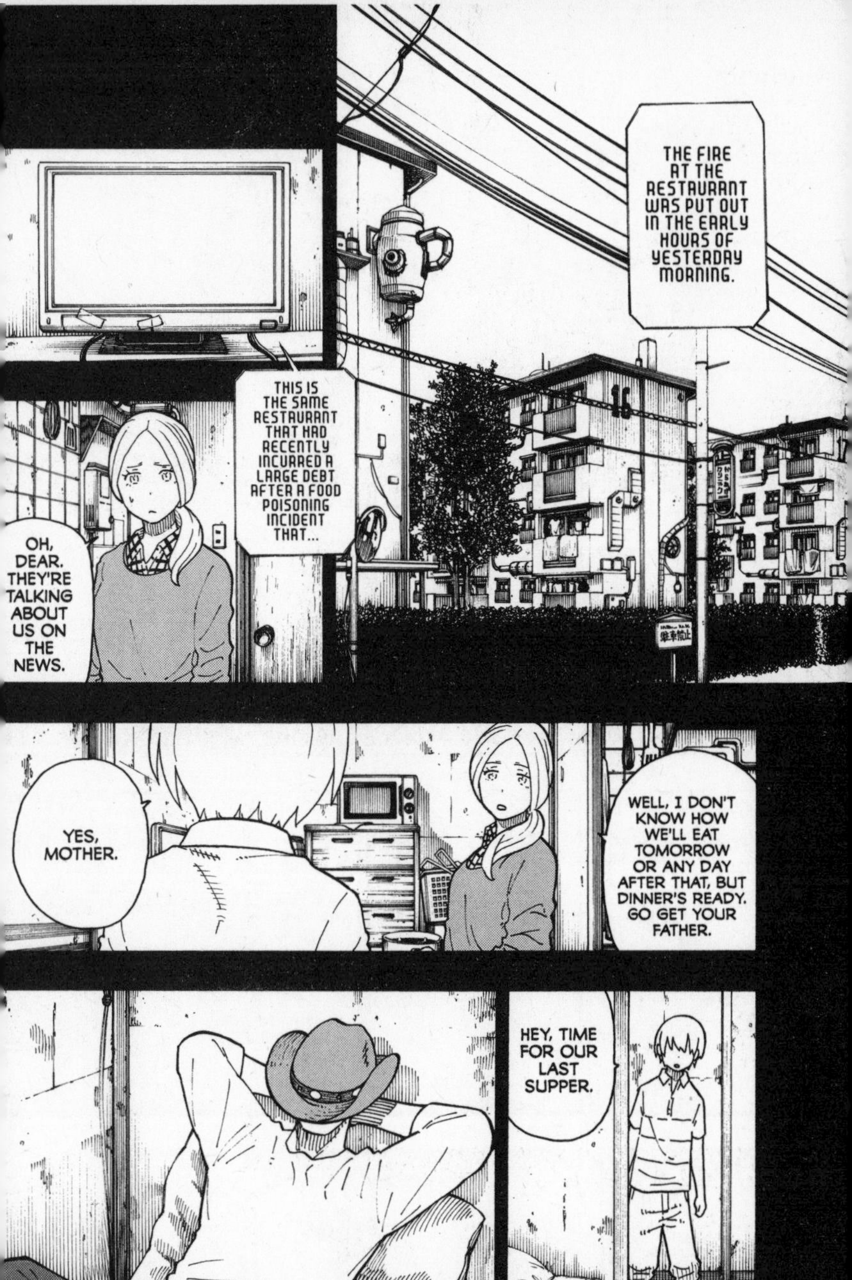
THE FIRE AT THE RESTAURANT WAS PUT OUT IN THE EARLY HOURS OF YESTERDAY MORNING.
THIS IS THE SAME RESTAURANT THAT HAD RECENTLY INCURRED A LARGE DEBT AFTER A FOOD POISONING INCIDENT THAT...
OH, DEAR. THEY'RE TALKING ABOUT US ON THE NEWS.
WELL, I DON'T KNOW HOW WE'LL EAT TOMORROW OR ANY DAY AFTER THAT, BUT DINNER'S READY. GO GET YOUR FATHER.
YES, MOTHER.
HEY, TIME FOR OUR LAST SUPPER.

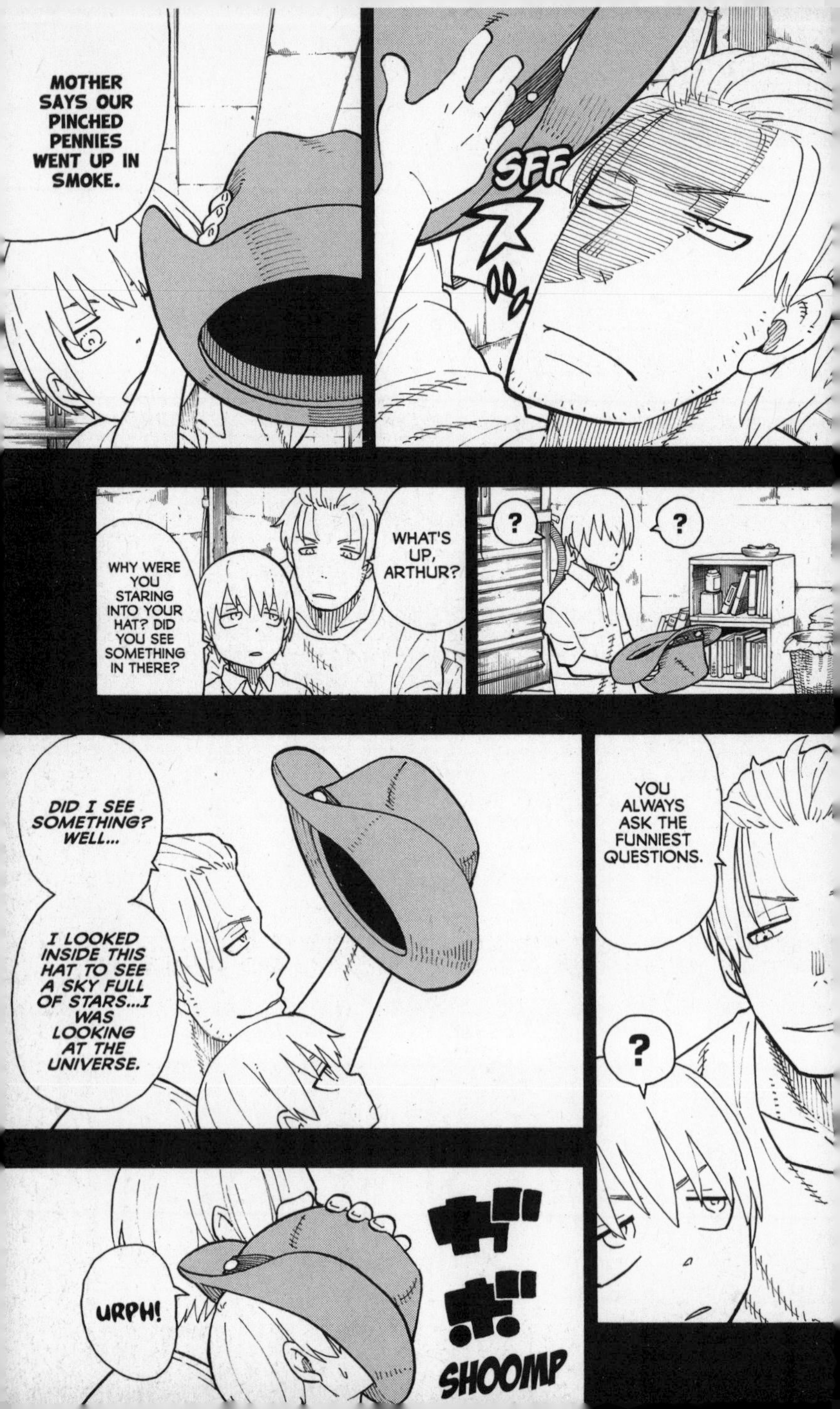
SFF
MOTHER SAYS OUR PINCHED PENNIES WENT UP IN SMOKE.
?
?
WHAT'S UP, ARTHUR?
WHY WERE YOU STARING INTO YOUR HAT? DID YOU SEE SOMETHING IN THERE?
YOU ALWAYS ASK THE FUNNIEST QUESTIONS.
?
DID I SEE SOMETHING? WELL...
I LOOKED INSIDE THIS HAT TO SEE A SKY FULL OF STARS...I WAS LOOKING AT THE UNIVERSE.
URPH!
SHOOMP

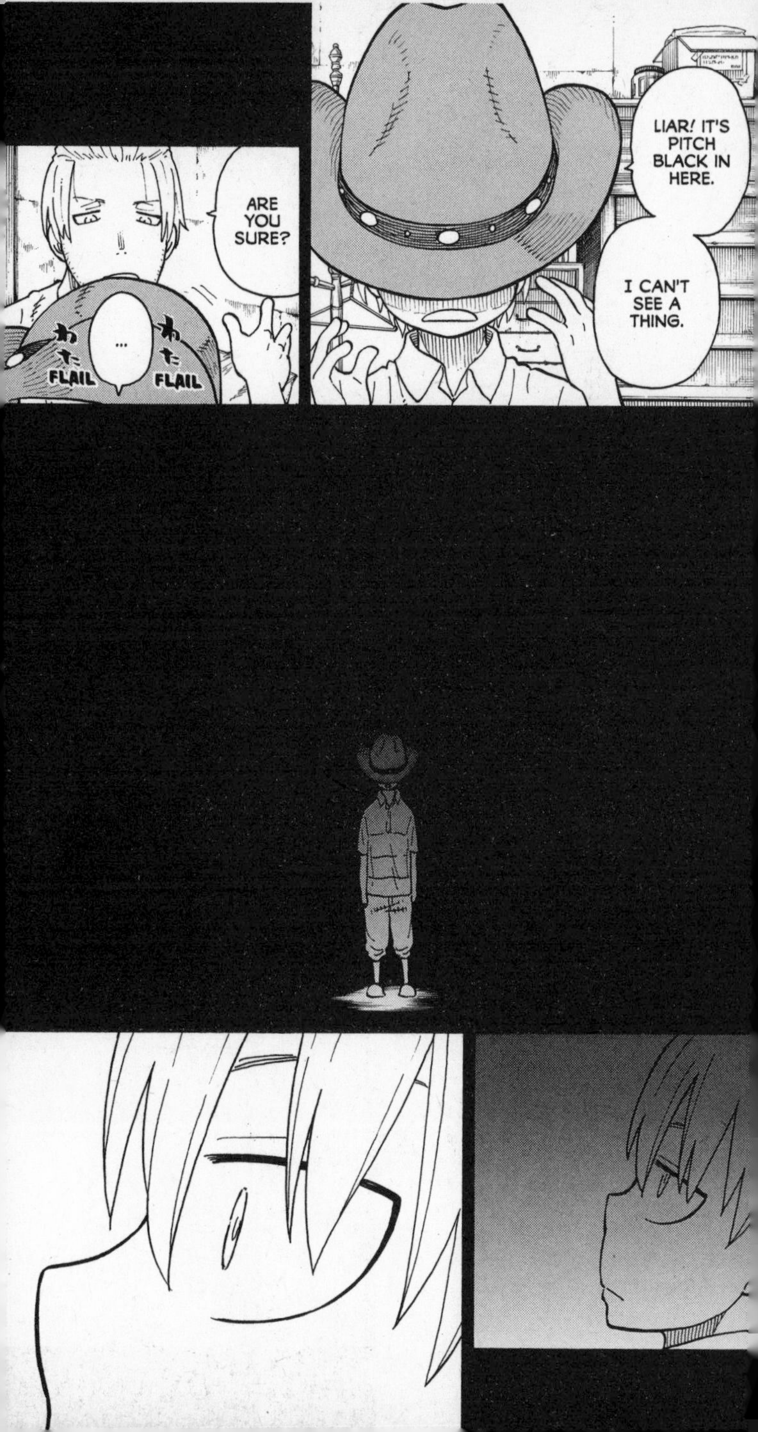
LIAR! IT'S PITCH BLACK IN HERE.
I CAN'T SEE A THING.
ARE YOU SURE?
...
FLAIL
FLAIL

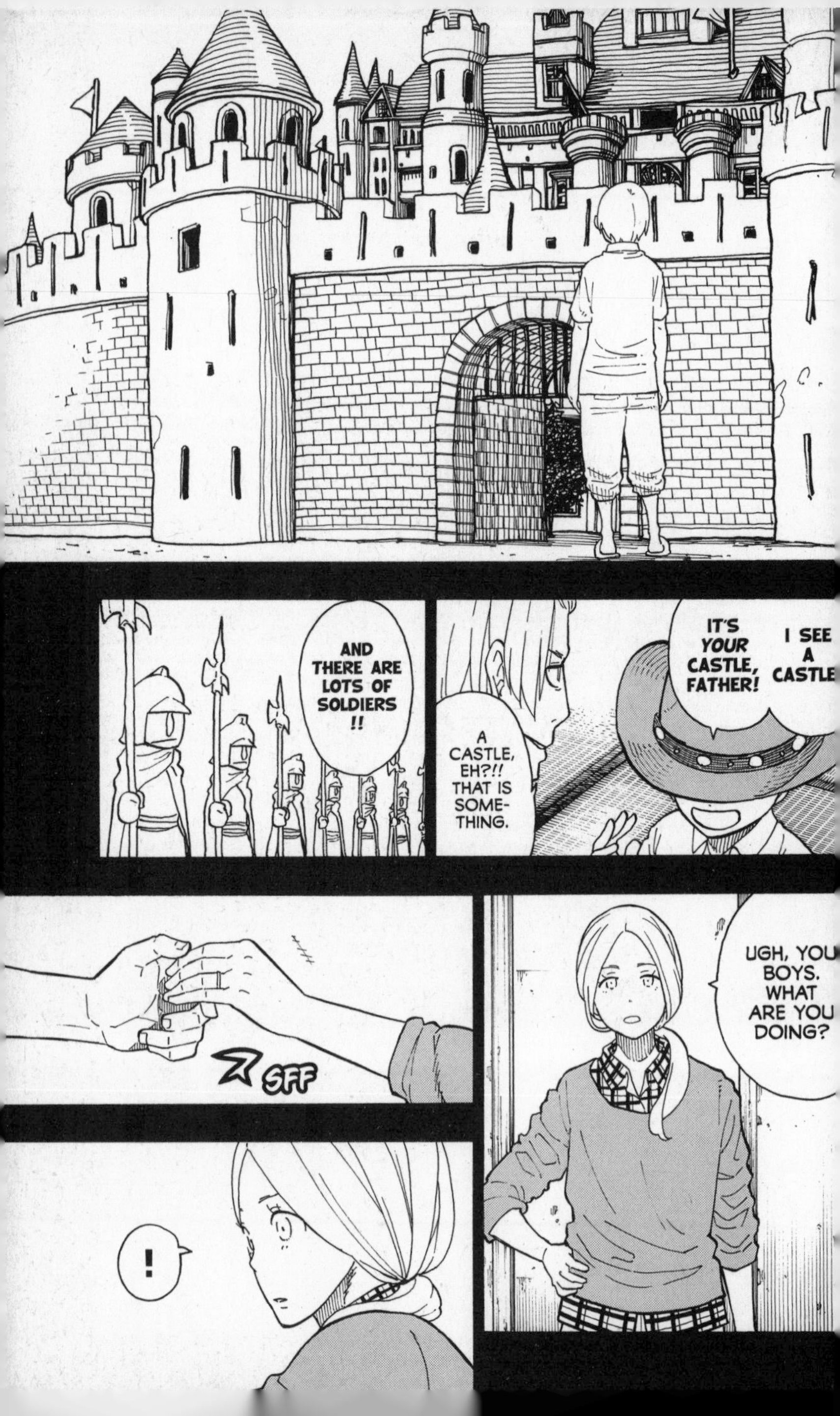
I SEE A CASTLE
IT'S *YOUR* CASTLE, FATHER!
A CASTLE, EH?!! THAT IS SOME-THING.
AND THERE ARE LOTS OF SOLDIERS !!
UGH, YOU BOYS. WHAT ARE YOU DOING?
SFF
!

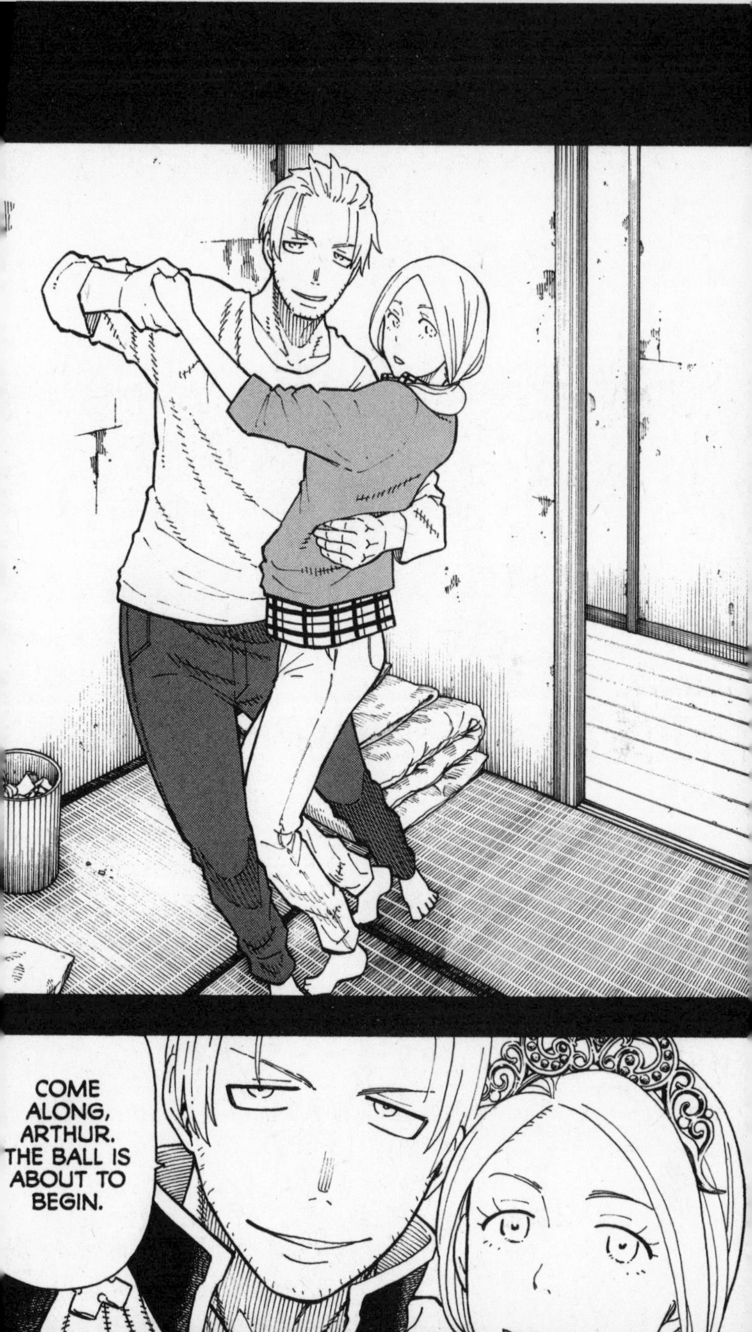
COME ALONG, ARTHUR. THE BALL IS ABOUT TO BEGIN.

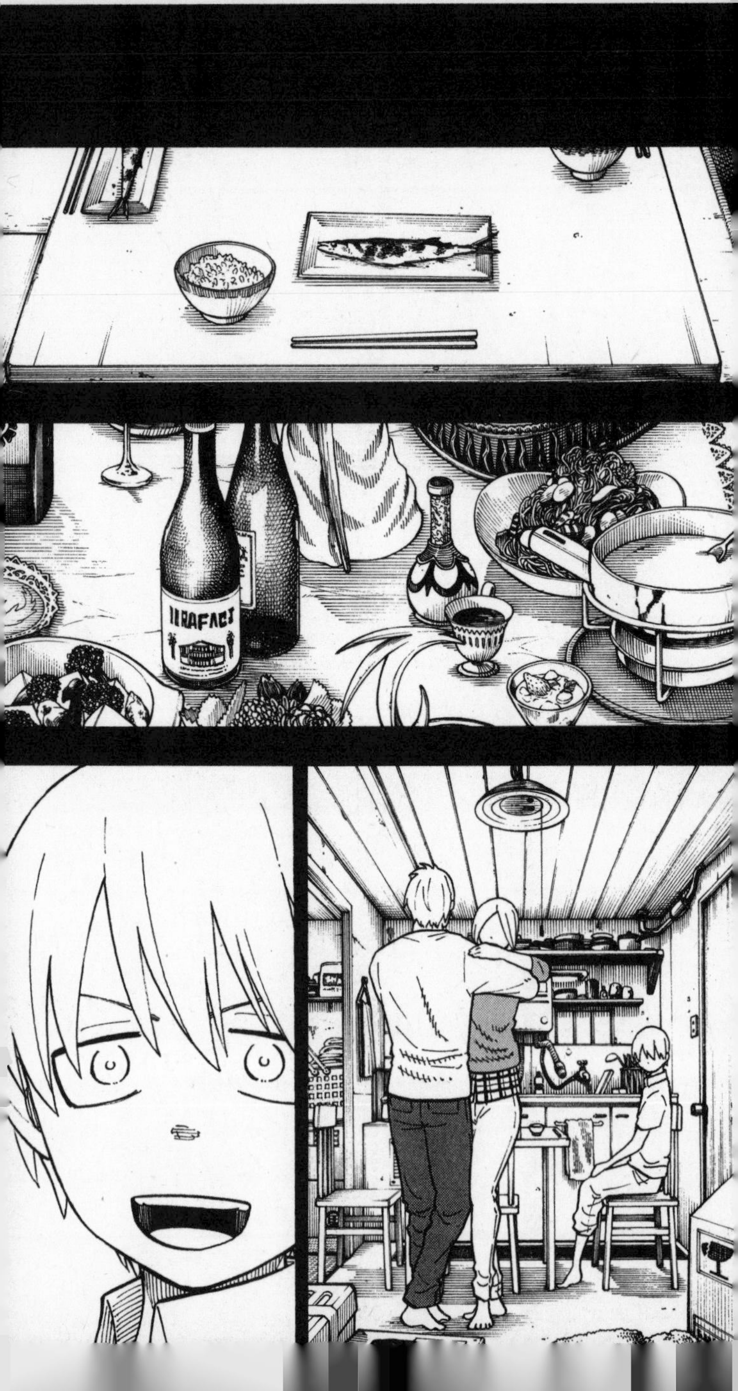

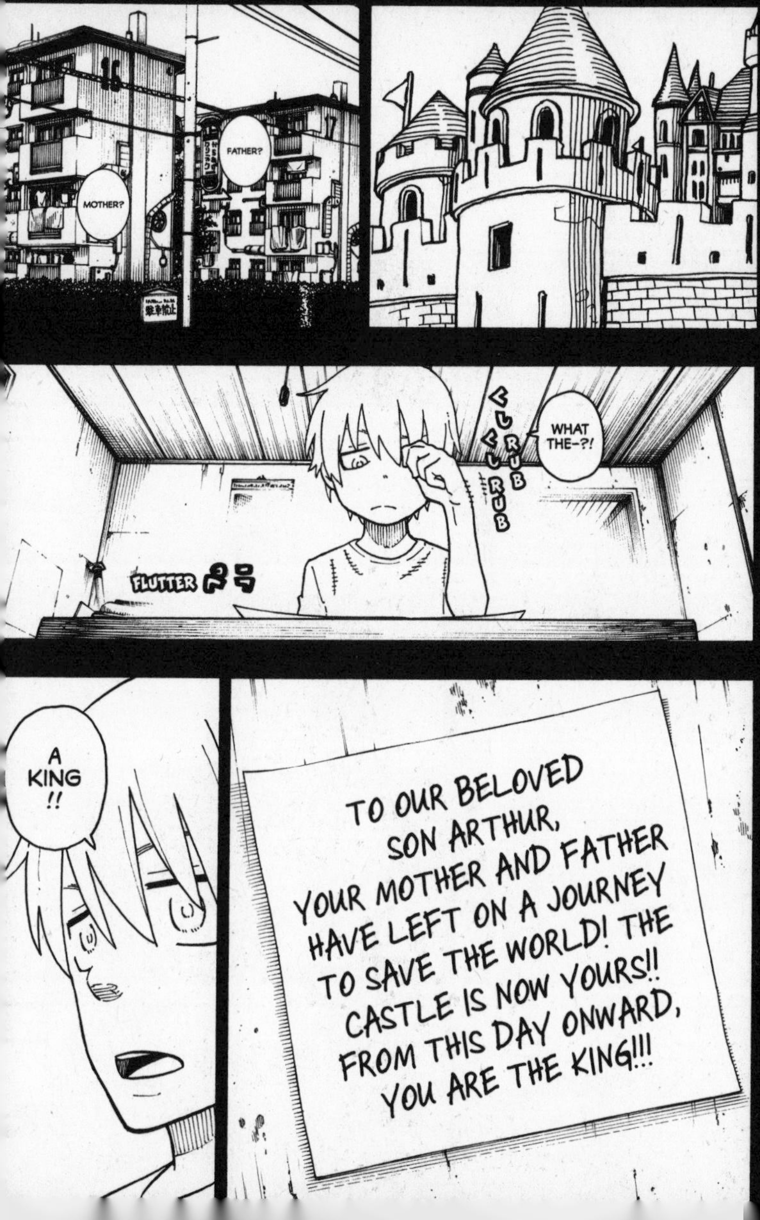
FATHER?
MOTHER?
WHAT THE-?!
RUB RUB
FLUTTER
TO OUR BELOVED SON ARTHUR, YOUR MOTHER AND FATHER HAVE LEFT ON A JOURNEY TO SAVE THE WORLD! THE CASTLE IS NOW YOURS!! FROM THIS DAY ONWARD, YOU ARE THE KING!!!
A KING !!

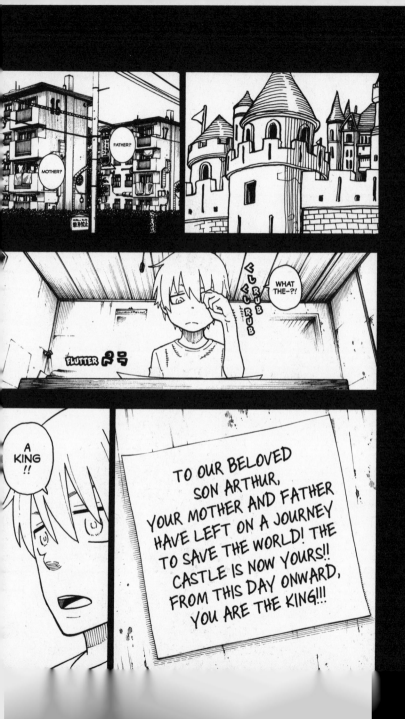

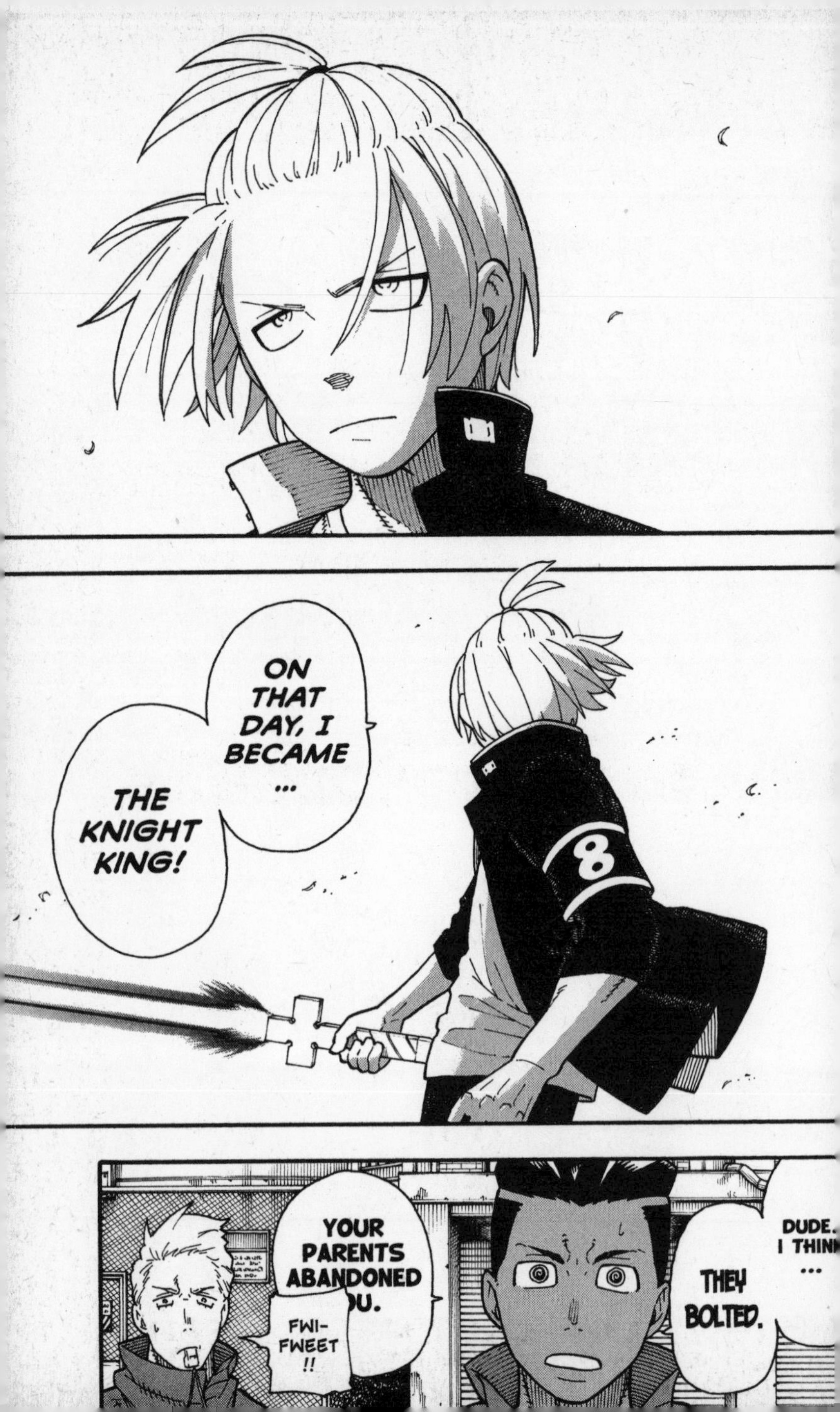
ON THAT DAY, I BECAME ...
THE KNIGHT KING!
DUDE. I THIN ...
THEY BOLTED.
YOUR PARENTS ABANDONED OU.
FWI-FWEET !!

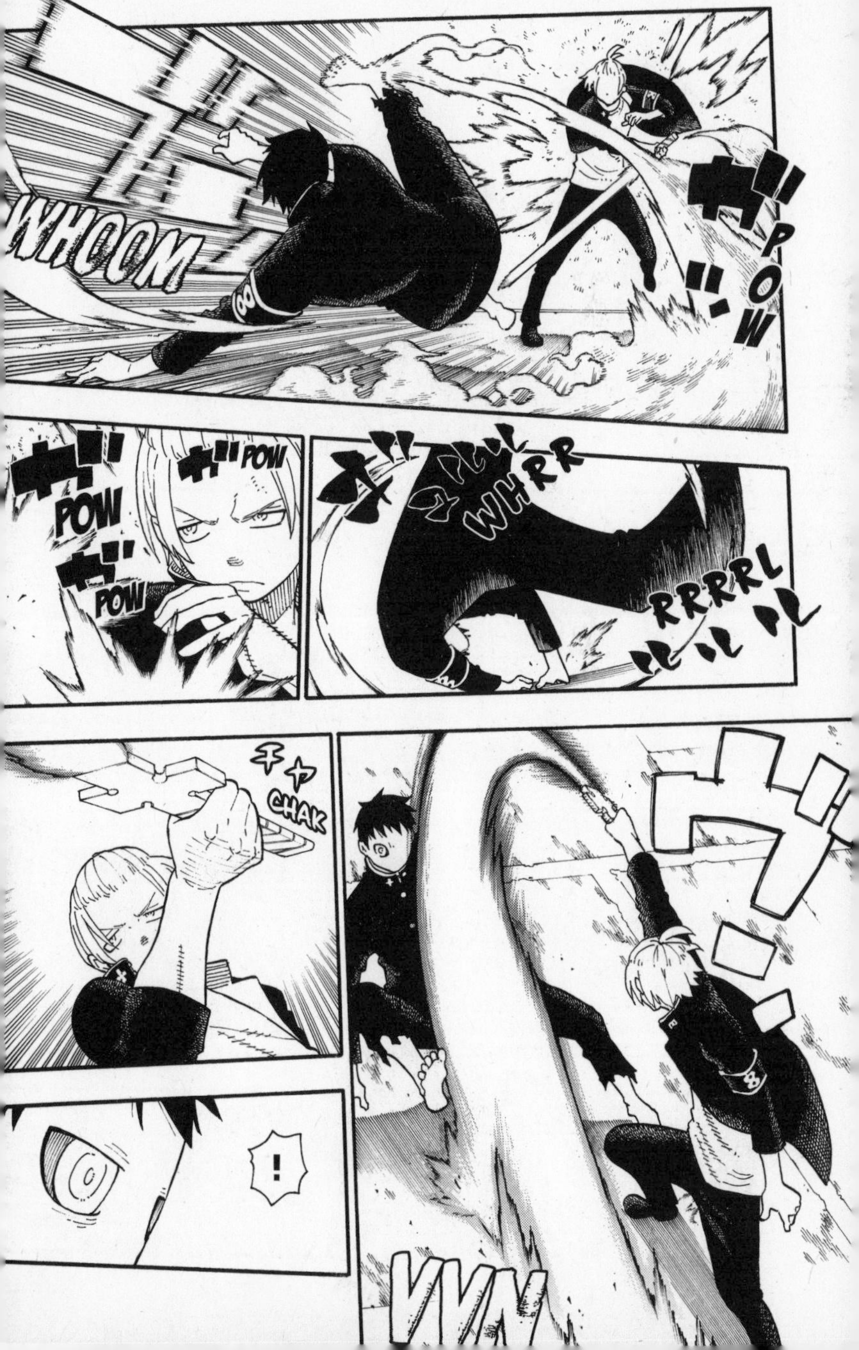
POW
WHOOM
WHRR
RRRRL
POW
POW
POW
VVN
チャ
CHAK
!

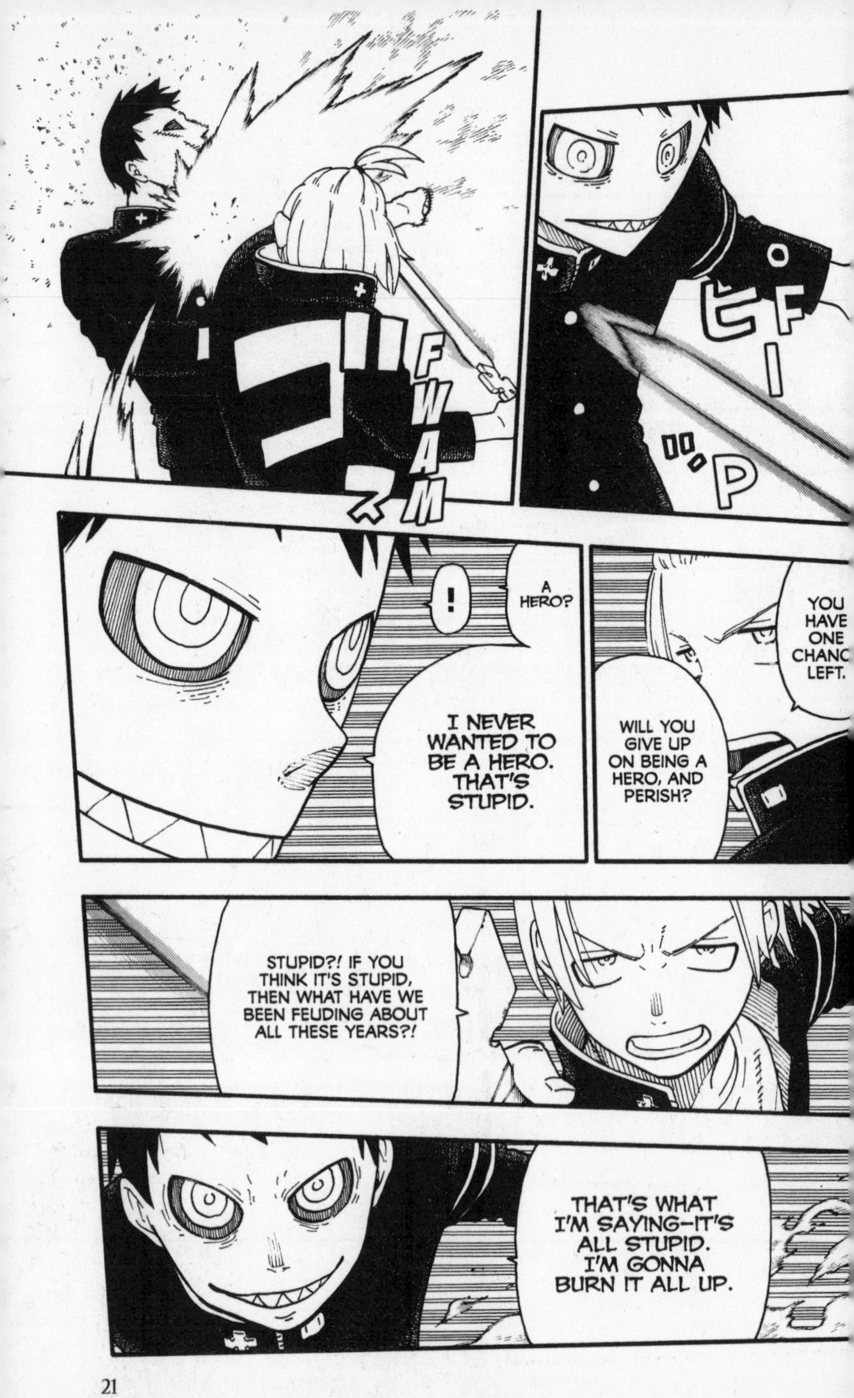
FIP
FWAM
YOU HAVE ONE CHANC LEFT.
WILL YOU GIVE UP ON BEING A HERO, AND PERISH?
A HERO?
!
I NEVER WANTED TO BE A HERO. THAT'S STUPID.
STUPID?! IF YOU THINK IT'S STUPID, THEN WHAT HAVE WE BEEN FEUDING ABOUT ALL THESE YEARS?!
THAT'S WHAT I'M SAYING—IT'S ALL STUPID. I'M GONNA BURN IT ALL UP.

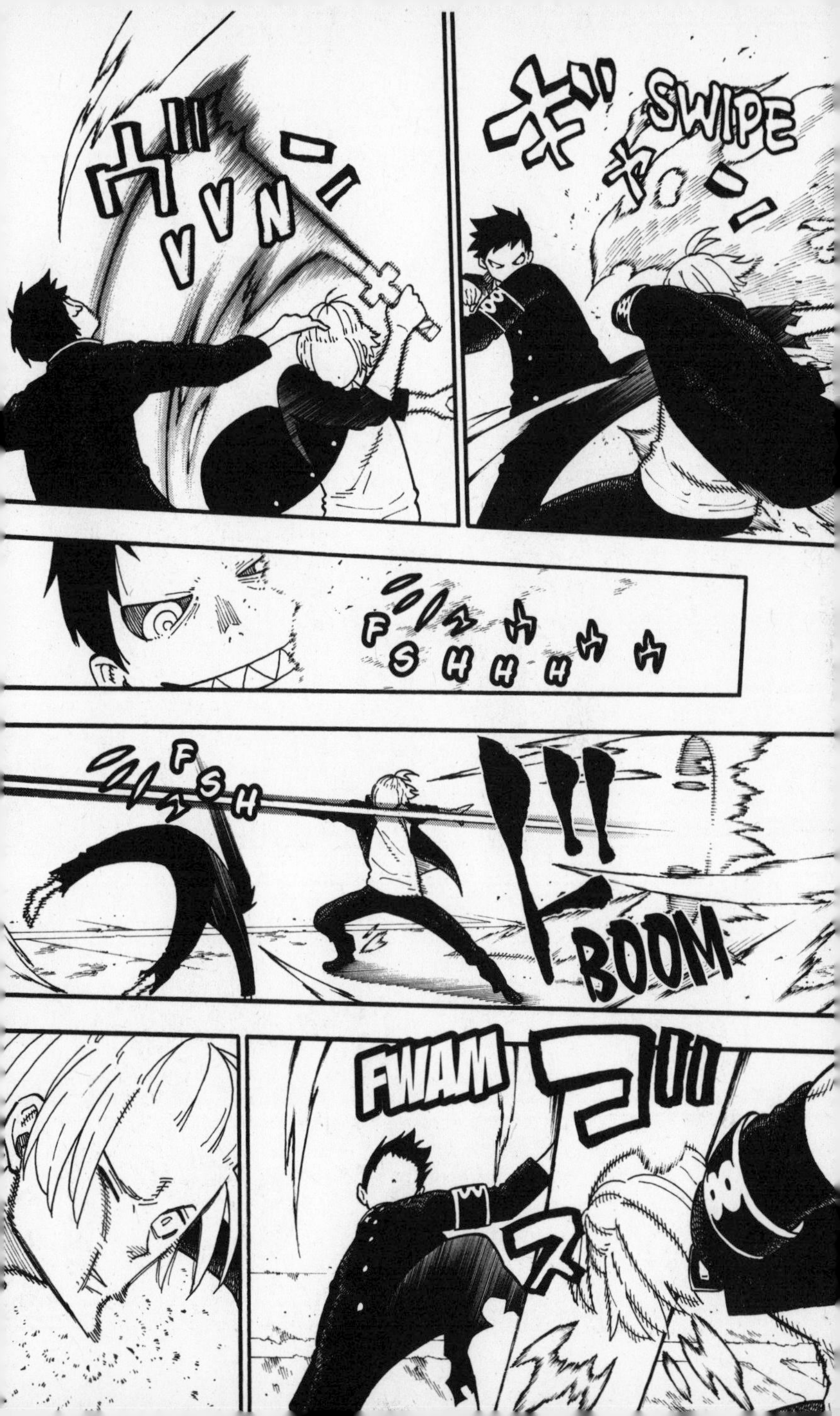
SWIPE
VVN
FSHHH
FSH
BOOM
FWAM

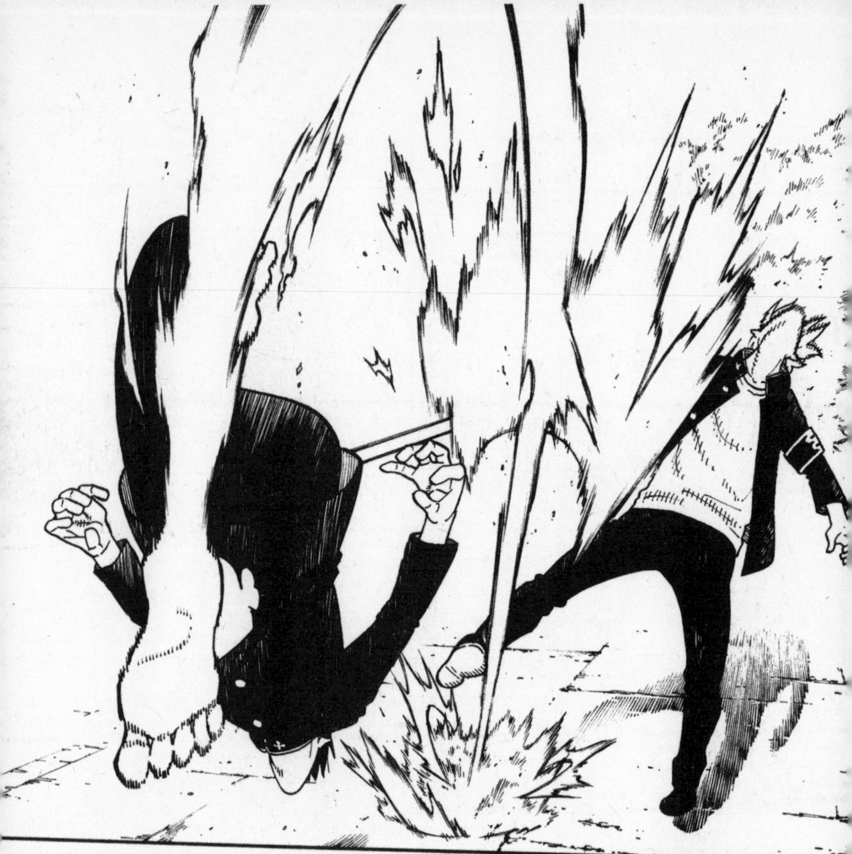

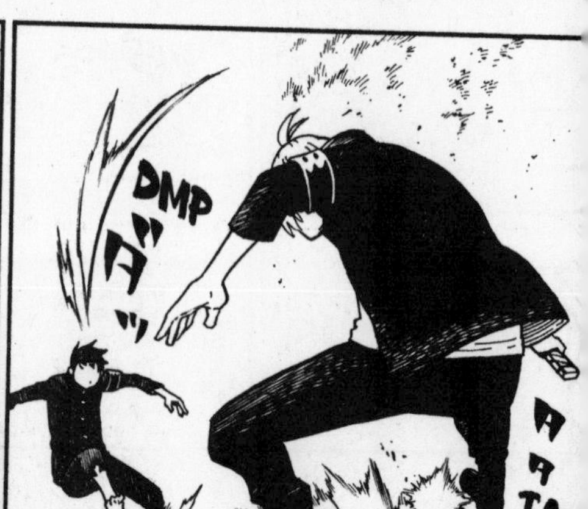
DMP
TA-TEP

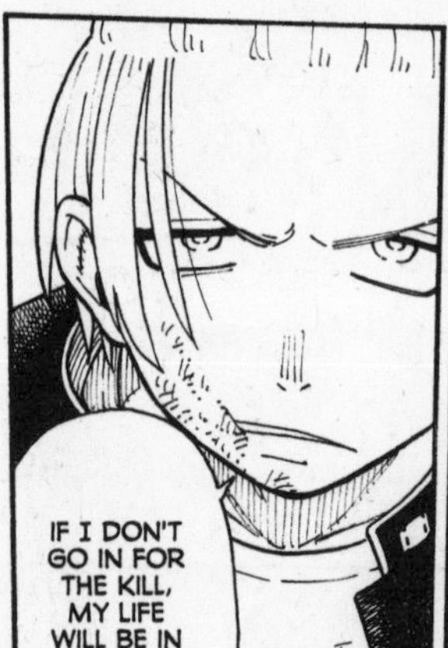
IF I DON'T GO IN FOR THE KILL, MY LIFE WILL BE IN DANGER.

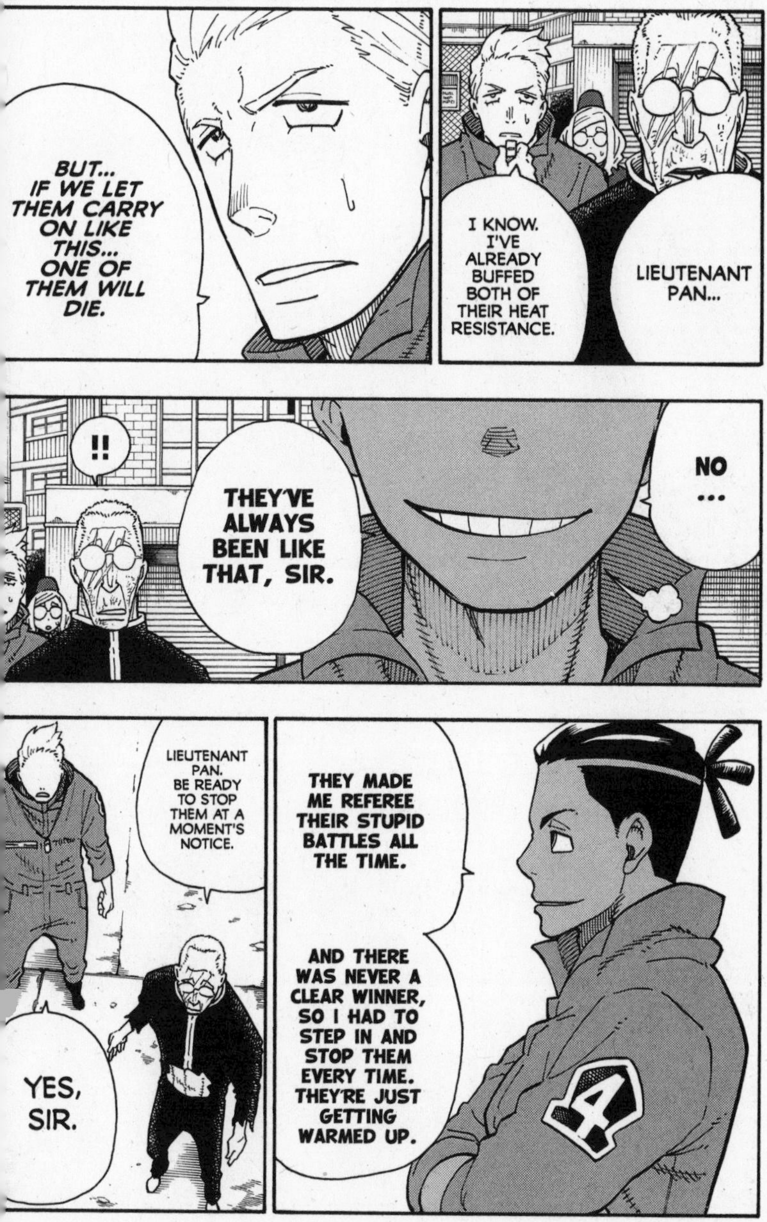
LIEUTENANT PAN...
I KNOW. I'VE ALREADY BUFFED BOTH OF THEIR HEAT RESISTANCE.
BUT... IF WE LET THEM CARRY ON LIKE THIS... ONE OF THEM WILL DIE.
NO ...
THEY'VE ALWAYS BEEN LIKE THAT, SIR.
!!
THEY MADE ME REFEREE THEIR STUPID BATTLES ALL THE TIME.
AND THERE WAS NEVER A CLEAR WINNER, SO I HAD TO STEP IN AND STOP THEM EVERY TIME. THEY'RE JUST GETTING WARMED UP.
LIEUTENANT PAN. BE READY TO STOP THEM AT A MOMENT'S NOTICE.
YES, SIR.

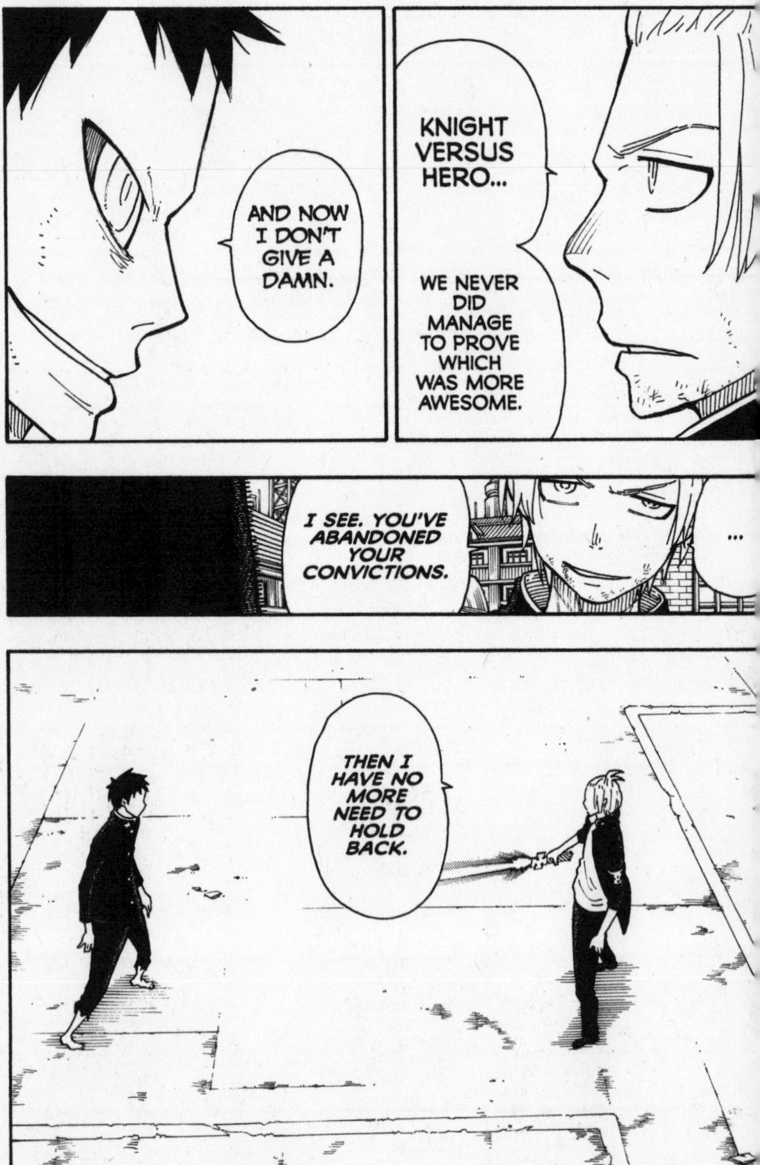
KNIGHT VERSUS HERO...
WE NEVER DID MANAGE TO PROVE WHICH WAS MORE AWESOME.
AND NOW I DON'T GIVE A DAMN.
...
I SEE. YOU'VE ABANDONED YOUR CONVICTIONS.
THEN I HAVE NO MORE NEED TO HOLD BACK.

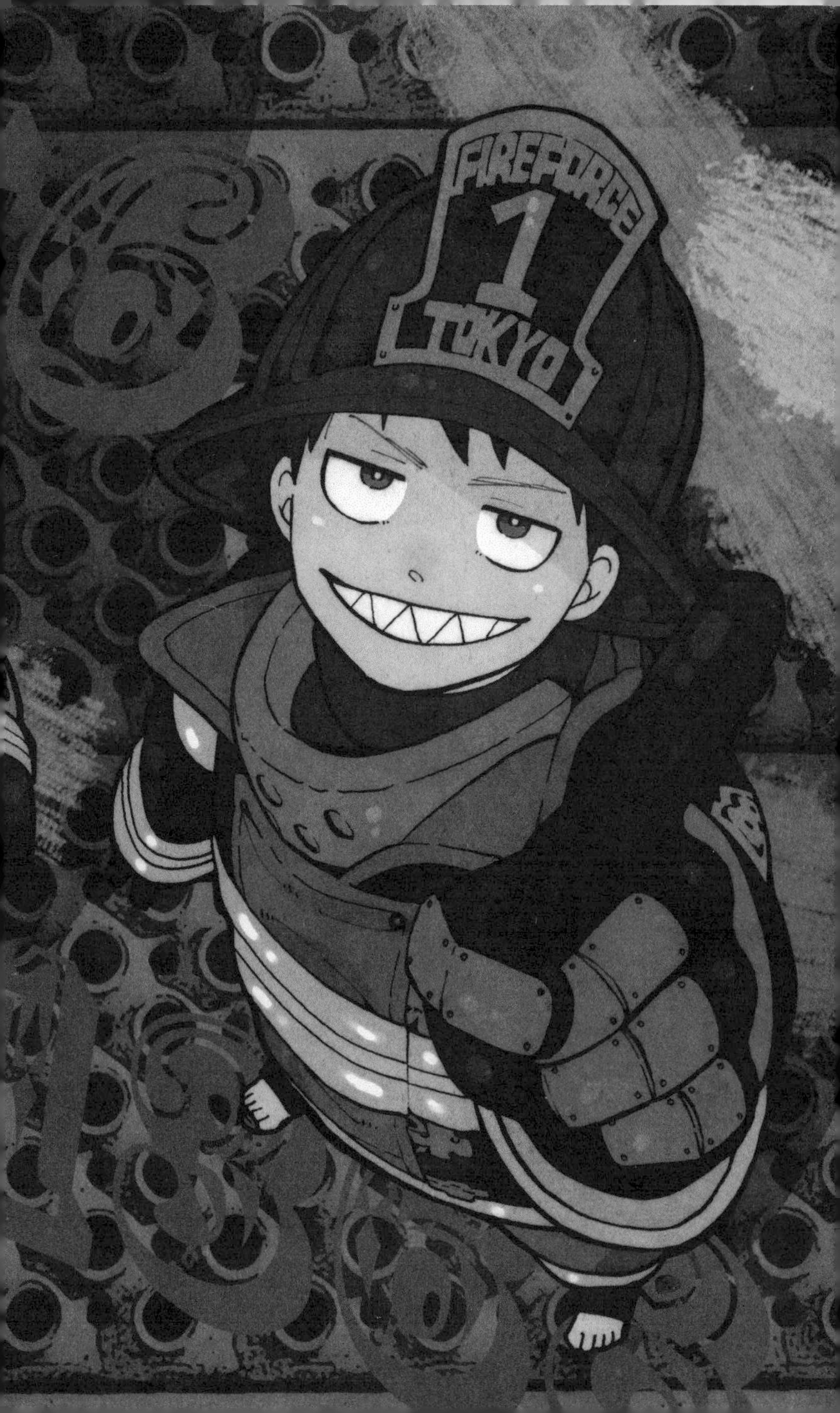
FIREFORCE
1
TOKYO

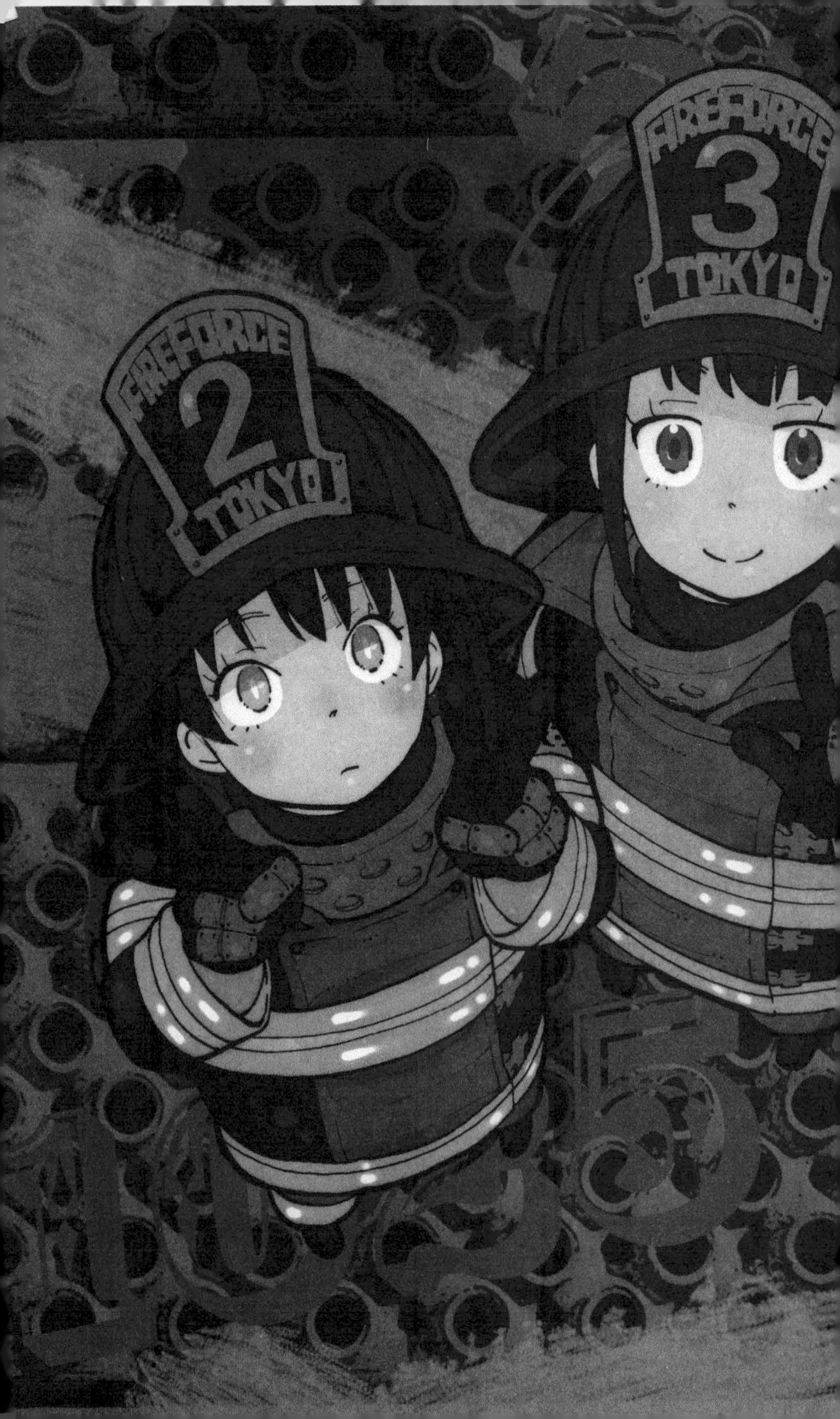
FIREFORCE
2
TOKYO
FIREFORCE
3
TOKYO

FIRE FORCE

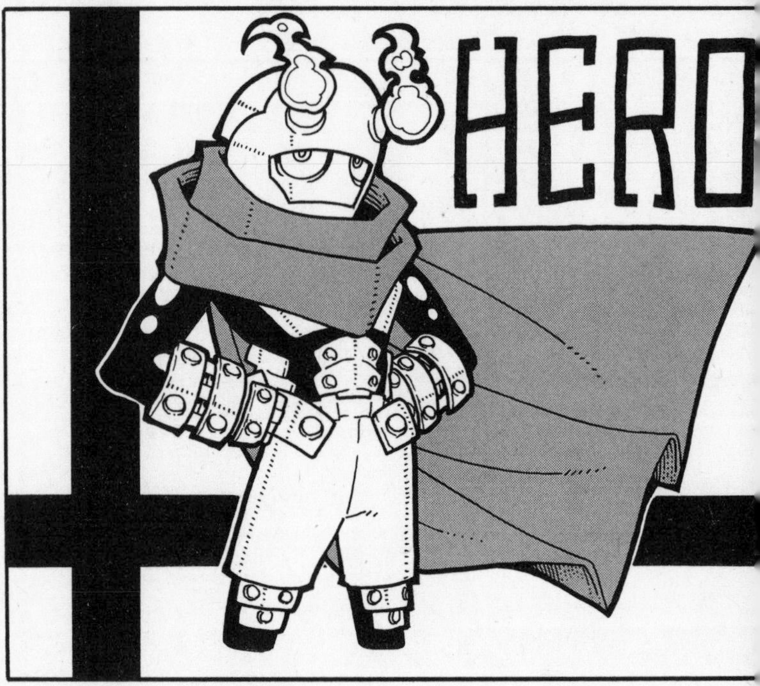
HERO

CHAPTER XCVIII: SHINRA VS. ARTHUR

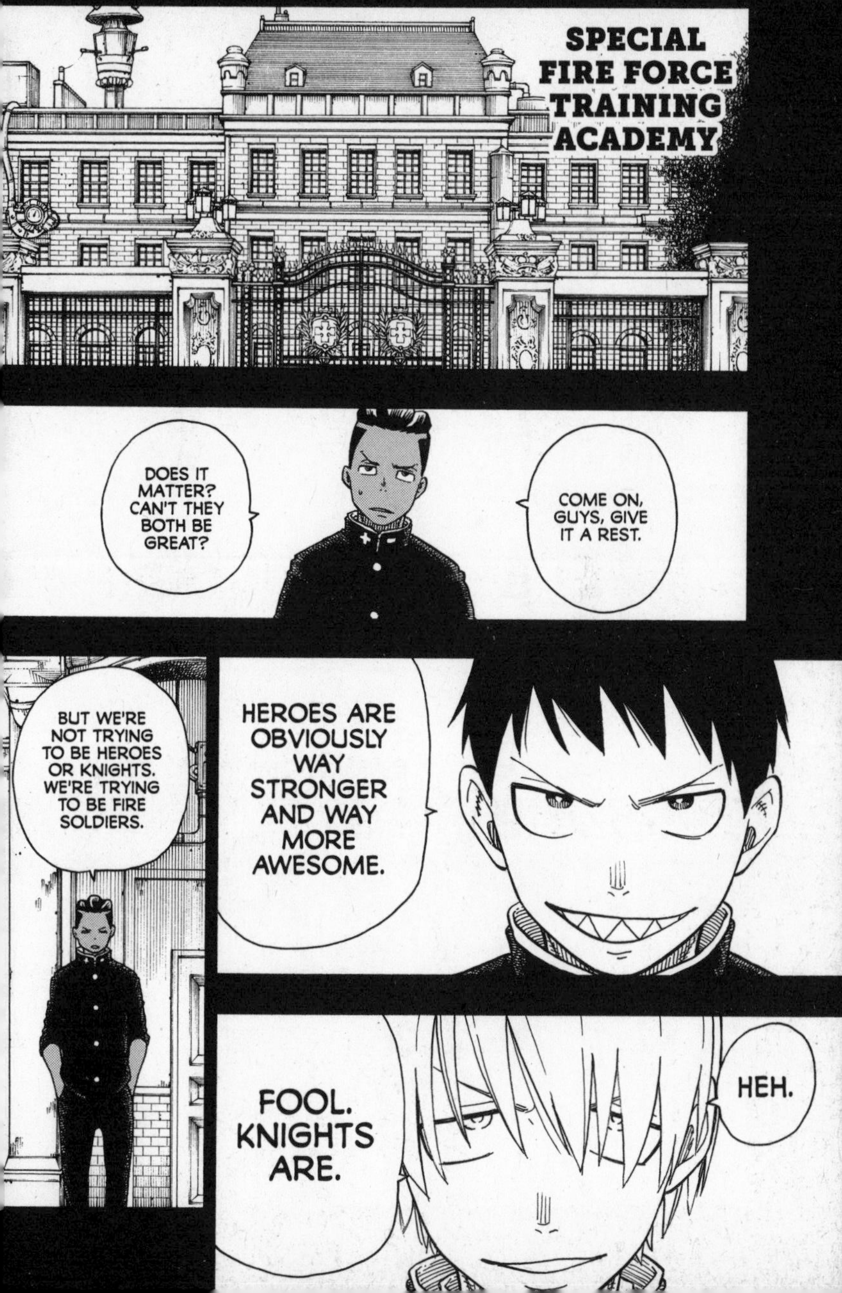
SPECIAL FIRE FORCE TRAINING ACADEMY
COME ON, GUYS, GIVE IT A REST.
DOES IT MATTER? CAN'T THEY BOTH BE GREAT?
HEROES ARE OBVIOUSLY WAY STRONGER AND WAY MORE AWESOME.
HEH.
FOOL. KNIGHTS ARE.
BUT WE'RE NOT TRYING TO BE HEROES OR KNIGHTS. WE'RE TRYING TO BE FIRE SOLDIERS.

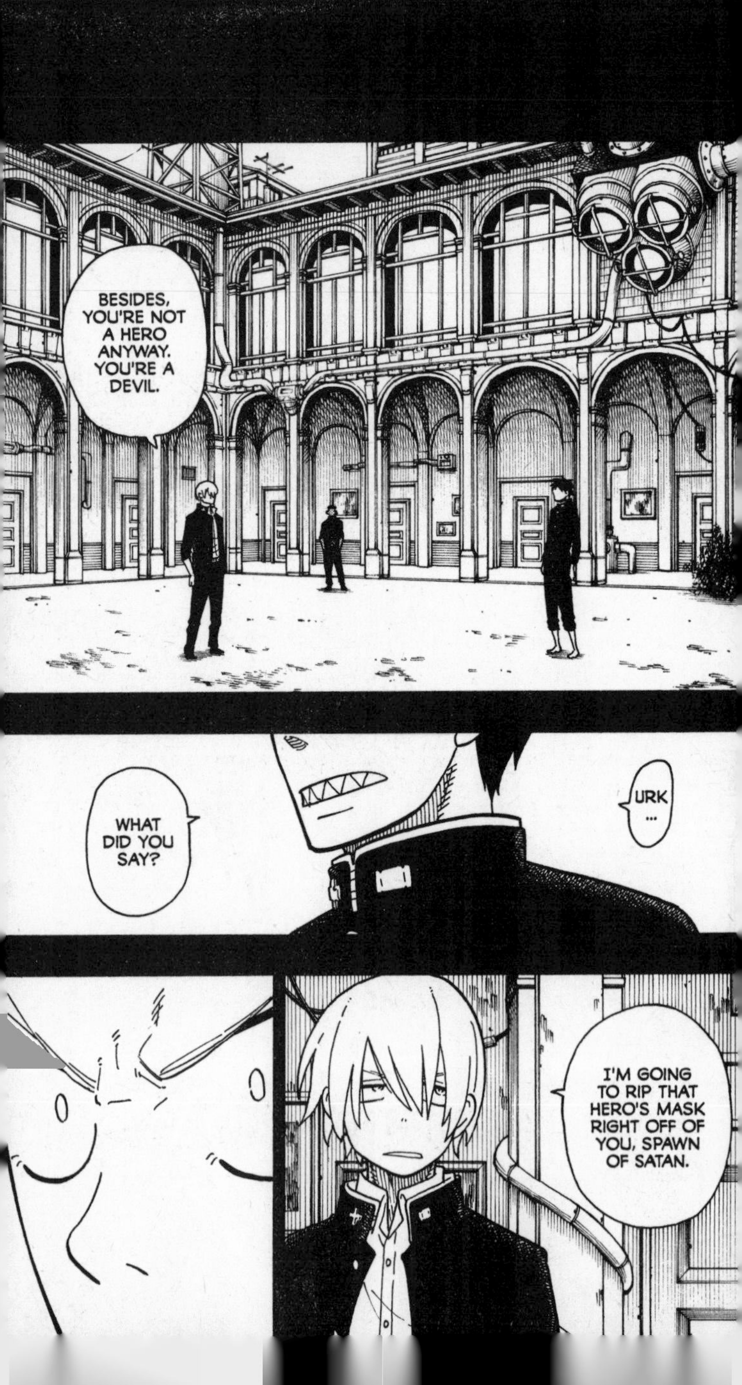
BESIDES, YOU'RE NOT A HERO ANYWAY. YOU'RE A DEVIL.
URK ...
WHAT DID YOU SAY?
I'M GOING TO RIP THAT HERO'S MASK RIGHT OFF OF YOU, SPAWN OF SATAN.

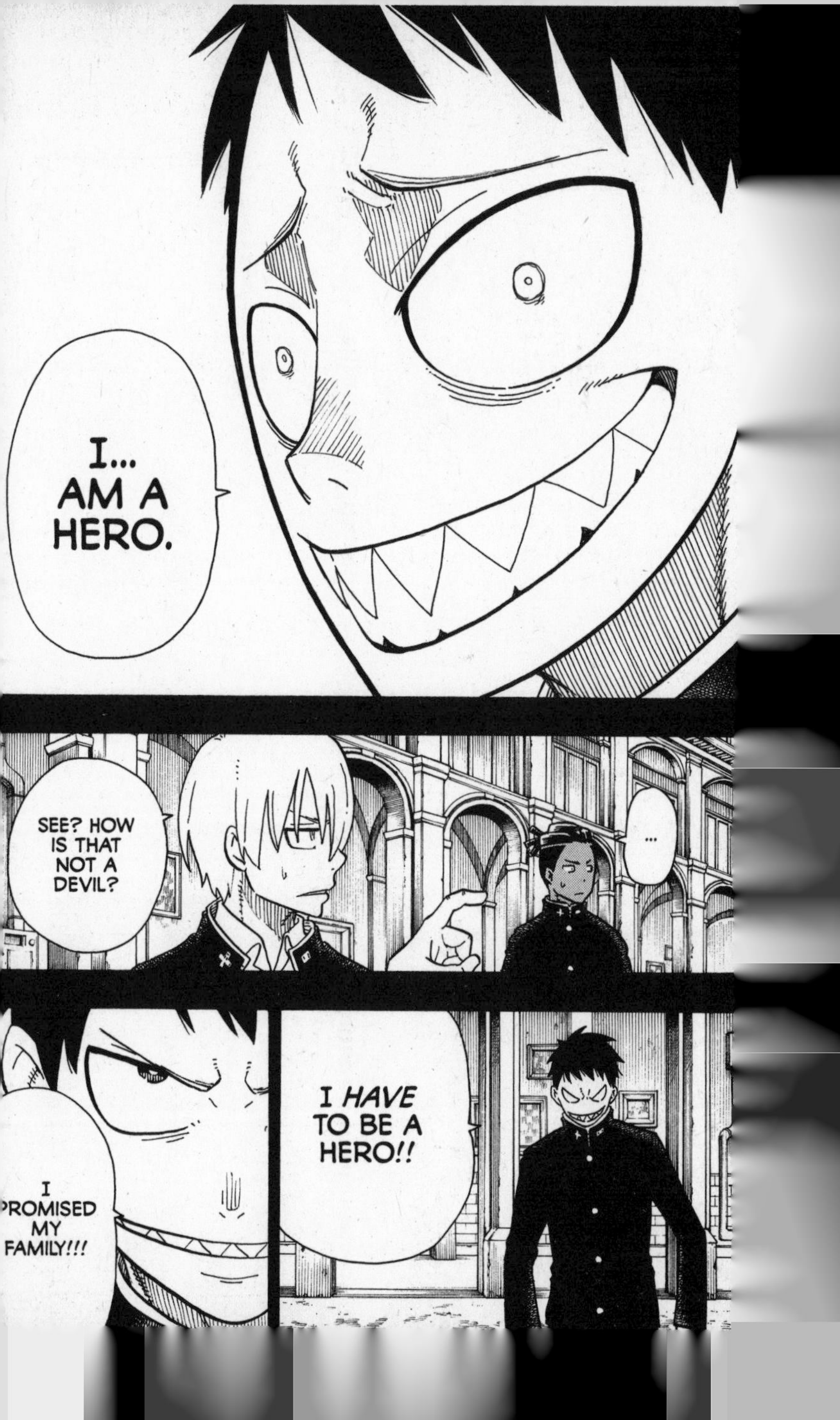
I... AM A HERO.
...
SEE? HOW IS THAT NOT A DEVIL?
I *HAVE* TO BE A HERO!!
I PROMISED MY FAMILY!!!

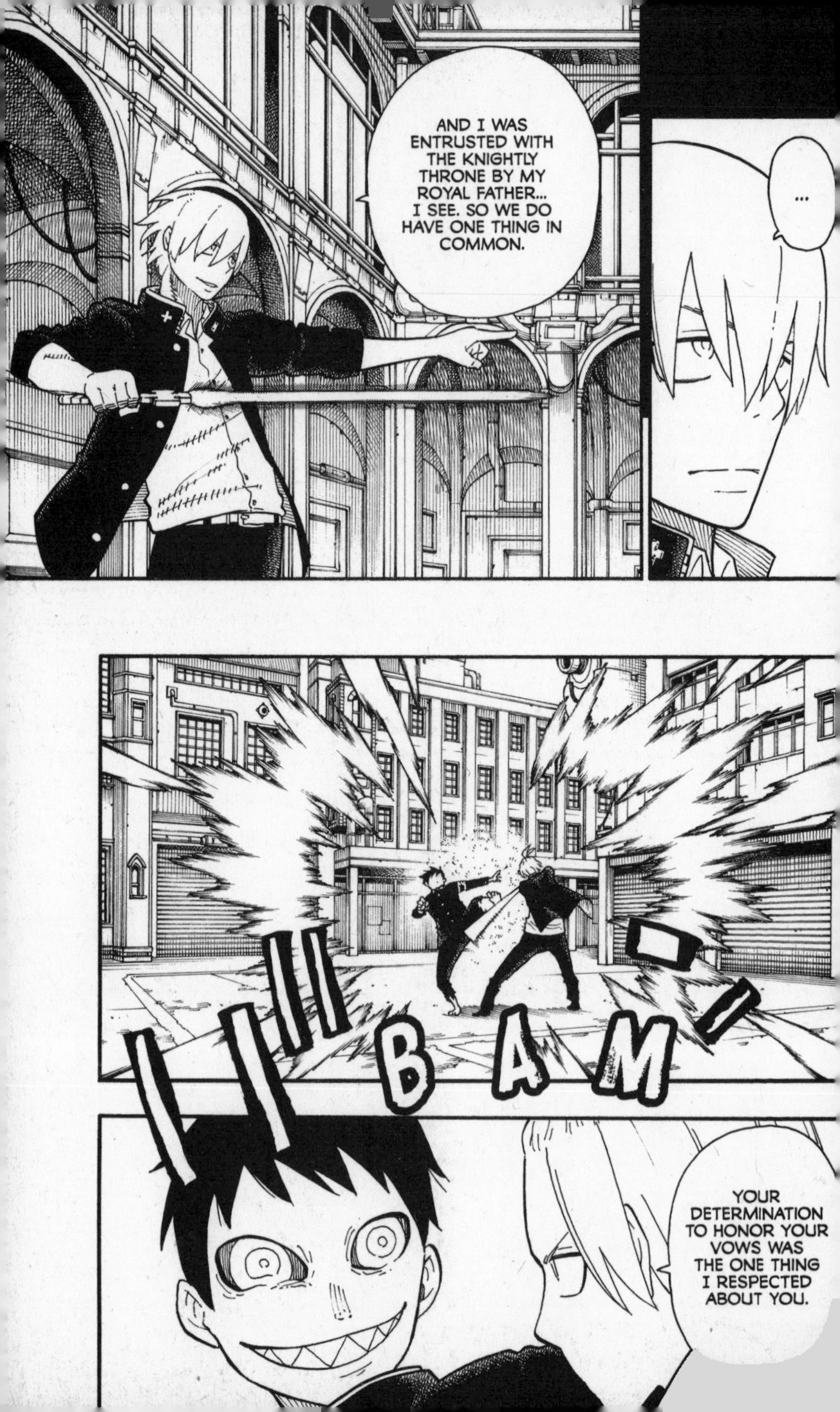
...
AND I WAS ENTRUSTED WITH THE KNIGHTLY THRONE BY MY ROYAL FATHER... I SEE. SO WE DO HAVE ONE THING IN COMMON.
BAM
YOUR DETERMINATION TO HONOR YOUR VOWS WAS THE ONE THING I RESPECTED ABOUT YOU.

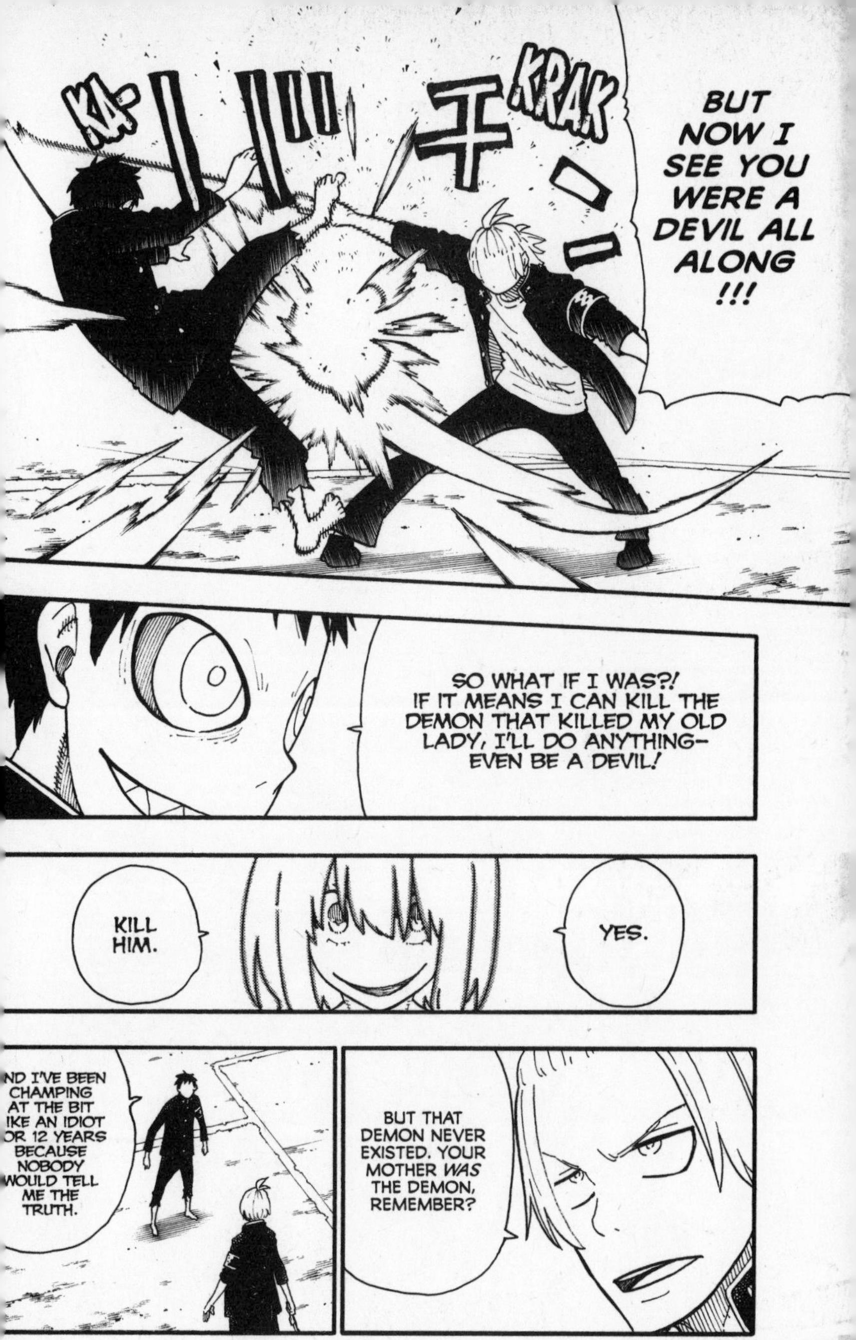
BUT NOW I SEE YOU WERE A DEVIL ALL ALONG!!!
KRAK
KA-
SO WHAT IF I WAS?! IF IT MEANS I CAN KILL THE DEMON THAT KILLED MY OLD LADY, I'LL DO ANYTHING— EVEN BE A DEVIL!
YES.
KILL HIM.
BUT THAT DEMON NEVER EXISTED. YOUR MOTHER *WAS* THE DEMON, REMEMBER?
ND I'VE BEEN CHAMPING AT THE BIT IKE AN IDIOT OR 12 YEARS BECAUSE NOBODY WOULD TELL ME THE TRUTH.

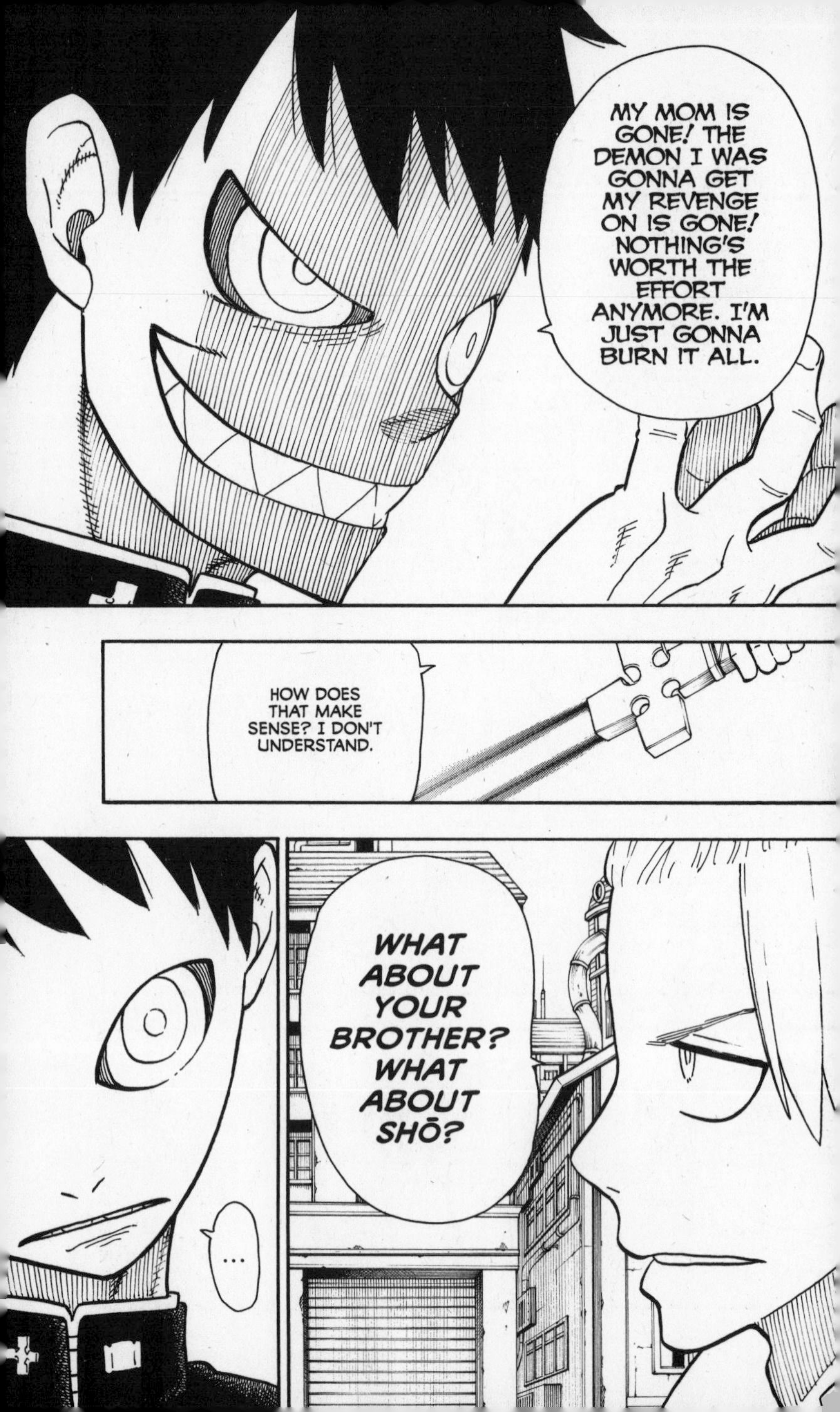
MY MOM IS GONE! THE DEMON I WAS GONNA GET MY REVENGE ON IS GONE! NOTHING'S WORTH THE EFFORT ANYMORE. I'M JUST GONNA BURN IT ALL.
HOW DOES THAT MAKE SENSE? I DON'T UNDERSTAND.
WHAT ABOUT YOUR BROTHER? WHAT ABOUT SHŌ?
...

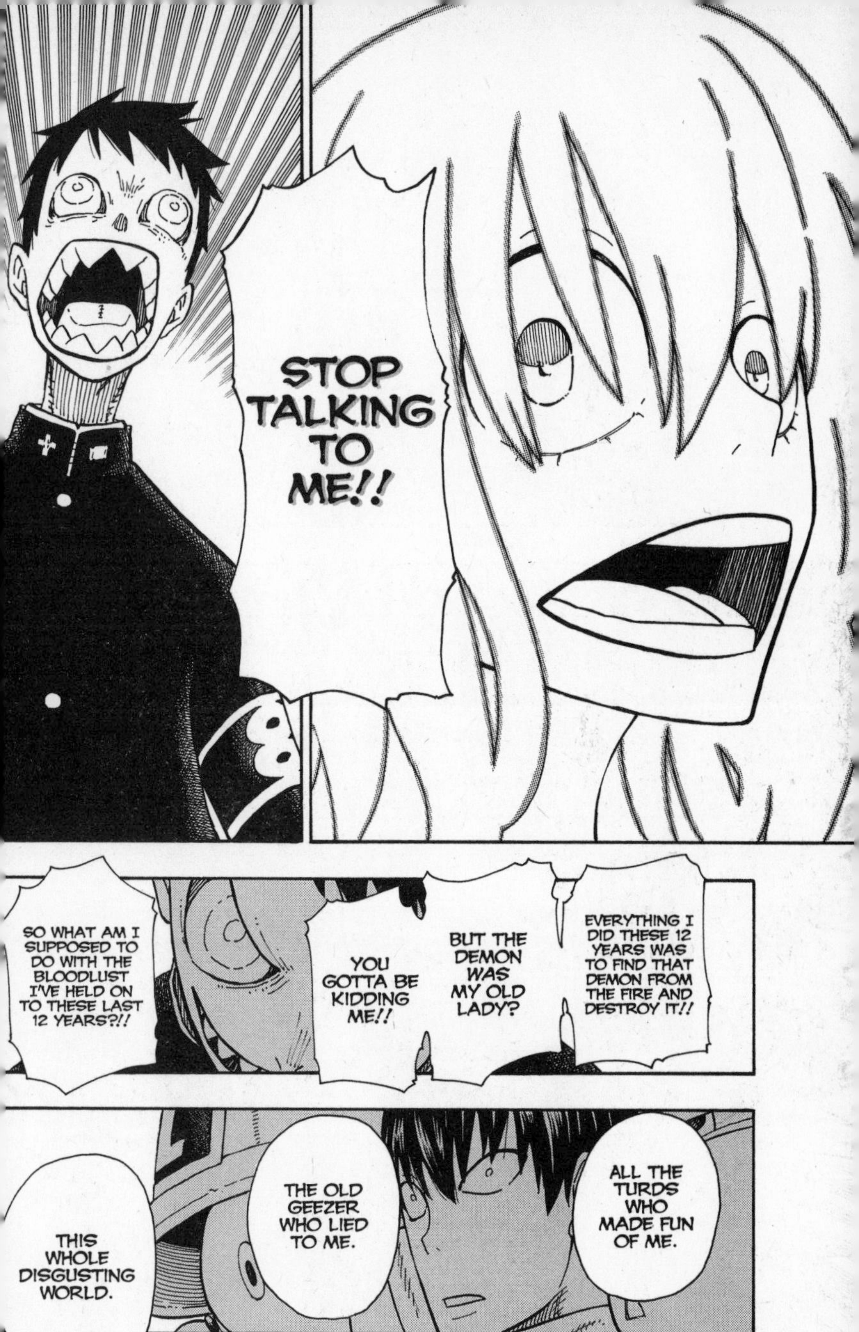
STOP TALKING TO ME!!
EVERYTHING I DID THESE 12 YEARS WAS TO FIND THAT DEMON FROM THE FIRE AND DESTROY IT!!
BUT THE DEMON *WAS* MY OLD LADY?
YOU GOTTA BE KIDDING ME!!
SO WHAT AM I SUPPOSED TO DO WITH THE BLOODLUST I'VE HELD ON TO THESE LAST 12 YEARS?!!
ALL THE TURDS WHO MADE FUN OF ME.
THE OLD GEEZER WHO LIED TO ME.
THIS WHOLE DISGUSTING WORLD.

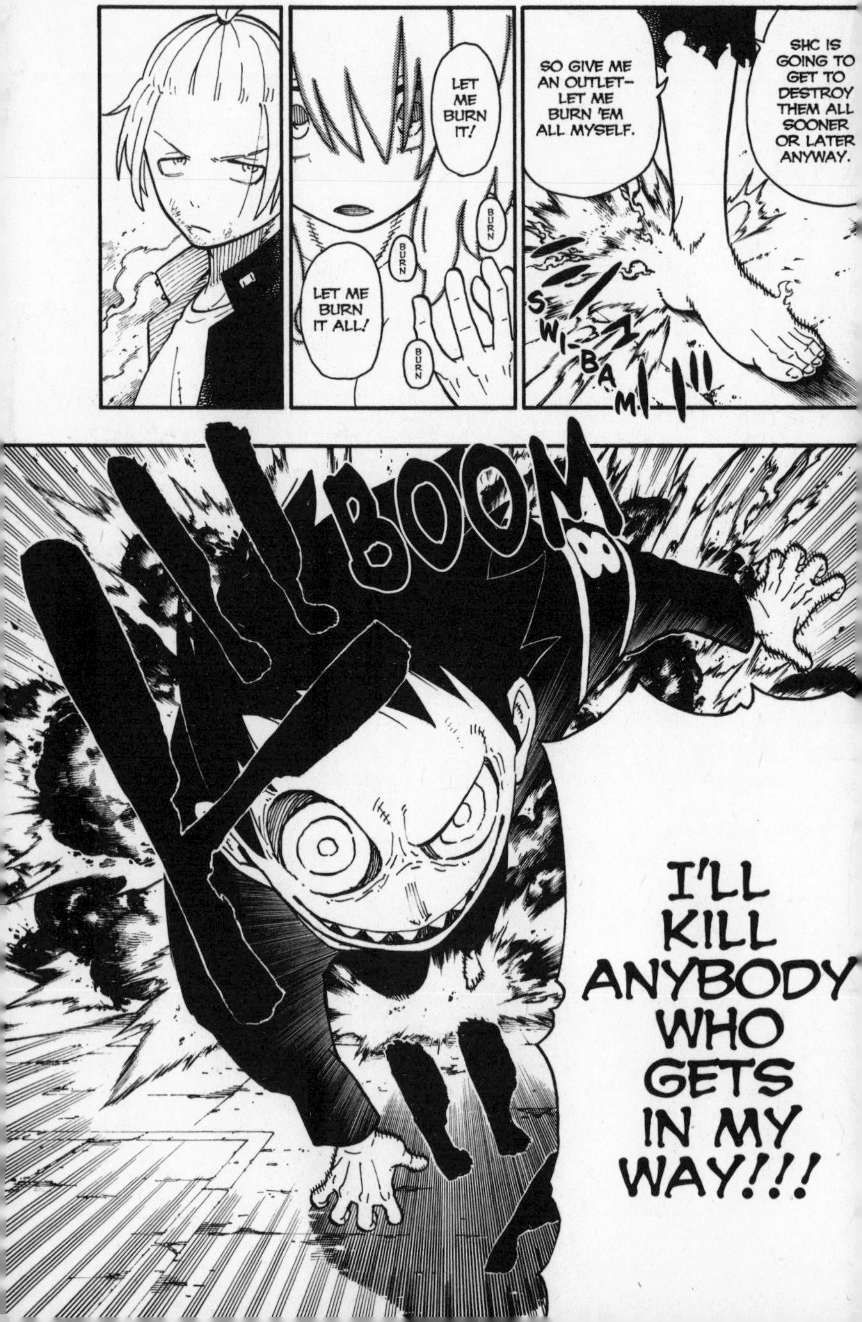
SHC IS GOING TO GET TO DESTROY THEM ALL SOONER OR LATER ANYWAY.
SO GIVE ME AN OUTLET—LET ME BURN 'EM ALL MYSELF.
SWI-BAM!!!
LET ME BURN IT!
BURN
BURN
LET ME BURN IT ALL!
BURN
KA-BOOM
I'LL KILL ANYBODY WHO GETS IN MY WAY!!!

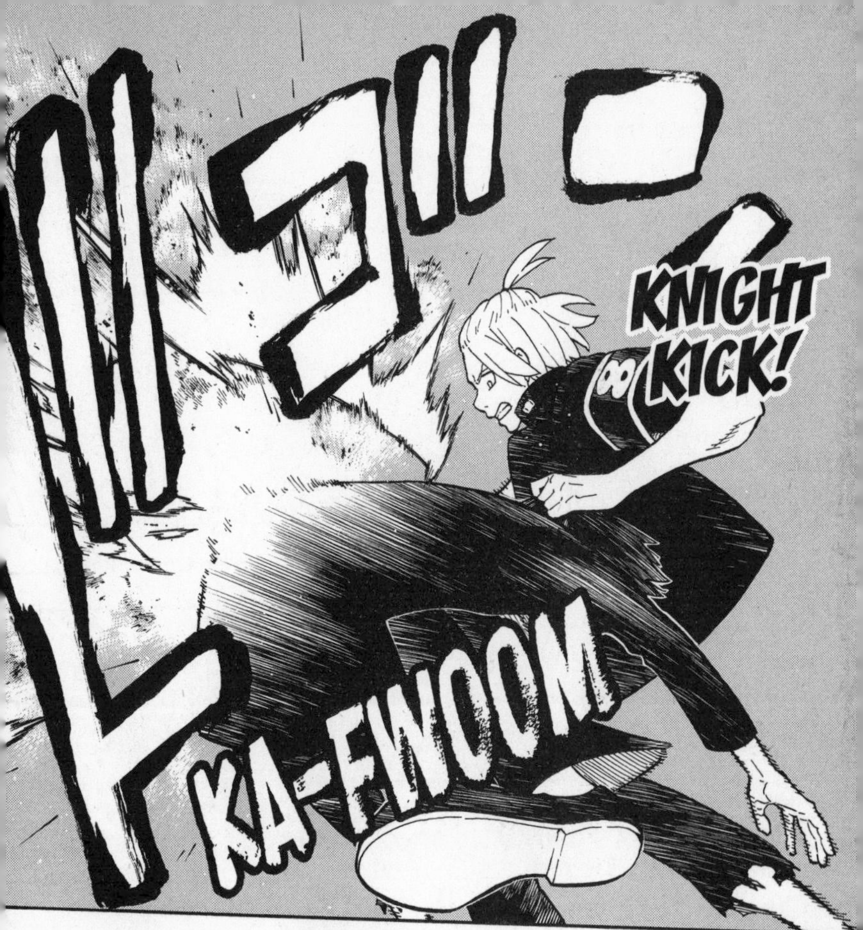
KNIGHT KICK!
KA-FWOOM
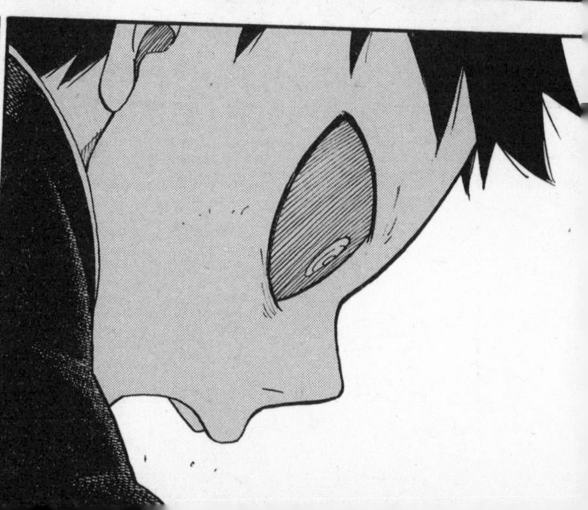
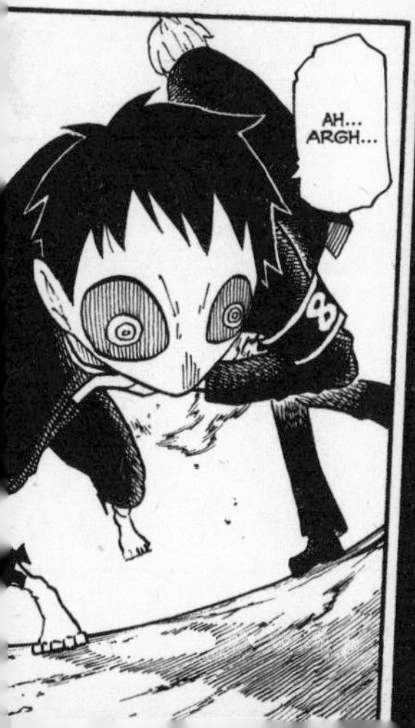
AH... ARGH...

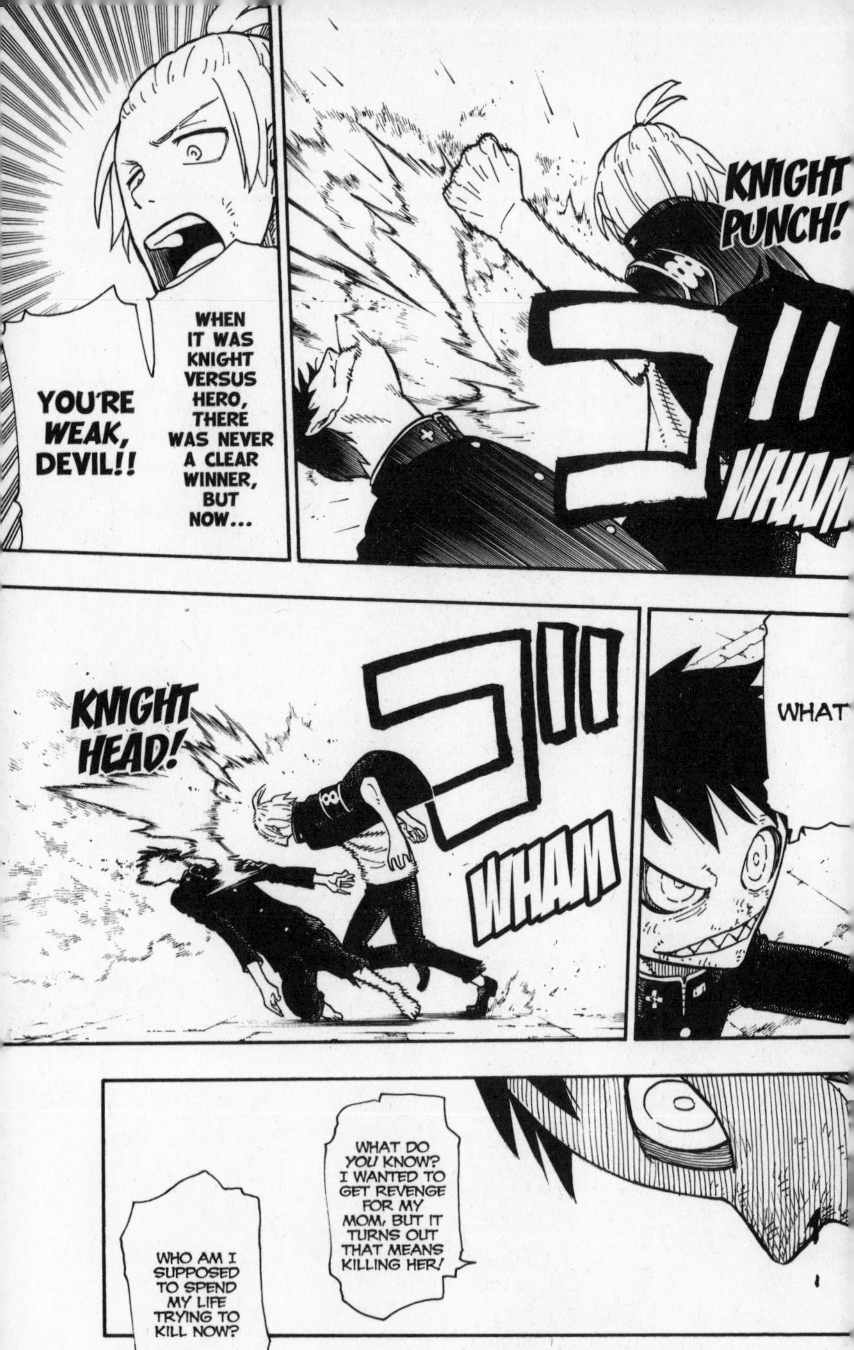
KNIGHT PUNCH!
WHAM
WHEN IT WAS KNIGHT VERSUS HERO, THERE WAS NEVER A CLEAR WINNER, BUT NOW...
YOU'RE WEAK, DEVIL!!
WHAT
WHAM
KNIGHT HEAD!
WHAT DO YOU KNOW? I WANTED TO GET REVENGE FOR MY MOM, BUT IT TURNS OUT THAT MEANS KILLING HER!
WHO AM I SUPPOSED TO SPEND MY LIFE TRYING TO KILL NOW?

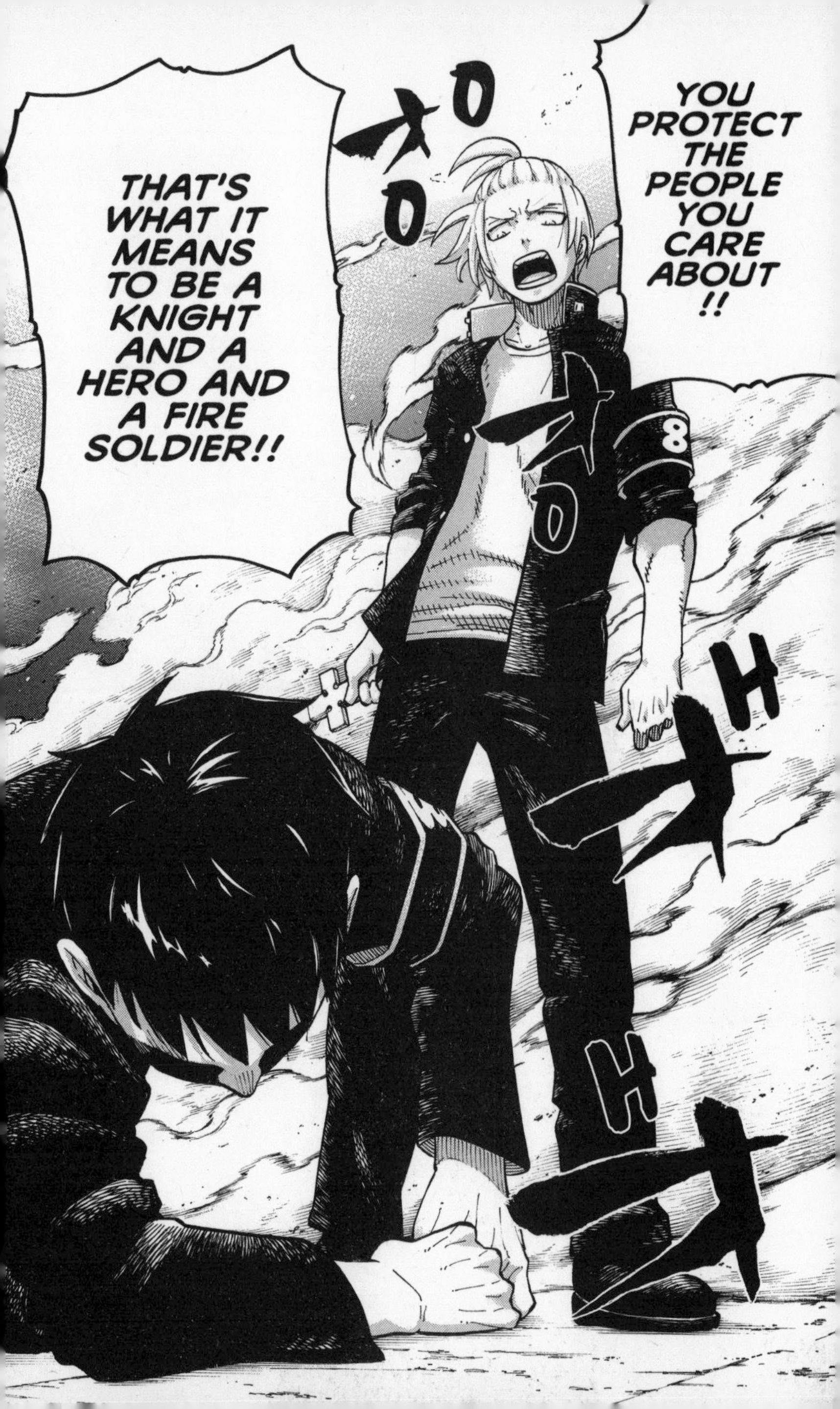
YOU PROTECT THE PEOPLE YOU CARE ABOUT!!
THAT'S WHAT IT MEANS TO BE A KNIGHT AND A HERO AND A FIRE SOLDIER!!

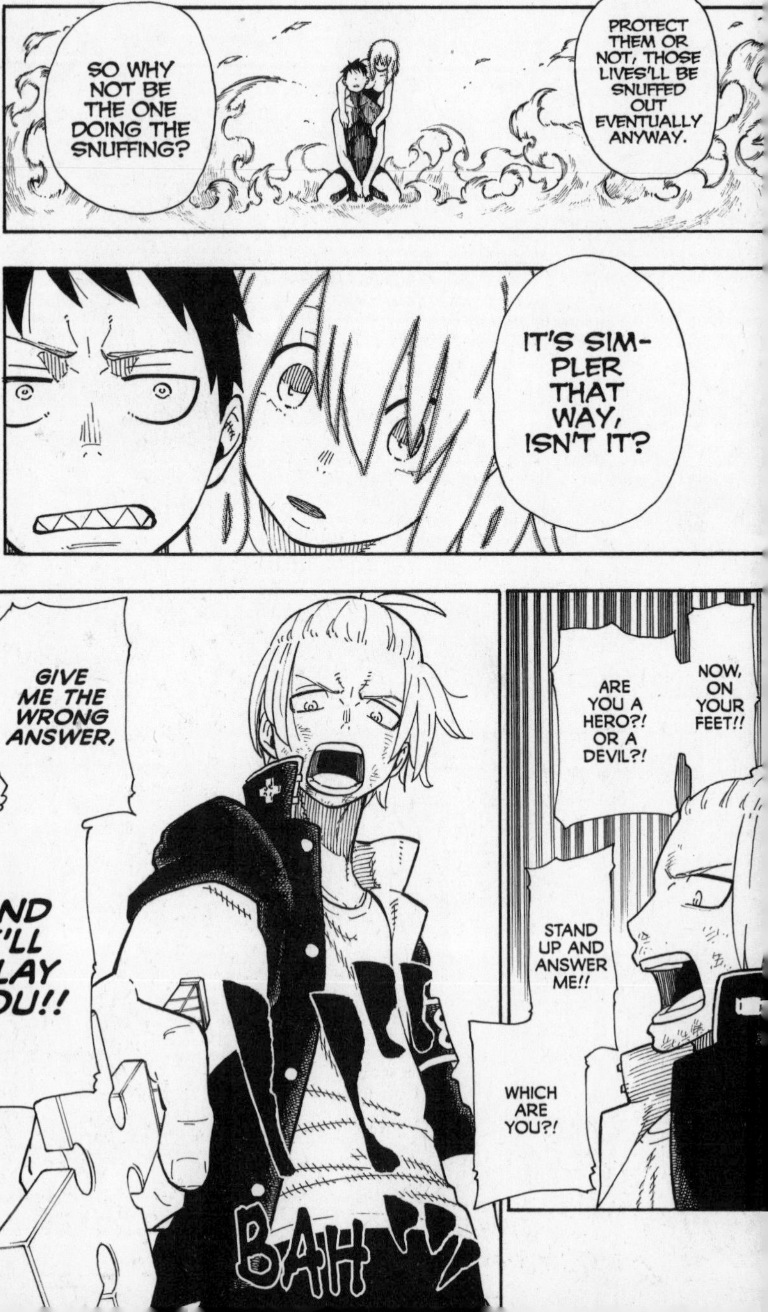
PROTECT THEM OR NOT, THOSE LIVES'LL BE SNUFFED OUT EVENTUALLY ANYWAY.
SO WHY NOT BE THE ONE DOING THE SNUFFING?
IT'S SIMPLER THAT WAY, ISN'T IT?
NOW, ON YOUR FEET!!
ARE YOU A HERO?! OR A DEVIL?!
STAND UP AND ANSWER ME!!
WHICH ARE YOU?!
GIVE ME THE WRONG ANSWER,
AND I'LL SLAY YOU!!
BAH

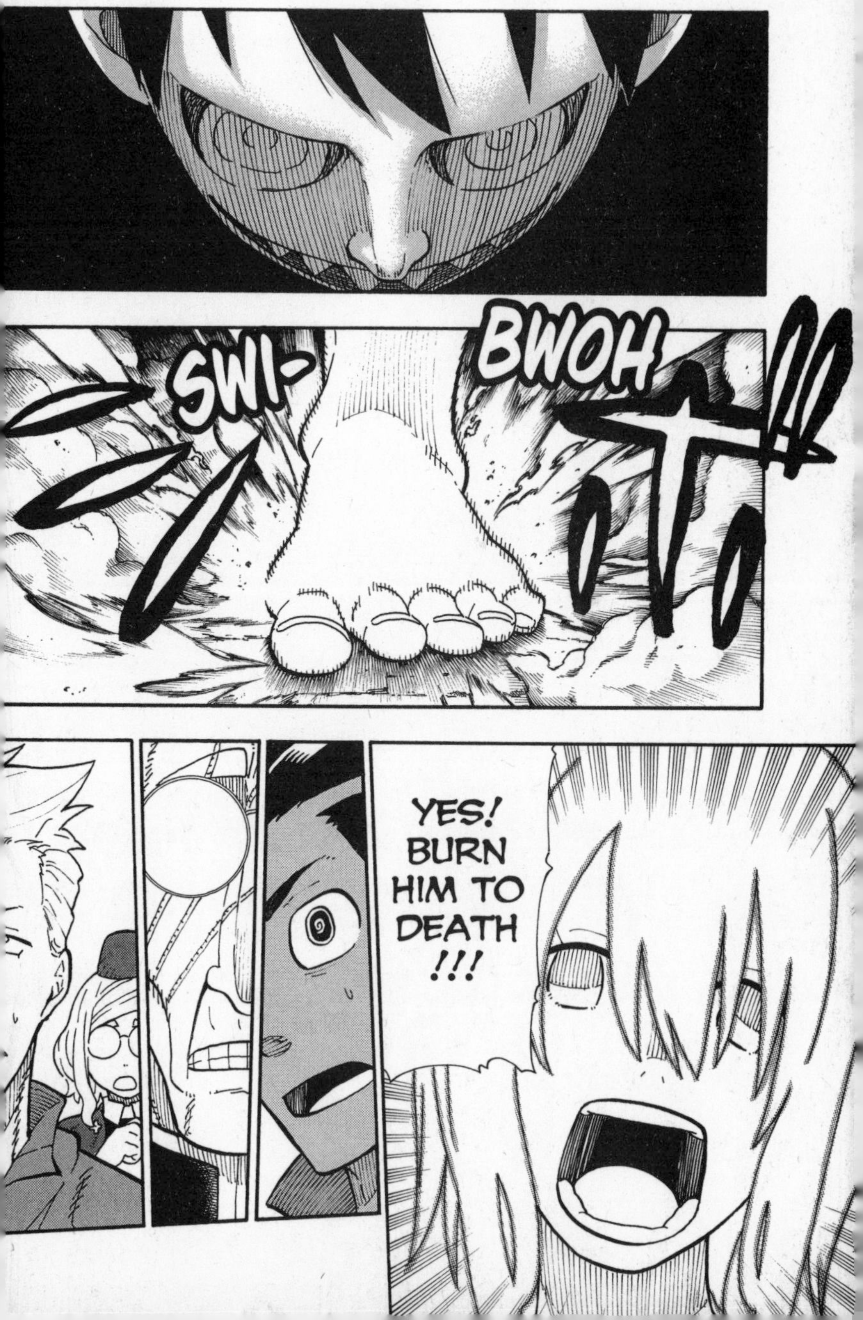
SWI-
BWOH
YES! BURN HIM TO DEATH !!!

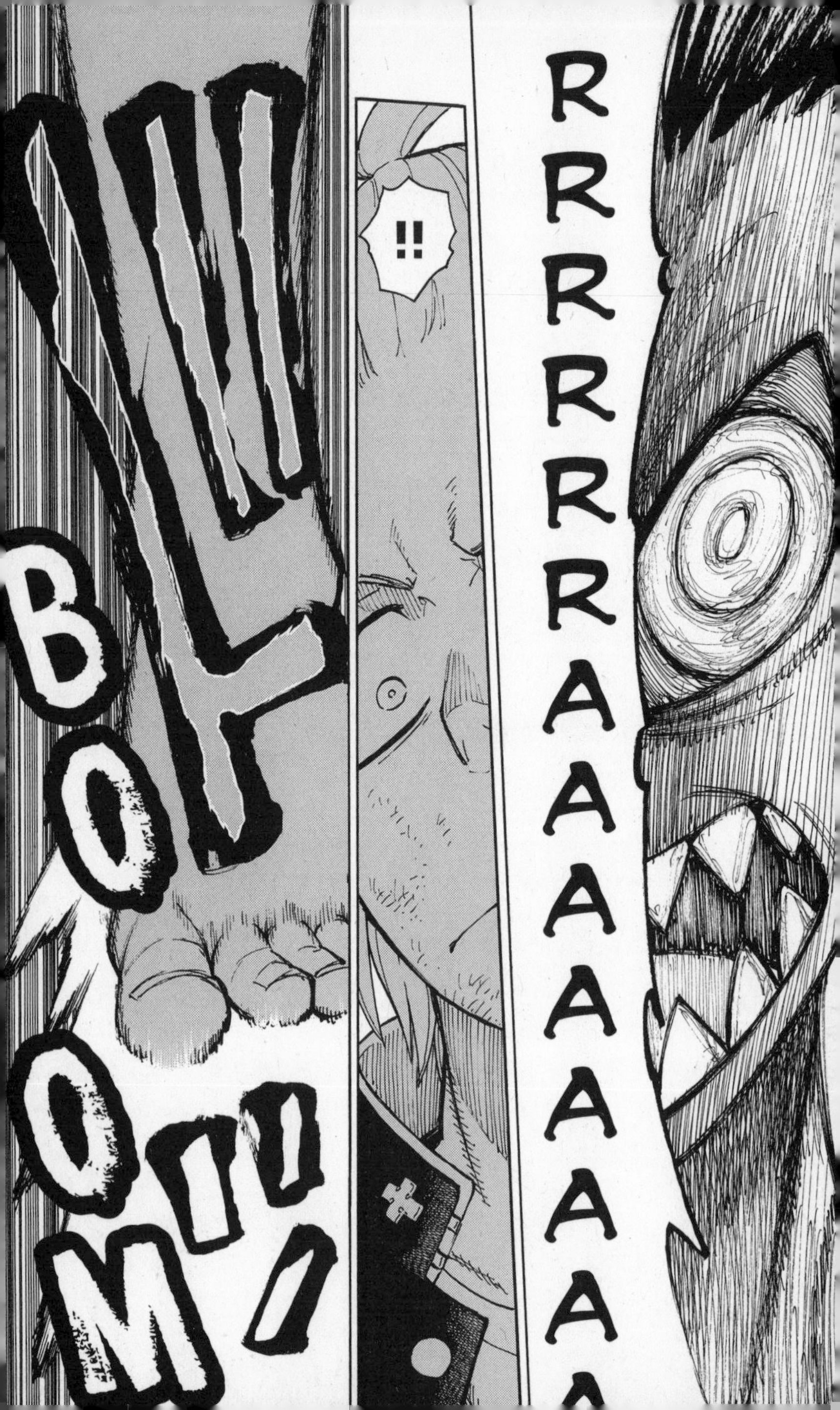
RRRRRRAAAAAAA
!!
BOOM!!

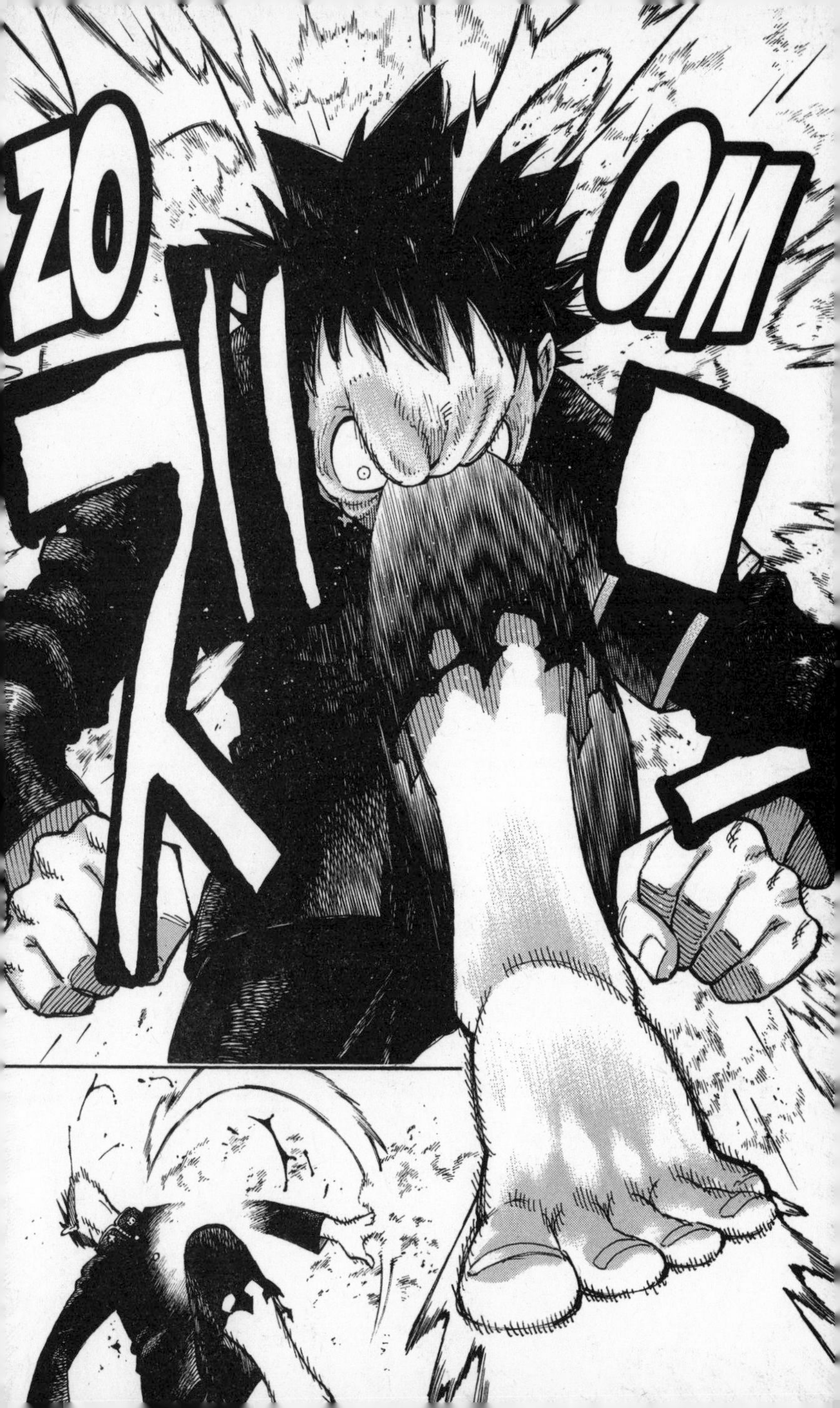
ZOOM

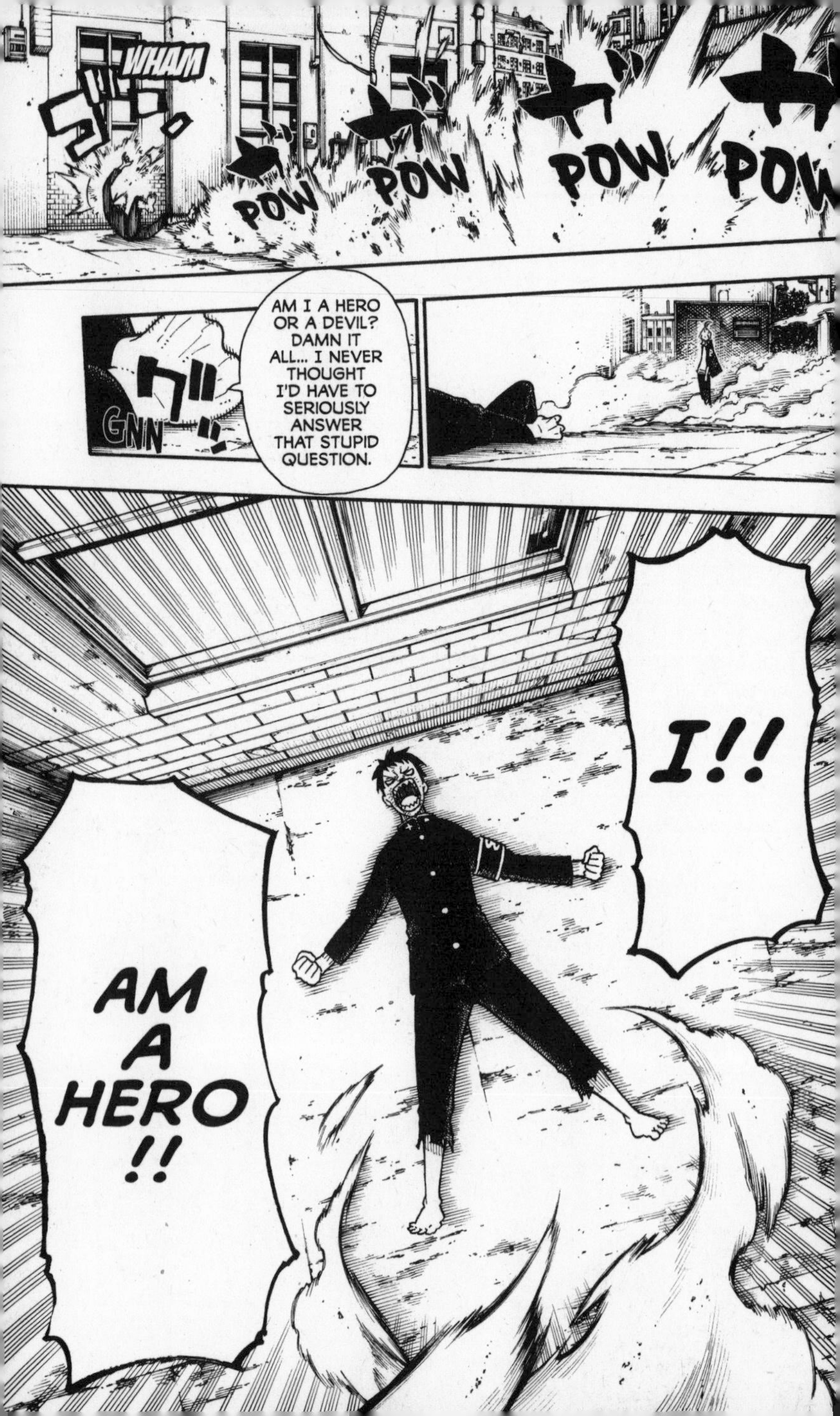
POW
POW
POW
POW
WHAM
AM I A HERO OR A DEVIL? DAMN IT ALL... I NEVER THOUGHT I'D HAVE TO SERIOUSLY ANSWER THAT STUPID QUESTION.
GNN
I!!
AM A HERO!!

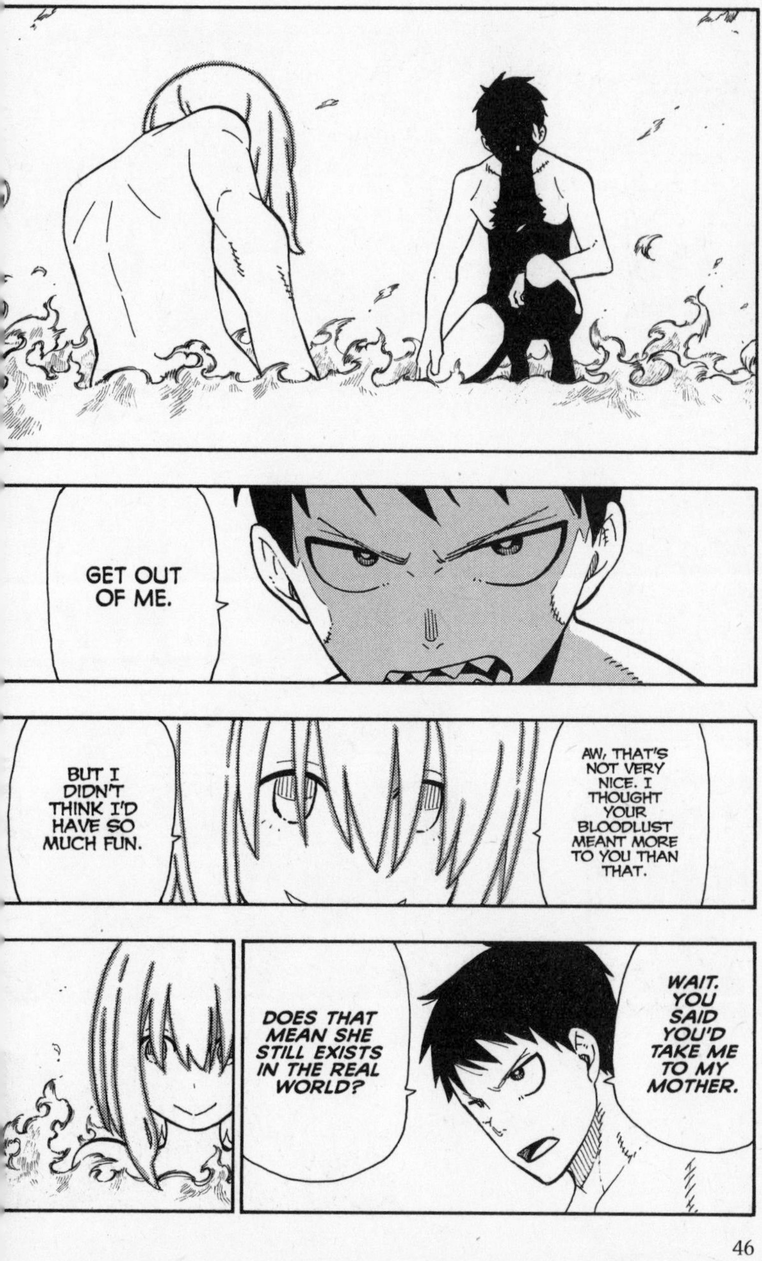
GET OUT OF ME.
AW, THAT'S NOT VERY NICE. I THOUGHT YOUR BLOODLUST MEANT MORE TO YOU THAN THAT.
BUT I DIDN'T THINK I'D HAVE SO MUCH FUN.
WAIT. YOU SAID YOU'D TAKE ME TO MY MOTHER.
DOES THAT MEAN SHE STILL EXISTS IN THE REAL WORLD?

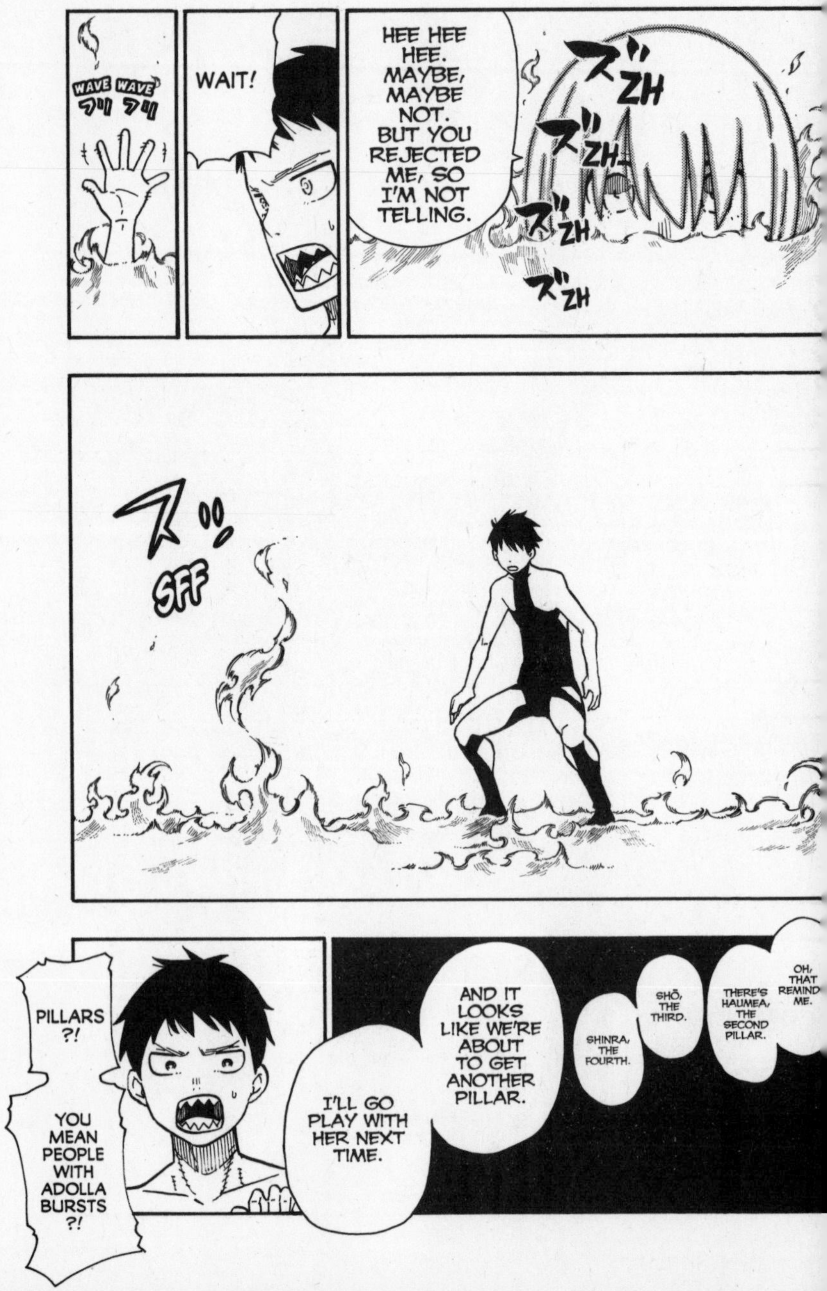
ズ ZH
ズ ZH
ズ ZH
ズ ZH
HEE HEE HEE. MAYBE, MAYBE NOT. BUT YOU REJECTED ME, SO I'M NOT TELLING.
WAIT!
WAVE WAVE フリフリ
ス SFF
OH, THAT REMIND ME.
THERE'S HAUMEA, THE SECOND PILLAR.
SHŌ, THE THIRD.
SHINRA, THE FOURTH.
AND IT LOOKS LIKE WE'RE ABOUT TO GET ANOTHER PILLAR.
I'LL GO PLAY WITH HER NEXT TIME.
PILLARS?!
YOU MEAN PEOPLE WITH ADOLLA BURSTS?!

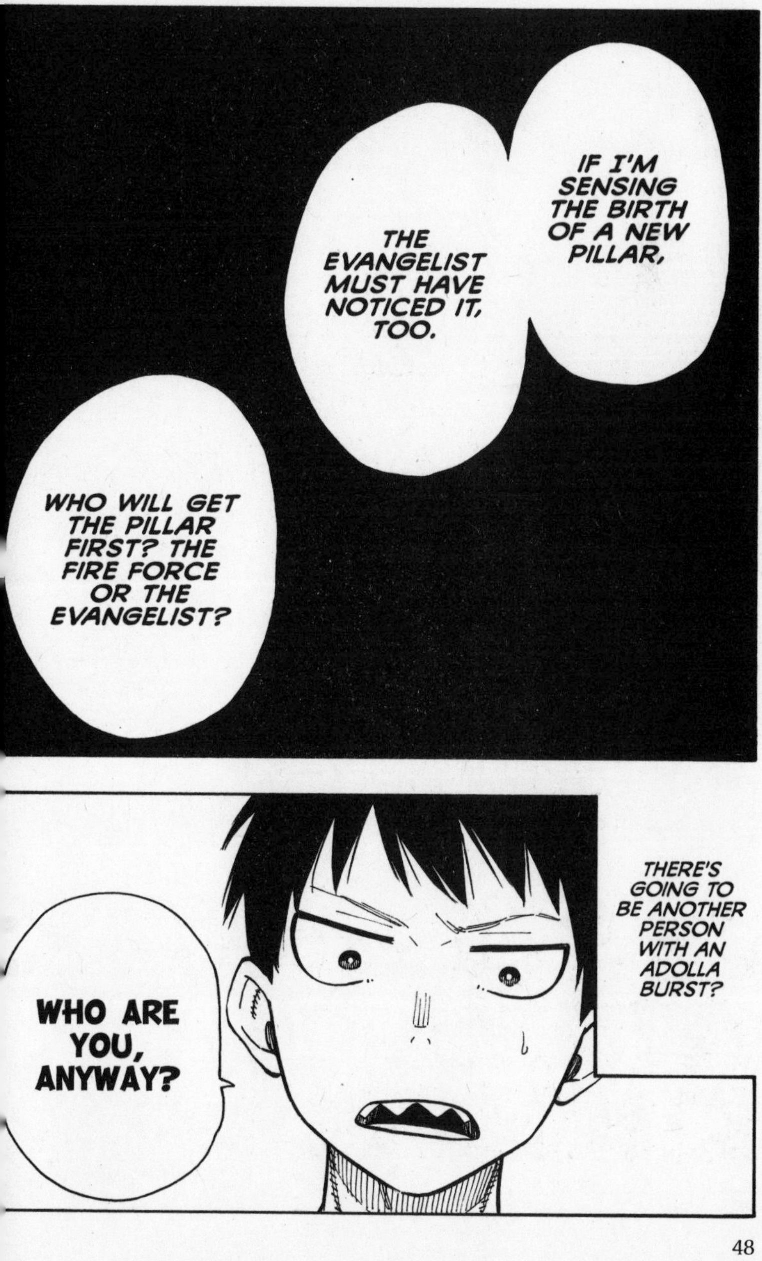
IF I'M SENSING THE BIRTH OF A NEW PILLAR,
THE EVANGELIST MUST HAVE NOTICED IT, TOO.
WHO WILL GET THE PILLAR FIRST? THE FIRE FORCE OR THE EVANGELIST?
THERE'S GOING TO BE ANOTHER PERSON WITH AN ADOLLA BURST?
WHO ARE YOU, ANYWAY?

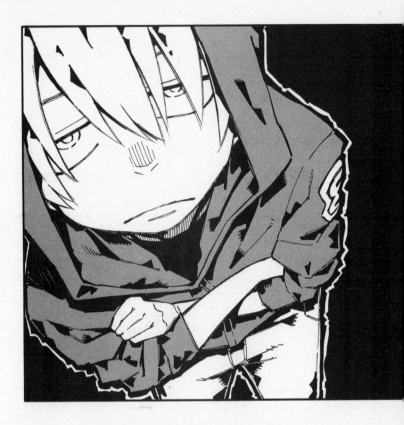

CHAPTER XCIX:
A NEW
KINDLING

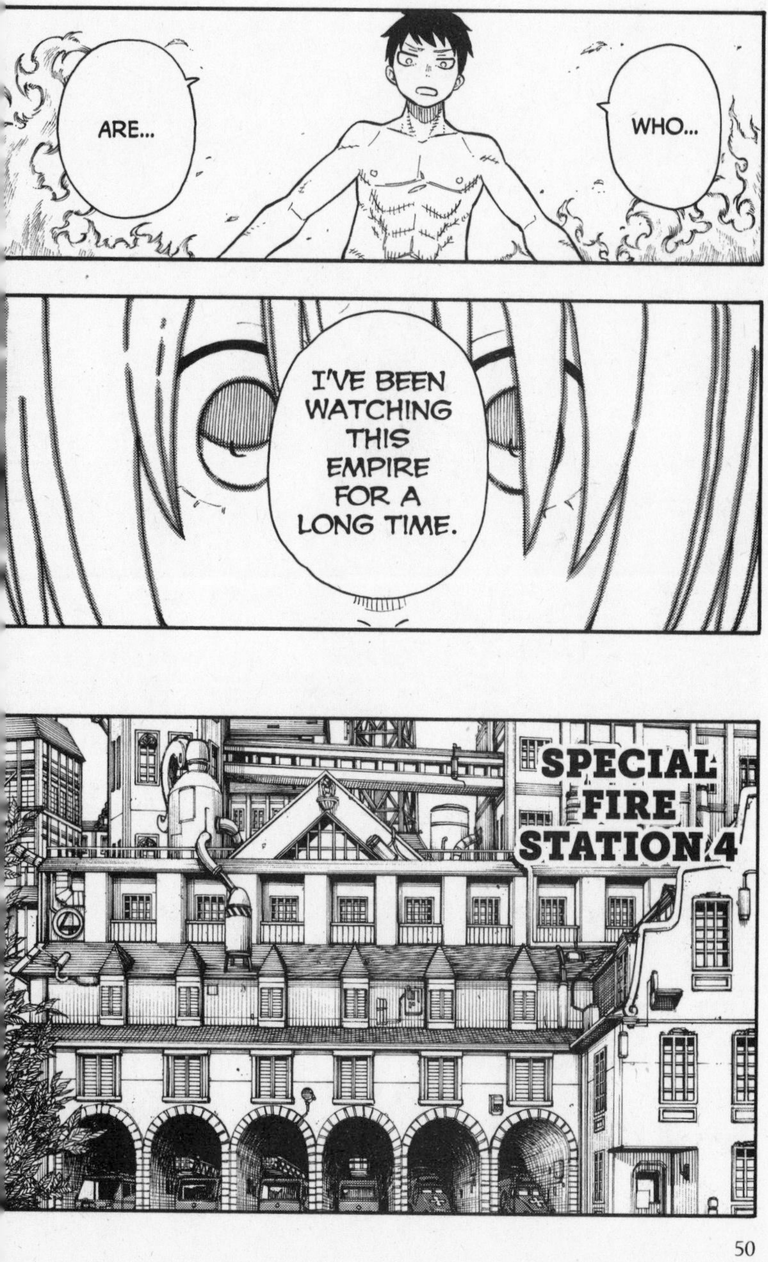
WHO...
ARE...
I'VE BEEN WATCHING THIS EMPIRE FOR A LONG TIME.
SPECIAL FIRE STATION 4

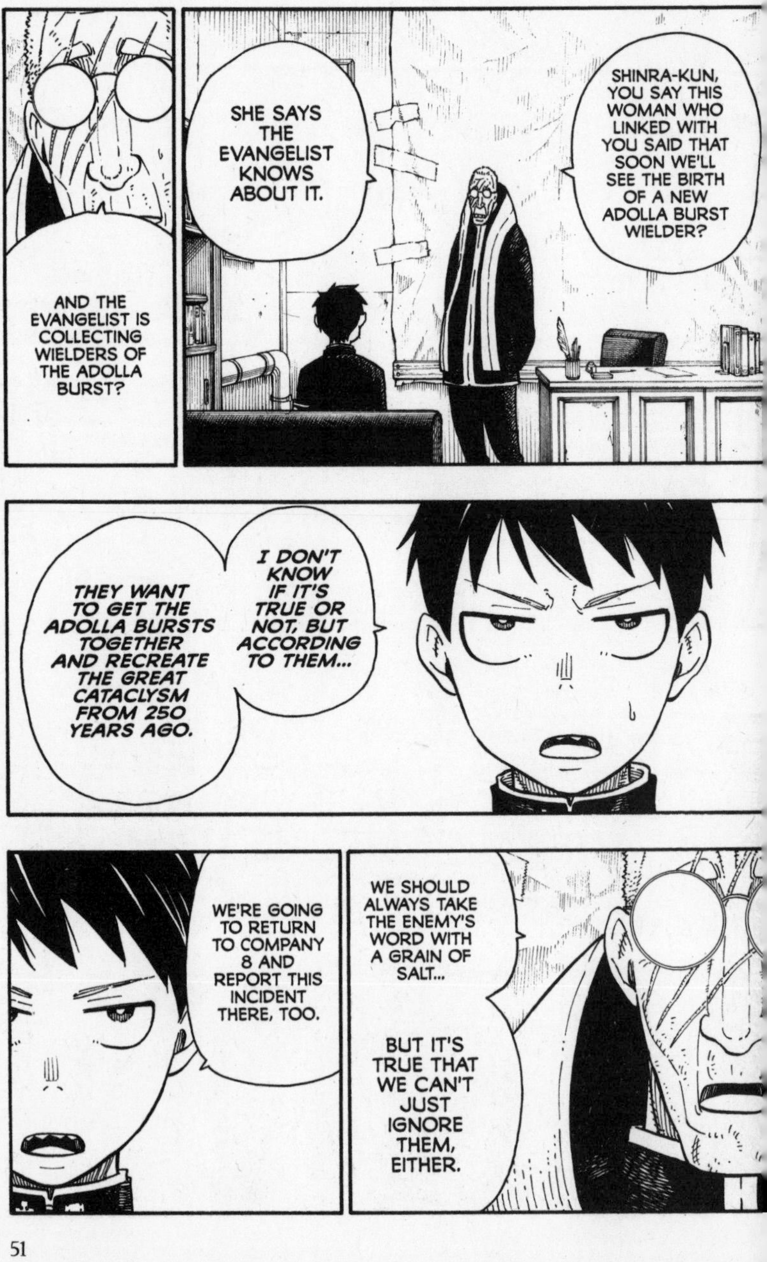
SHINRA-KUN, YOU SAY THIS WOMAN WHO LINKED WITH YOU SAID THAT SOON WE'LL SEE THE BIRTH OF A NEW ADOLLA BURST WIELDER?
SHE SAYS THE EVANGELIST KNOWS ABOUT IT.
AND THE EVANGELIST IS COLLECTING WIELDERS OF THE ADOLLA BURST?
I DON'T KNOW IF IT'S TRUE OR NOT, BUT ACCORDING TO THEM...
THEY WANT TO GET THE ADOLLA BURSTS TOGETHER AND RECREATE THE GREAT CATACLYSM FROM 250 YEARS AGO.
WE SHOULD ALWAYS TAKE THE ENEMY'S WORD WITH A GRAIN OF SALT...
BUT IT'S TRUE THAT WE CAN'T JUST IGNORE THEM, EITHER.
WE'RE GOING TO RETURN TO COMPANY 8 AND REPORT THIS INCIDENT THERE, TOO.

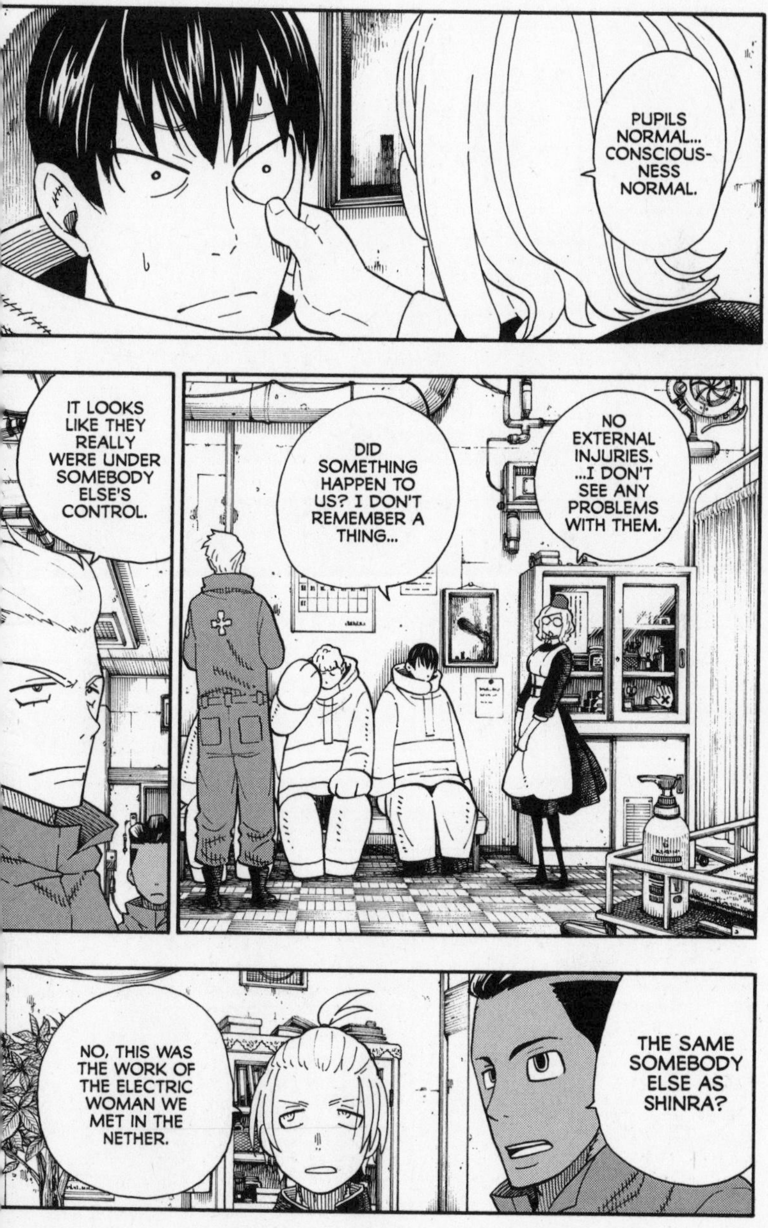
PUPILS NORMAL... CONSCIOUS-NESS NORMAL.
NO EXTERNAL INJURIES. ...I DON'T SEE ANY PROBLEMS WITH THEM.
DID SOMETHING HAPPEN TO US? I DON'T REMEMBER A THING...
IT LOOKS LIKE THEY REALLY WERE UNDER SOMEBODY ELSE'S CONTROL.
THE SAME SOMEBODY ELSE AS SHINRA?
NO, THIS WAS THE WORK OF THE ELECTRIC WOMAN WE MET IN THE NETHER.

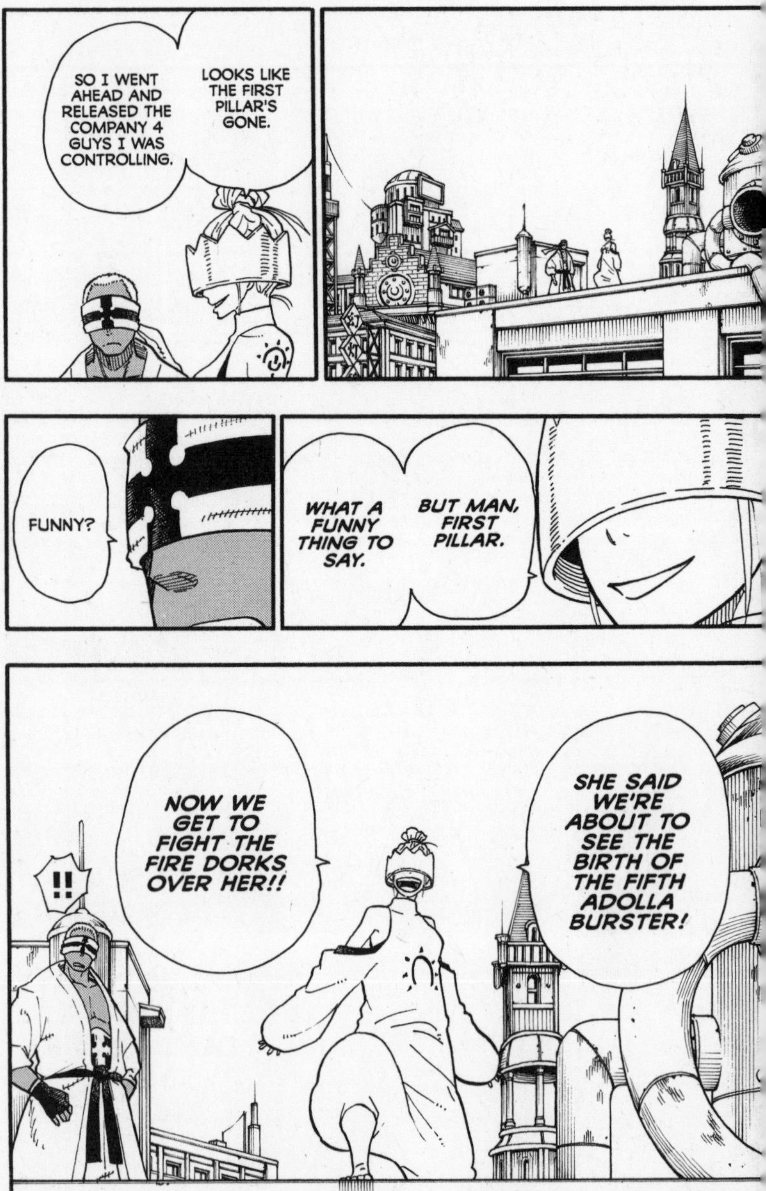
LOOKS LIKE THE FIRST PILLAR'S GONE.
SO I WENT AHEAD AND RELEASED THE COMPANY 4 GUYS I WAS CONTROLLING.
BUT MAN, FIRST PILLAR.
WHAT A FUNNY THING TO SAY.
FUNNY?
SHE SAID WE'RE ABOUT TO SEE THE BIRTH OF THE FIFTH ADOLLA BURSTER!
NOW WE GET TO FIGHT THE FIRE DORKS OVER HER!!
!!

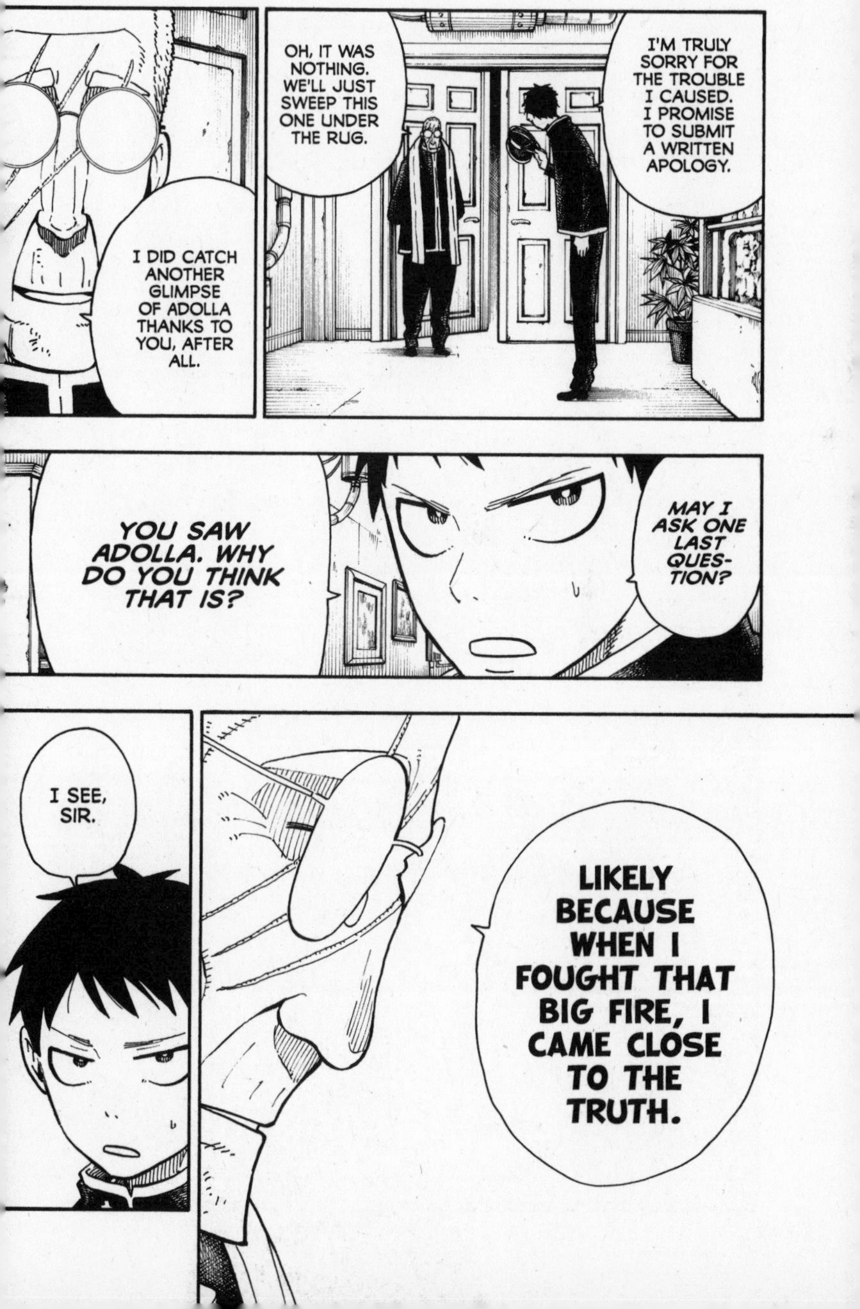
I'M TRULY SORRY FOR THE TROUBLE I CAUSED. I PROMISE TO SUBMIT A WRITTEN APOLOGY.
OH, IT WAS NOTHING. WE'LL JUST SWEEP THIS ONE UNDER THE RUG.
I DID CATCH ANOTHER GLIMPSE OF ADOLLA THANKS TO YOU, AFTER ALL.
MAY I ASK ONE LAST QUES-TION?
YOU SAW ADOLLA. WHY DO YOU THINK THAT IS?
LIKELY BECAUSE WHEN I FOUGHT THAT BIG FIRE, I CAME CLOSE TO THE TRUTH.
I SEE, SIR.

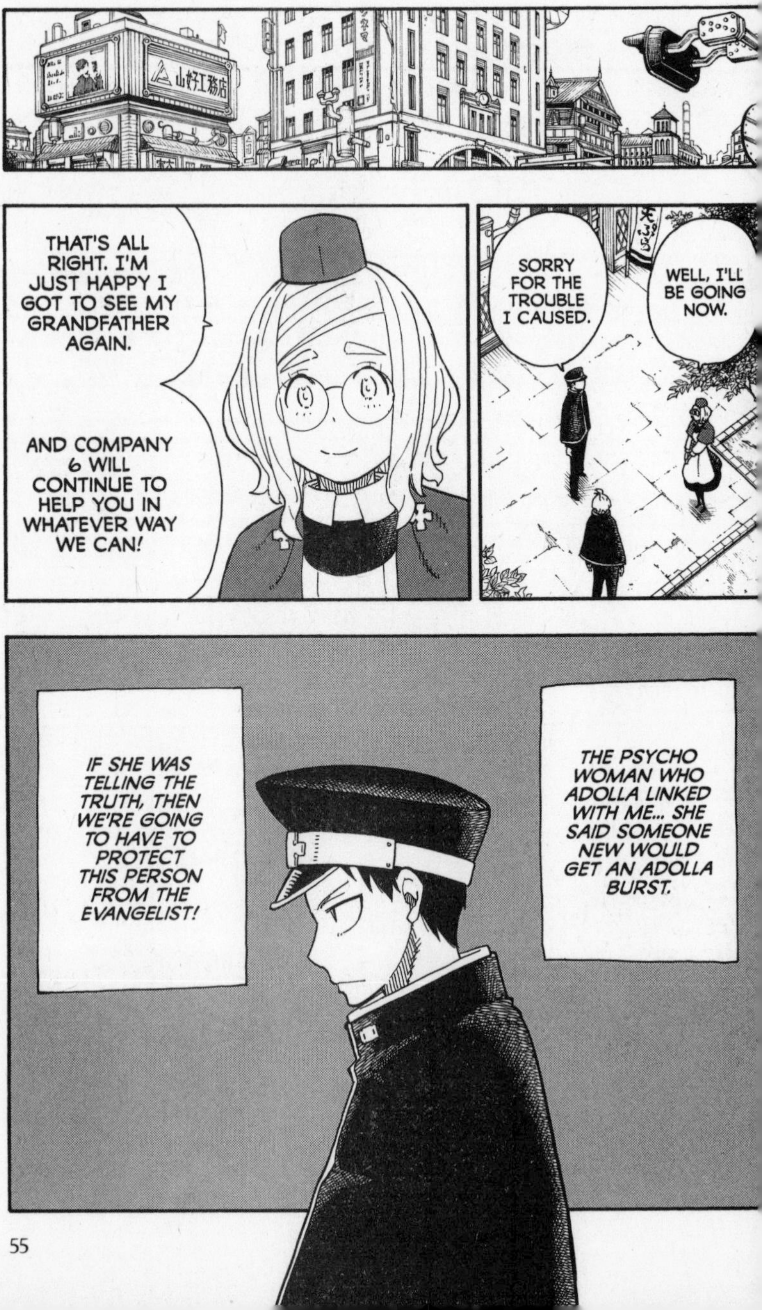

山好工務店
WELL, I'LL BE GOING NOW.
SORRY FOR THE TROUBLE I CAUSED.
THAT'S ALL RIGHT. I'M JUST HAPPY I GOT TO SEE MY GRANDFATHER AGAIN.
AND COMPANY 6 WILL CONTINUE TO HELP YOU IN WHATEVER WAY WE CAN!
THE PSYCHO WOMAN WHO ADOLLA LINKED WITH ME... SHE SAID SOMEONE NEW WOULD GET AN ADOLLA BURST.
IF SHE WAS TELLING THE TRUTH, THEN WE'RE GOING TO HAVE TO PROTECT THIS PERSON FROM THE EVANGELIST!

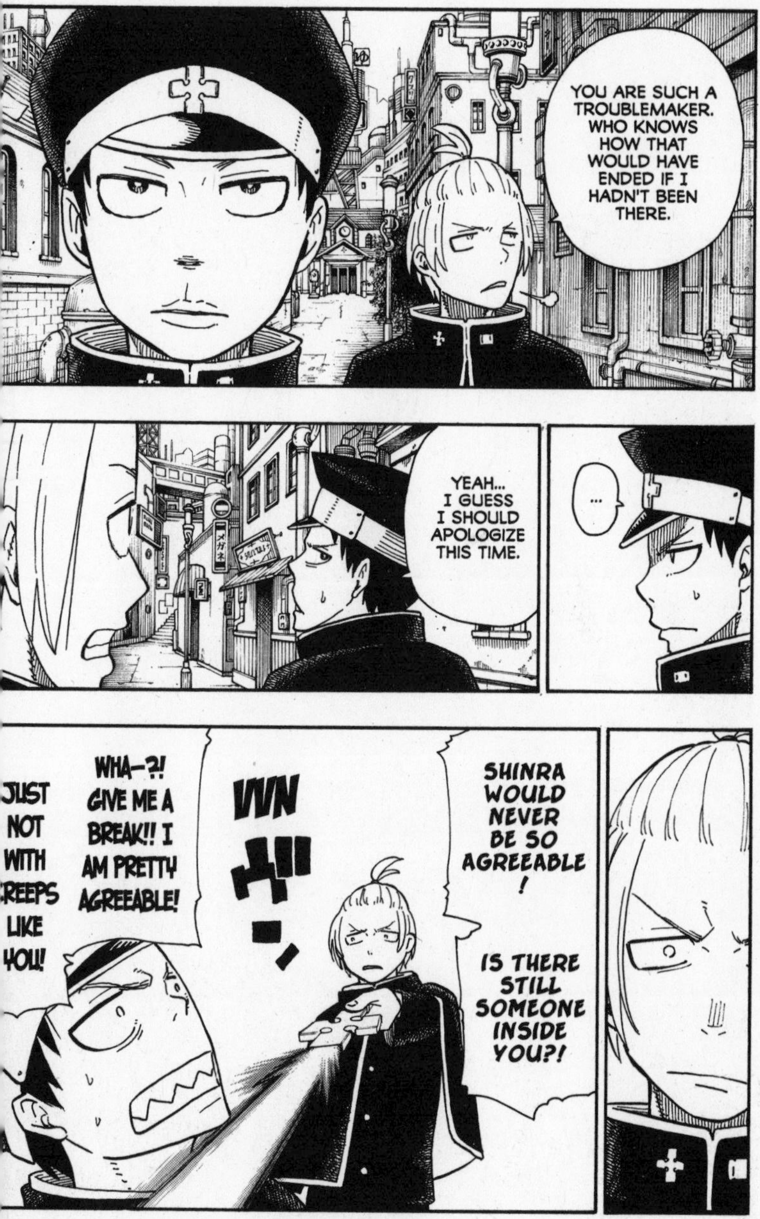

YOU ARE SUCH A TROUBLEMAKER. WHO KNOWS HOW THAT WOULD HAVE ENDED IF I HADN'T BEEN THERE.
...
YEAH... I GUESS I SHOULD APOLOGIZE THIS TIME.
SHINRA WOULD NEVER BE SO AGREEABLE!
IS THERE STILL SOMEONE INSIDE YOU?!
VVN
WHA-?! GIVE ME A BREAK!! I AM PRETTY AGREEABLE!
JUST NOT WITH CREEPS LIKE YOU!

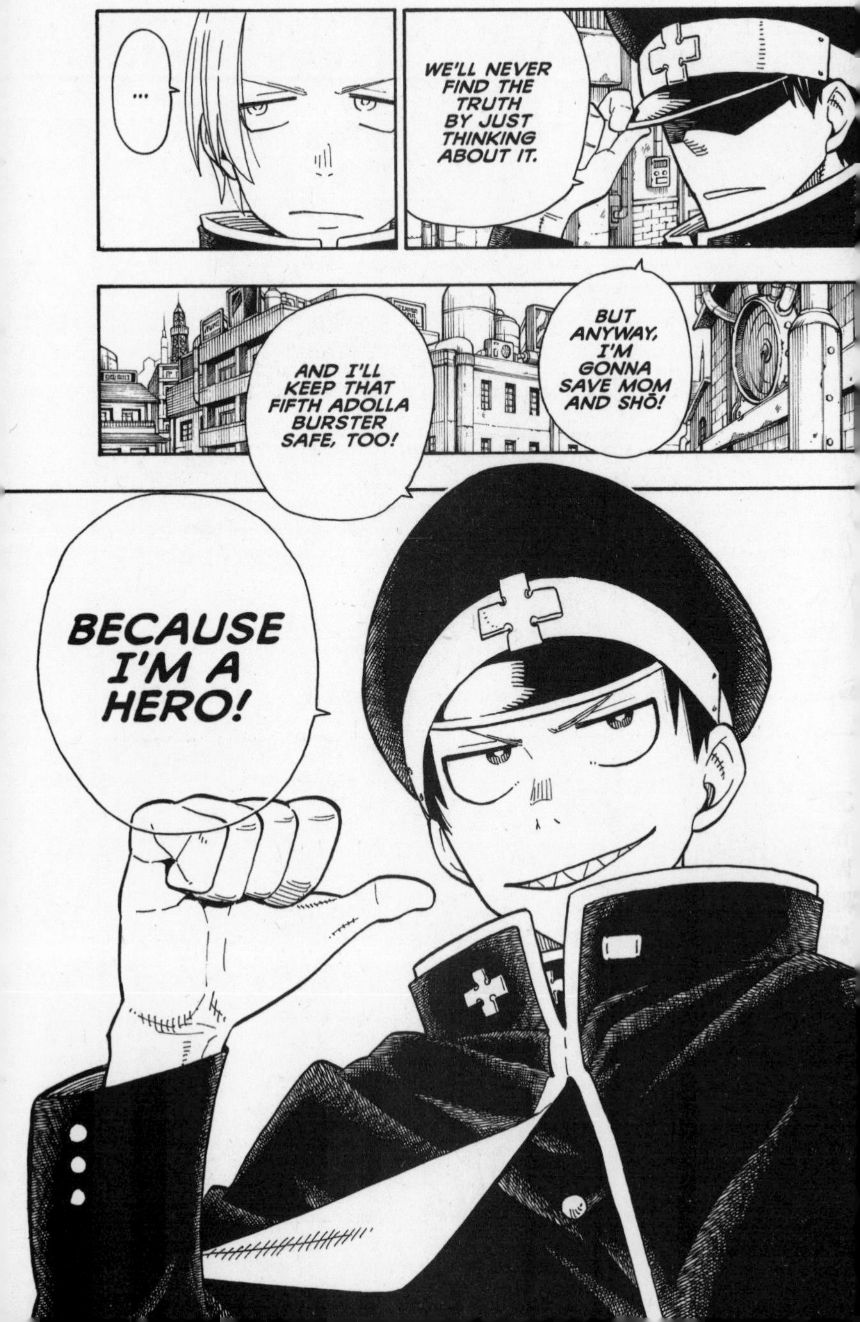
WE'LL NEVER FIND THE TRUTH BY JUST THINKING ABOUT IT.
...
BUT ANYWAY, I'M GONNA SAVE MOM AND SHŌ!
AND I'LL KEEP THAT FIFTH ADOLLA BURSTER SAFE, TOO!
BECAUSE I'M A HERO!

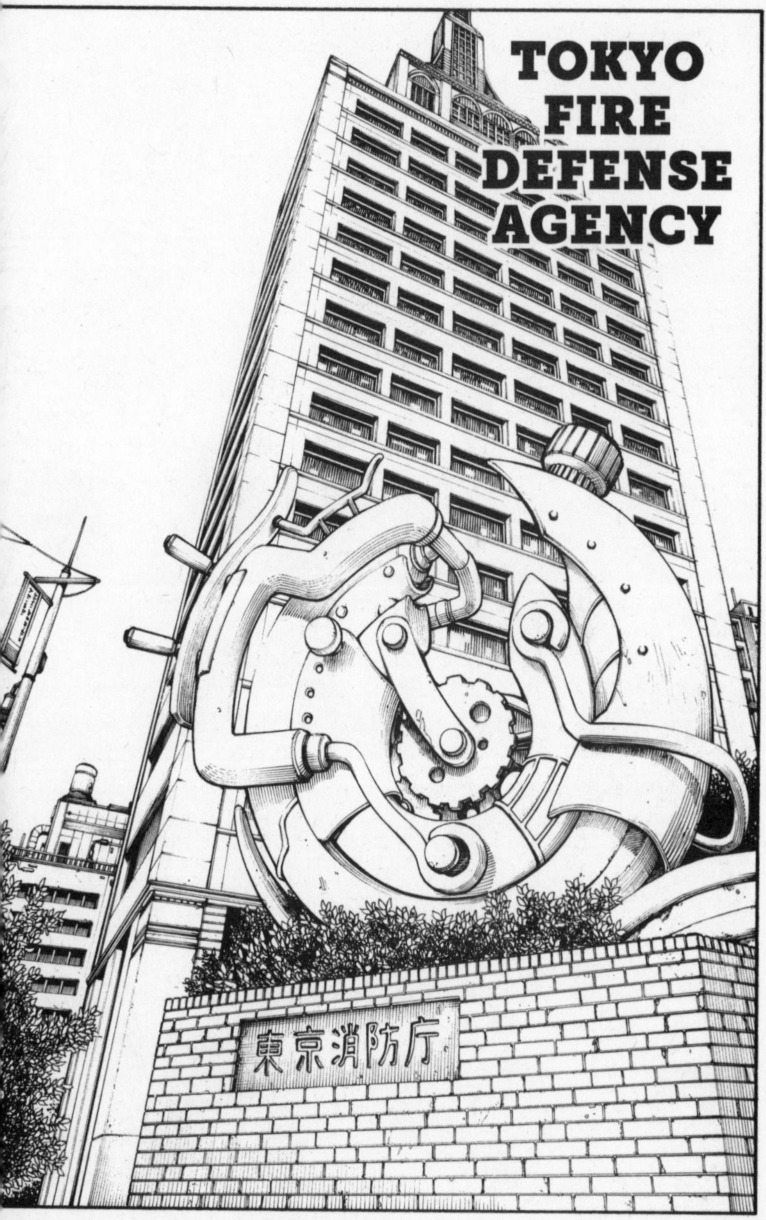
TOKYO FIRE DEFENSE AGENCY
東京消防庁

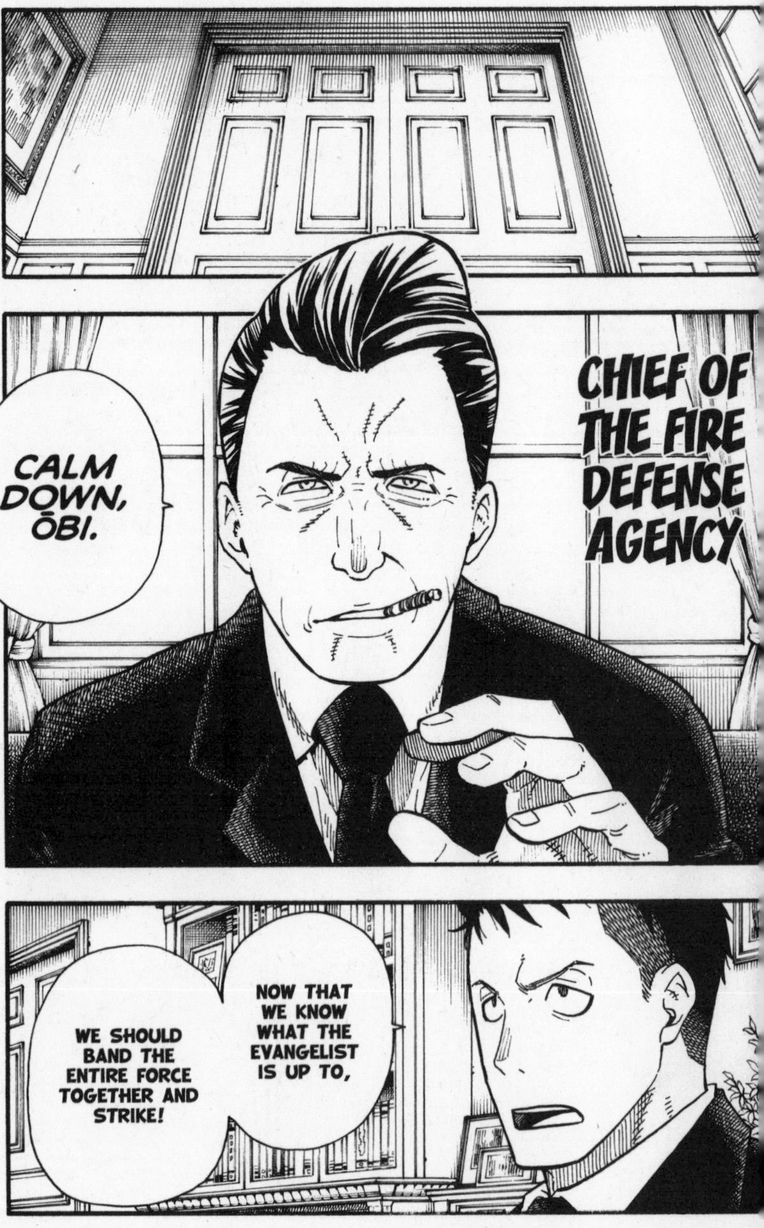
CHIEF OF THE FIRE DEFENSE AGENCY
CALM DOWN, ŌBI.
NOW THAT WE KNOW WHAT THE EVANGELIST IS UP TO,
WE SHOULD BAND THE ENTIRE FORCE TOGETHER AND STRIKE!

Sign: Perseverance

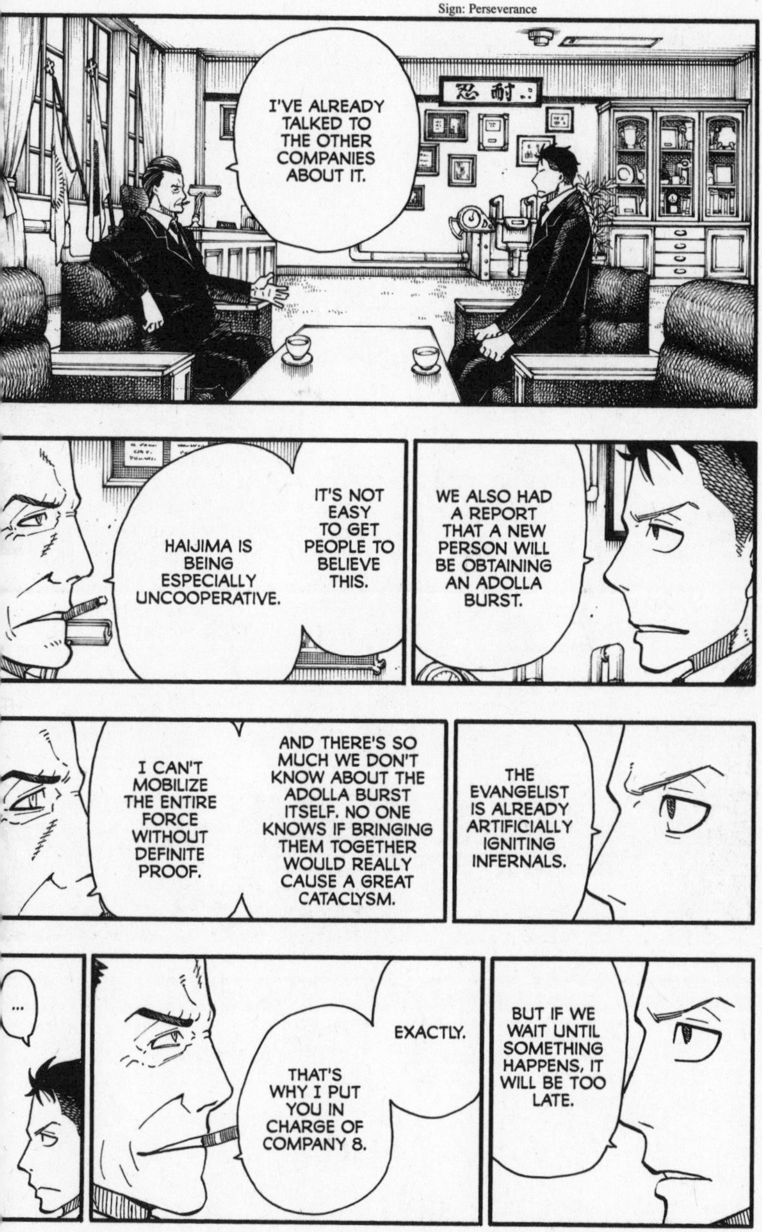

I'VE ALREADY TALKED TO THE OTHER COMPANIES ABOUT IT.
WE ALSO HAD A REPORT THAT A NEW PERSON WILL BE OBTAINING AN ADOLLA BURST.
IT'S NOT EASY TO GET PEOPLE TO BELIEVE THIS.
HAIJIMA IS BEING ESPECIALLY UNCOOPERATIVE.
THE EVANGELIST IS ALREADY ARTIFICIALLY IGNITING INFERNALS.
AND THERE'S SO MUCH WE DON'T KNOW ABOUT THE ADOLLA BURST ITSELF. NO ONE KNOWS IF BRINGING THEM TOGETHER WOULD REALLY CAUSE A GREAT CATACLYSM.
I CAN'T MOBILIZE THE ENTIRE FORCE WITHOUT DEFINITE PROOF.
BUT IF WE WAIT UNTIL SOMETHING HAPPENS, IT WILL BE TOO LATE.
EXACTLY.
THAT'S WHY I PUT YOU IN CHARGE OF COMPANY 8.
...

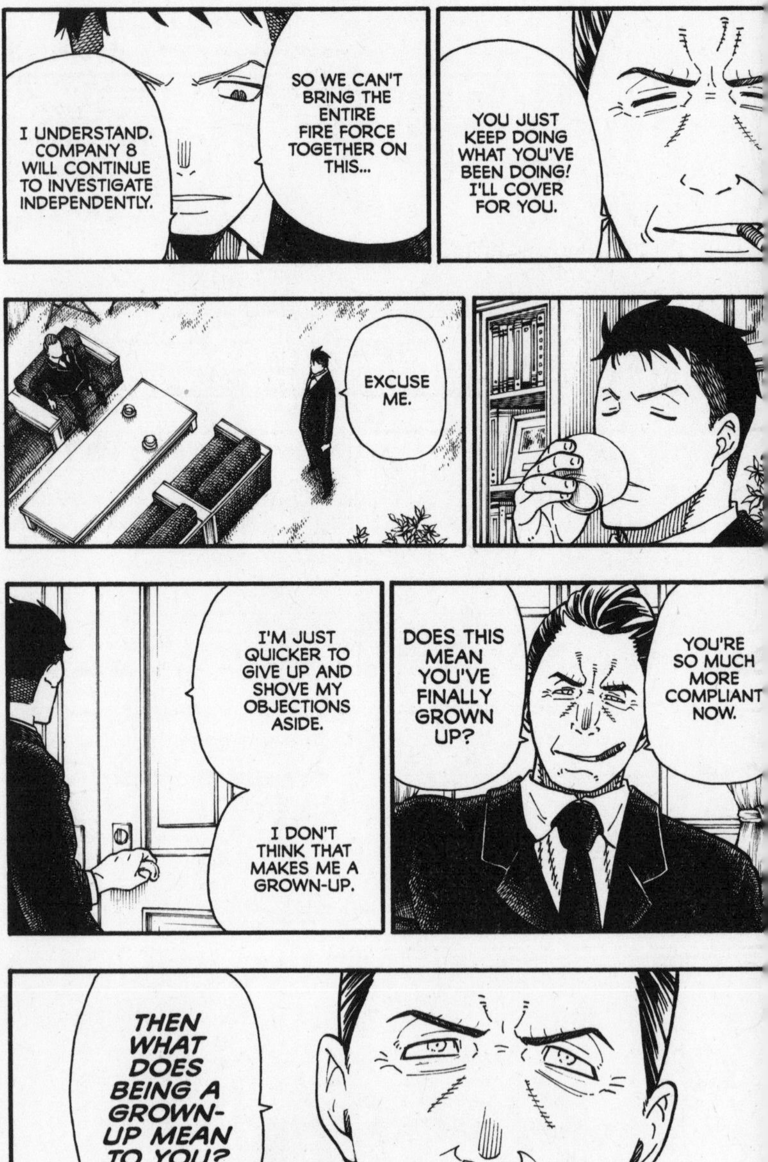
YOU JUST KEEP DOING WHAT YOU'VE BEEN DOING! I'LL COVER FOR YOU.
SO WE CAN'T BRING THE ENTIRE FIRE FORCE TOGETHER ON THIS...
I UNDERSTAND. COMPANY 8 WILL CONTINUE TO INVESTIGATE INDEPENDENTLY.
EXCUSE ME.
YOU'RE SO MUCH MORE COMPLIANT NOW.
DOES THIS MEAN YOU'VE FINALLY GROWN UP?
I'M JUST QUICKER TO GIVE UP AND SHOVE MY OBJECTIONS ASIDE.
I DON'T THINK THAT MAKES ME A GROWN-UP.
THEN WHAT DOES BEING A GROWN-UP MEAN TO YOU?

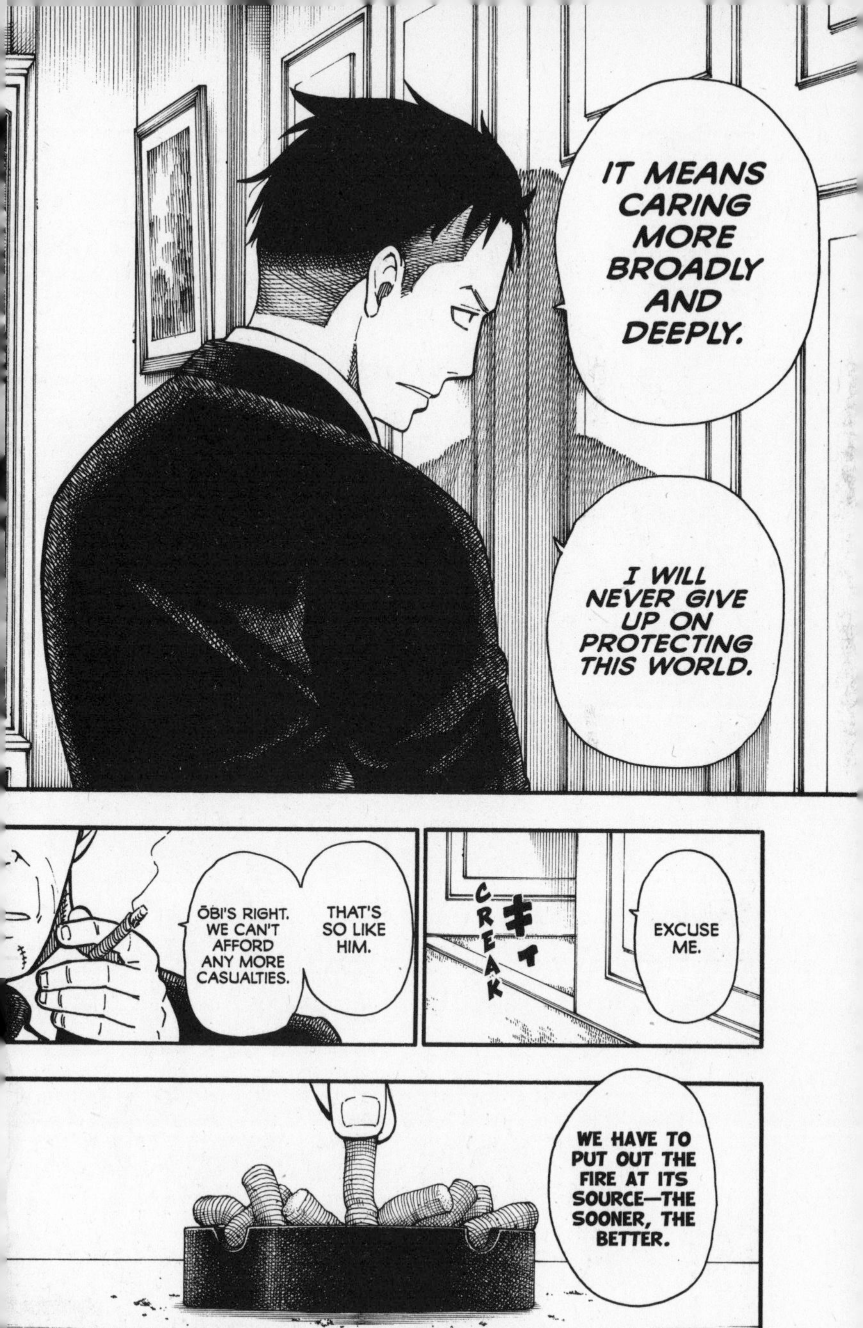

IT MEANS CARING MORE BROADLY AND DEEPLY.
I WILL NEVER GIVE UP ON PROTECTING THIS WORLD.
EXCUSE ME.
CREAK
キイ
THAT'S SO LIKE HIM.
ŌBI'S RIGHT. WE CAN'T AFFORD ANY MORE CASUALTIES.
WE HAVE TO PUT OUT THE FIRE AT ITS SOURCE—THE SOONER, THE BETTER.

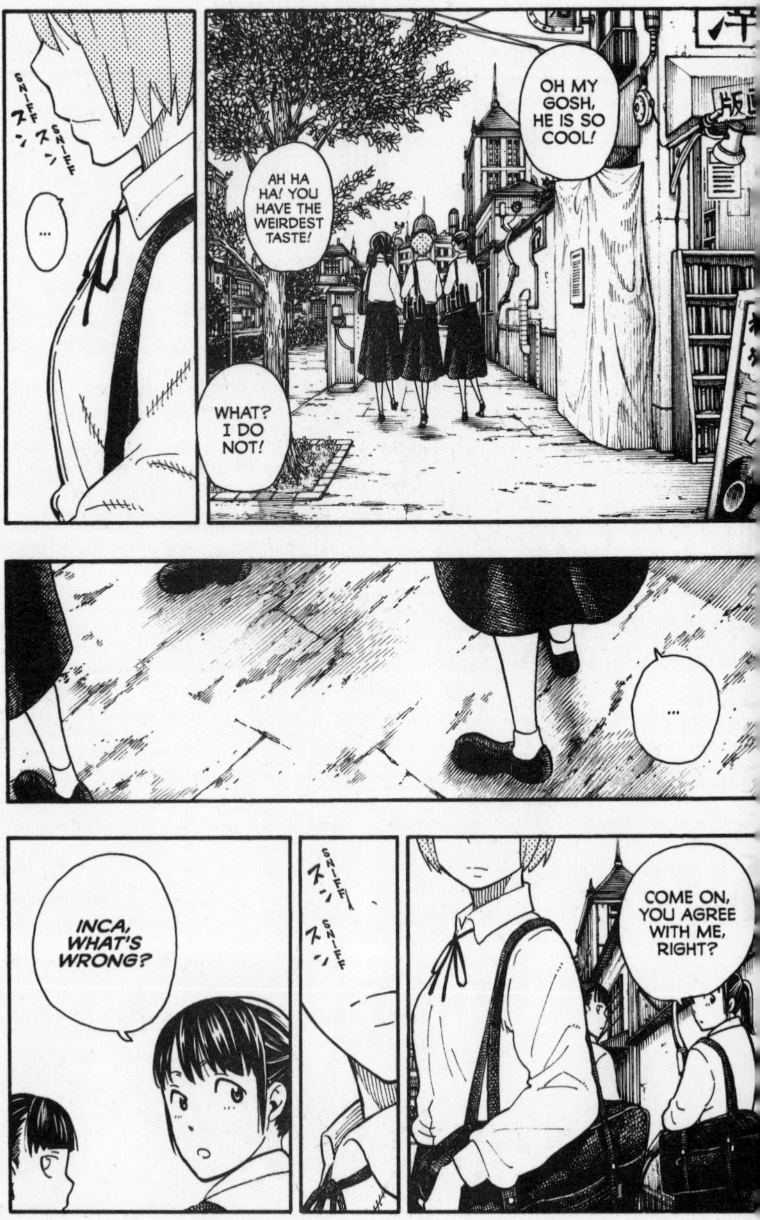

OH MY GOSH, HE IS SO COOL!
AH HA HA! YOU HAVE THE WEIRDEST TASTE!
WHAT? I DO NOT!
SNIFF
スン
SNIFF
スン
...
...
COME ON, YOU AGREE WITH ME, RIGHT?
SNIFF
スン
SNIFF
スン
INCA, WHAT'S WRONG?

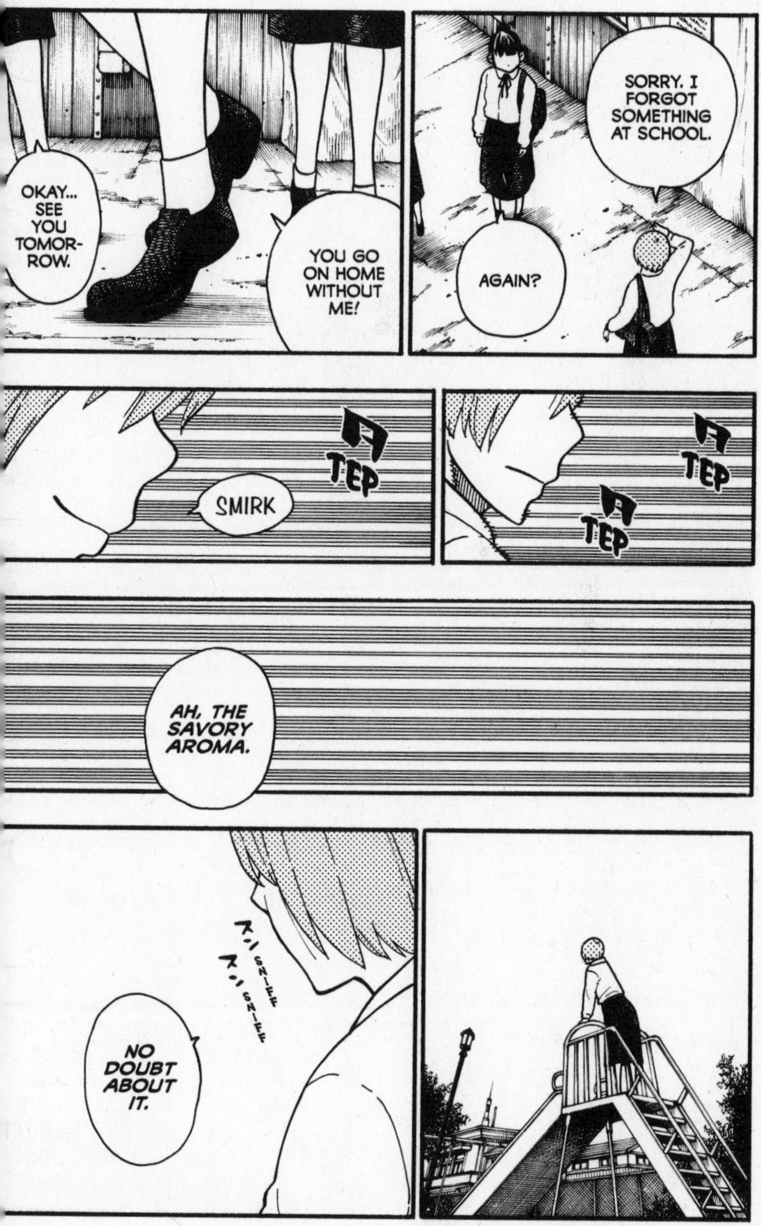
SORRY. I FORGOT SOMETHING AT SCHOOL.
AGAIN?
YOU GO ON HOME WITHOUT ME!
OKAY... SEE YOU TOMOR-ROW.
TEP
TEP
TEP
SMIRK
AH, THE SAVORY AROMA.
SNIFF
SNIFF
NO DOUBT ABOUT IT.

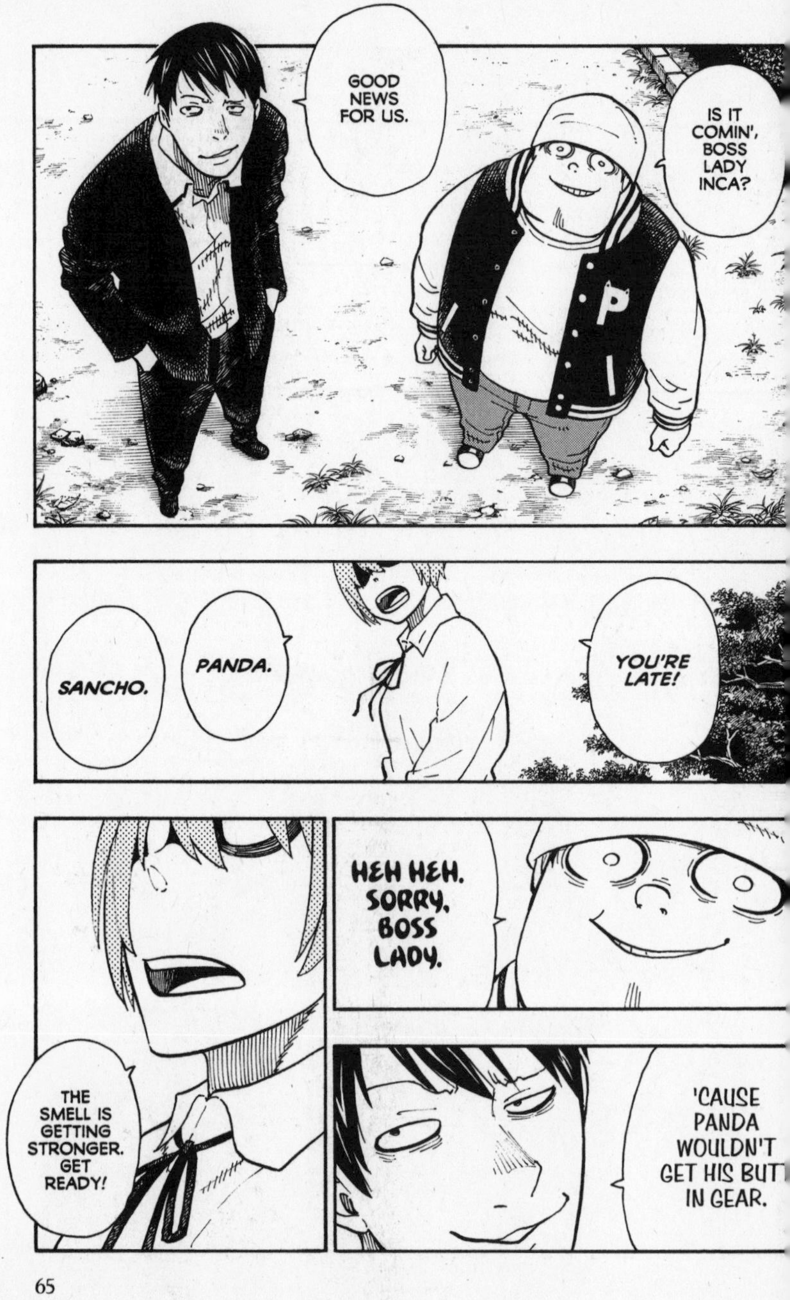
IS IT COMIN', BOSS LADY INCA?
GOOD NEWS FOR US.
YOU'RE LATE!
PANDA.
SANCHO.
HEH HEH. SORRY, BOSS LADY.
'CAUSE PANDA WOULDN'T GET HIS BUT IN GEAR.
THE SMELL IS GETTING STRONGER. GET READY!

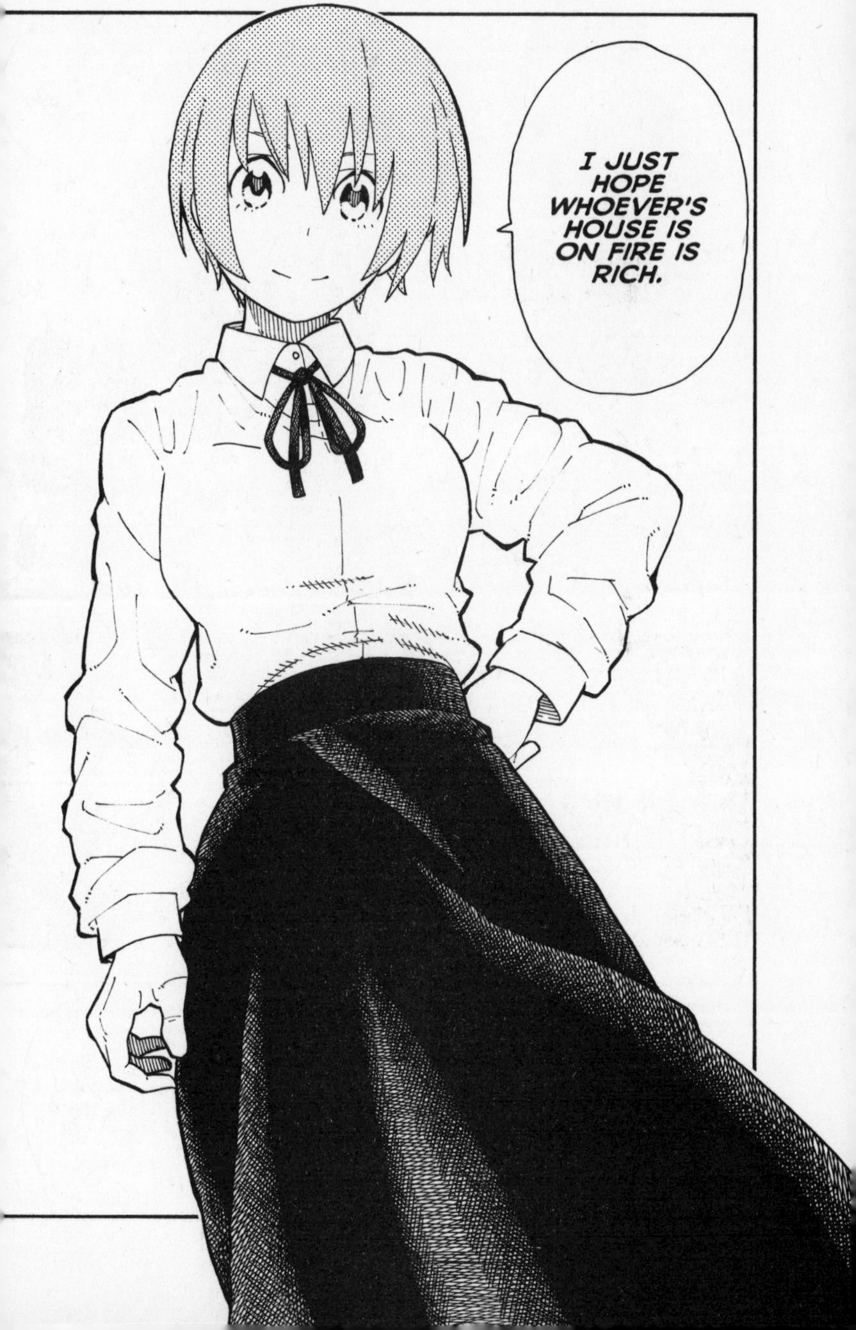
I JUST HOPE WHOEVER'S HOUSE IS ON FIRE IS RICH.

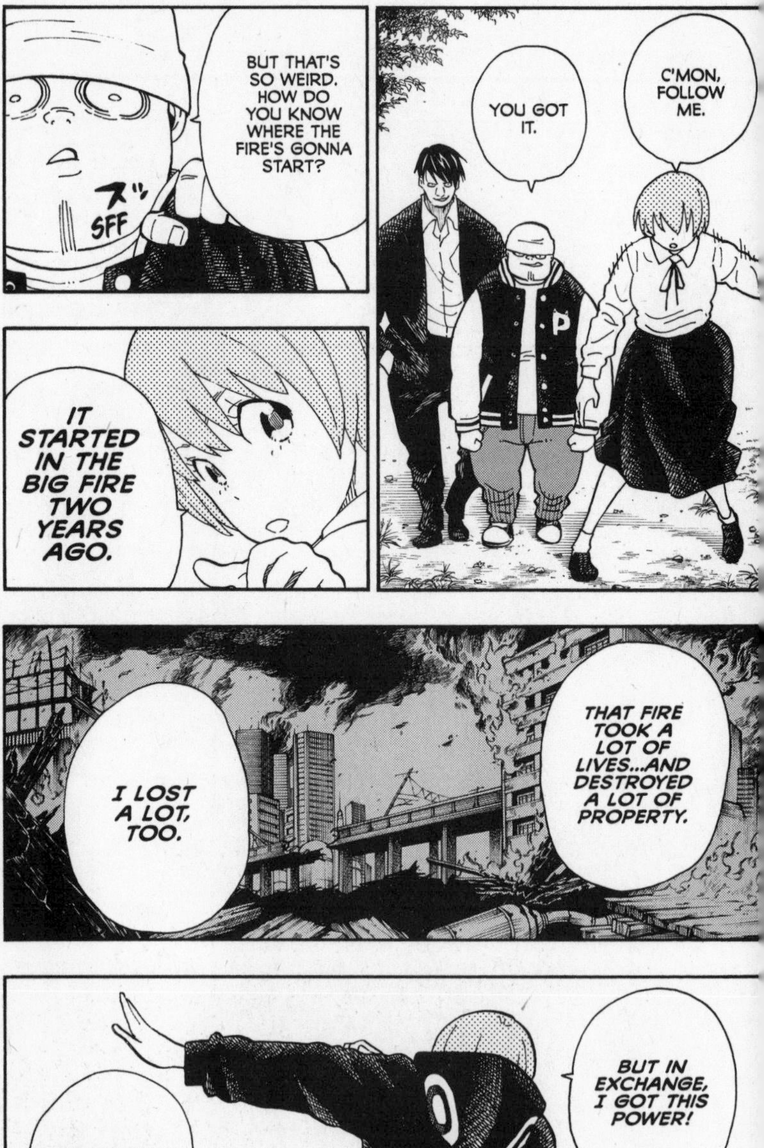
C'MON, FOLLOW ME.
YOU GOT IT.
BUT THAT'S SO WEIRD. HOW DO YOU KNOW WHERE THE FIRE'S GONNA START?
ズッ
SFF
IT STARTED IN THE BIG FIRE TWO YEARS AGO.
THAT FIRE TOOK A LOT OF LIVES...AND DESTROYED A LOT OF PROPERTY.
I LOST A LOT, TOO.
BUT IN EXCHANGE, I GOT THIS POWER!
COME ON! THE FIRE'S STARTING!!

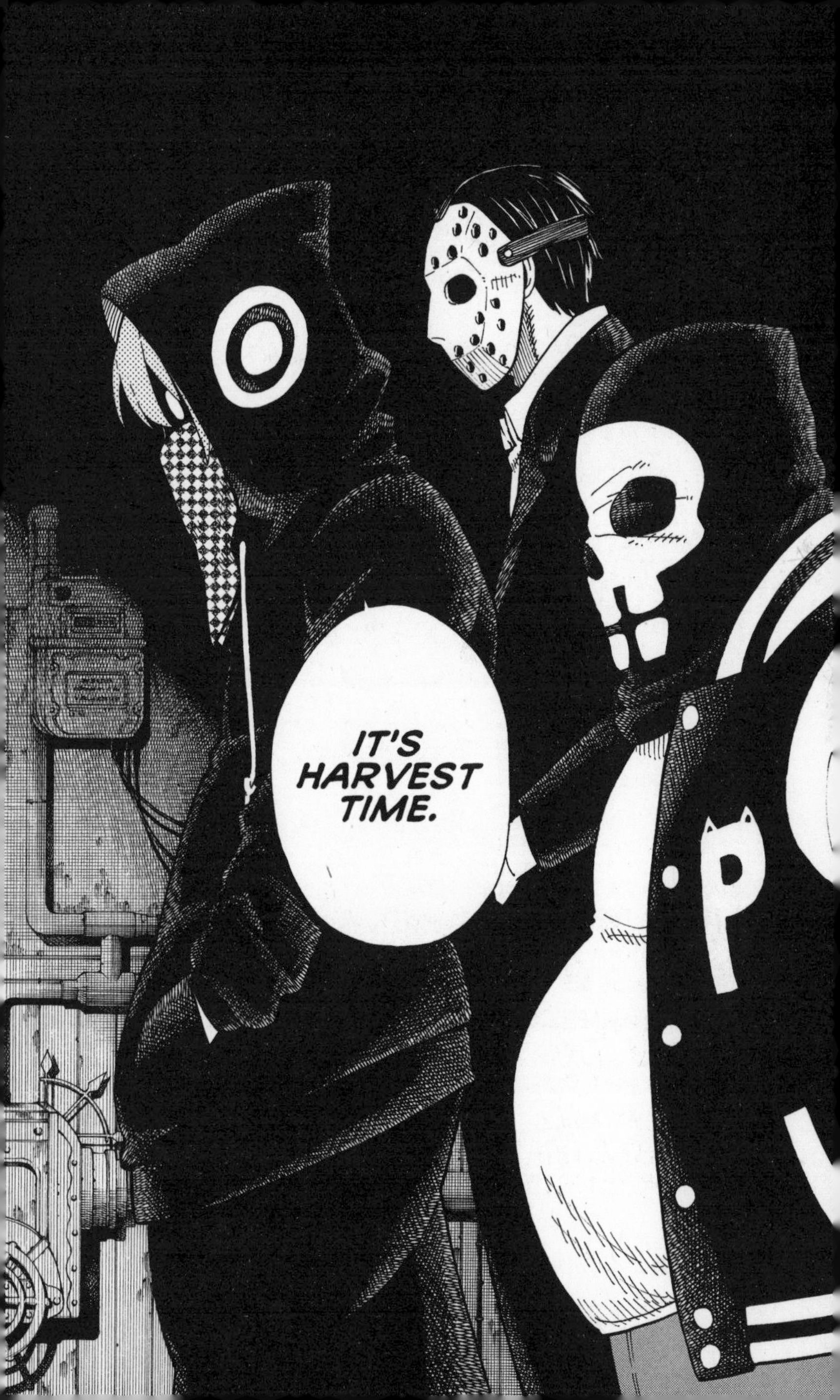
IT'S HARVEST TIME.

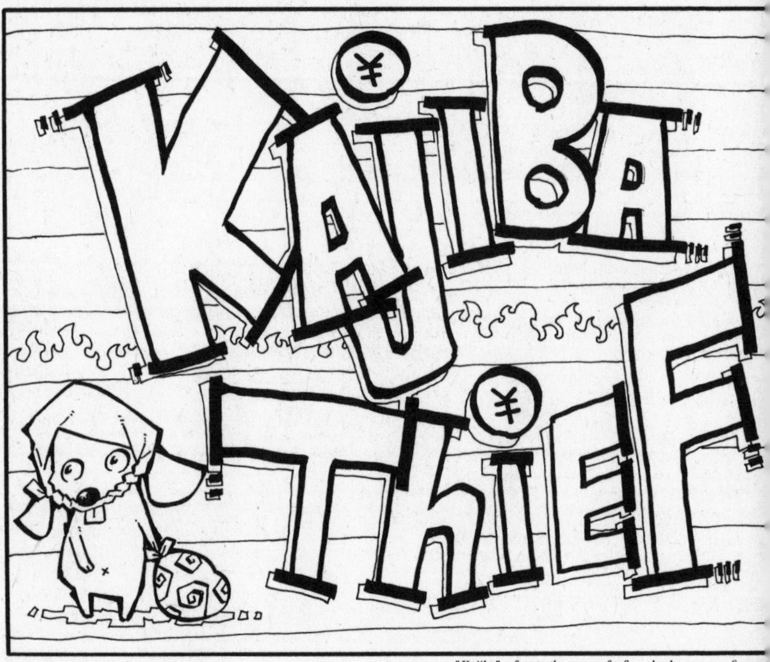
KAJIBA
THIEF

"*Kajiba*" refers to the scene of a fire, also known as a firegro

CHAPTER C: THE SCENT OF THE FLAME

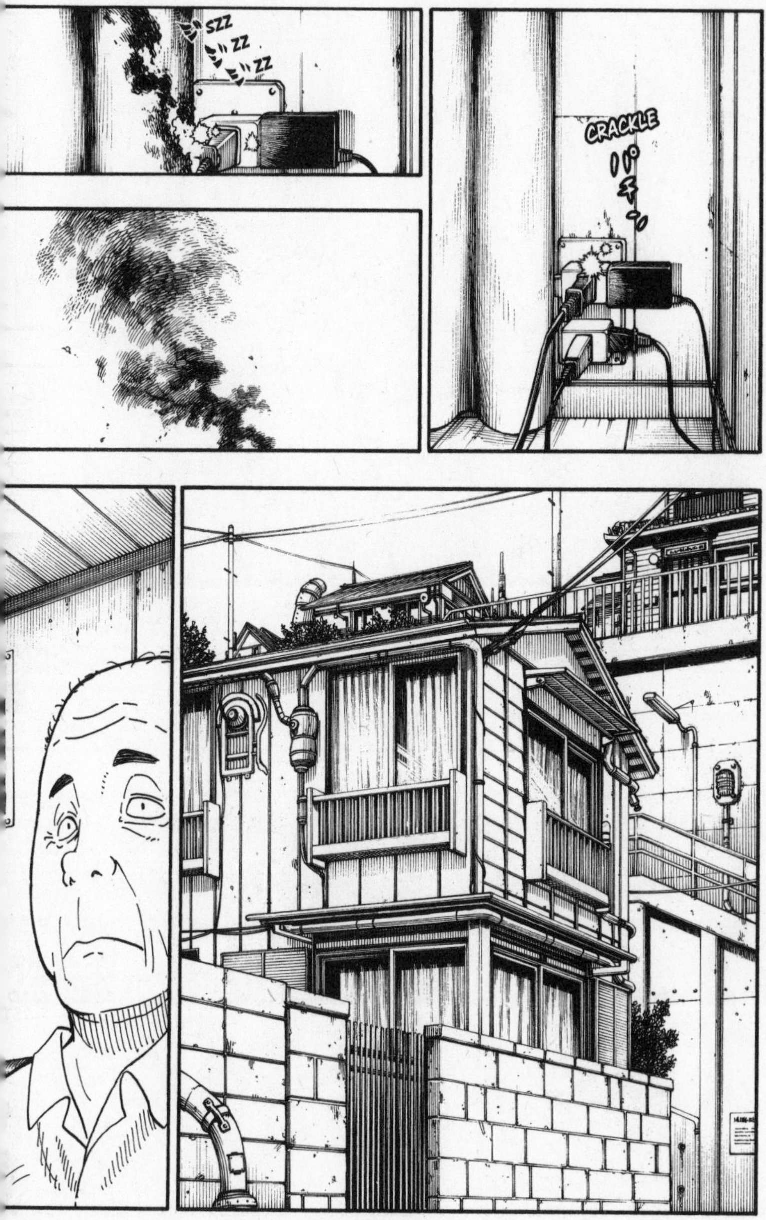
CRACKLE
SZZ
ZZ
ZZ

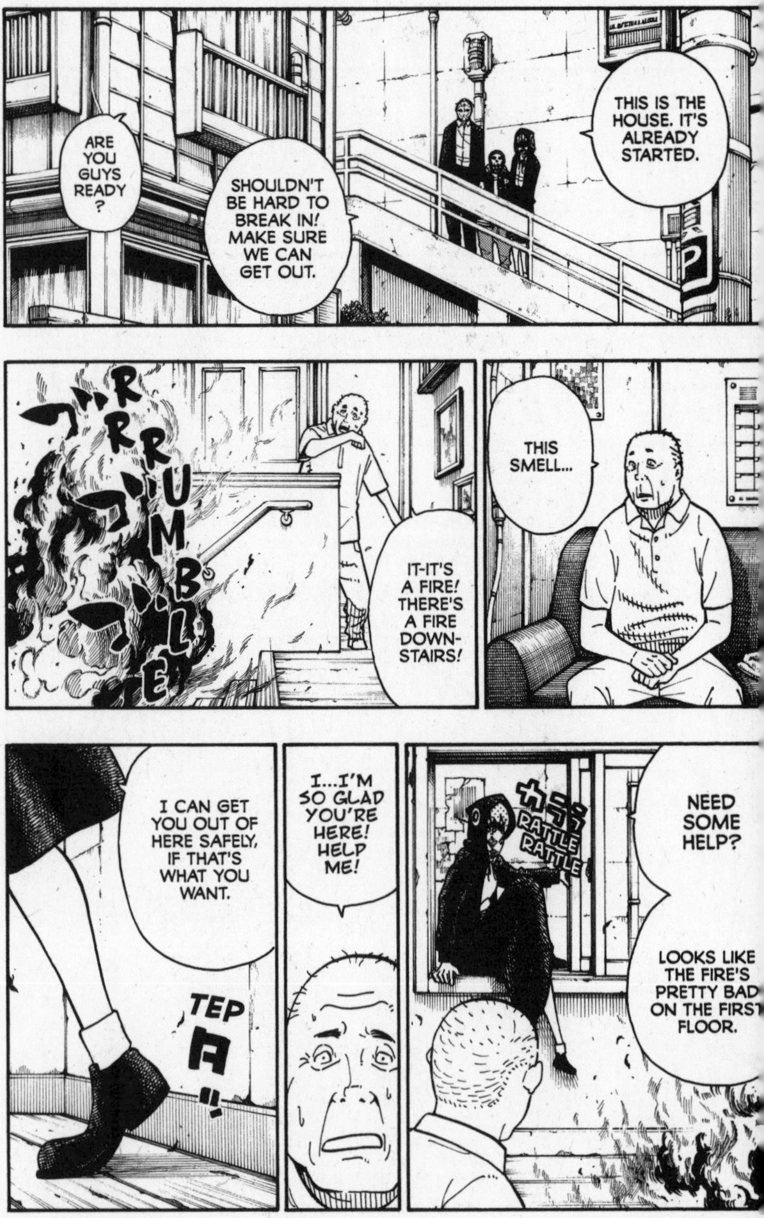
THIS IS THE HOUSE. IT'S ALREADY STARTED.
SHOULDN'T BE HARD TO BREAK IN! MAKE SURE WE CAN GET OUT.
ARE YOU GUYS READY?
THIS SMELL...
IT-IT'S A FIRE! THERE'S A FIRE DOWN-STAIRS!
RRRUMBLE
NEED SOME HELP?
RATTLE RATTLE
LOOKS LIKE THE FIRE'S PRETTY BAD ON THE FIRST FLOOR.
I...I'M SO GLAD YOU'RE HERE! HELP ME!
I CAN GET YOU OUT OF HERE SAFELY, IF THAT'S WHAT YOU WANT.
TEP

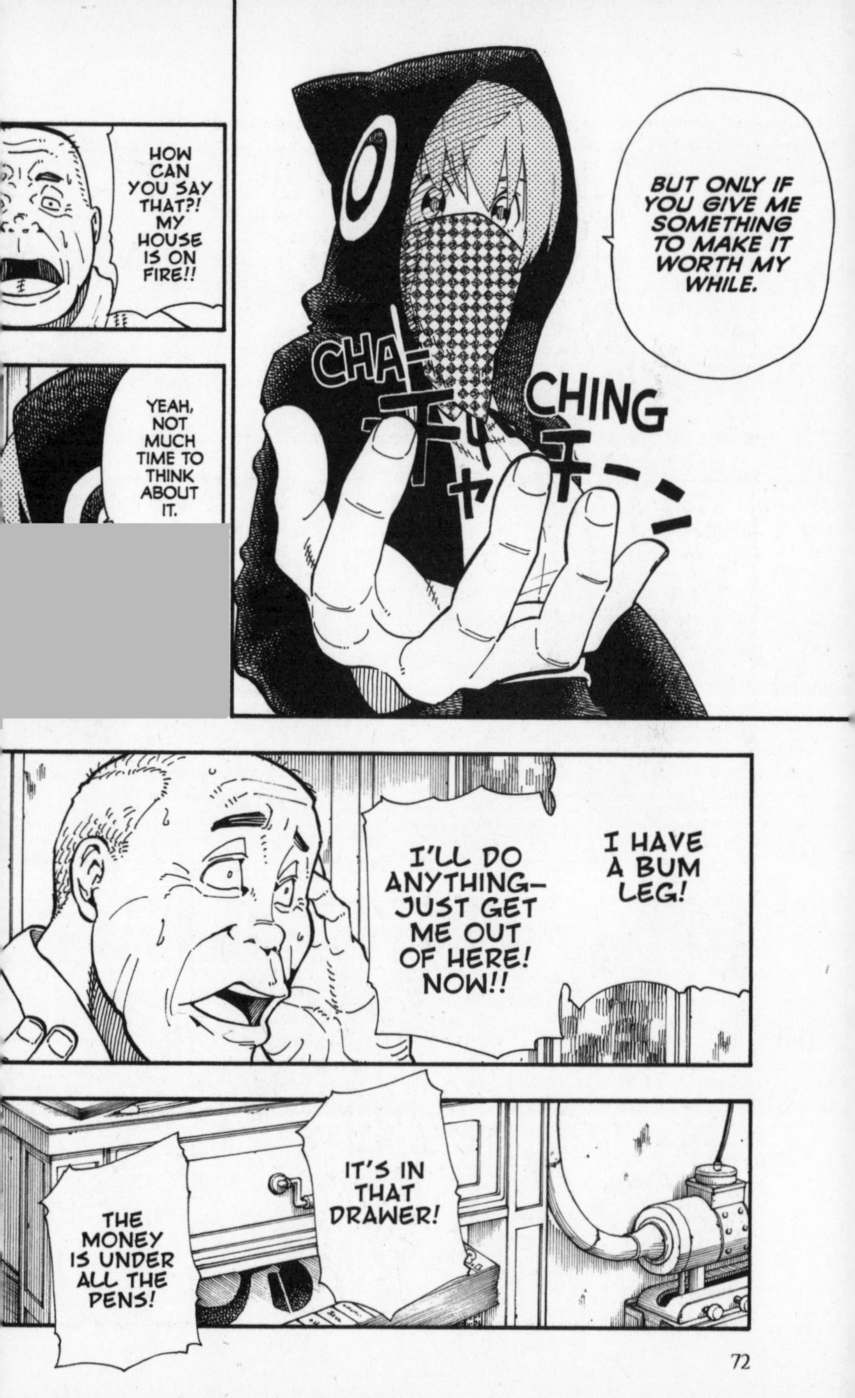
BUT ONLY IF YOU GIVE ME SOMETHING TO MAKE IT WORTH MY WHILE.
CHA-CHING
HOW CAN YOU SAY THAT?! MY HOUSE IS ON FIRE!!
YEAH, NOT MUCH TIME TO THINK ABOUT IT.
I HAVE A BUM LEG!
I'LL DO ANYTHING— JUST GET ME OUT OF HERE! NOW!!
IT'S IN THAT DRAWER!
THE MONEY IS UNDER ALL THE PENS!

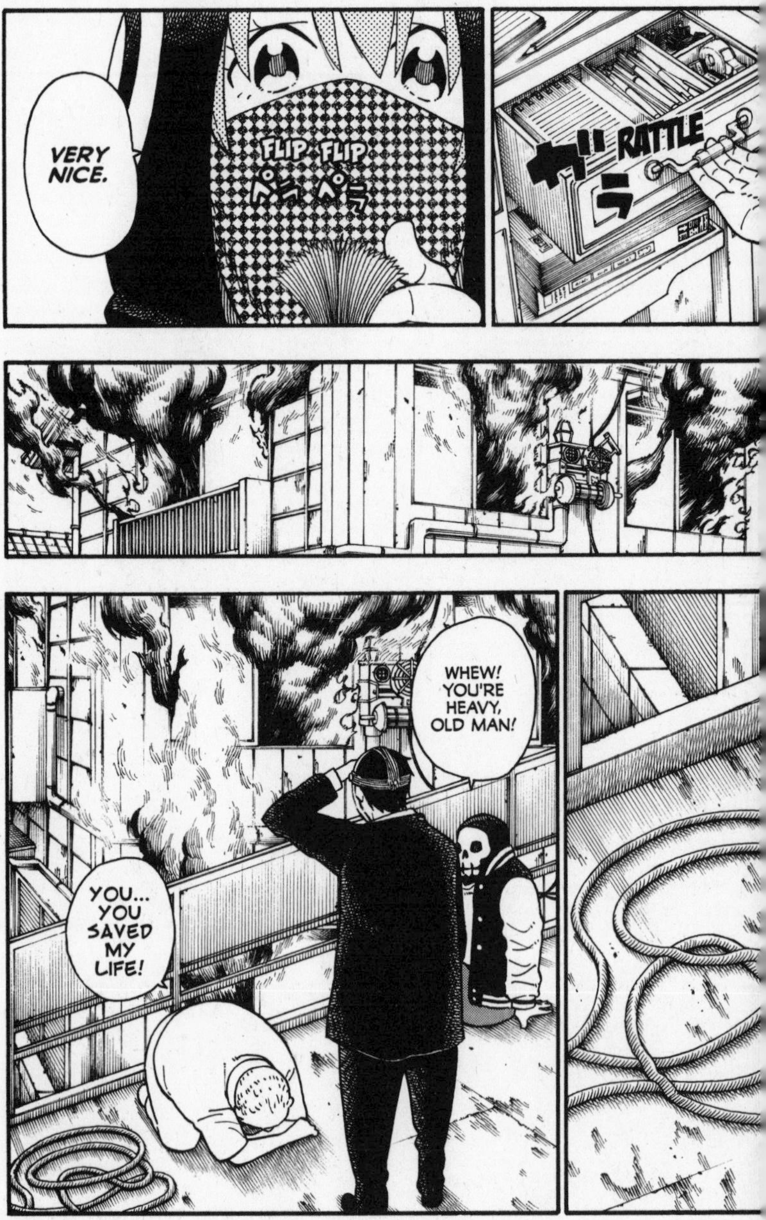
RATTLE
FLIP FLIP
ぺらぺら
VERY NICE.
WHEW! YOU'RE HEAVY, OLD MAN!
YOU... YOU SAVED MY LIFE!

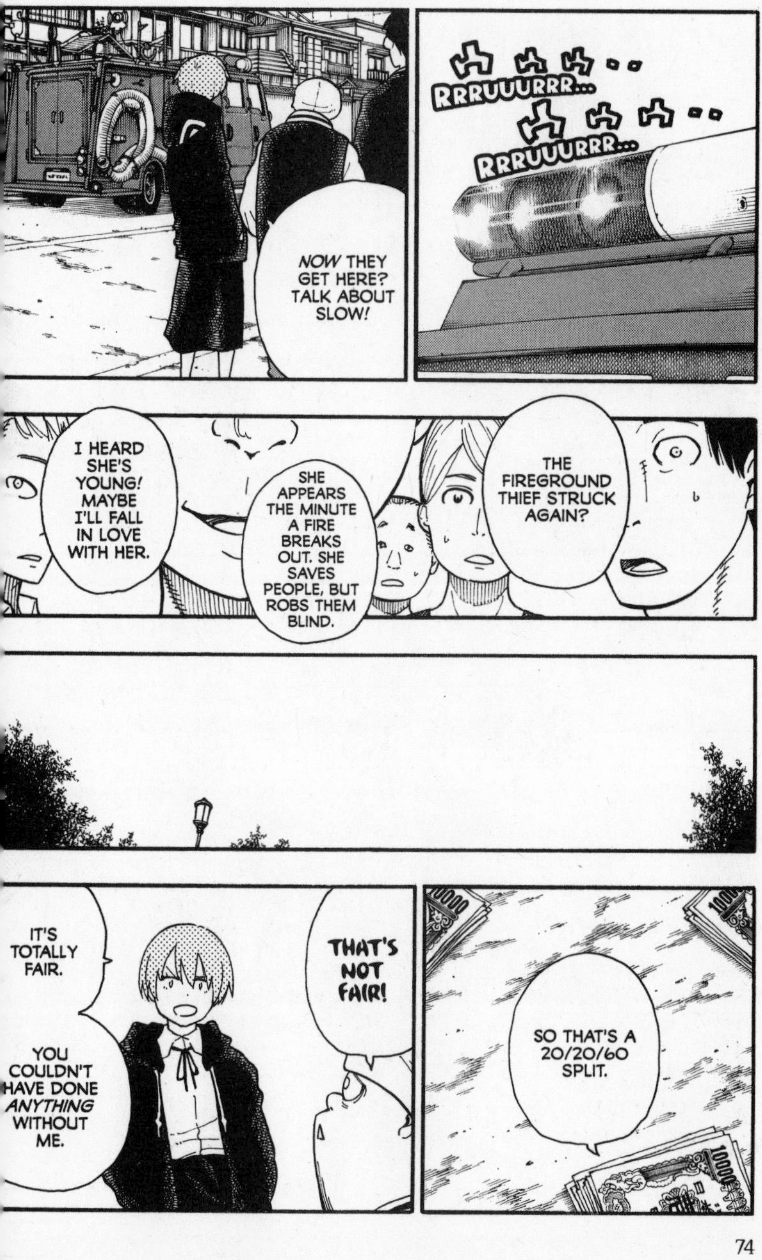
RRRUUURRR...
RRRUUURRR...
NOW THEY GET HERE? TALK ABOUT SLOW!
THE FIREGROUND THIEF STRUCK AGAIN?
SHE APPEARS THE MINUTE A FIRE BREAKS OUT. SHE SAVES PEOPLE, BUT ROBS THEM BLIND.
I HEARD SHE'S YOUNG! MAYBE I'LL FALL IN LOVE WITH HER.
SO THAT'S A 20/20/60 SPLIT.
THAT'S NOT FAIR!
IT'S TOTALLY FAIR.
YOU COULDN'T HAVE DONE ANYTHING WITHOUT ME.

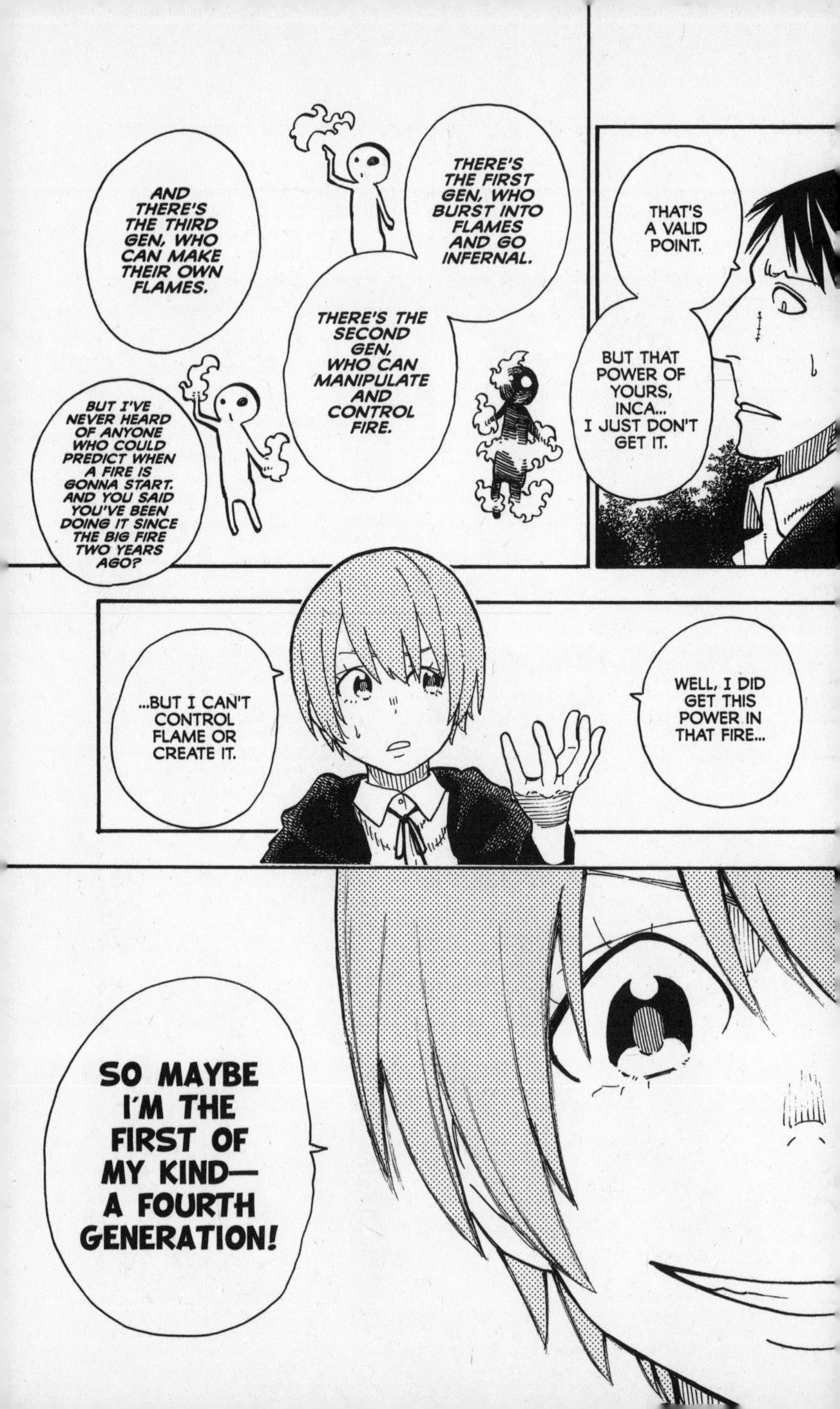
THAT'S A VALID POINT.
BUT THAT POWER OF YOURS, INCA... I JUST DON'T GET IT.
THERE'S THE FIRST GEN, WHO BURST INTO FLAMES AND GO INFERNAL.
THERE'S THE SECOND GEN, WHO CAN MANIPULATE AND CONTROL FIRE.
AND THERE'S THE THIRD GEN, WHO CAN MAKE THEIR OWN FLAMES.
BUT I'VE NEVER HEARD OF ANYONE WHO COULD PREDICT WHEN A FIRE IS GONNA START. AND YOU SAID YOU'VE BEEN DOING IT SINCE THE BIG FIRE TWO YEARS AGO?
WELL, I DID GET THIS POWER IN THAT FIRE...
...BUT I CAN'T CONTROL FLAME OR CREATE IT.
SO MAYBE I'M THE FIRST OF MY KIND—A FOURTH GENERATION!

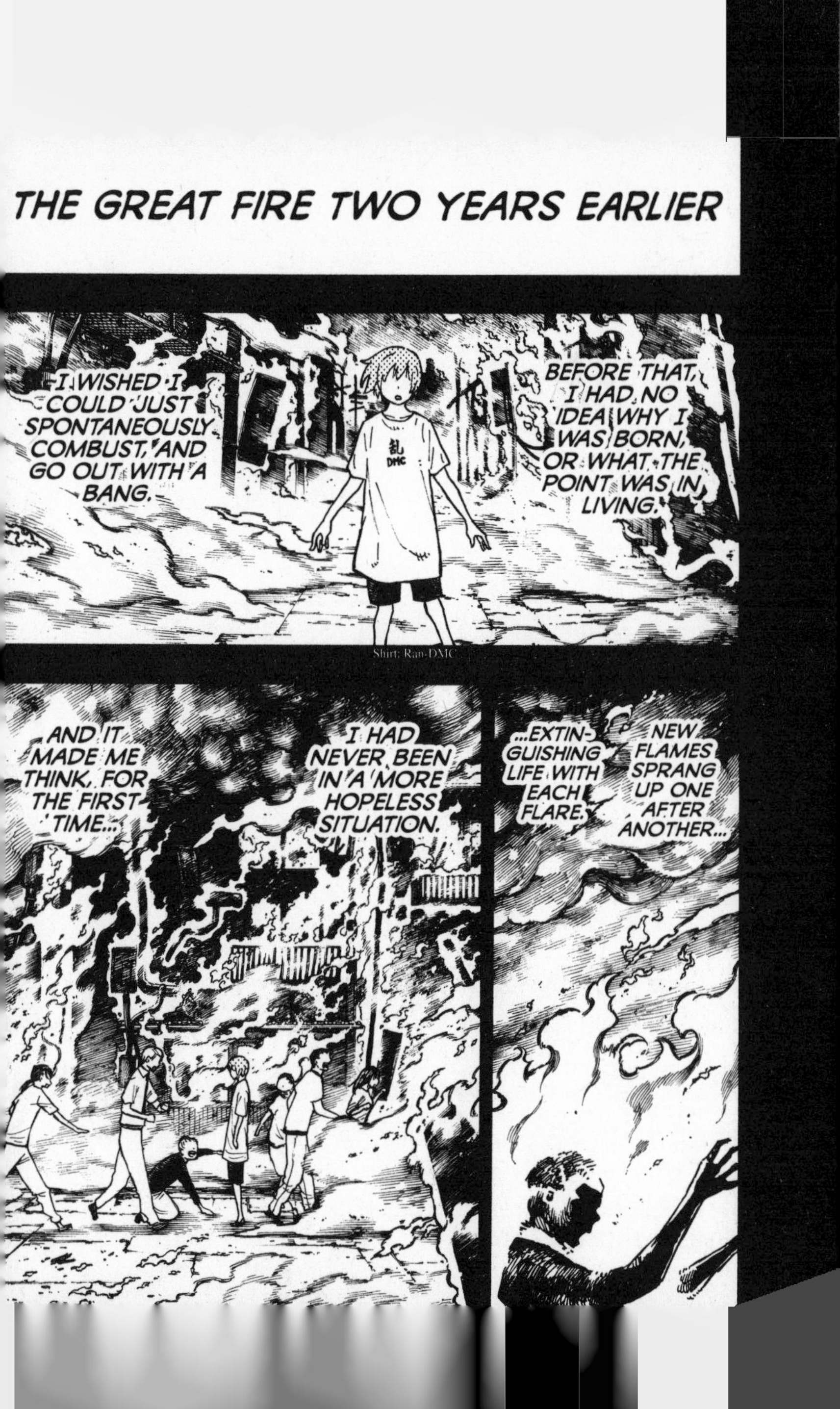
THE GREAT FIRE TWO YEARS EARLIER
BEFORE THAT, I HAD NO IDEA WHY I WAS BORN, OR WHAT THE POINT WAS IN LIVING.
I WISHED I COULD JUST SPONTANEOUSLY COMBUST, AND GO OUT WITH A BANG.
Shirt: Ran-DMC
NEW FLAMES SPRANG UP ONE AFTER ANOTHER...
...EXTIN-GUISHING LIFE WITH EACH FLARE.
I HAD NEVER BEEN IN A MORE HOPELESS SITUATION.
AND IT MADE ME THINK, FOR THE FIRST TIME...

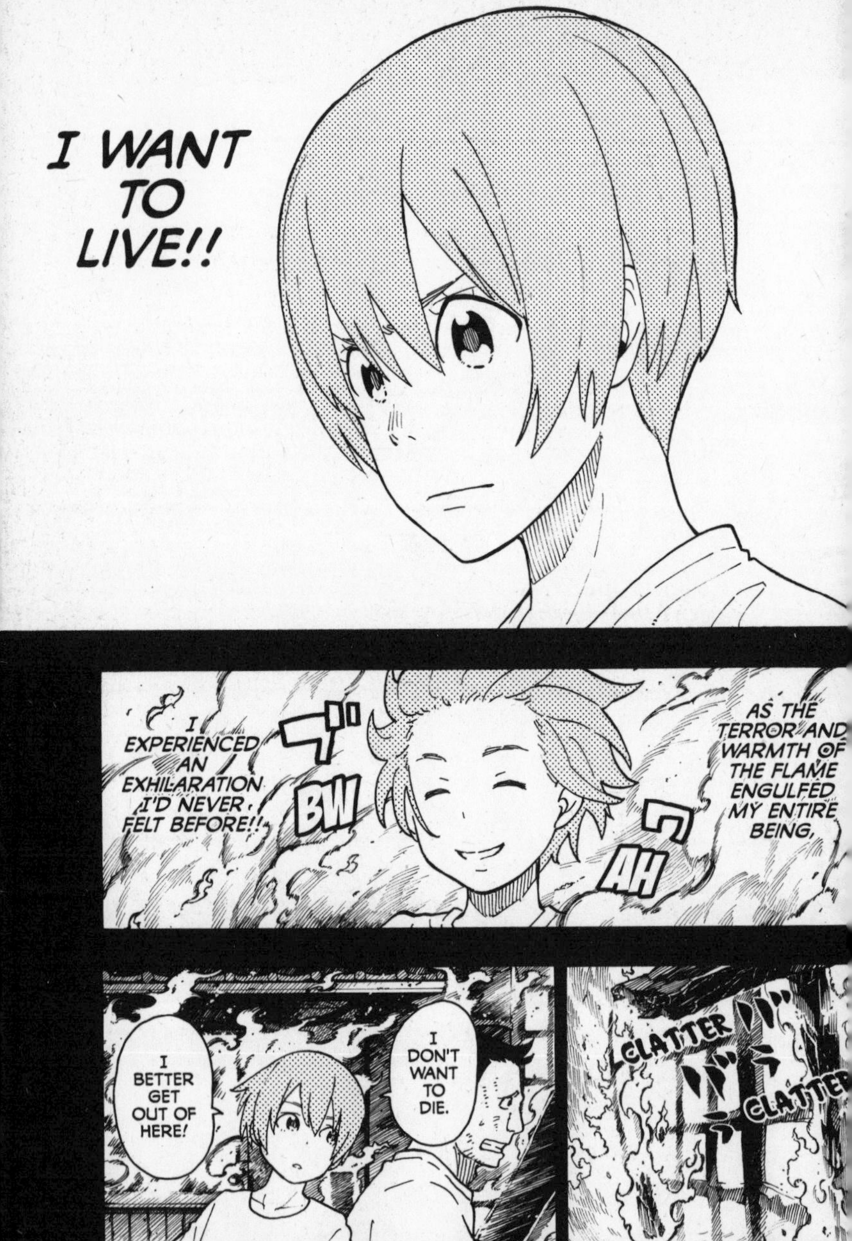
I WANT TO LIVE!!
AS THE TERROR AND WARMTH OF THE FLAME ENGULFED MY ENTIRE BEING,
AH
BW
I EXPERIENCED AN EXHILARATION I'D NEVER FELT BEFORE!!
CLATTER
CLATTER
I DON'T WANT TO DIE.
I BETTER GET OUT OF HERE!

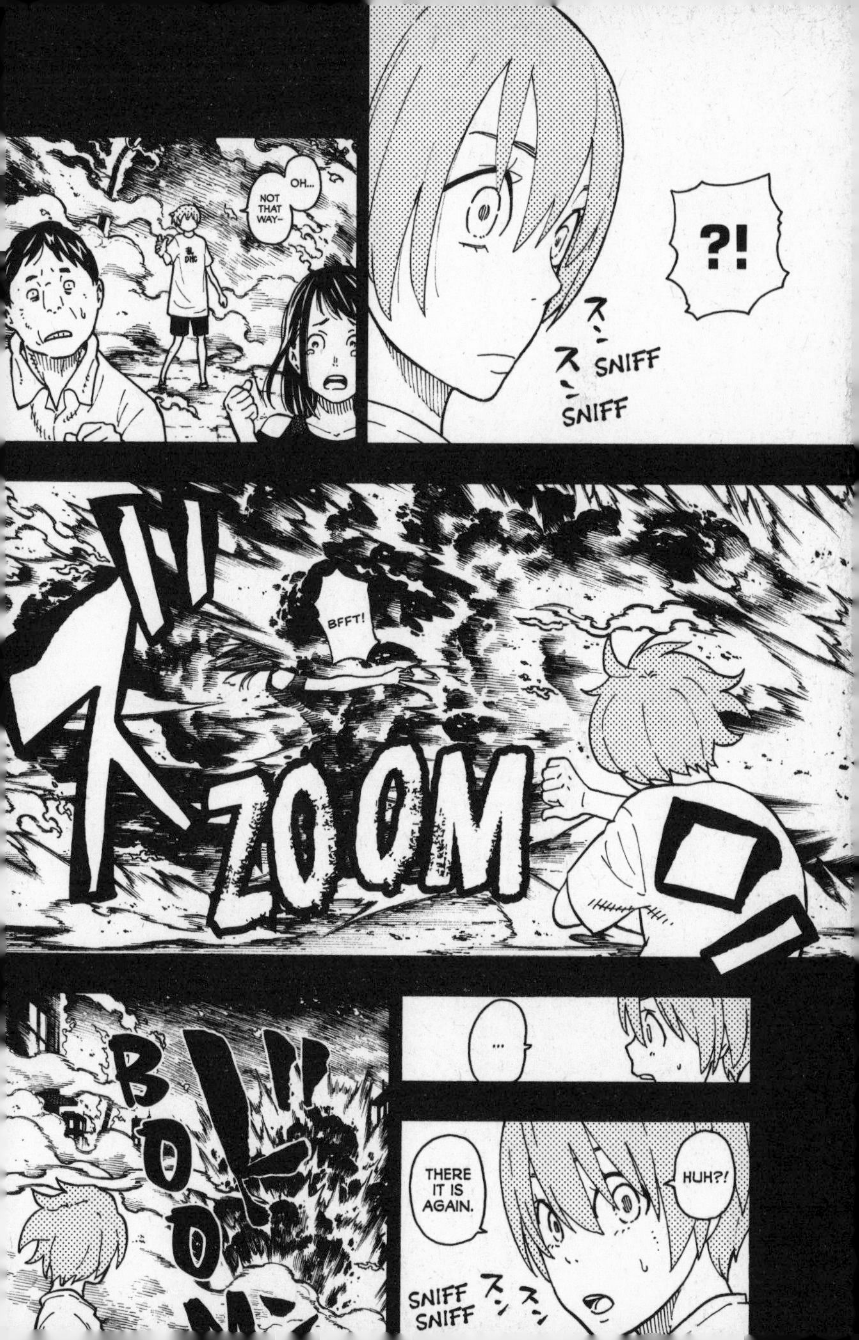
?!
スン SNIFF
スン SNIFF
OH... NOT THAT WAY-
BFFT!
ZOOM
...
HUH?!
THERE IT IS AGAIN.
SNIFF SNIFF
BOOM

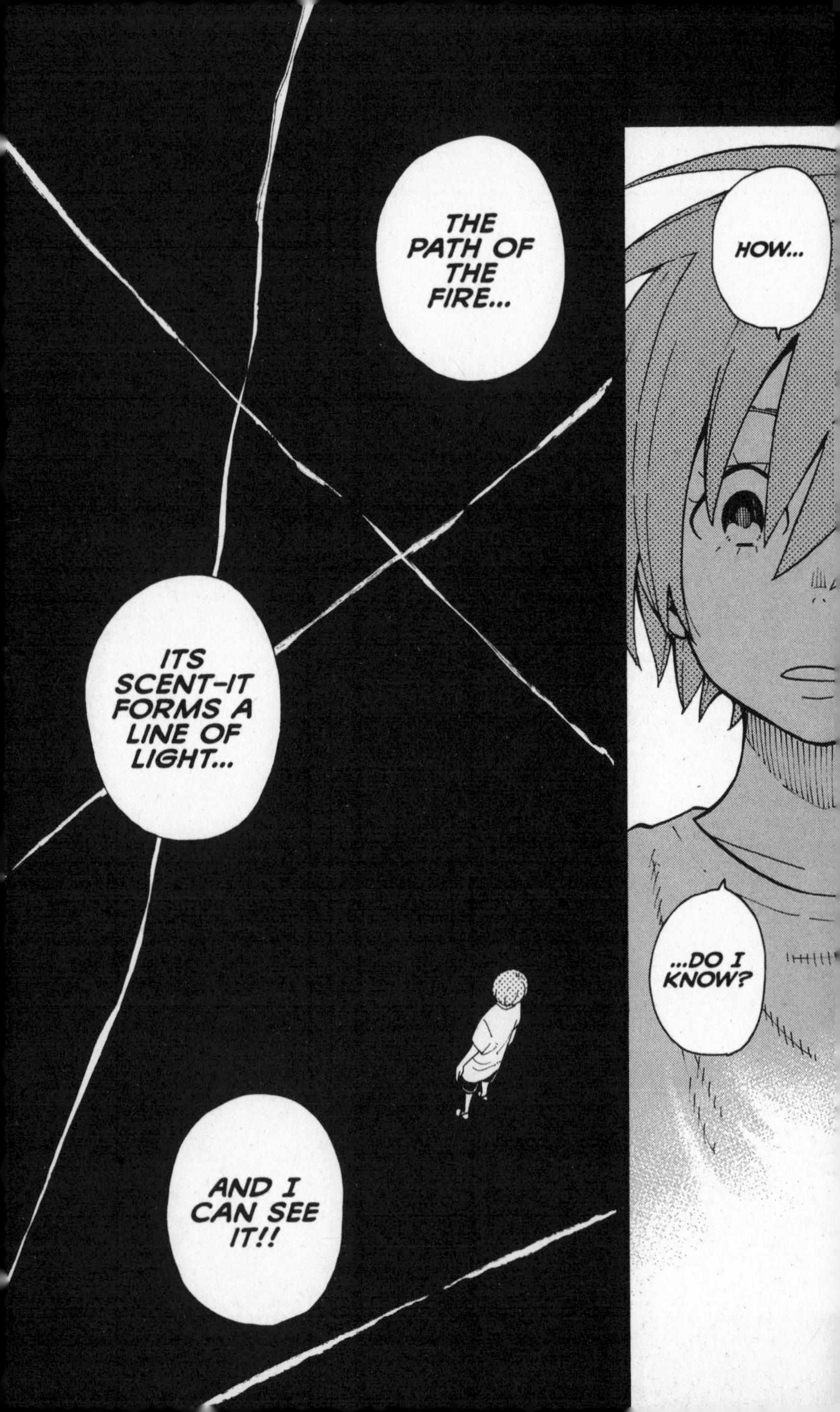
HOW...
...DO I KNOW?
THE PATH OF THE FIRE...
ITS SCENT–IT FORMS A LINE OF LIGHT...
AND I CAN SEE IT!!

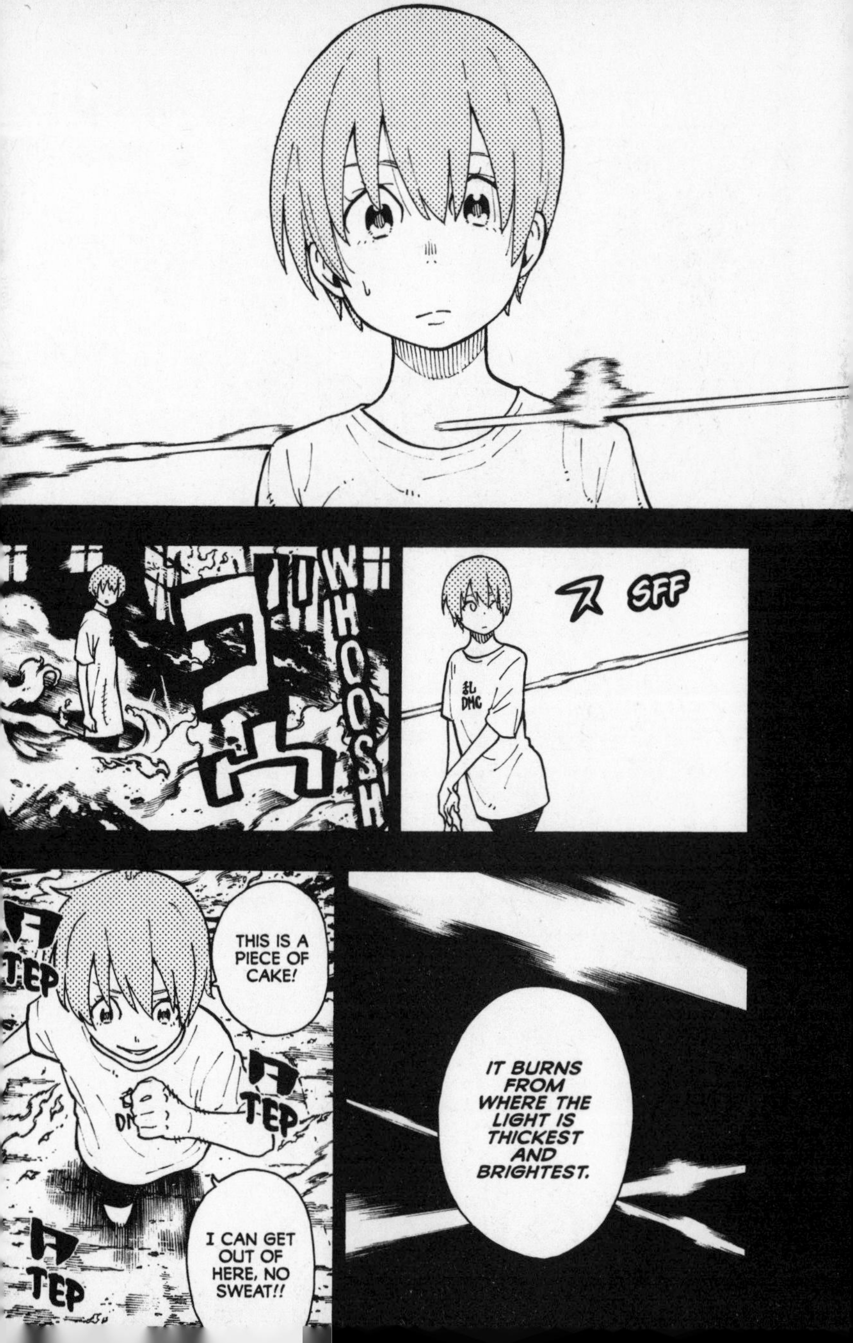
ス
SFF
DMC
WHOOSH
IT BURNS FROM WHERE THE LIGHT IS THICKEST AND BRIGHTEST.
THIS IS A PIECE OF CAKE!
TEP
TEP
I CAN GET OUT OF HERE, NO SWEAT!!
TEP

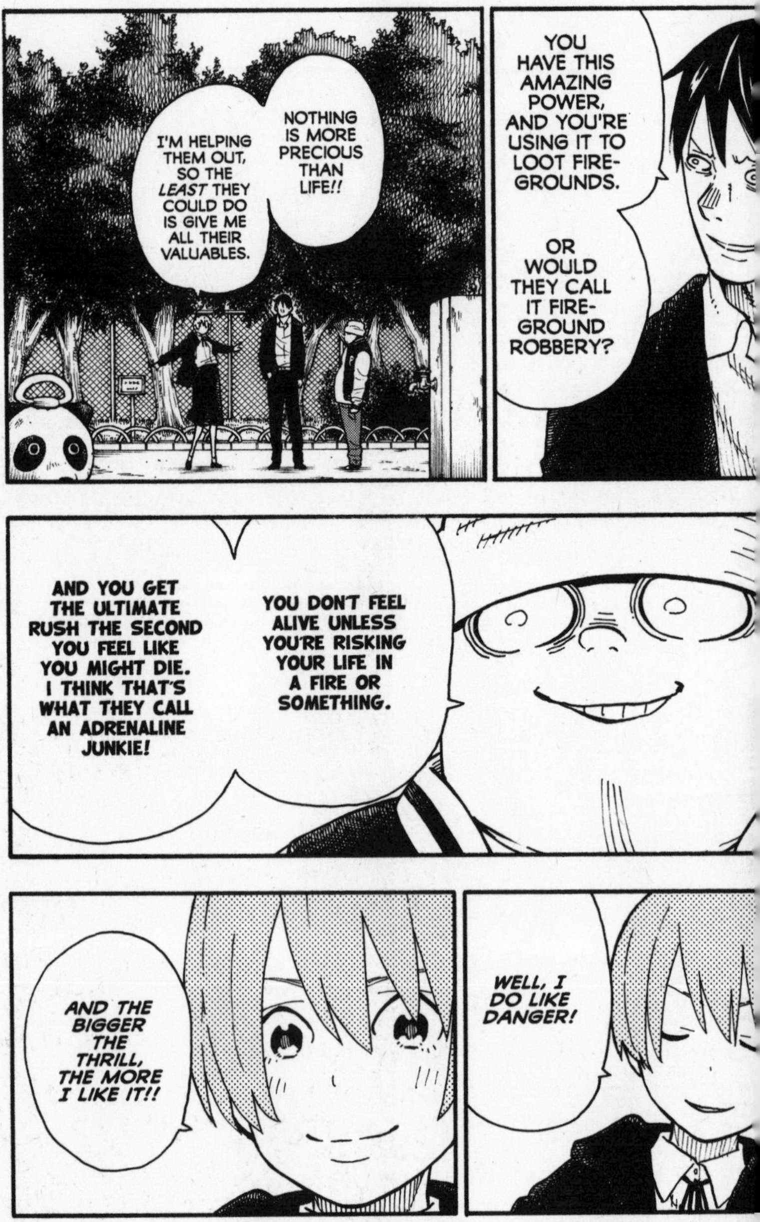

YOU HAVE THIS AMAZING POWER, AND YOU'RE USING IT TO LOOT FIRE-GROUNDS.
OR WOULD THEY CALL IT FIRE-GROUND ROBBERY?
NOTHING IS MORE PRECIOUS THAN LIFE!!
I'M HELPING THEM OUT, SO THE *LEAST* THEY COULD DO IS GIVE ME ALL THEIR VALUABLES.
YOU DON'T FEEL ALIVE UNLESS YOU'RE RISKING YOUR LIFE IN A FIRE OR SOMETHING.
AND YOU GET THE ULTIMATE RUSH THE SECOND YOU FEEL LIKE YOU MIGHT DIE. I THINK THAT'S WHAT THEY CALL AN ADRENALINE JUNKIE!
WELL, I DO LIKE DANGER!
AND THE BIGGER THE THRILL, THE MORE I LIKE IT!!

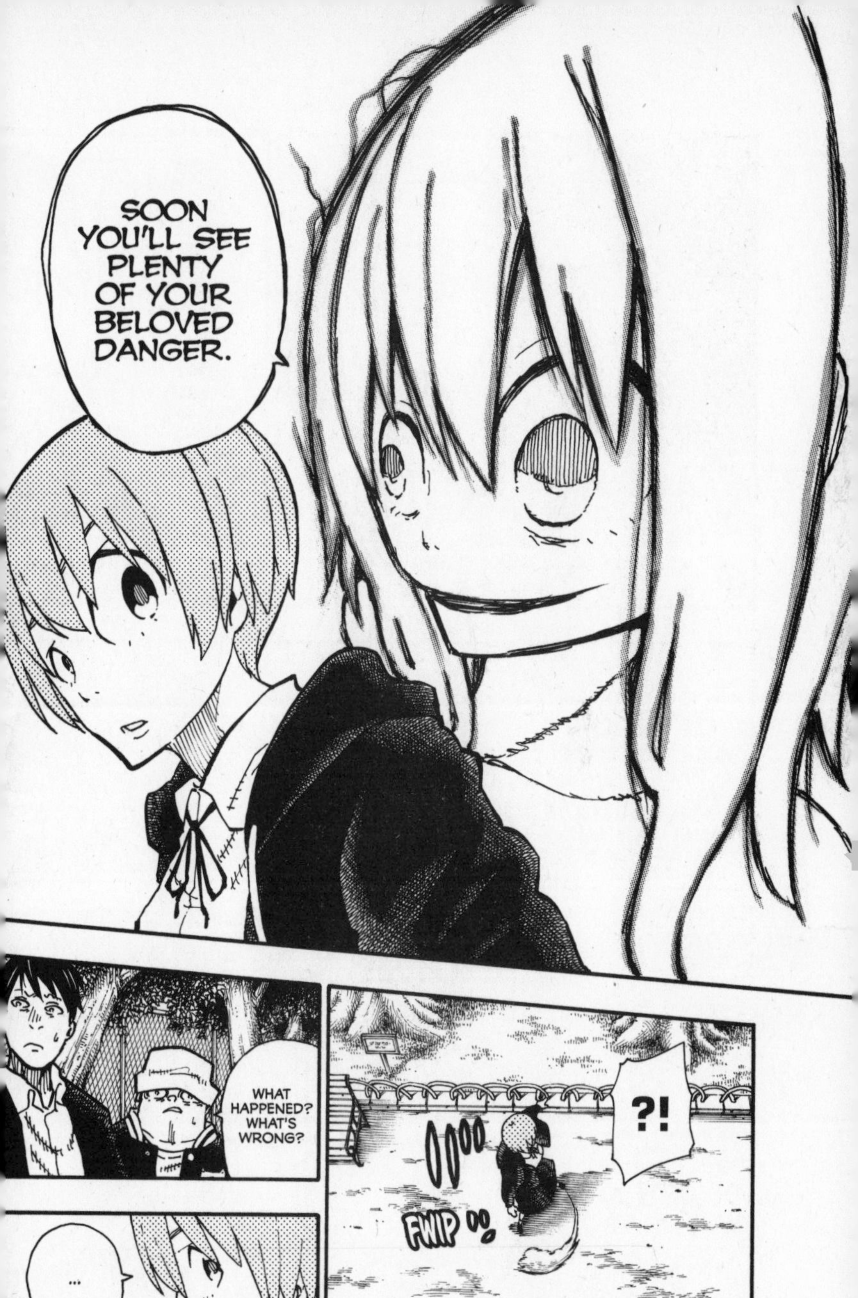
SOON YOU'LL SEE PLENTY OF YOUR BELOVED DANGER.
?!
FWIP
WHAT HAPPENED? WHAT'S WRONG?
...

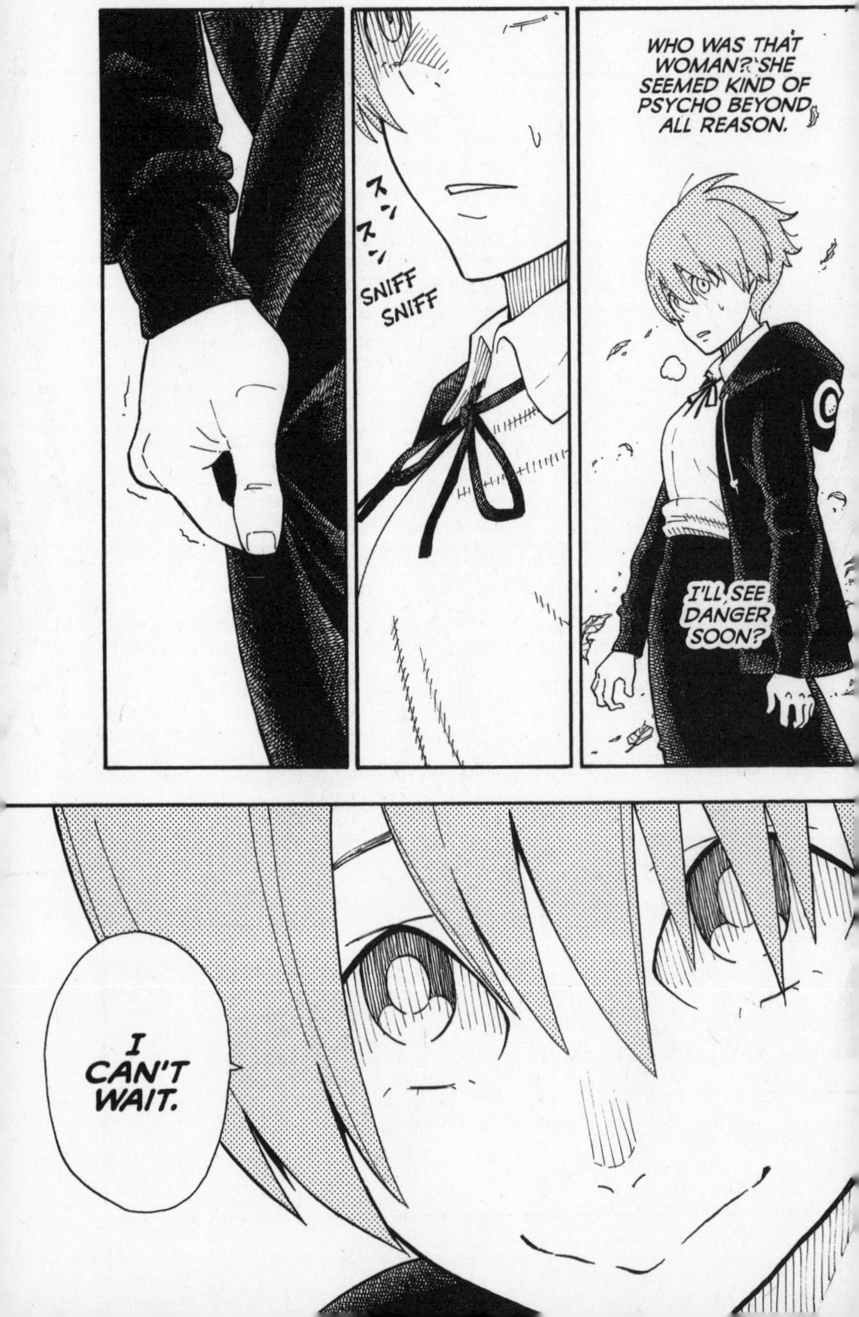
WHO WAS THAT WOMAN?! SHE SEEMED KIND OF PSYCHO BEYOND ALL REASON.
I'LL SEE DANGER SOON?
SNIFF SNIFF
I CAN'T WAIT.

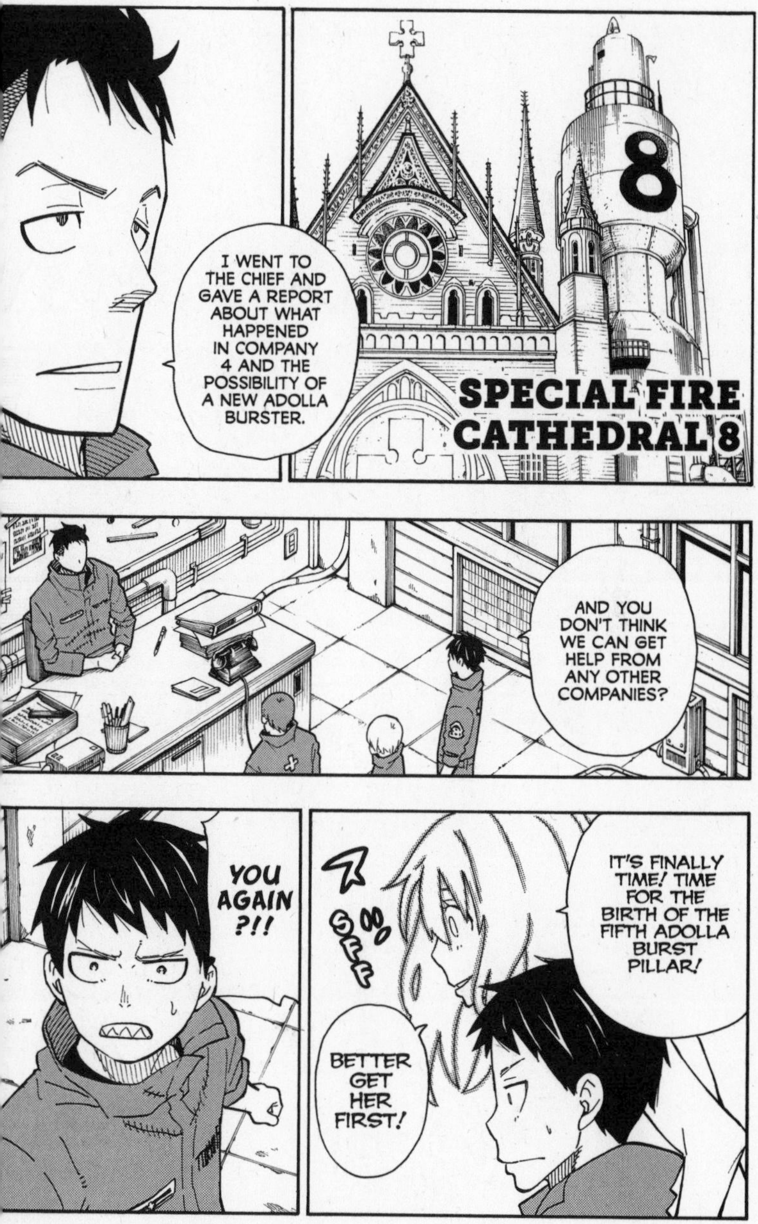
SPECIAL FIRE CATHEDRAL 8
I WENT TO THE CHIEF AND GAVE A REPORT ABOUT WHAT HAPPENED IN COMPANY 4 AND THE POSSIBILITY OF A NEW ADOLLA BURSTER.
AND YOU DON'T THINK WE CAN GET HELP FROM ANY OTHER COMPANIES?
IT'S FINALLY TIME! TIME FOR THE BIRTH OF THE FIFTH ADOLLA BURST PILLAR!
SFF
BETTER GET HER FIRST!
YOU AGAIN ?!!

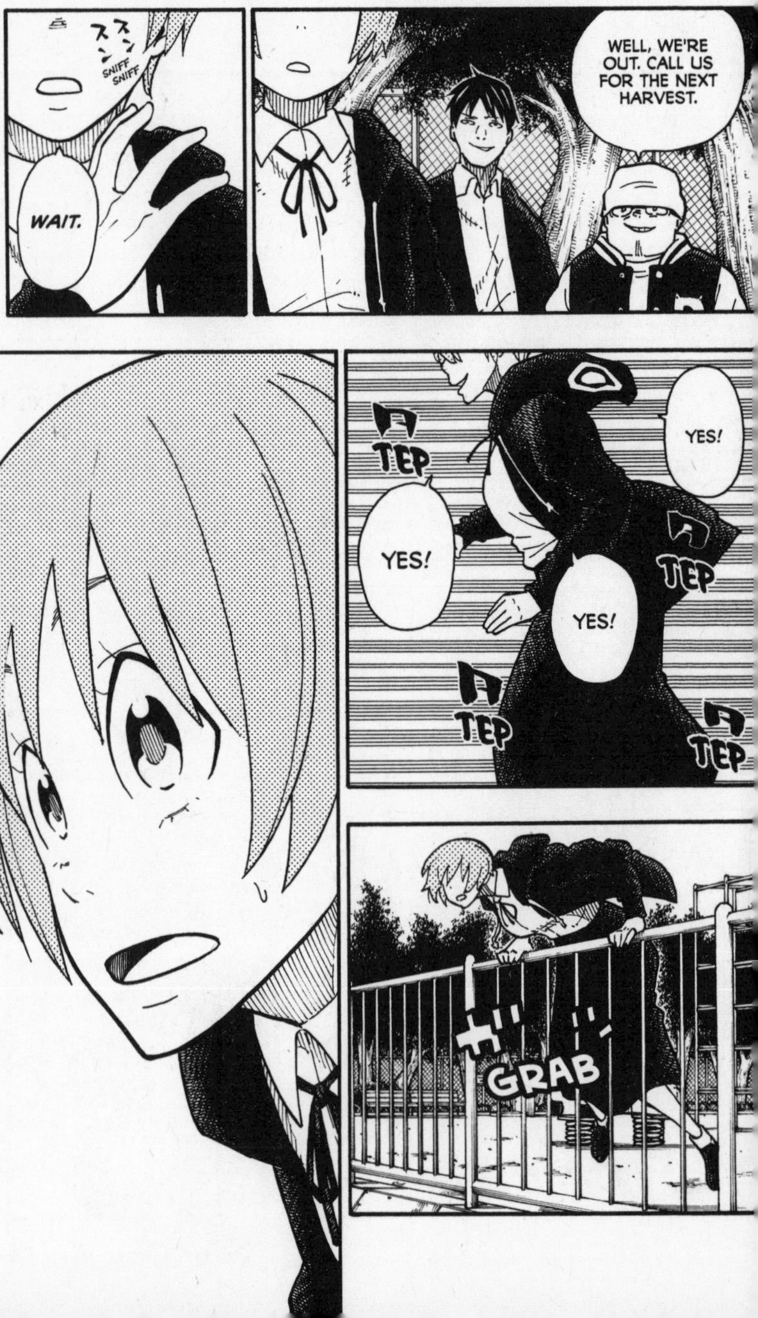
WELL, WE'RE OUT. CALL US FOR THE NEXT HARVEST.
スン スン
SNIFF SNIFF
WAIT.
YES!
TEP
TEP
YES!
YES!
TEP
TEP
GRAB

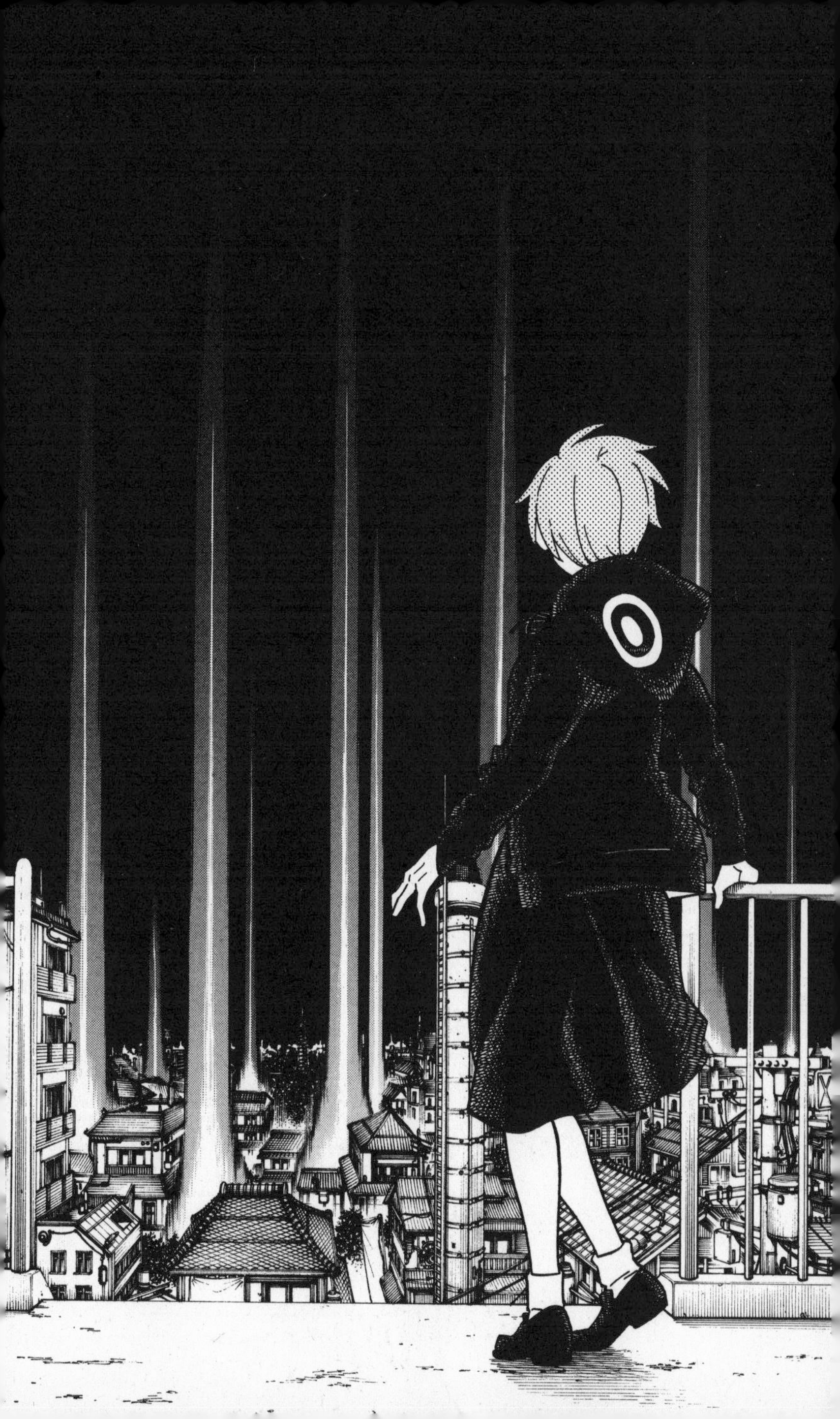

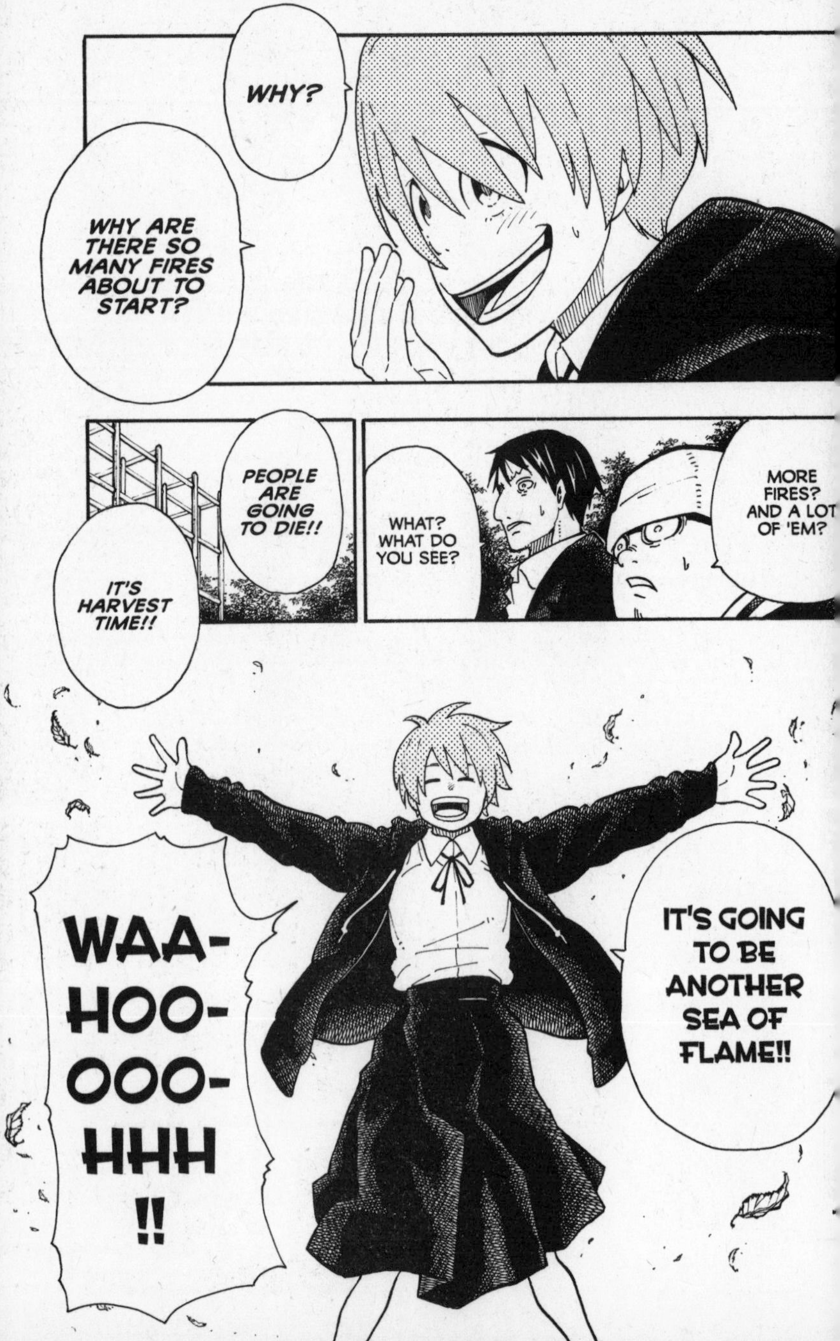
WHY?
WHY ARE THERE SO MANY FIRES ABOUT TO START?
MORE FIRES? AND A LOT OF 'EM?
WHAT? WHAT DO YOU SEE?
PEOPLE ARE GOING TO DIE!!
IT'S HARVEST TIME!!
IT'S GOING TO BE ANOTHER SEA OF FLAME!!
WAA-HOO-OOO-HHH!!

FIRE FORCE

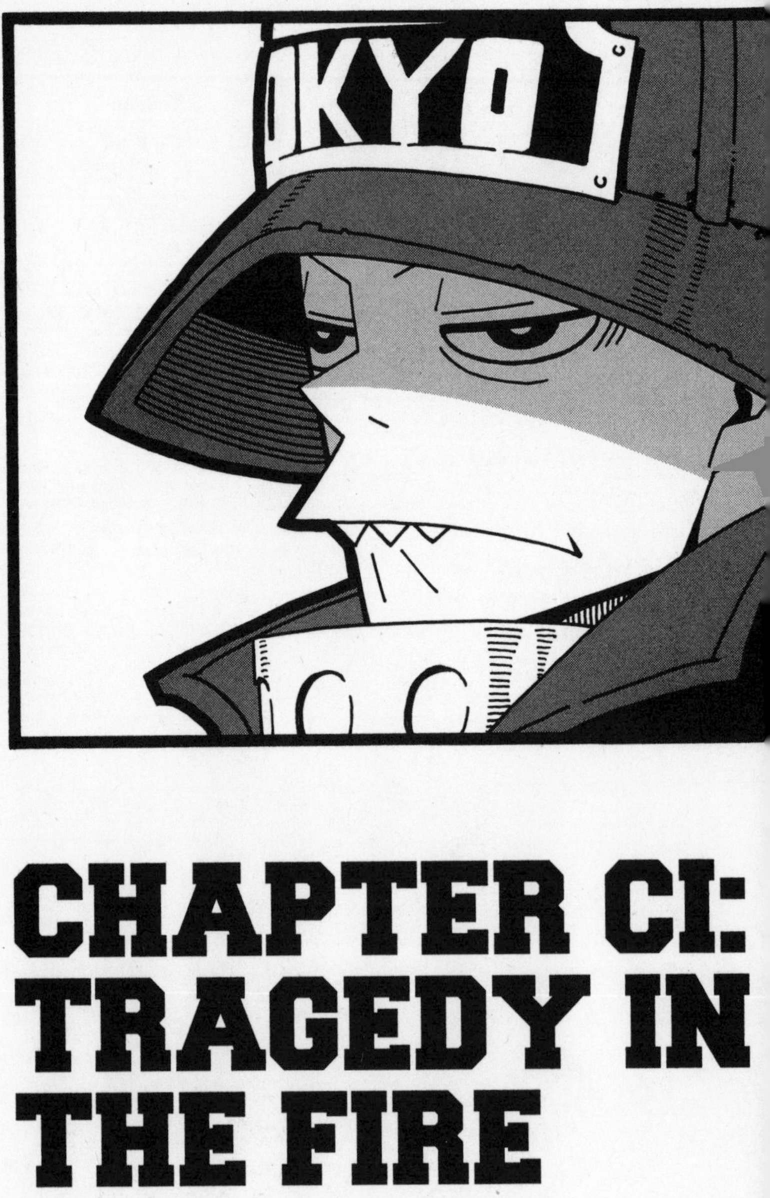
OKYO

CHAPTER CI: TRAGEDY IN THE FIRE

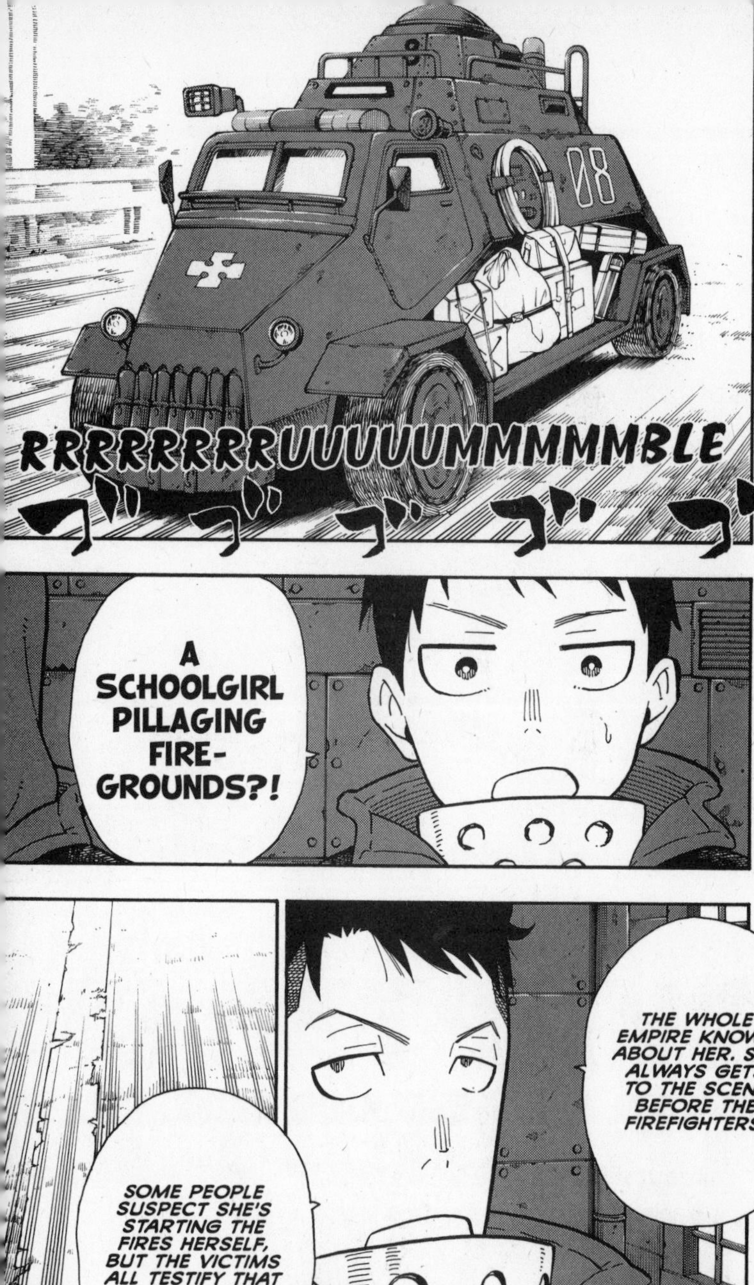
RRRRRRRRUUUUUUMMMMMBLE
ゴゴゴゴゴ
A SCHOOLGIRL PILLAGING FIRE-GROUNDS?!
THE WHOLE EMPIRE KNOWS ABOUT HER. SHE ALWAYS GETS TO THE SCENE BEFORE THE FIREFIGHTERS.
SOME PEOPLE SUSPECT SHE'S STARTING THE FIRES HERSELF, BUT THE VICTIMS ALL TESTIFY THAT SHE'S NOT.

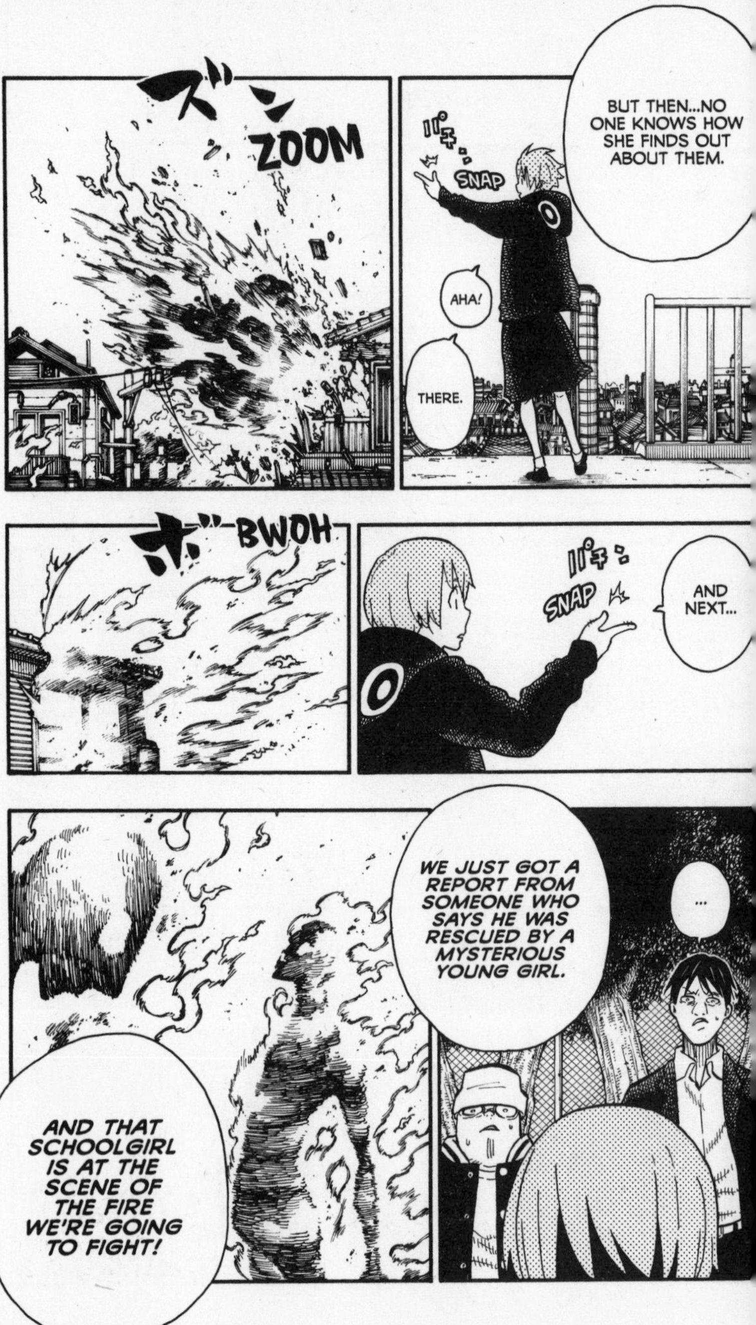
BUT THEN...NO ONE KNOWS HOW SHE FINDS OUT ABOUT THEM.
SNAP
AHA!
THERE.
ZOOM
AND NEXT...
SNAP
BWOH
...
WE JUST GOT A REPORT FROM SOMEONE WHO SAYS HE WAS RESCUED BY A MYSTERIOUS YOUNG GIRL.
AND THAT SCHOOLGIRL IS AT THE SCENE OF THE FIRE WE'RE GOING TO FIGHT!

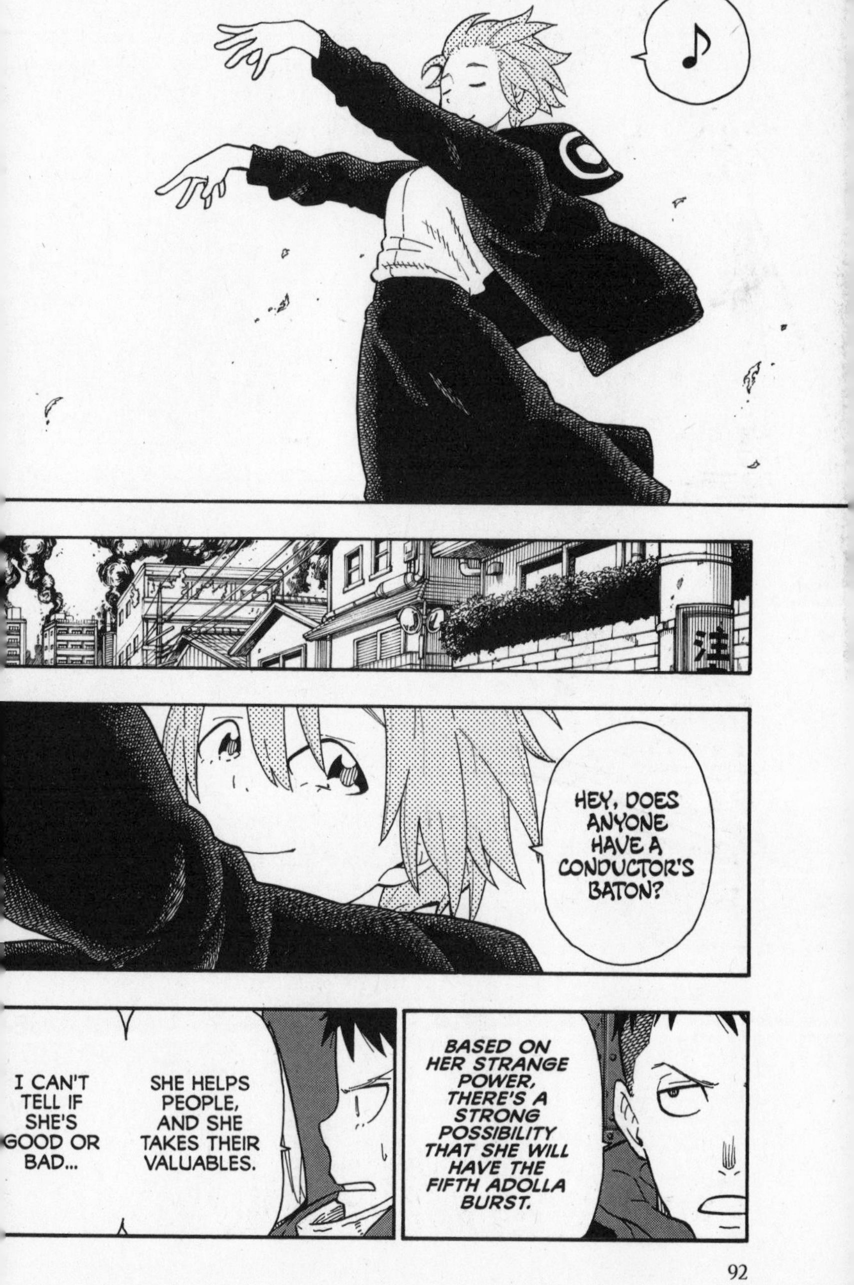
♪
注
HEY, DOES ANYONE HAVE A CONDUCTOR'S BATON?
BASED ON HER STRANGE POWER, THERE'S A STRONG POSSIBILITY THAT SHE WILL HAVE THE FIFTH ADOLLA BURST.
SHE HELPS PEOPLE, AND SHE TAKES THEIR VALUABLES.
I CAN'T TELL IF SHE'S GOOD OR BAD...

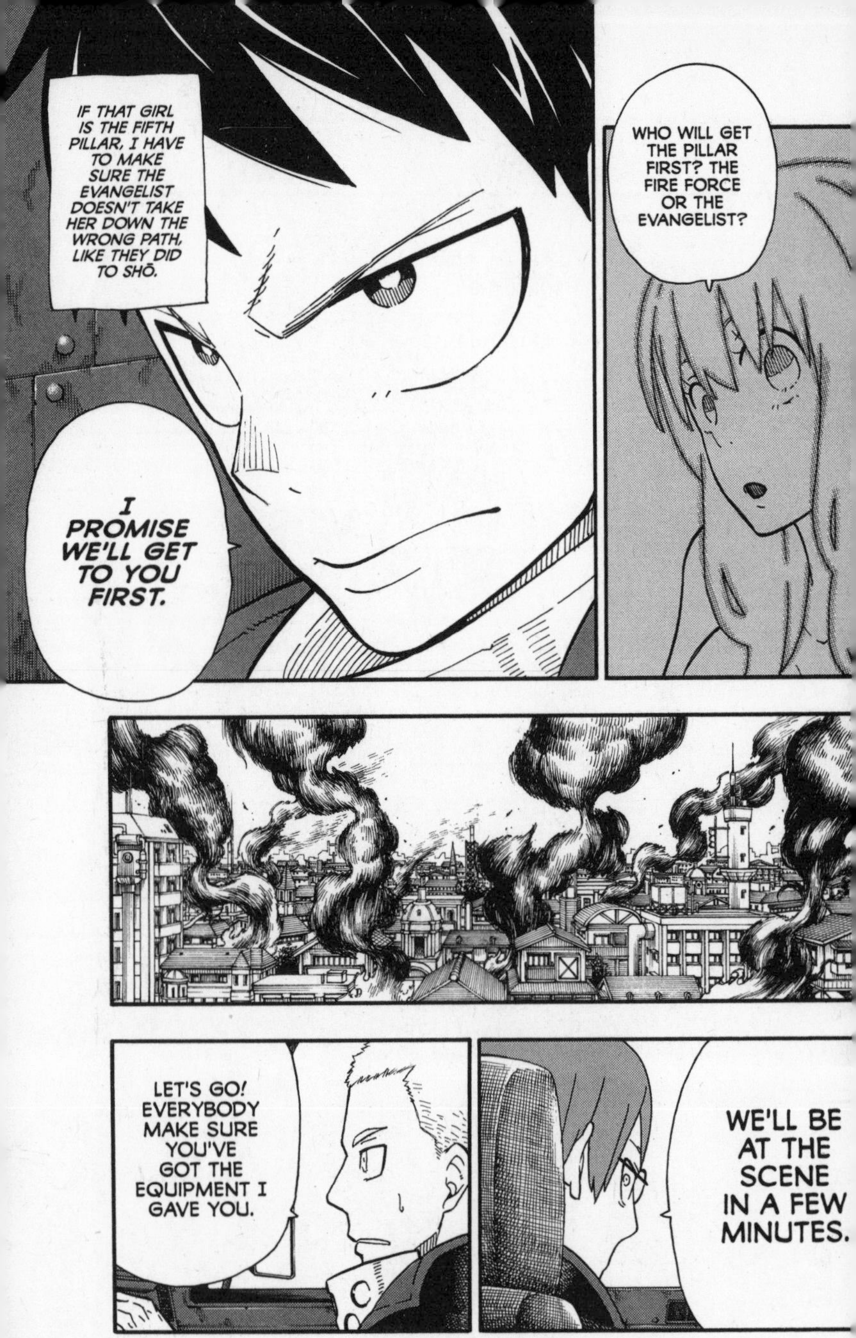
WHO WILL GET THE PILLAR FIRST? THE FIRE FORCE OR THE EVANGELIST?
IF THAT GIRL IS THE FIFTH PILLAR, I HAVE TO MAKE SURE THE EVANGELIST DOESN'T TAKE HER DOWN THE WRONG PATH, LIKE THEY DID TO SHŌ.
I PROMISE WE'LL GET TO YOU FIRST.
WE'LL BE AT THE SCENE IN A FEW MINUTES.
LET'S GO! EVERYBODY MAKE SURE YOU'VE GOT THE EQUIPMENT I GAVE YOU.

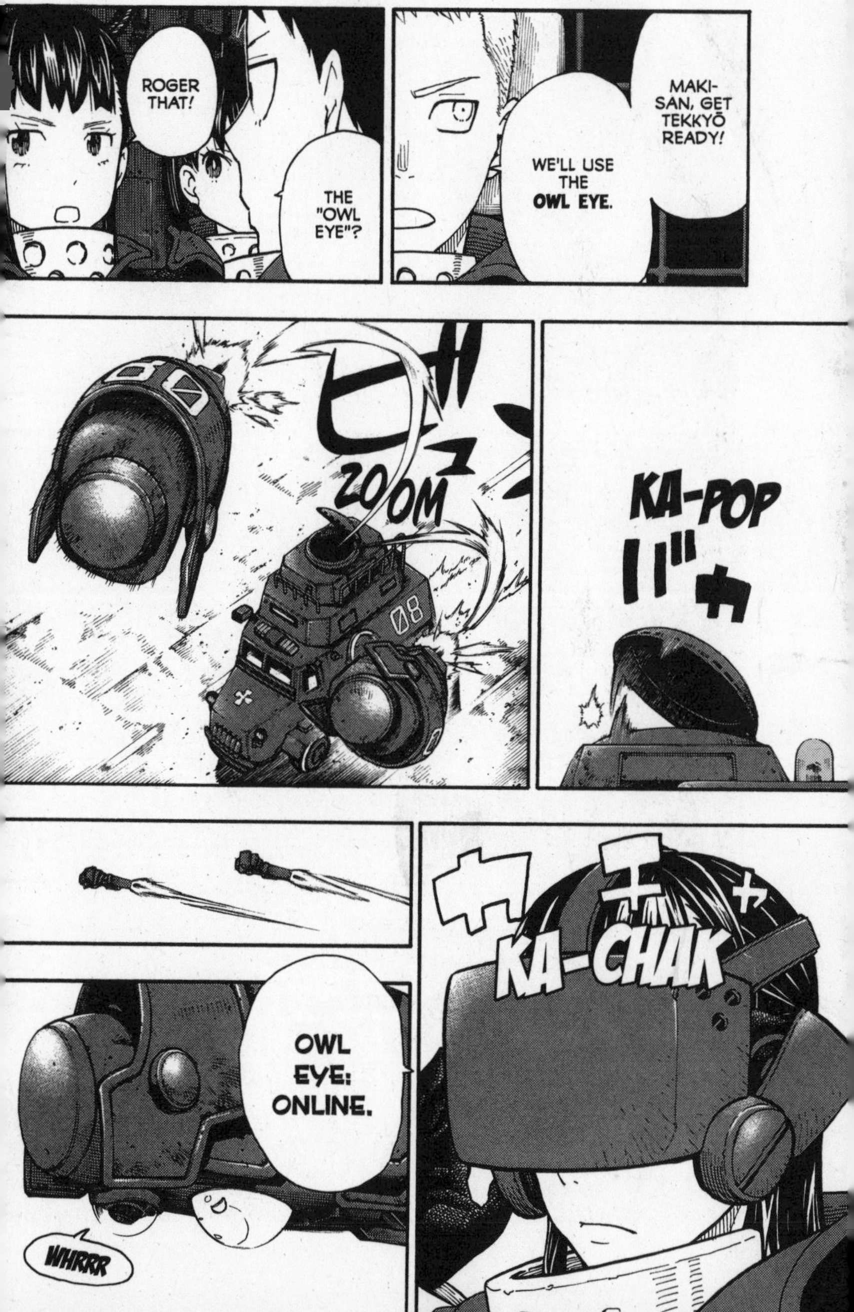
MAKI-SAN, GET TEKKYŌ READY!
WE'LL USE THE OWL EYE.
ROGER THAT!
THE "OWL EYE"?
KA-POP
ZOOM
KA-CHAK
OWL EYE: ONLINE.
WHRRR

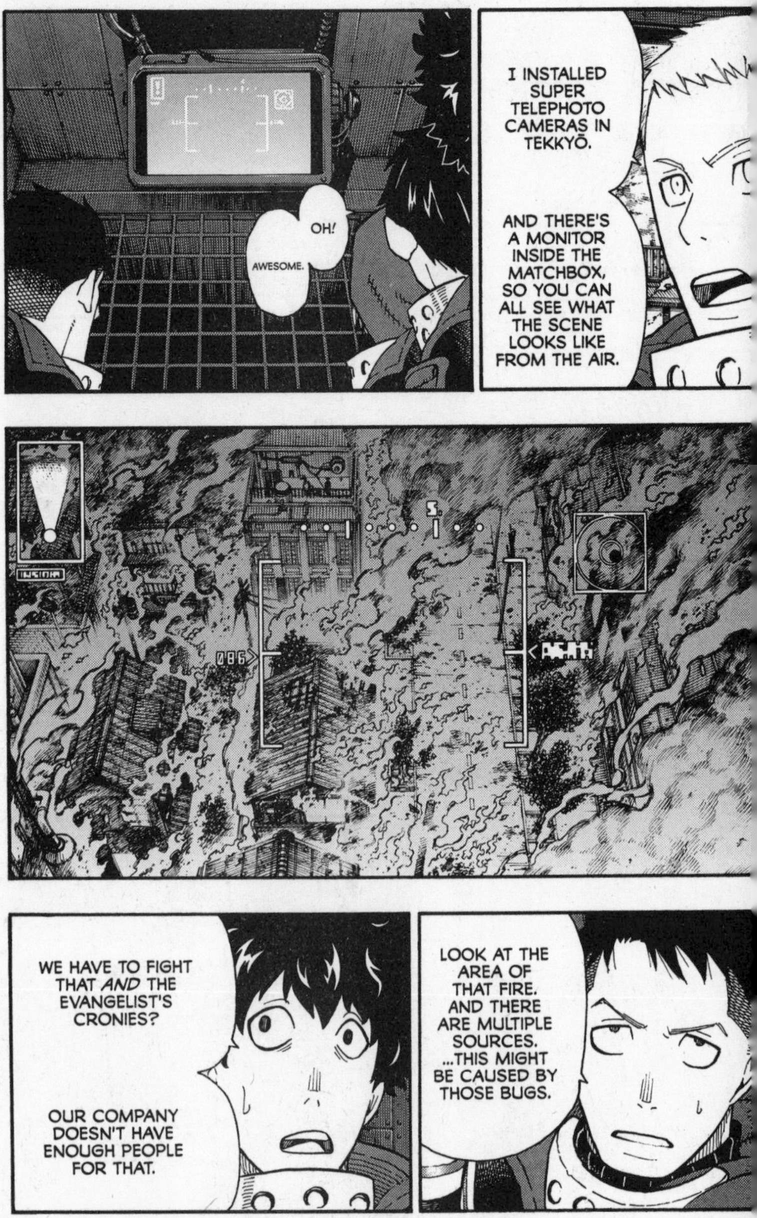
I INSTALLED SUPER TELEPHOTO CAMERAS IN TEKKYŌ.
AND THERE'S A MONITOR INSIDE THE MATCHBOX, SO YOU CAN ALL SEE WHAT THE SCENE LOOKS LIKE FROM THE AIR.
OH!
AWESOME.
LOOK AT THE AREA OF THAT FIRE. AND THERE ARE MULTIPLE SOURCES. ...THIS MIGHT BE CAUSED BY THOSE BUGS.
WE HAVE TO FIGHT THAT *AND* THE EVANGELIST'S CRONIES?
OUR COMPANY DOESN'T HAVE ENOUGH PEOPLE FOR THAT.

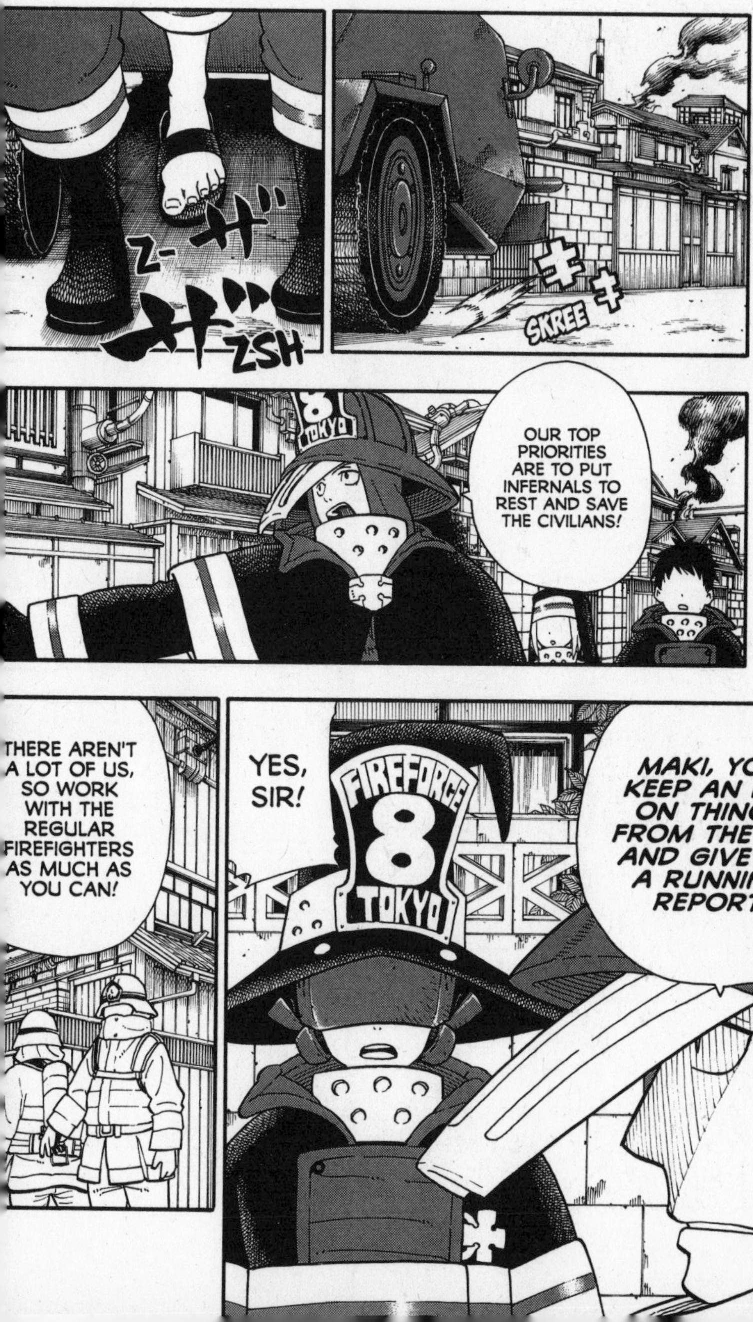
SKREE
ZSH
OUR TOP PRIORITIES ARE TO PUT INFERNALS TO REST AND SAVE THE CIVILIANS!
MAKI, YOU KEEP AN EYE ON THINGS FROM THE AIR AND GIVE ME A RUNNING REPORT.
YES, SIR!
THERE AREN'T A LOT OF US, SO WORK WITH THE REGULAR FIREFIGHTERS AS MUCH AS YOU CAN!

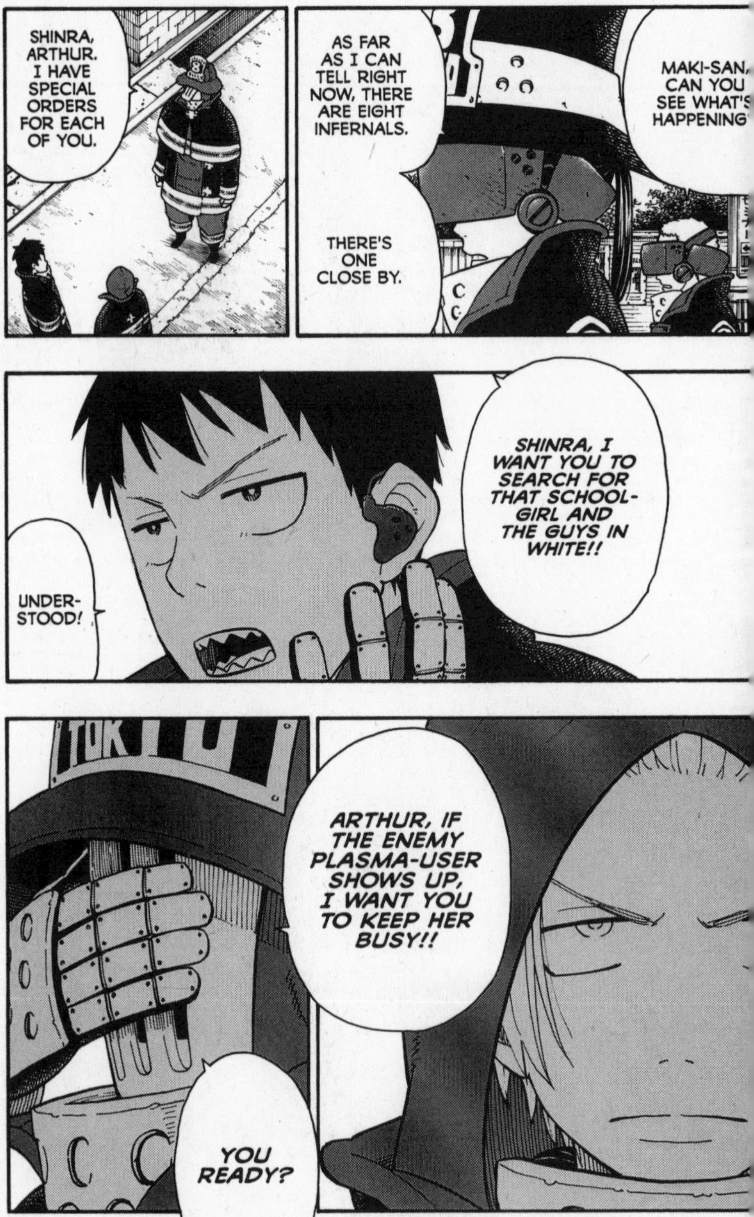
MAKI-SAN, CAN YOU SEE WHAT'S HAPPENING?
AS FAR AS I CAN TELL RIGHT NOW, THERE ARE EIGHT INFERNALS.
THERE'S ONE CLOSE BY.
SHINRA, ARTHUR. I HAVE SPECIAL ORDERS FOR EACH OF YOU.
SHINRA, I WANT YOU TO SEARCH FOR THAT SCHOOL-GIRL AND THE GUYS IN WHITE!!
UNDER-STOOD!
ARTHUR, IF THE ENEMY PLASMA-USER SHOWS UP, I WANT YOU TO KEEP HER BUSY!!
YOU READY?

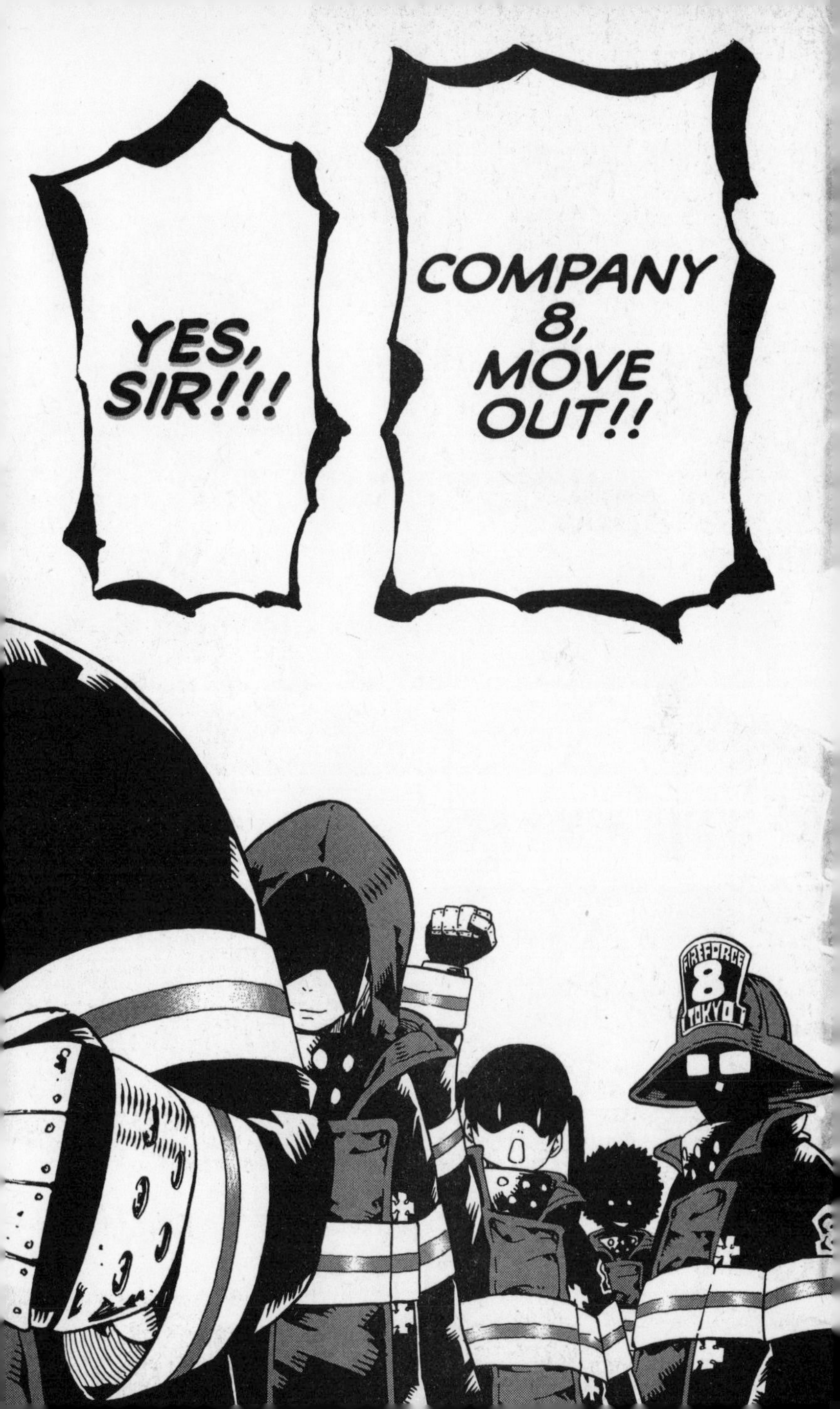
COMPANY 8, MOVE OUT!!
YES, SIR!!!
FIRE FORCE 8 TOKYO

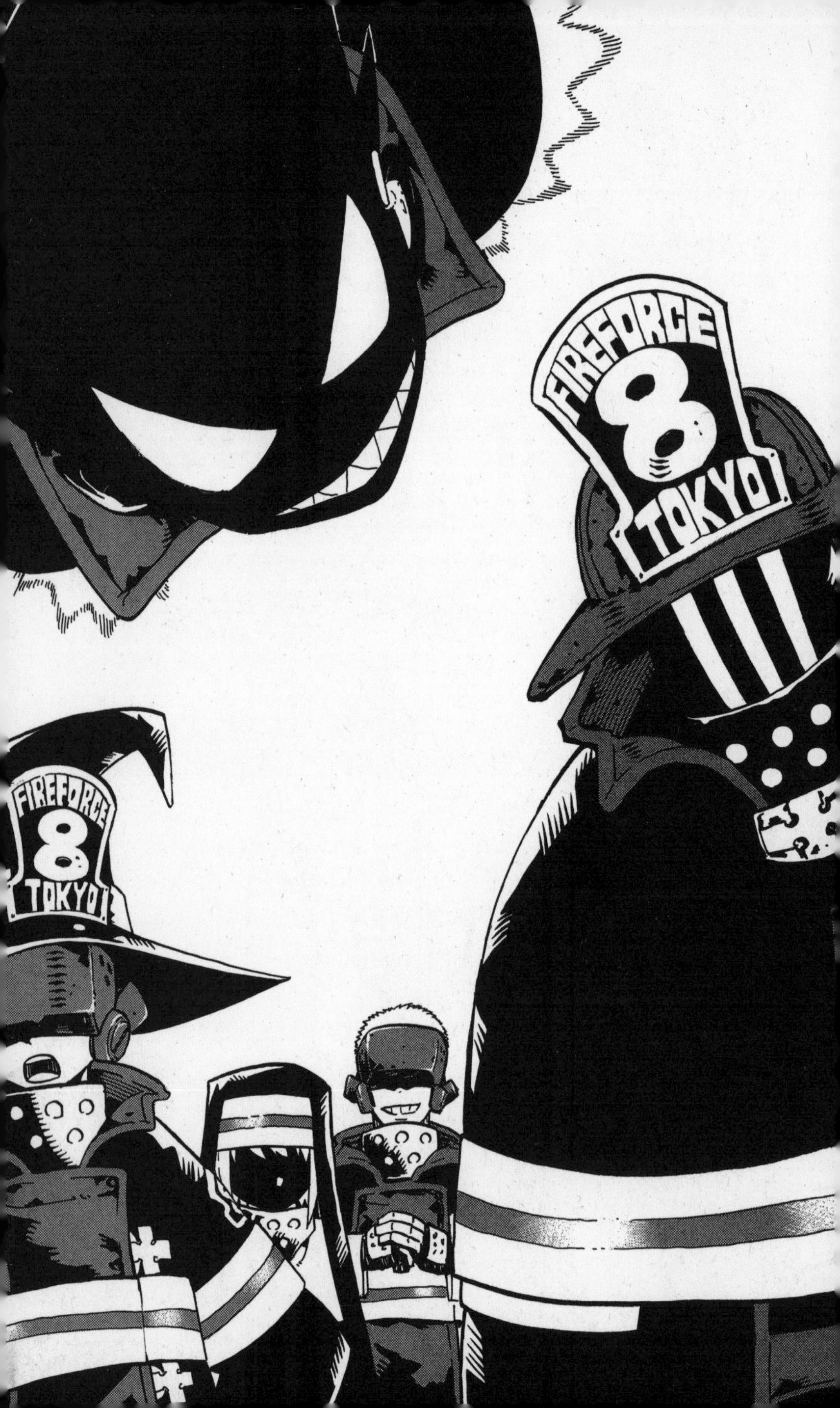
FIREFORCE
8
TOKYO
FIREFORCE
8
TOKYO

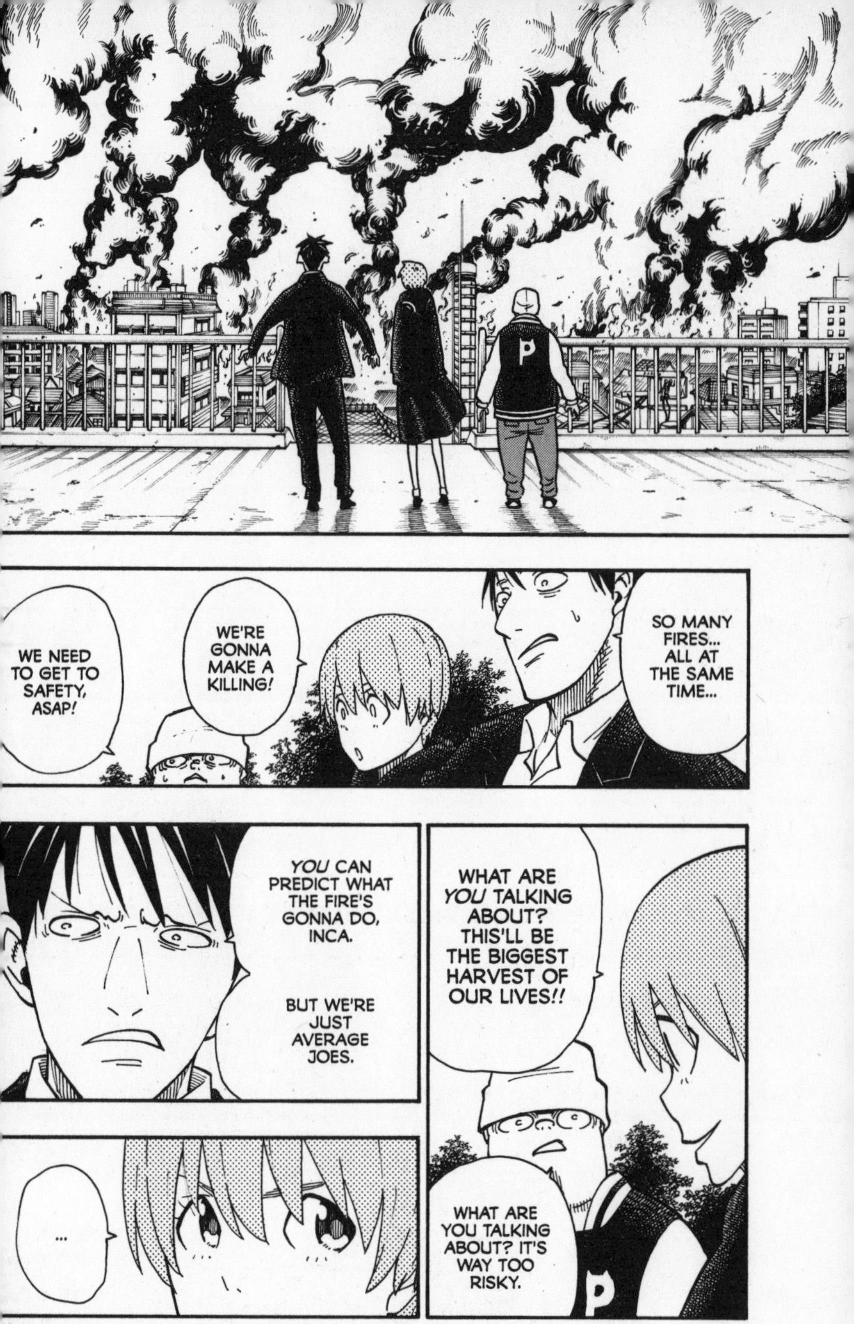

SO MANY FIRES... ALL AT THE SAME TIME...
WE'RE GONNA MAKE A KILLING!
WE NEED TO GET TO SAFETY, ASAP!
WHAT ARE *YOU* TALKING ABOUT? THIS'LL BE THE BIGGEST HARVEST OF OUR LIVES!!
WHAT ARE YOU TALKING ABOUT? IT'S WAY TOO RISKY.
YOU CAN PREDICT WHAT THE FIRE'S GONNA DO, INCA.
BUT WE'RE JUST AVERAGE JOES.
...

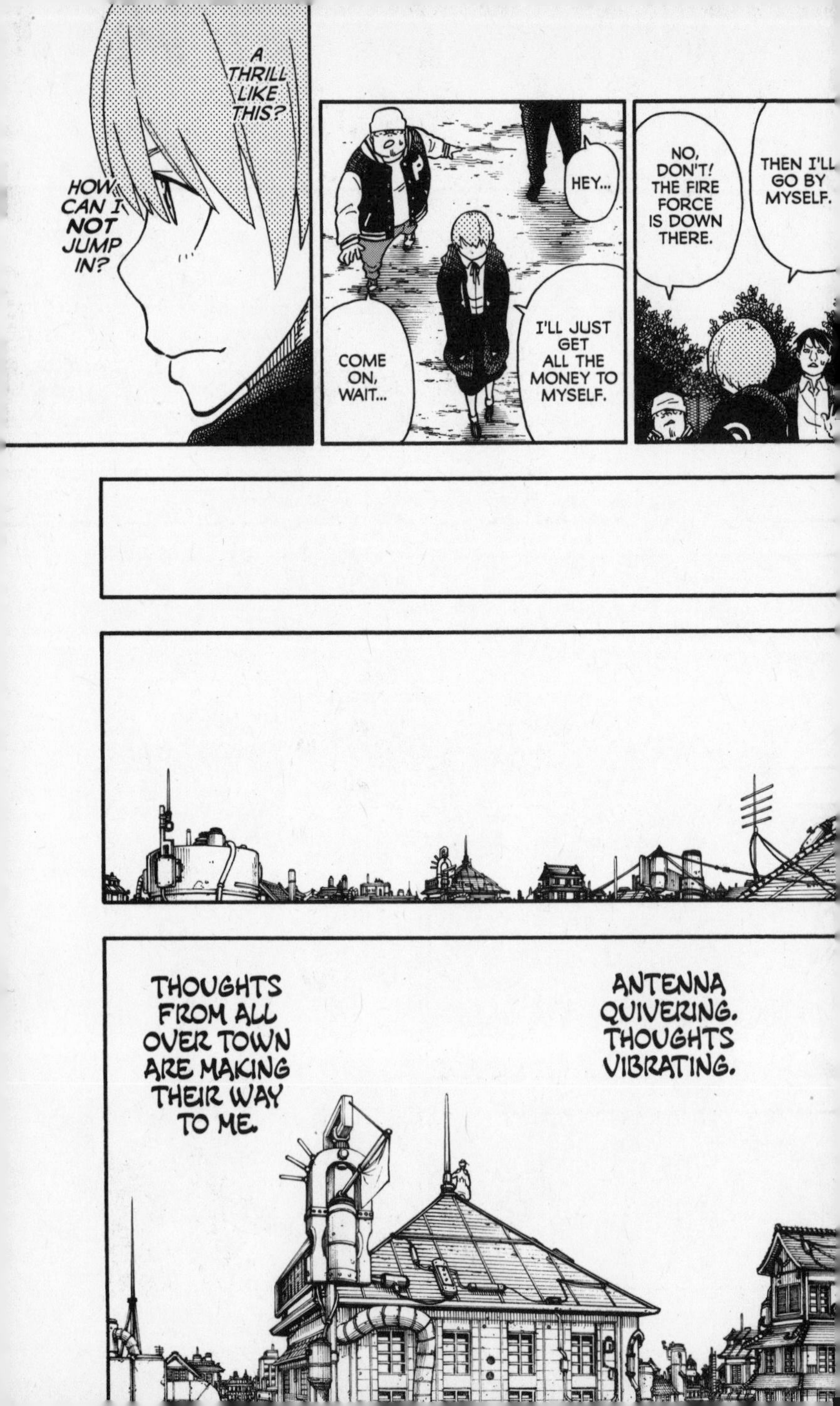
THEN I'LL GO BY MYSELF.
NO, DON'T! THE FIRE FORCE IS DOWN THERE.
HEY...
I'LL JUST GET ALL THE MONEY TO MYSELF.
COME ON, WAIT...
A THRILL LIKE THIS?
HOW CAN I NOT JUMP IN?
ANTENNA QUIVERING. THOUGHTS VIBRATING.
THOUGHTS FROM ALL OVER TOWN ARE MAKING THEIR WAY TO ME.

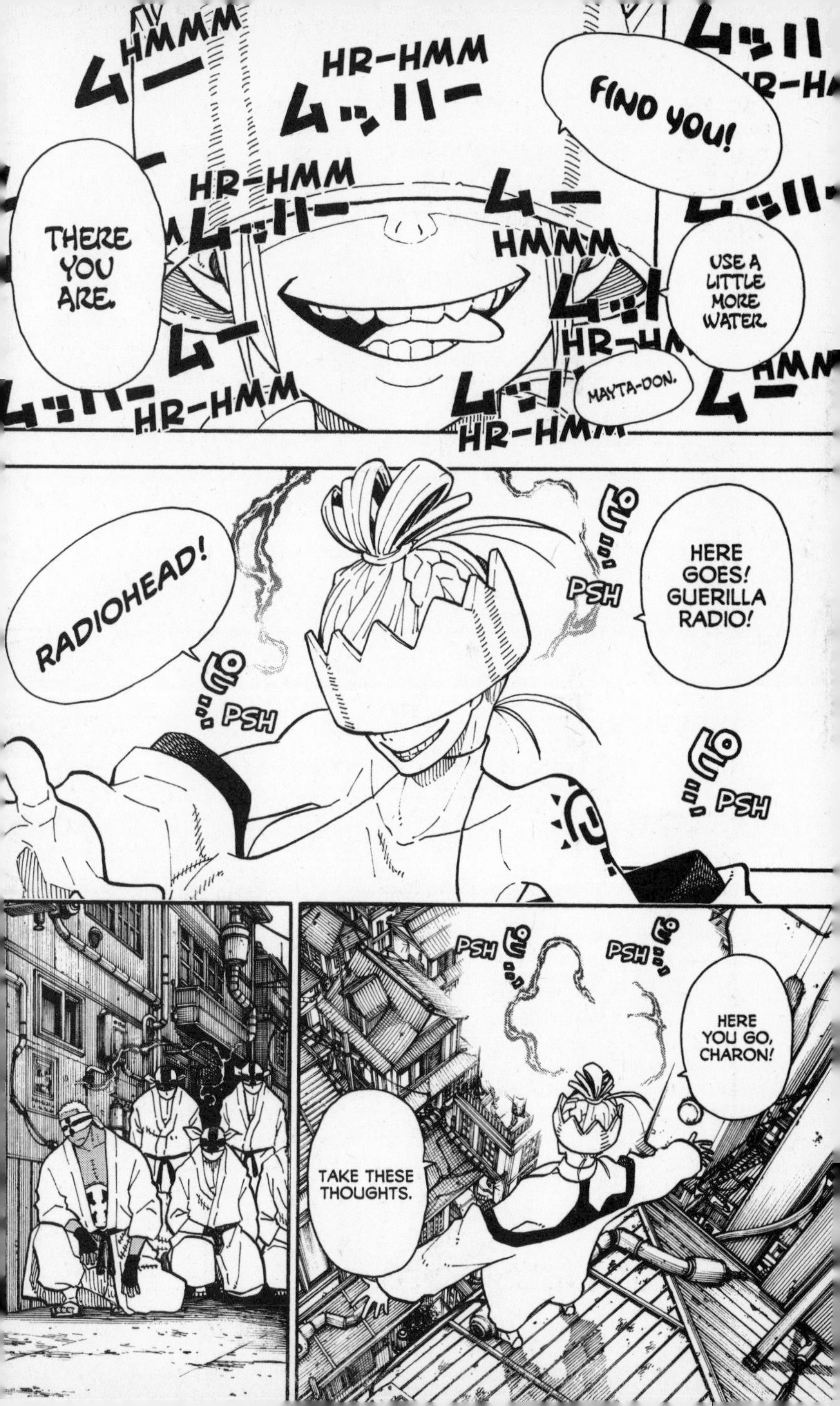
FIND YOU!
USE A LITTLE MORE WATER.
MAYTA-DON.
HR-HMM
HMMM
HR-HMM
HR-HMM
THERE YOU ARE.
HR-HMM
HMMM
HERE GOES! GUERILLA RADIO!
PSH
PSH
RADIOHEAD!
PSH
HERE YOU GO, CHARON!
PSH
PSH
TAKE THESE THOUGHTS.

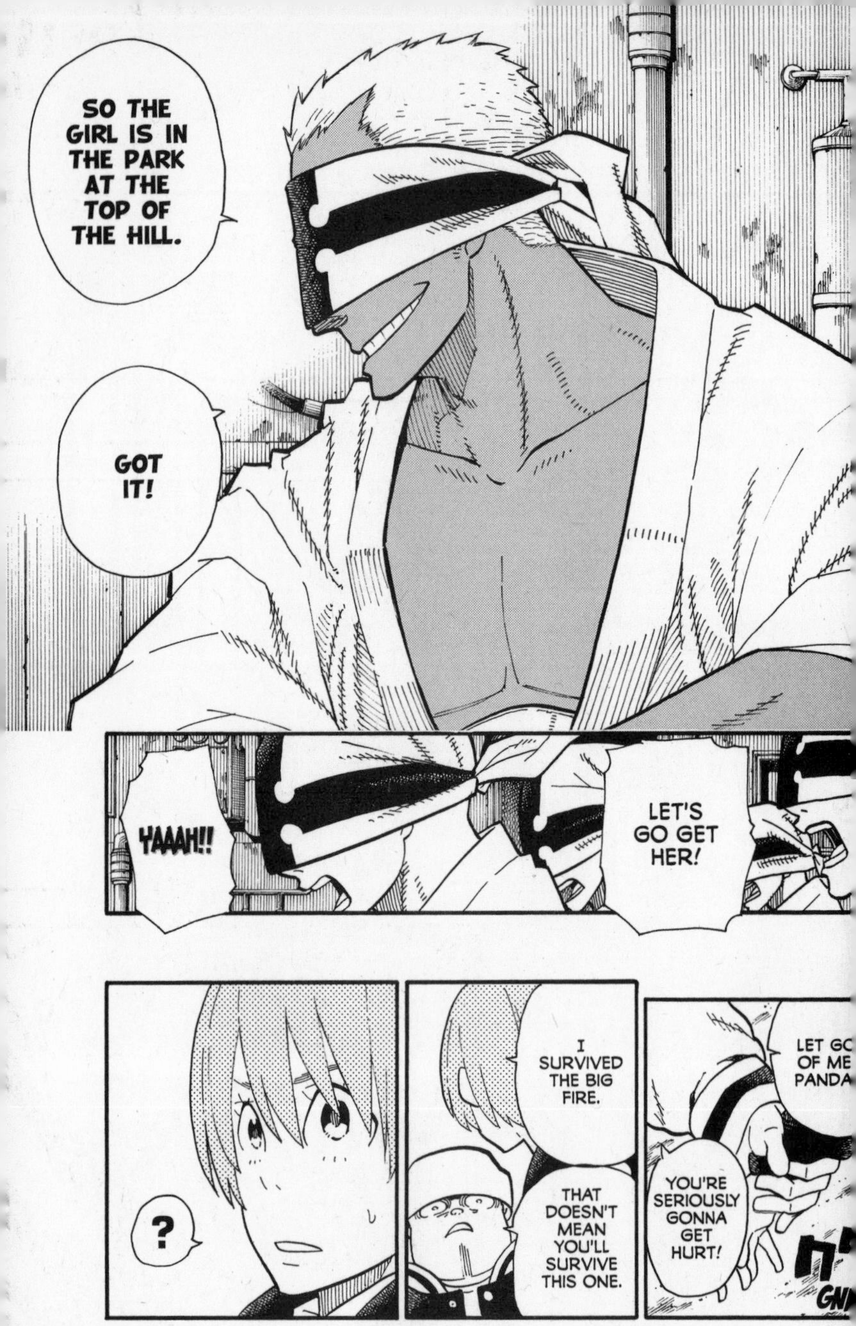
SO THE GIRL IS IN THE PARK AT THE TOP OF THE HILL.
GOT IT!
LET'S GO GET HER!
YAAAH!!
LET GO OF ME PANDA
YOU'RE SERIOUSLY GONNA GET HURT!
I SURVIVED THE BIG FIRE.
THAT DOESN'T MEAN YOU'LL SURVIVE THIS ONE.
?

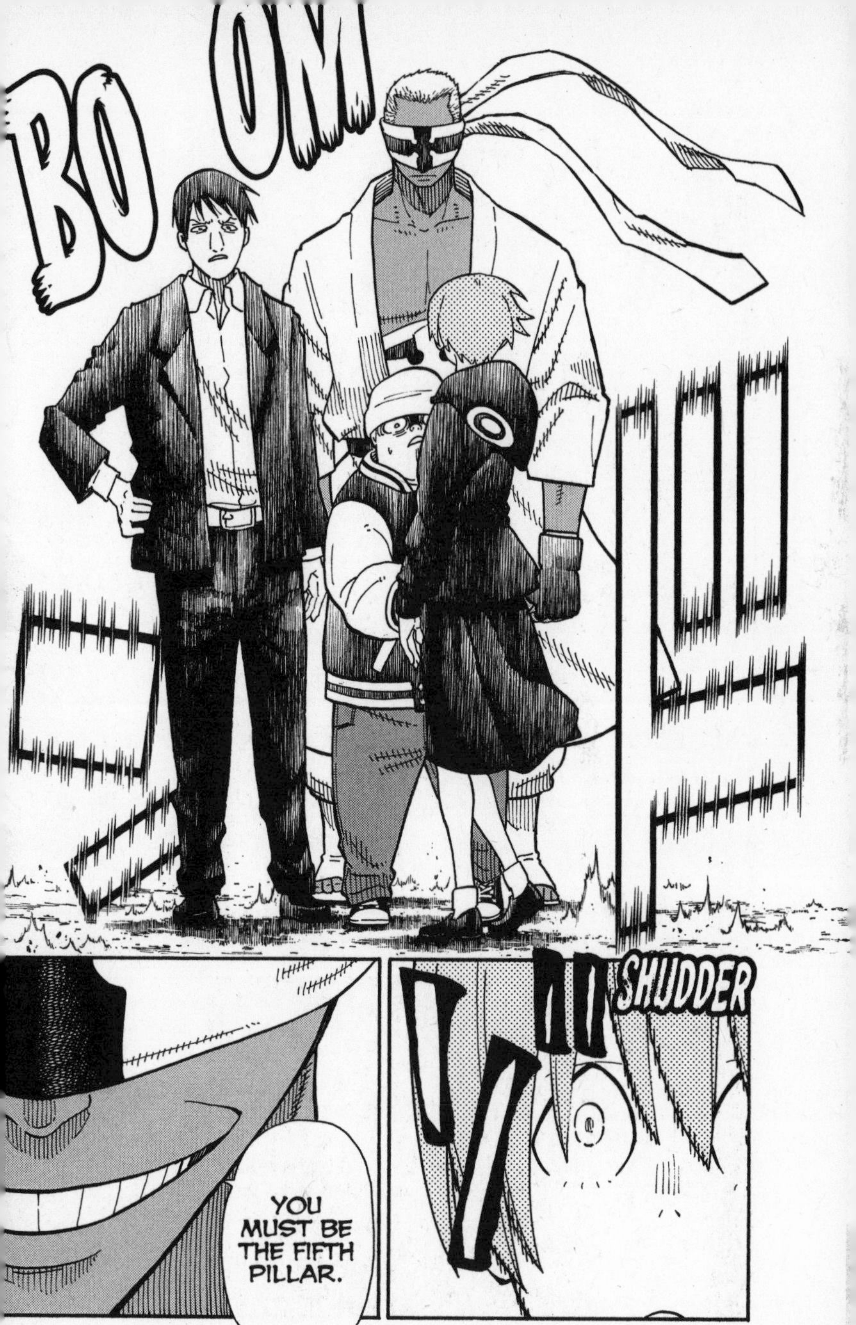
BOOM
SHUDDER
YOU MUST BE THE FIFTH PILLAR.

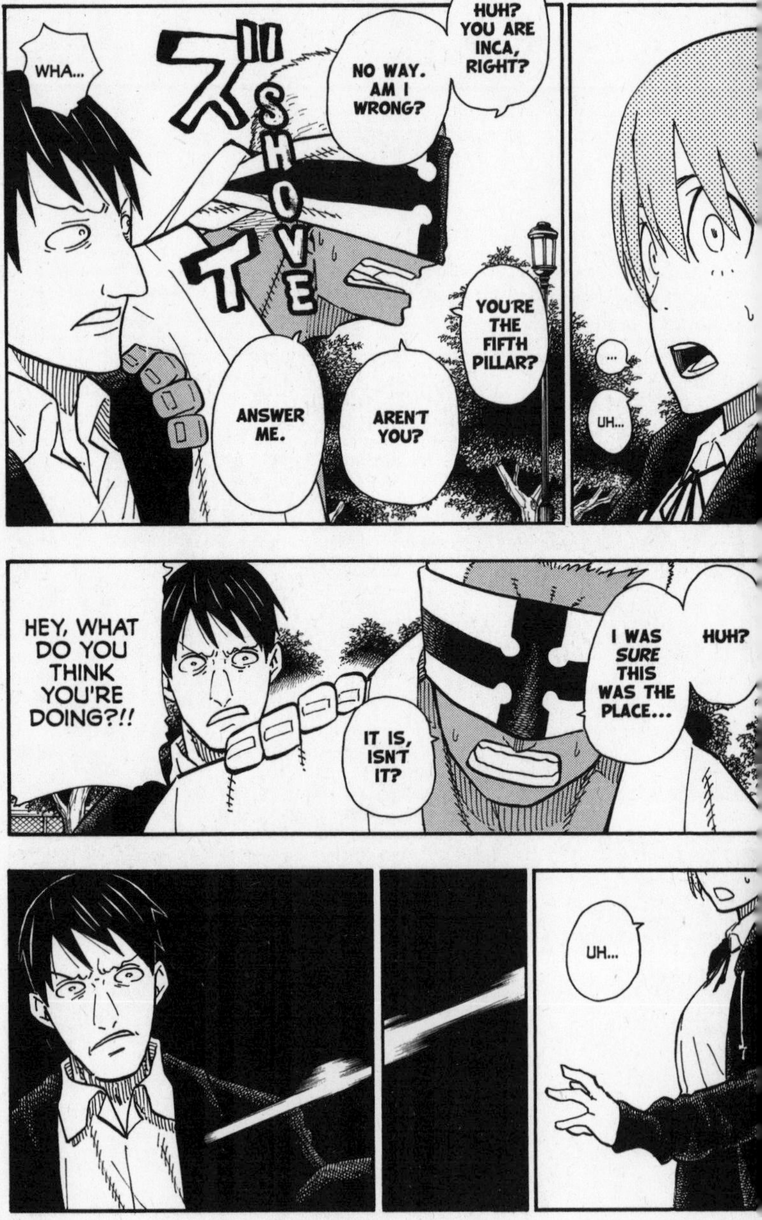
...
UH...
HUH? YOU ARE INCA, RIGHT?
NO WAY. AM I WRONG?
YOU'RE THE FIFTH PILLAR?
ズ
SHOVE
AREN'T YOU?
ANSWER ME.
WHA...
HUH?
I WAS *SURE* THIS WAS THE PLACE...
IT IS, ISN'T IT?
HEY, WHAT DO YOU THINK YOU'RE DOING?!!
UH...

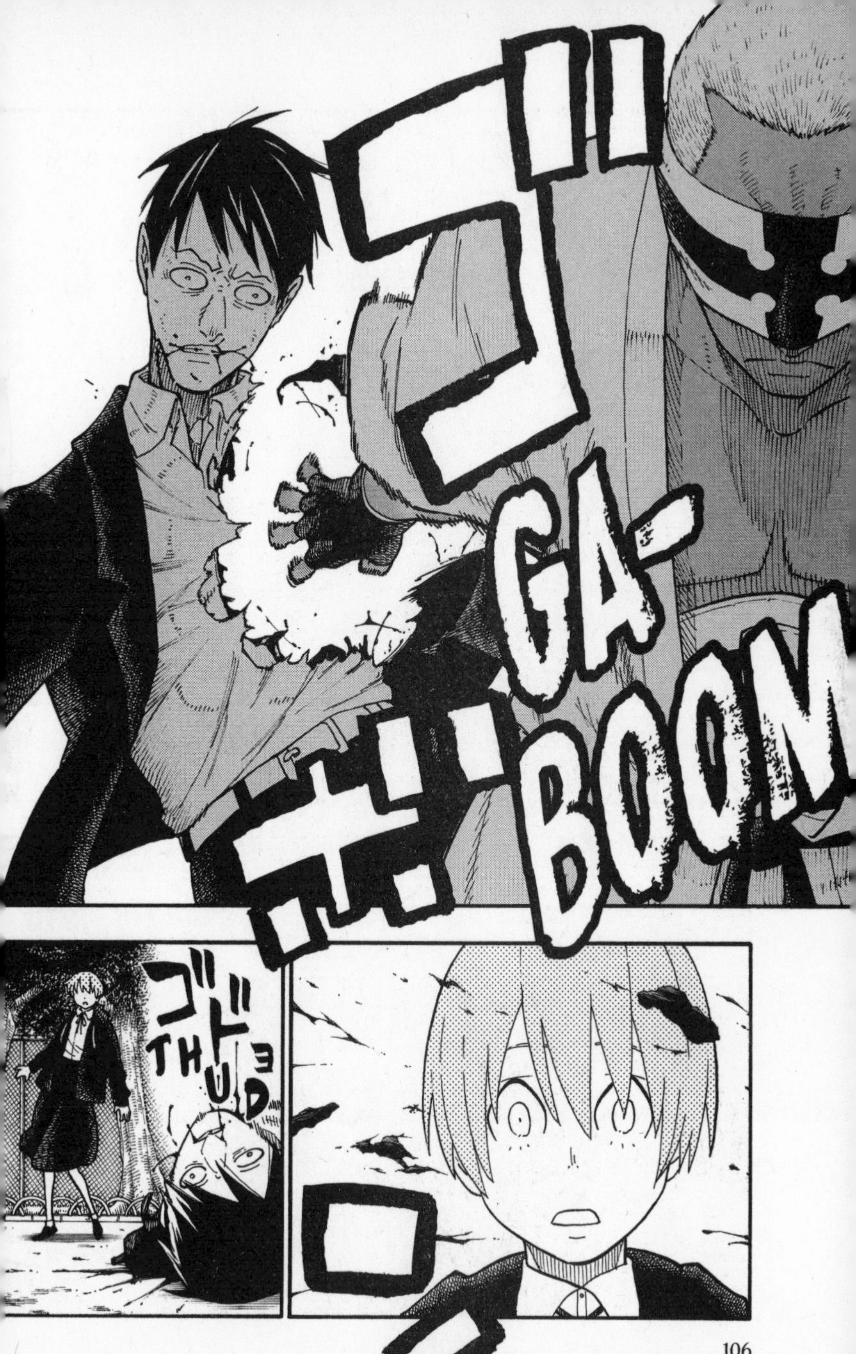
GA-BOOM
THUD

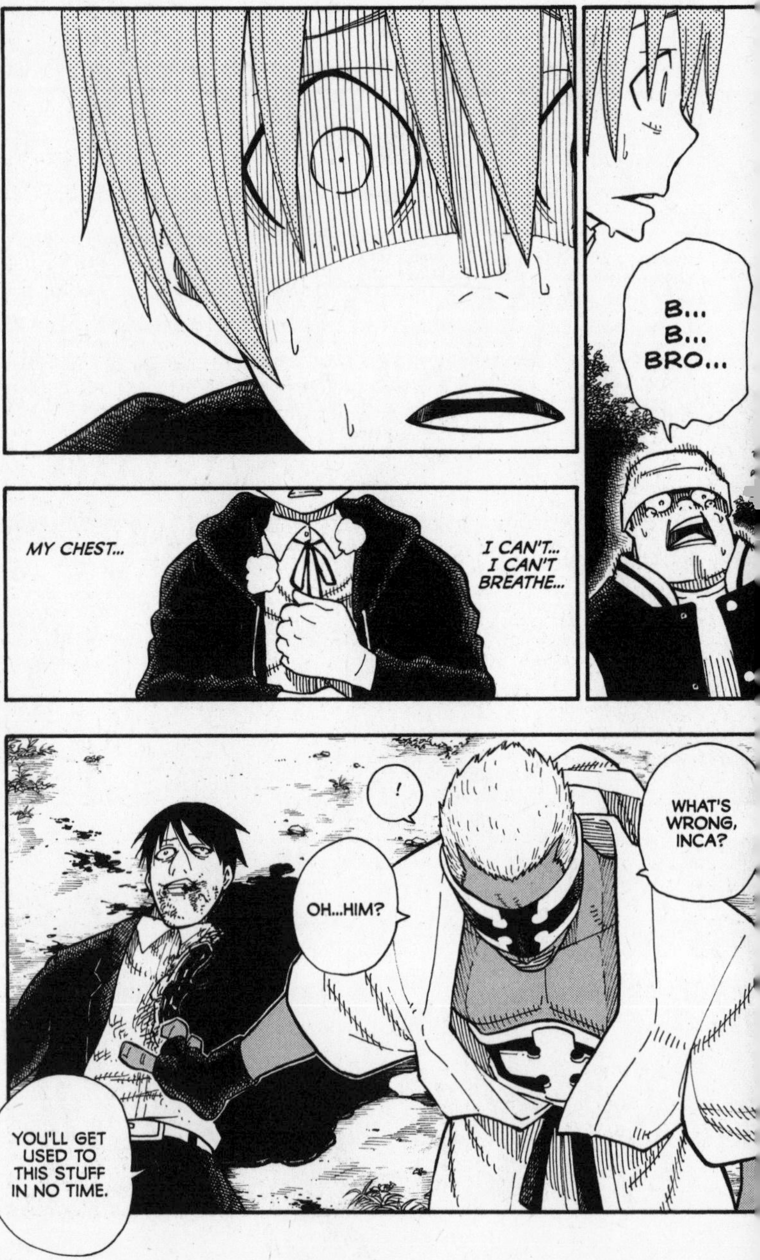
B... B... BRO...
I CAN'T... I CAN'T BREATHE...
MY CHEST...
WHAT'S WRONG, INCA?
!
OH...HIM?
YOU'LL GET USED TO THIS STUFF IN NO TIME.

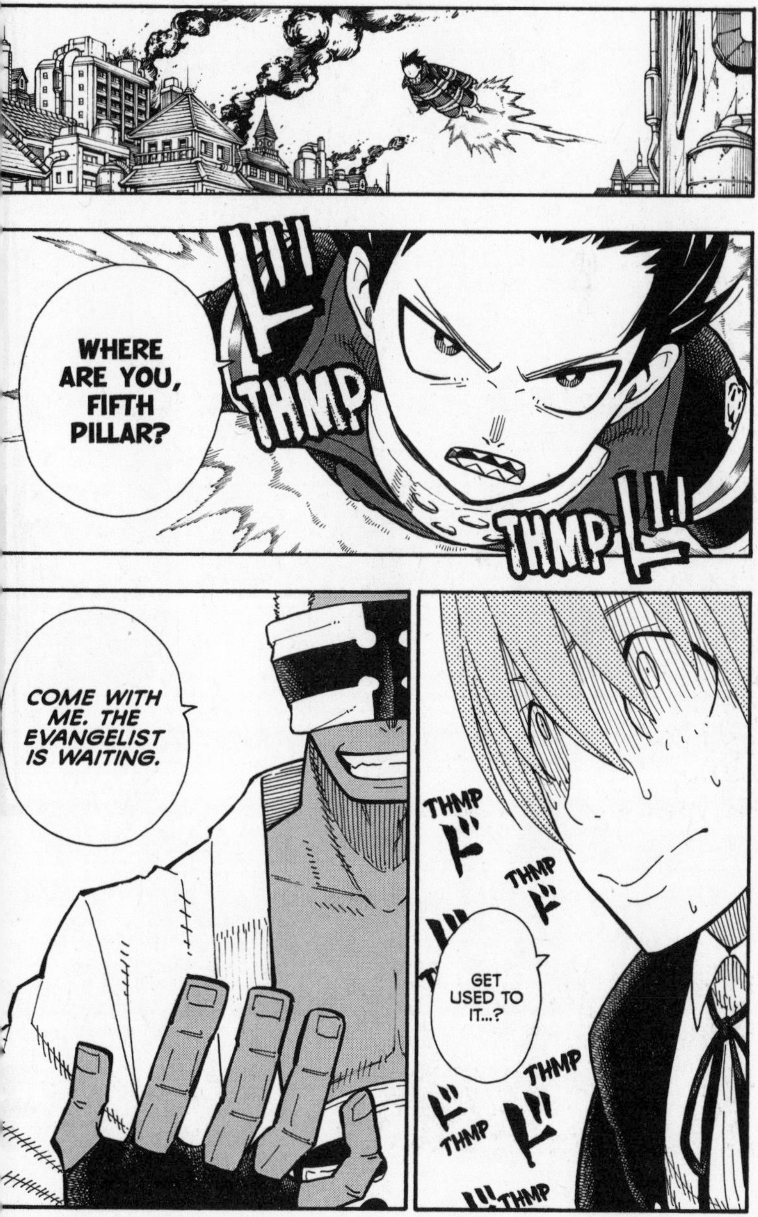
ドッ
THMP
WHERE ARE YOU, FIFTH PILLAR?
THMP
ドッ
THMP
ド
THMP
ド
GET USED TO IT...?
THMP
ドッ
THMP
ド
THMP
COME WITH ME. THE EVANGELIST IS WAITING.

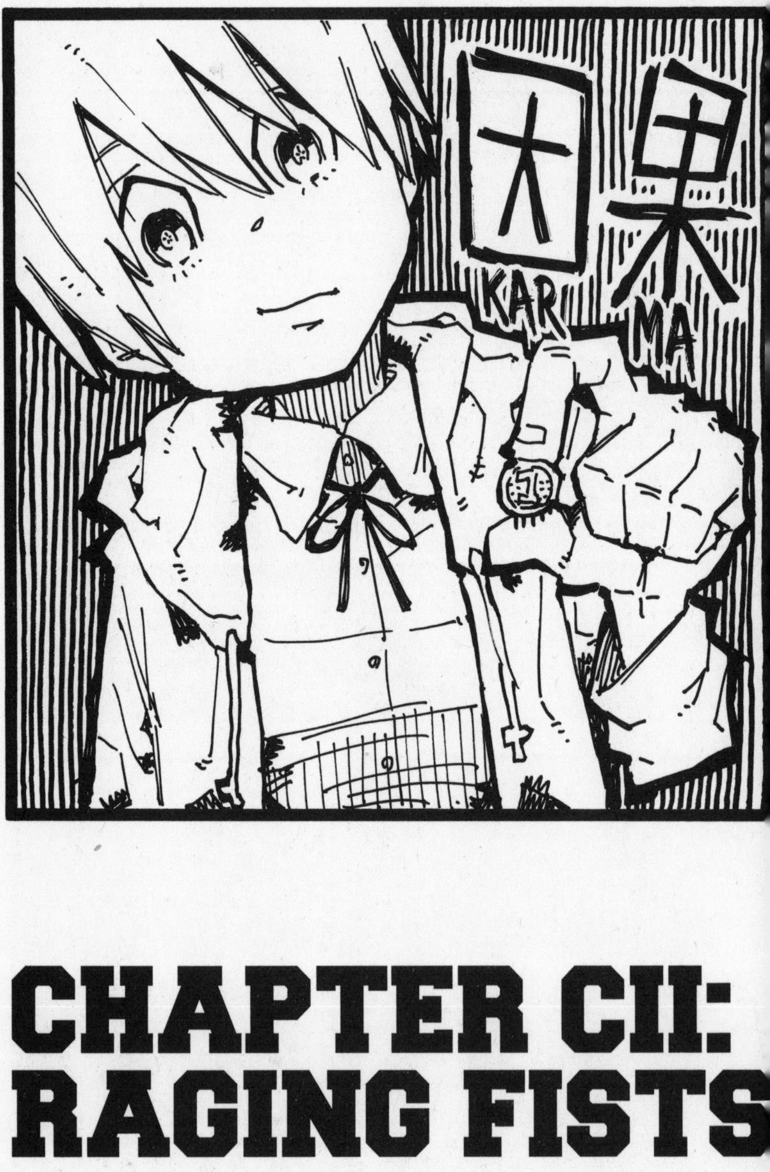
因果
KARMA

CHAPTER CII: RAGING FISTS

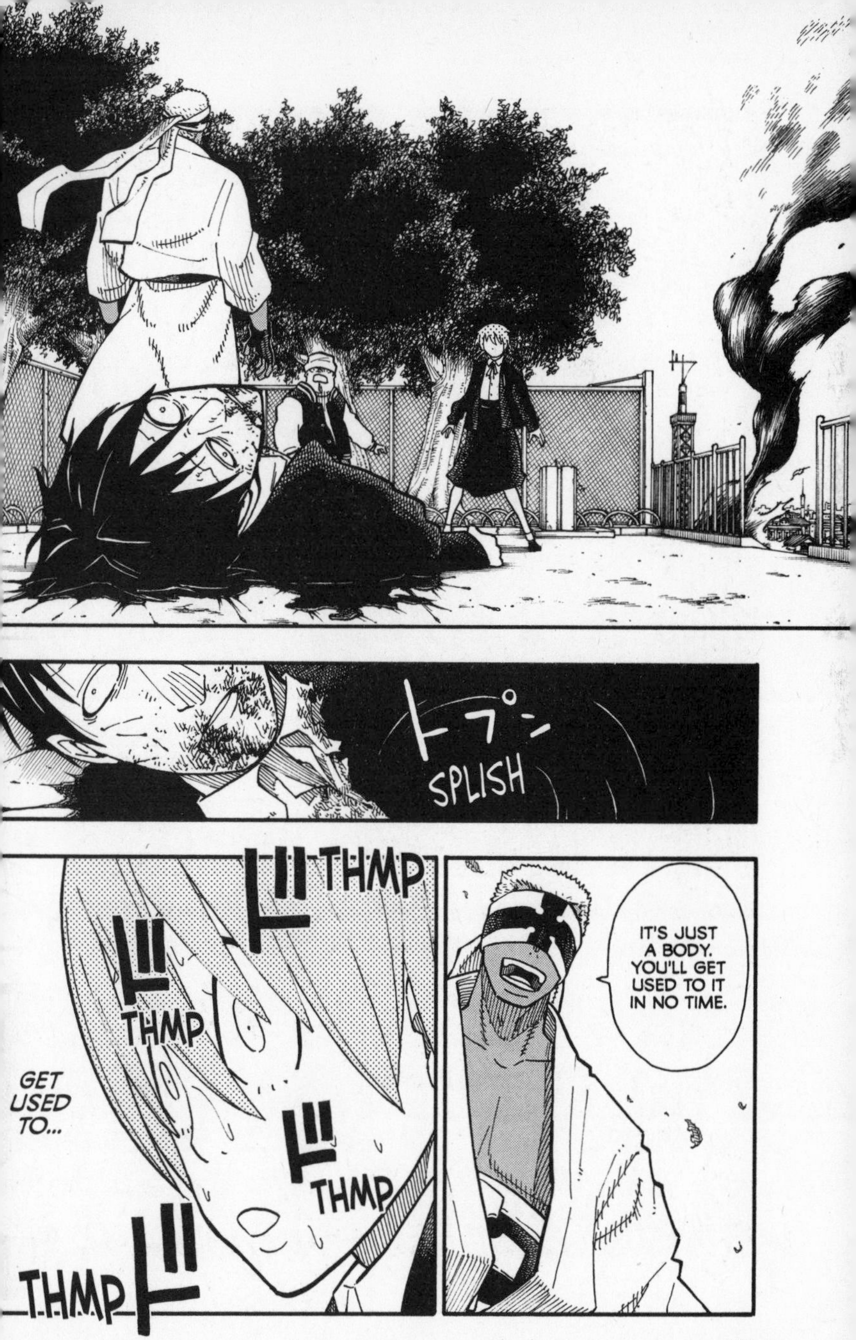
SPLISH
IT'S JUST A BODY. YOU'LL GET USED TO IT IN NO TIME.
THMP
THMP
GET USED TO...
THMP
THMP

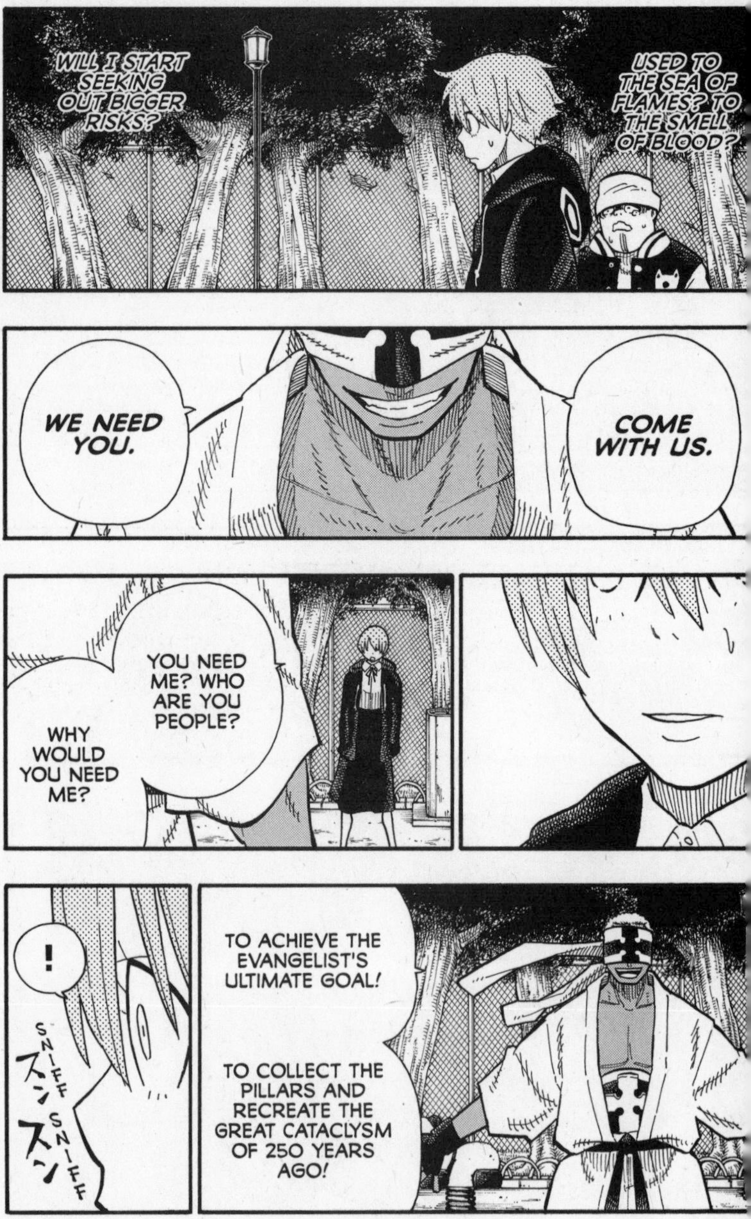
USED TO THE SEA OF FLAMES? TO THE SMELL OF BLOOD?
WILL I START SEEKING OUT BIGGER RISKS?
COME WITH US.
WE NEED YOU.
YOU NEED ME? WHO ARE YOU PEOPLE?
WHY WOULD YOU NEED ME?
TO ACHIEVE THE EVANGELIST'S ULTIMATE GOAL!
TO COLLECT THE PILLARS AND RECREATE THE GREAT CATACLYSM OF 250 YEARS AGO!
!
SNIFF スン
SNIFF スン

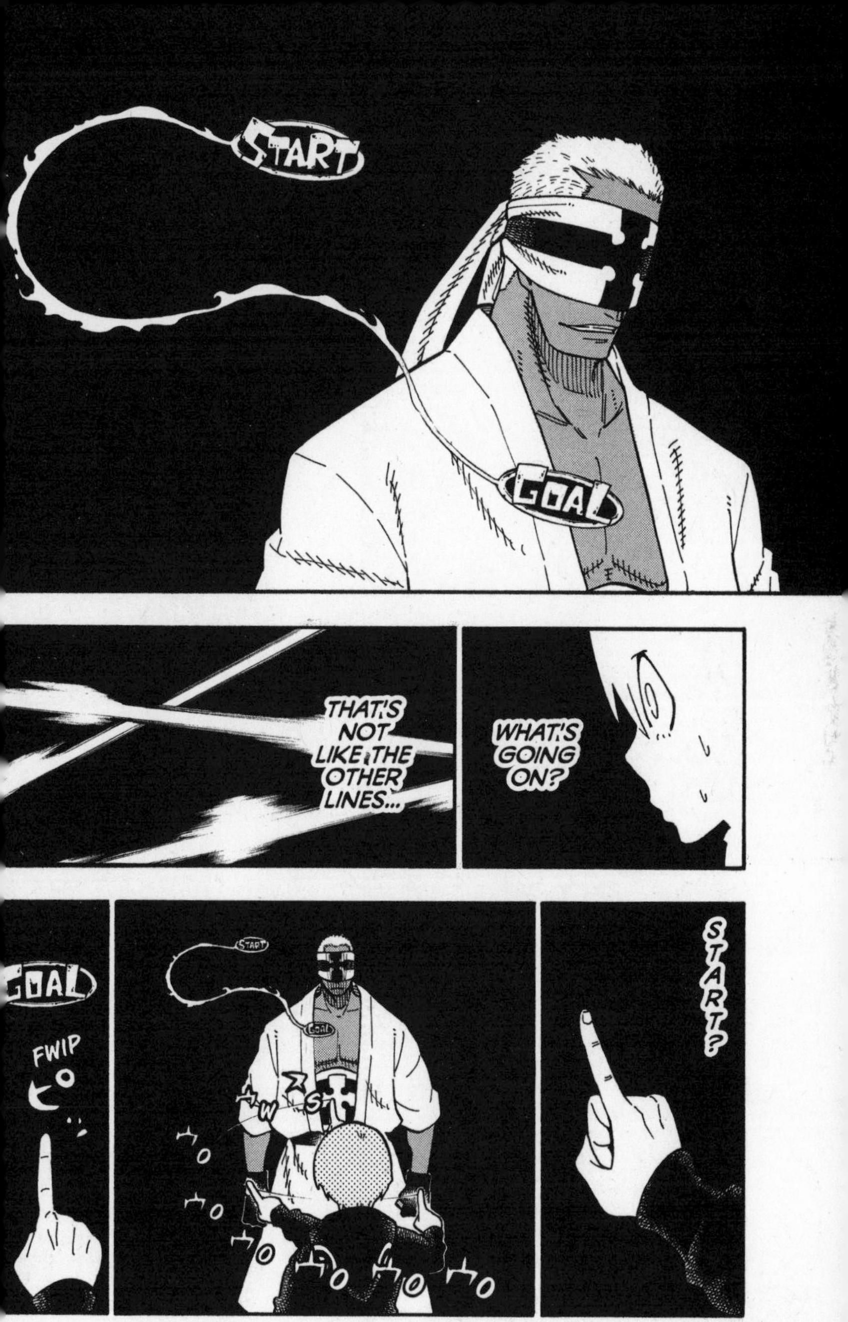
START
GOAL
WHAT'S GOING ON?
THAT'S NOT LIKE THE OTHER LINES...
START?
START
GOAL
GOAL
FWIP

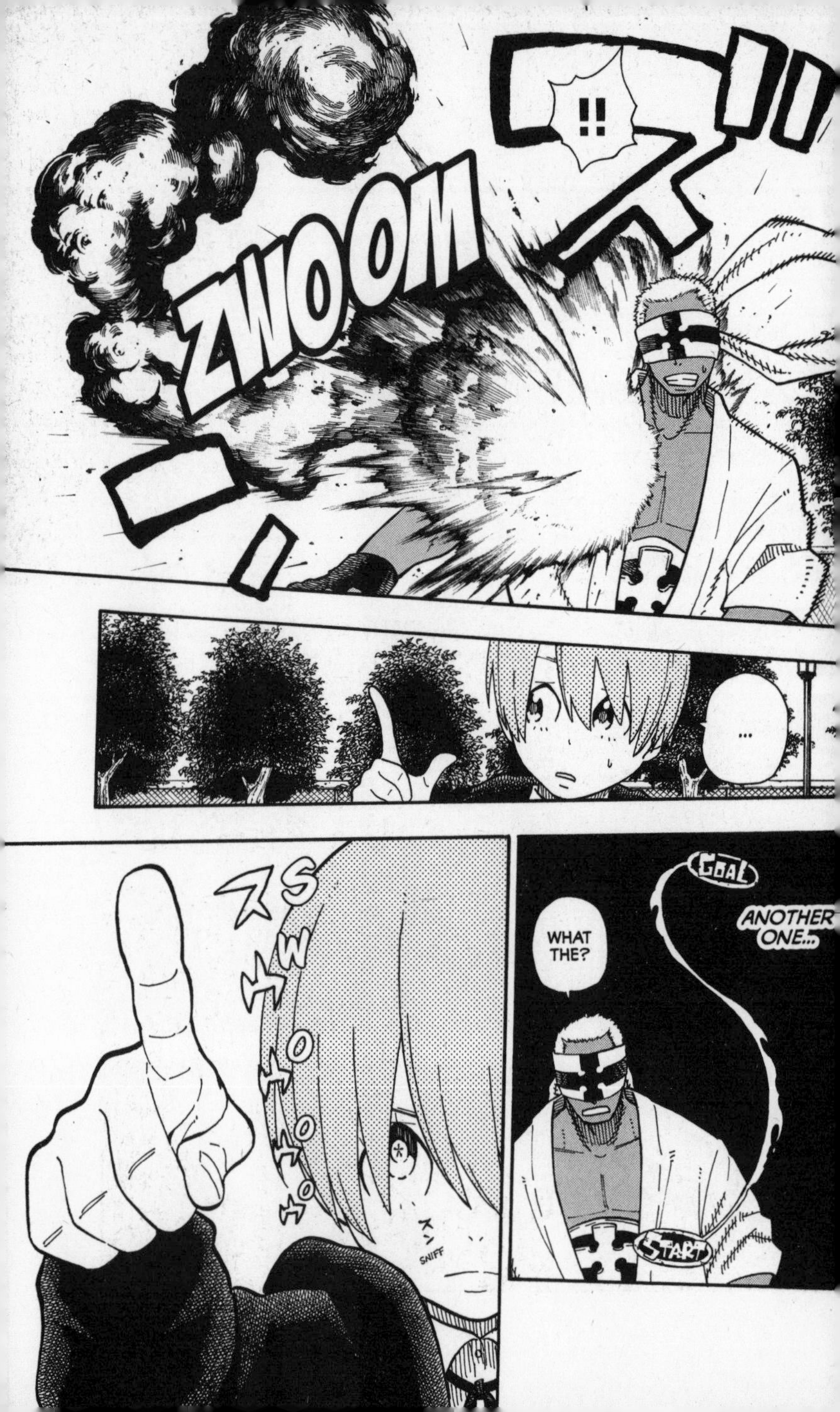
!!
ZWOOM
...
GOAL
ANOTHER ONE...
WHAT THE?
START
SWOOO
SNIFF

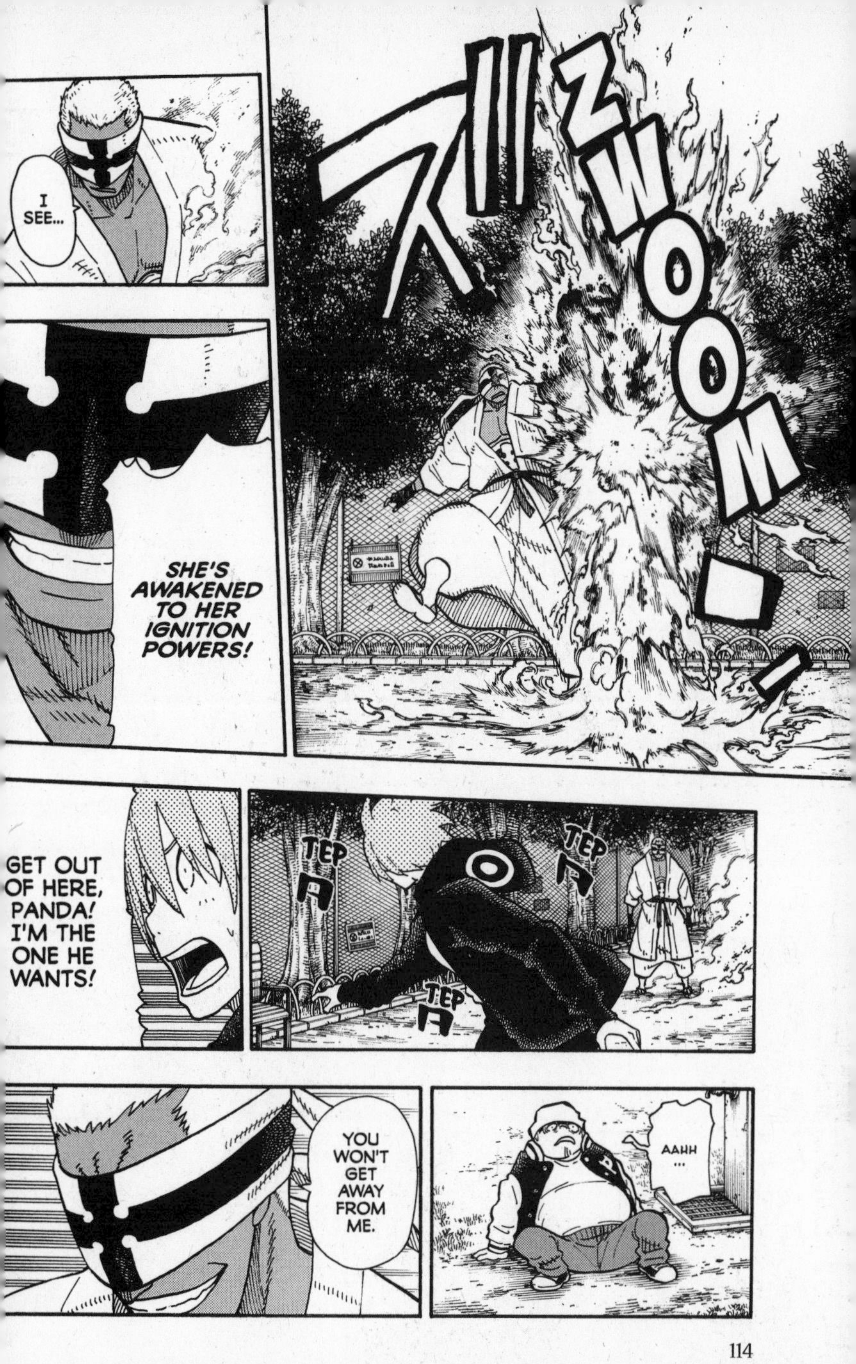
ZWOOOM!!
I SEE...
SHE'S AWAKENED TO HER IGNITION POWERS!
TEP
TEP
TEP
GET OUT OF HERE, PANDA! I'M THE ONE HE WANTS!
AAHH ...
YOU WON'T GET AWAY FROM ME.

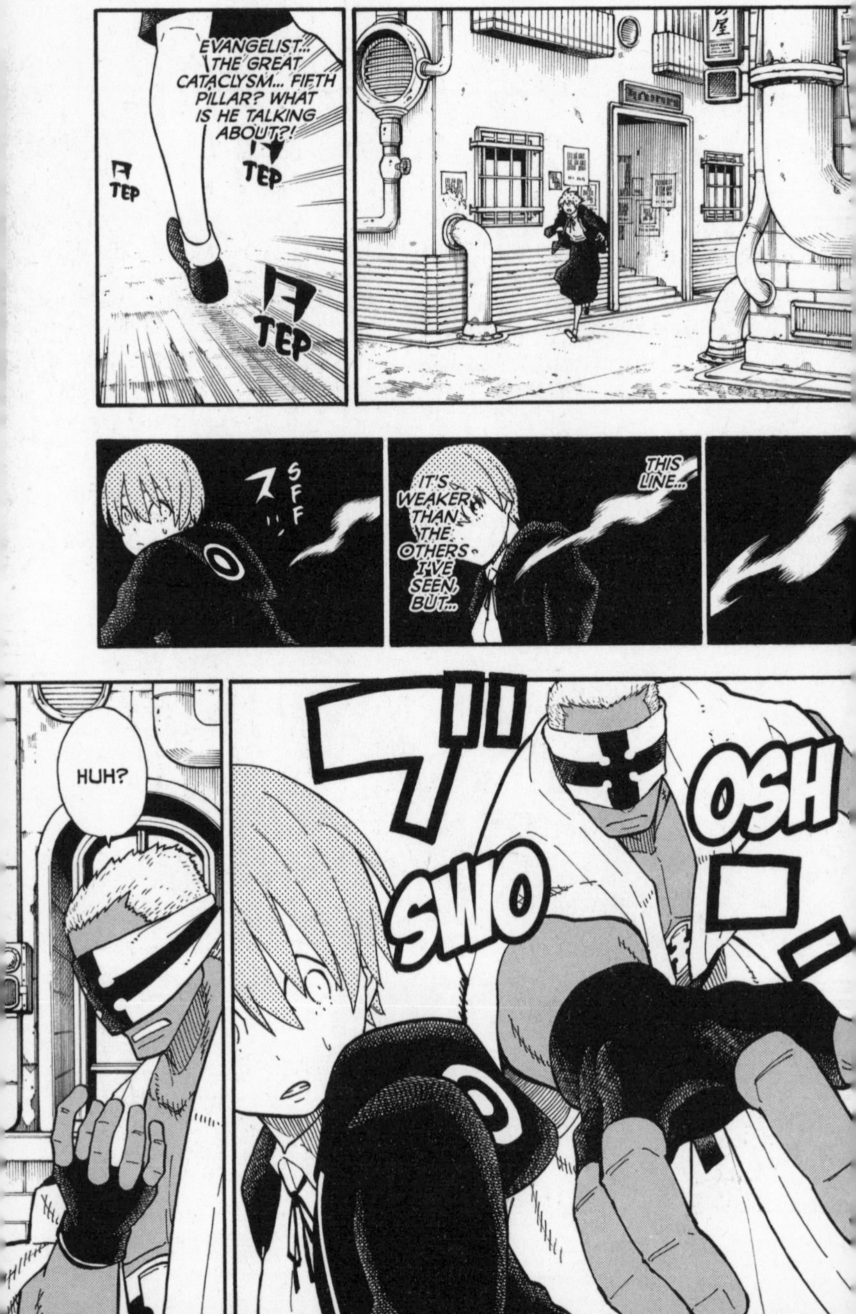
EVANGELIST... THE GREAT CATACLYSM... FIFTH PILLAR? WHAT IS HE TALKING ABOUT?!
TEP
TEP
TEP
THIS LINE...
IT'S WEAKER THAN THE OTHERS I'VE SEEN, BUT...
SFF
SWO
OSH
HUH?

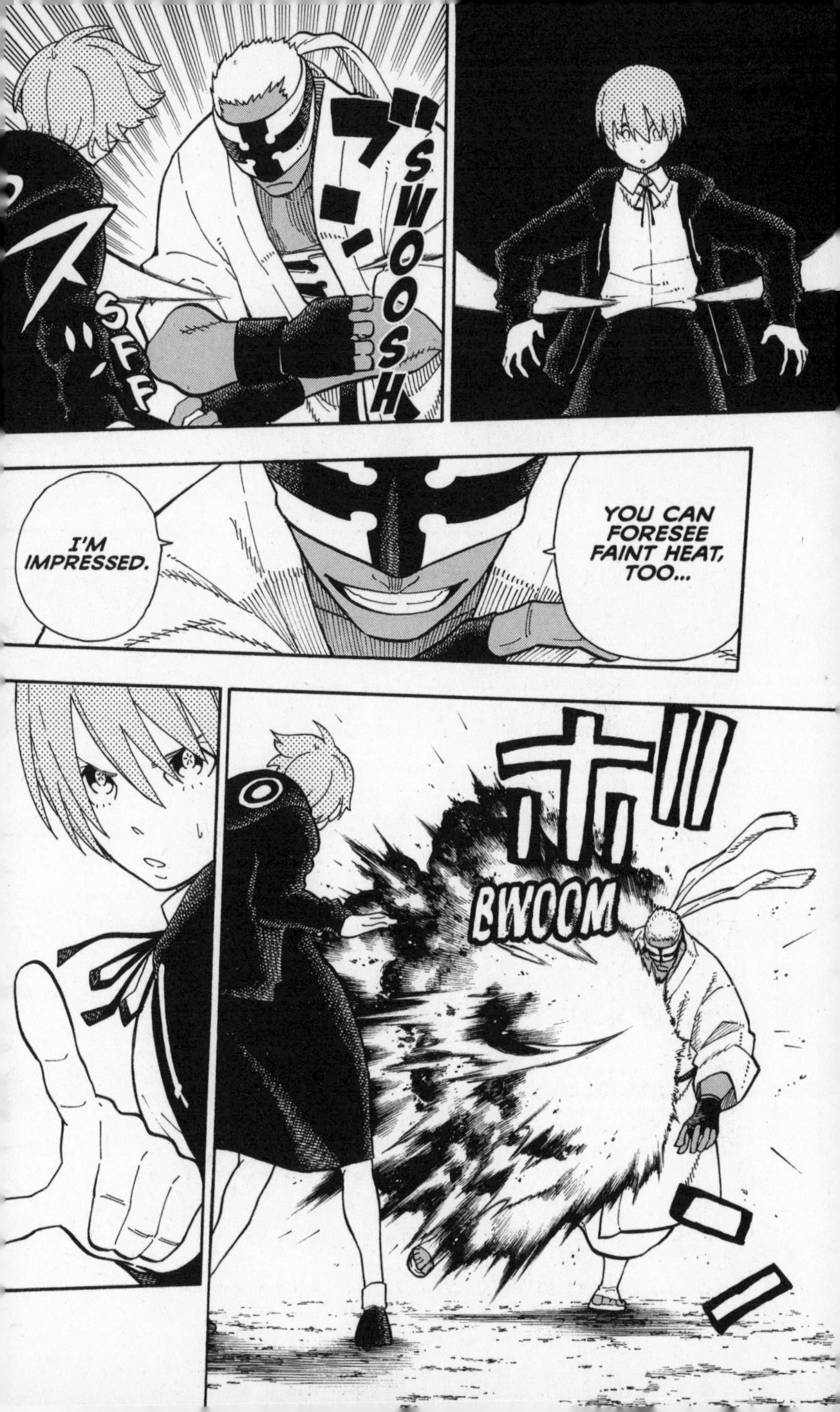
SWOOSH
SFF
YOU CAN FORESEE FAINT HEAT, TOO...
I'M IMPRESSED.
BWOOM

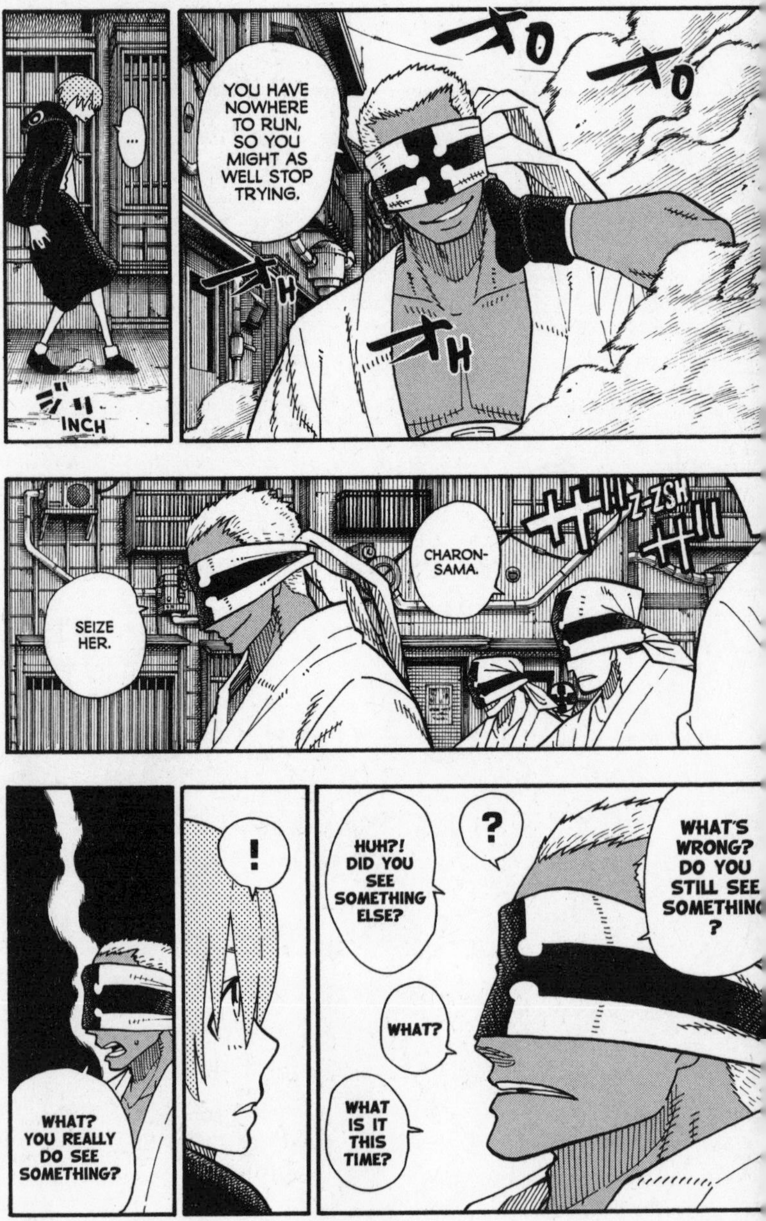
YOU HAVE NOWHERE TO RUN, SO YOU MIGHT AS WELL STOP TRYING.
...
INCH
Z-ZSH
CHARON-SAMA.
SEIZE HER.
WHAT'S WRONG? DO YOU STILL SEE SOMETHING?
?
HUH?! DID YOU SEE SOMETHING ELSE?
WHAT?
WHAT IS IT THIS TIME?
!
WHAT? YOU REALLY DO SEE SOMETHING?

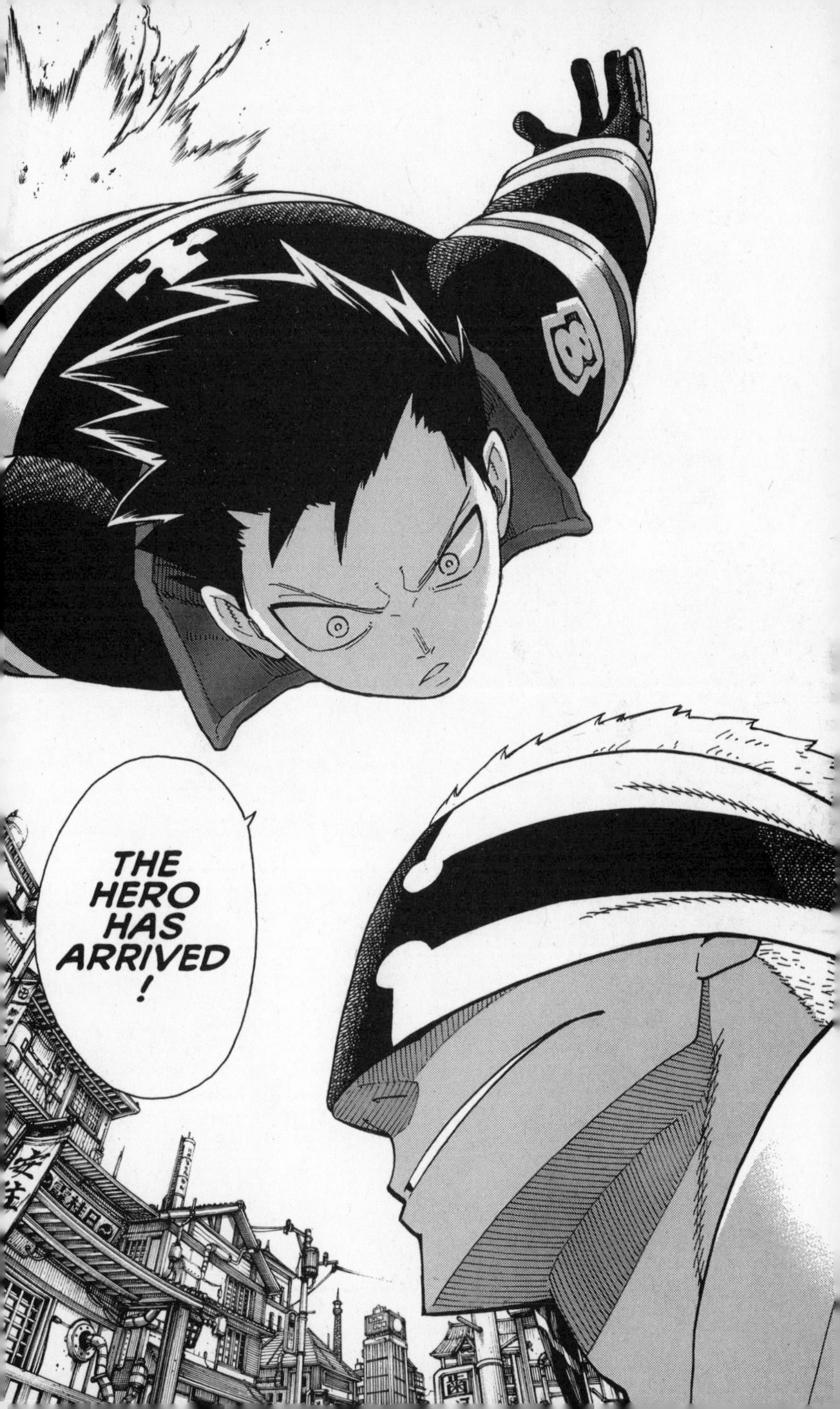
THE HERO HAS ARRIVED!

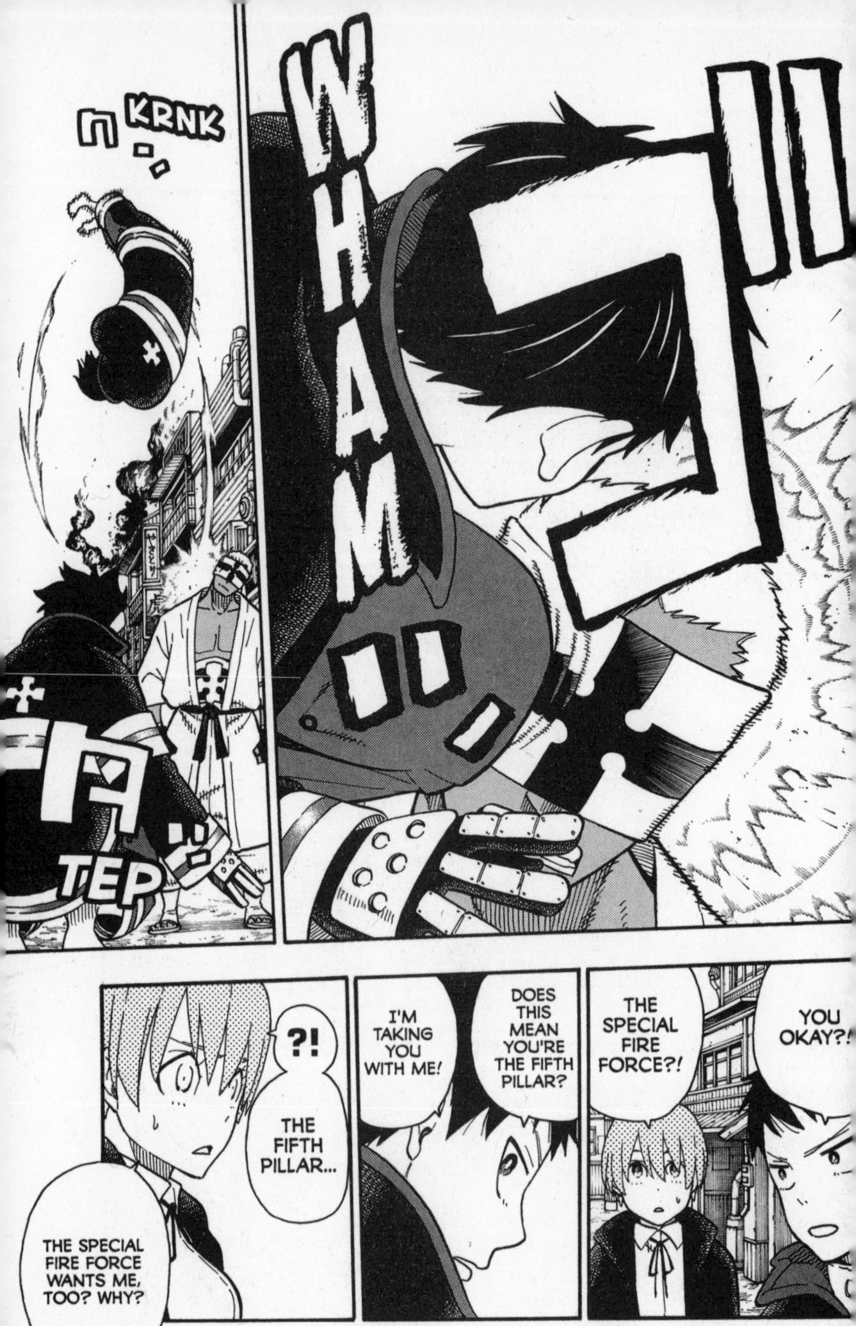
WHAM
KRNK
TEP
YOU OKAY?!
THE SPECIAL FIRE FORCE?!
DOES THIS MEAN YOU'RE THE FIFTH PILLAR?
I'M TAKING YOU WITH ME!
?!
THE FIFTH PILLAR...
THE SPECIAL FIRE FORCE WANTS ME, TOO? WHY?

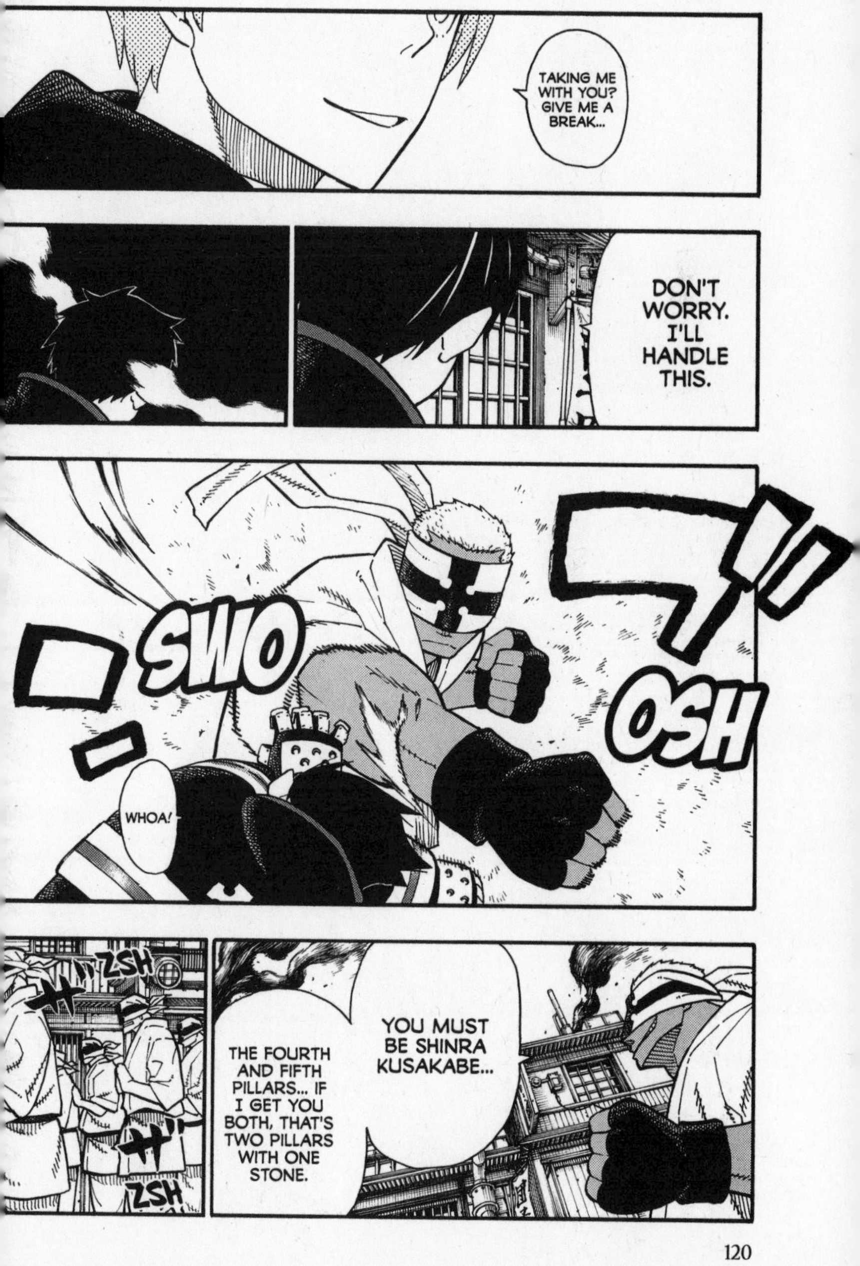
TAKING ME WITH YOU? GIVE ME A BREAK...
DON'T WORRY. I'LL HANDLE THIS.
SWO
OSH
WHOA!
YOU MUST BE SHINRA KUSAKABE...
THE FOURTH AND FIFTH PILLARS... IF I GET YOU BOTH, THAT'S TWO PILLARS WITH ONE STONE.
ZSH
ZSH

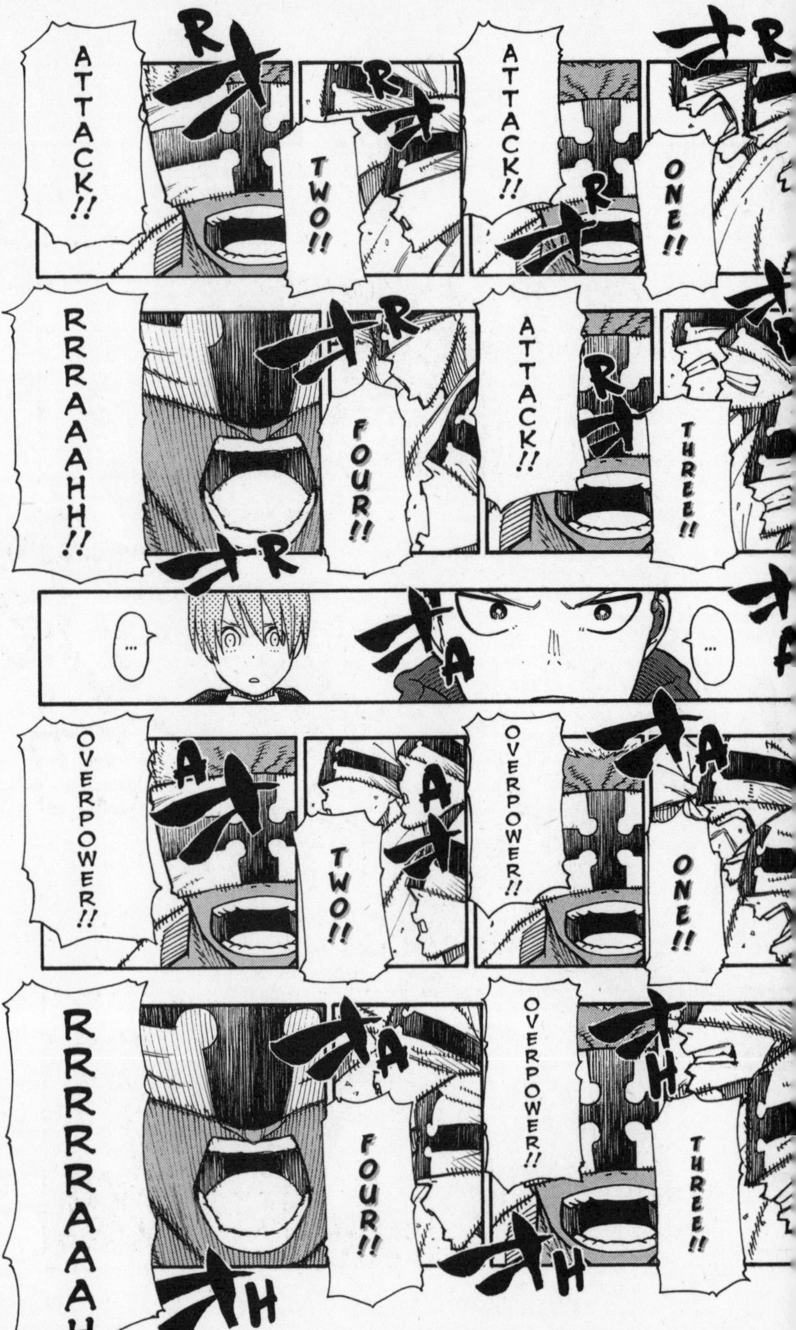
ONE!!
ATTACK!!
TWO!!
ATTACK!!
THREE!!
ATTACK!!
FOUR!!
RRRAAAHH!!
...
...
ONE!!
OVERPOWER!!
TWO!!
OVERPOWER!!
THREE!!
OVERPOWER!!
FOUR!!
RRRRRAAAH

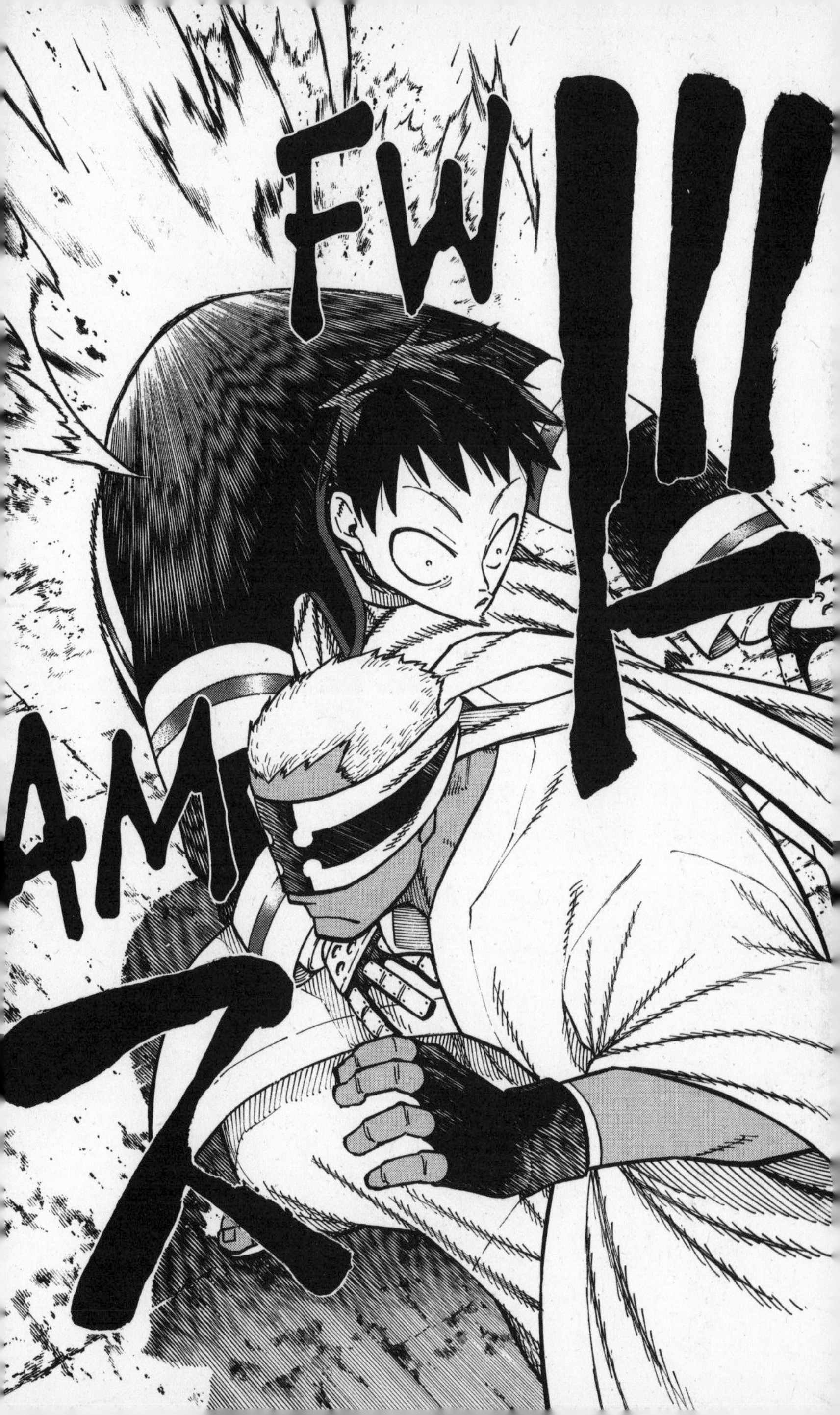
FW
AM

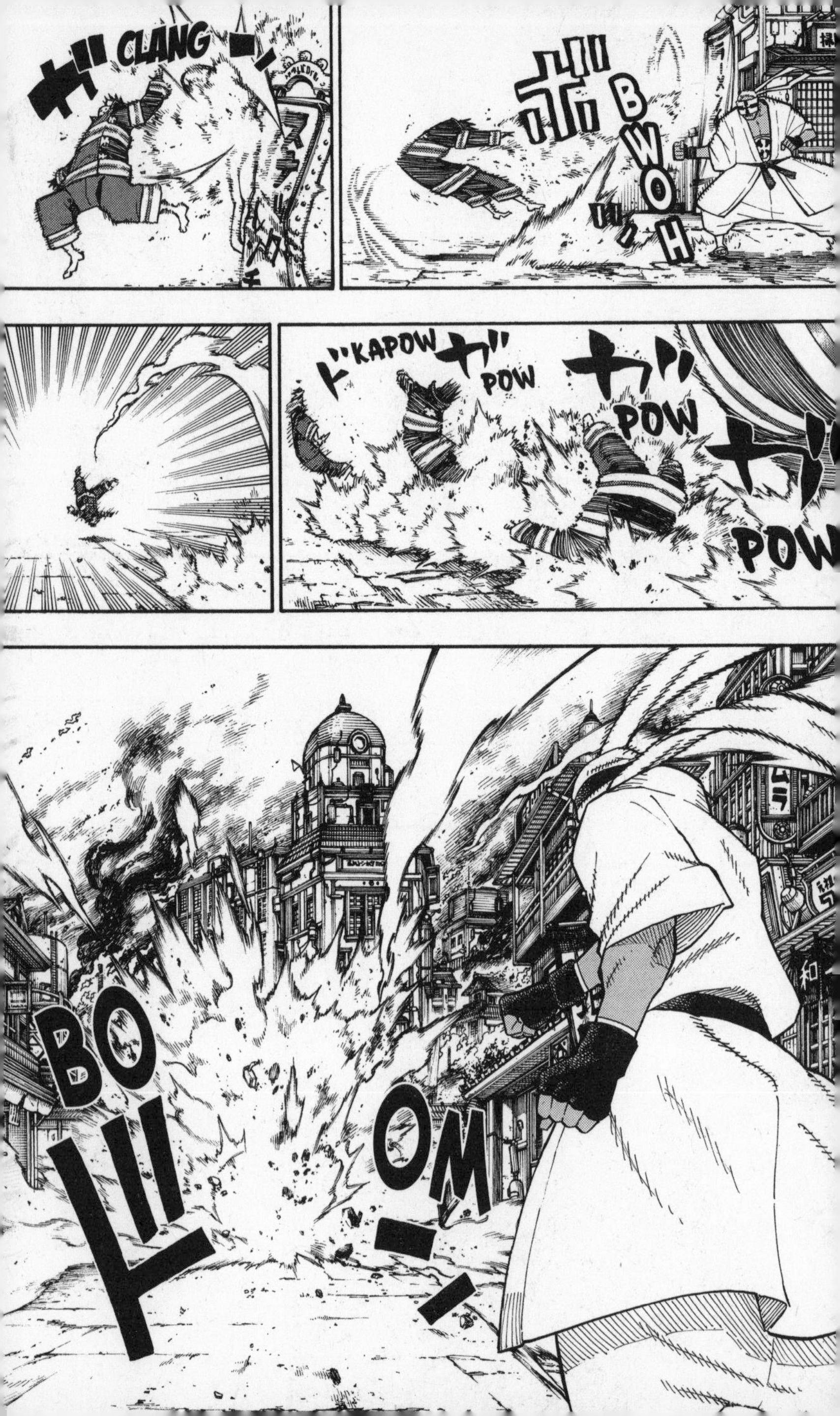
BWOH
CLANG
KAPOW
POW
POW
POW
BO
-OM

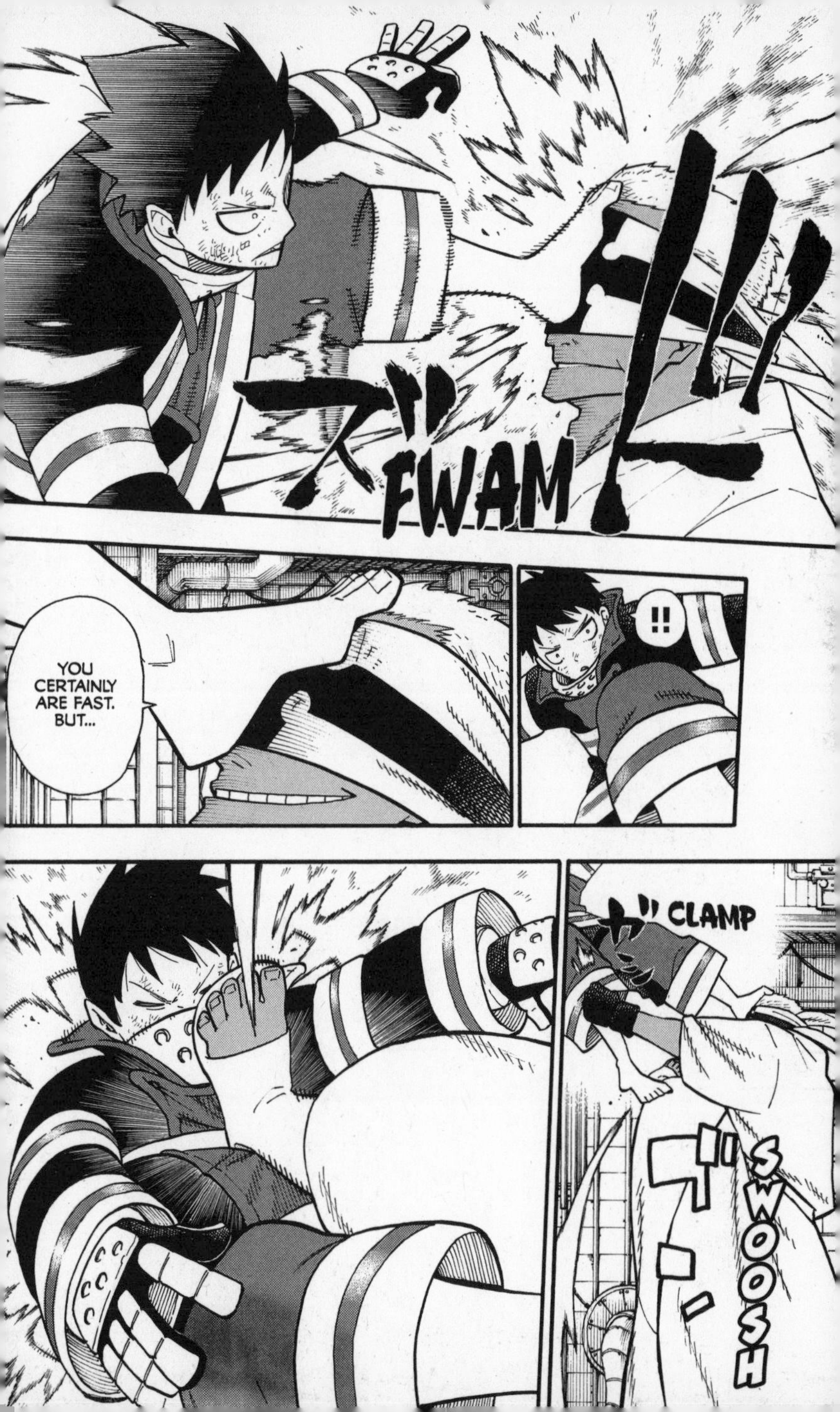
FWAM
!!
YOU CERTAINLY ARE FAST. BUT...
CLAMP
SWOOSH

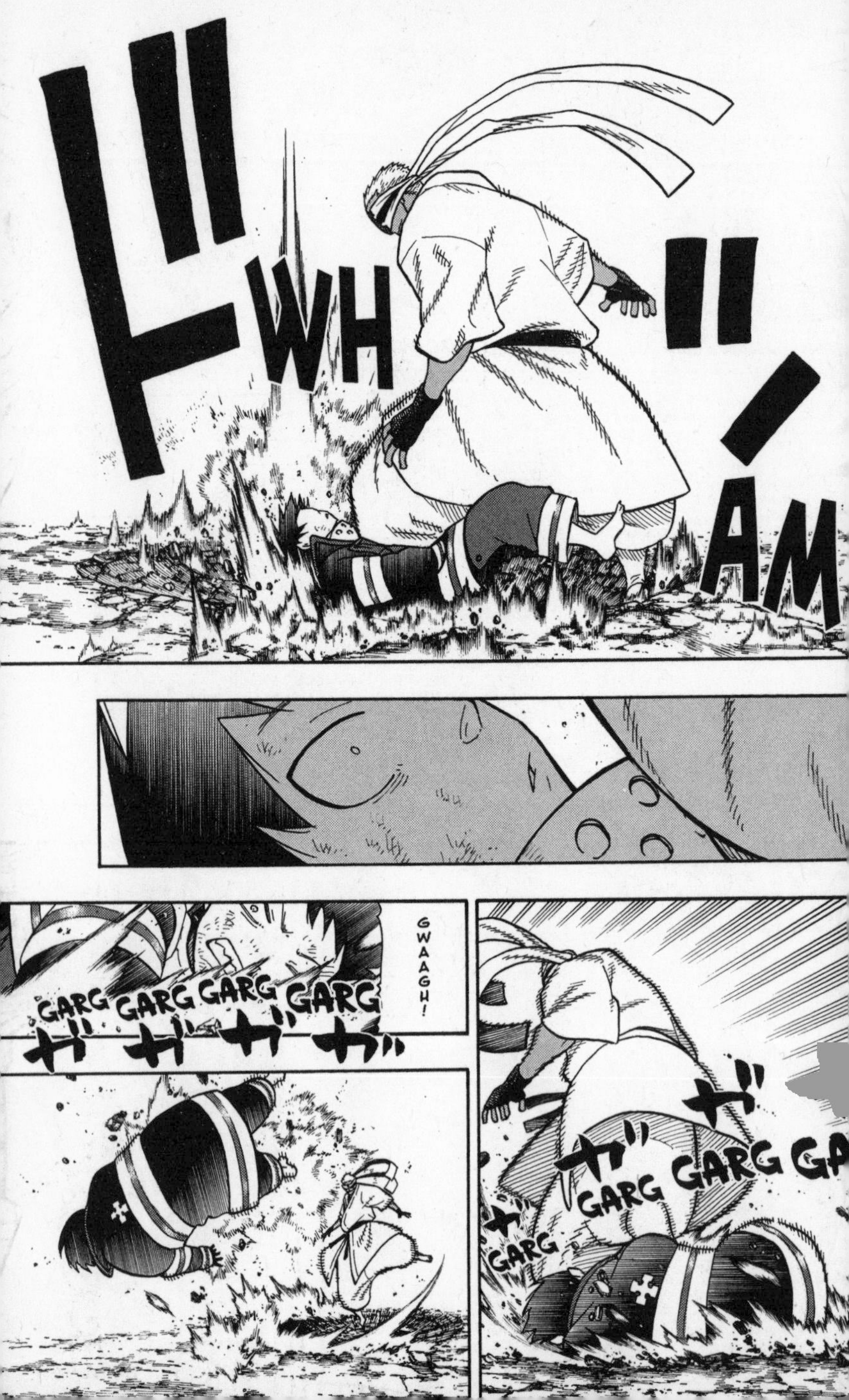
WH
AM
GARG GA
GARG
GARG
GWAAGH!
GARG GARG GARG GARG

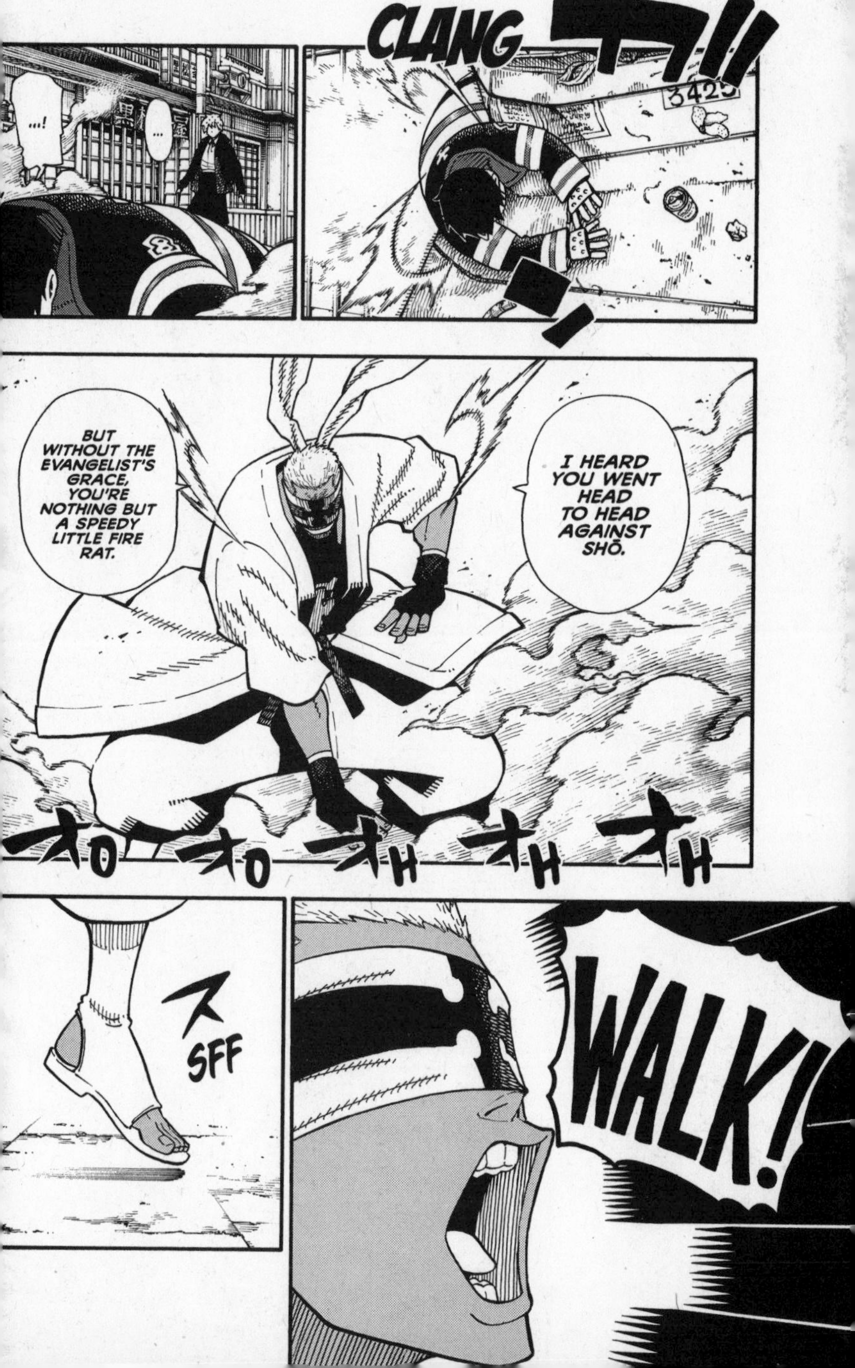
CLANG
...
...!
I HEARD YOU WENT HEAD TO HEAD AGAINST SHŌ.
BUT WITHOUT THE EVANGELIST'S GRACE, YOU'RE NOTHING BUT A SPEEDY LITTLE FIRE RAT.
OH OH OH OH OH
WALK!
SFF

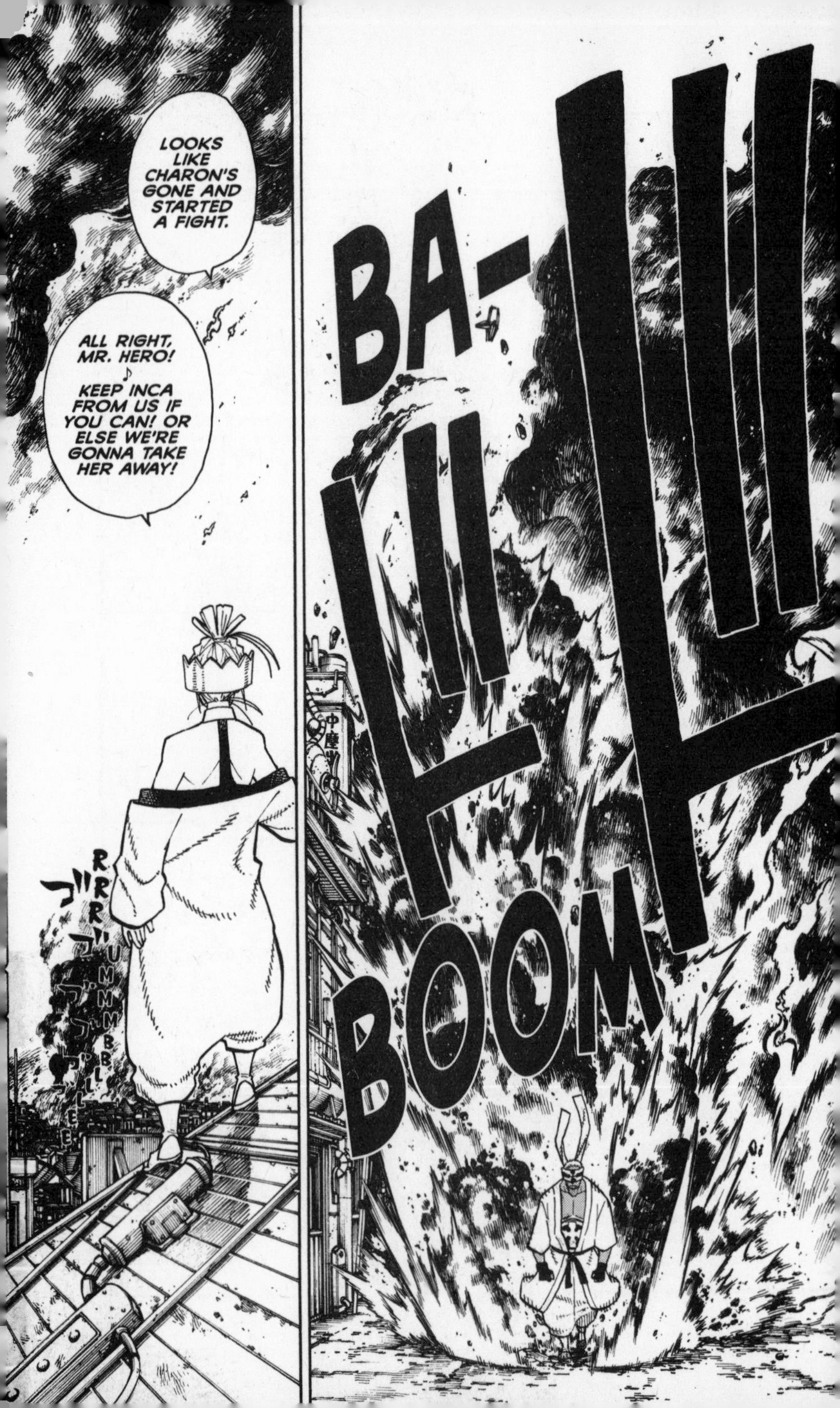
BA-
BOOM
LOOKS LIKE CHARON'S GONE AND STARTED A FIGHT.
ALL RIGHT, MR. HERO! ♪ KEEP INCA FROM US IF YOU CAN! OR ELSE WE'RE GONNA TAKE HER AWAY!
RRRRUMMMBBLLEE

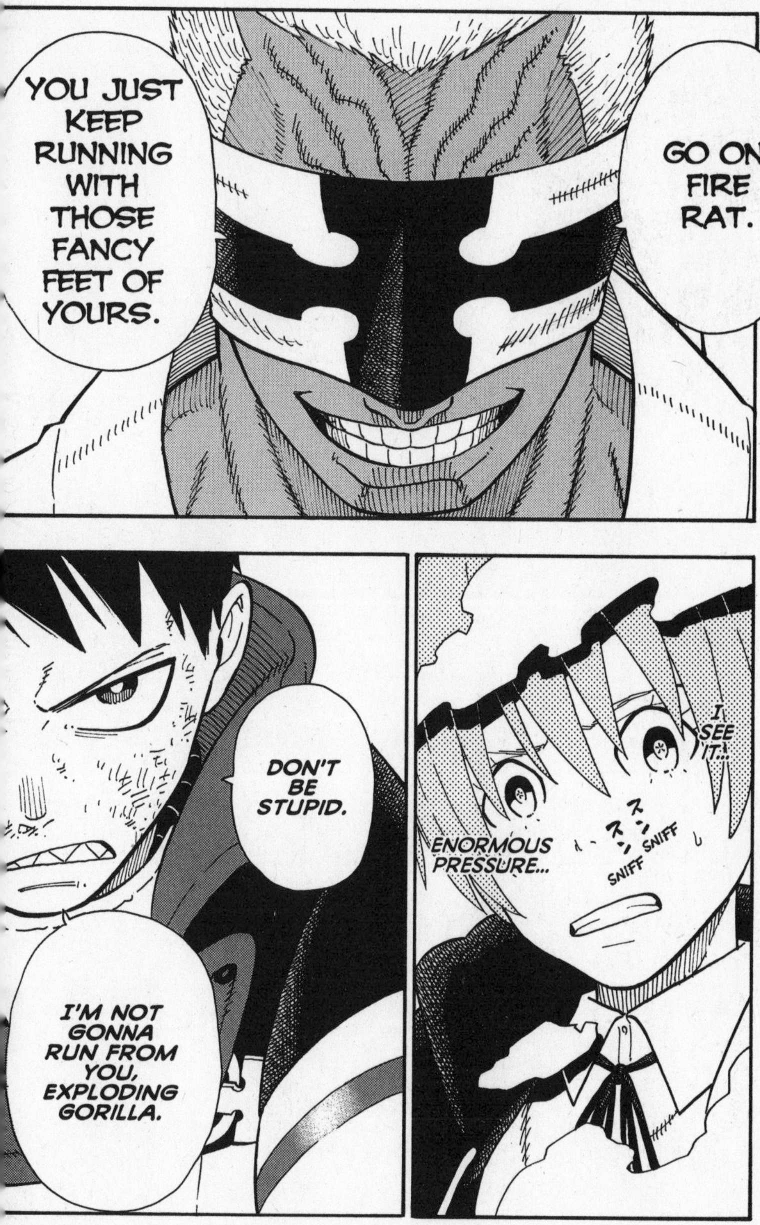
GO ON, FIRE RAT.
YOU JUST KEEP RUNNING WITH THOSE FANCY FEET OF YOURS.
I SEE IT...
ENORMOUS PRESSURE...
スン スン
SNIFF SNIFF
DON'T BE STUPID.
I'M NOT GONNA RUN FROM YOU, EXPLODING GORILLA.

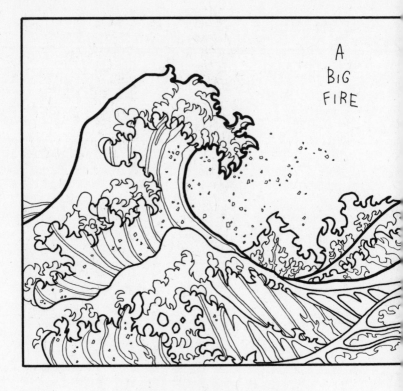

A
BIG
FIRE

CHAPTER CIII: GROPING THROUGH THE FLAMES

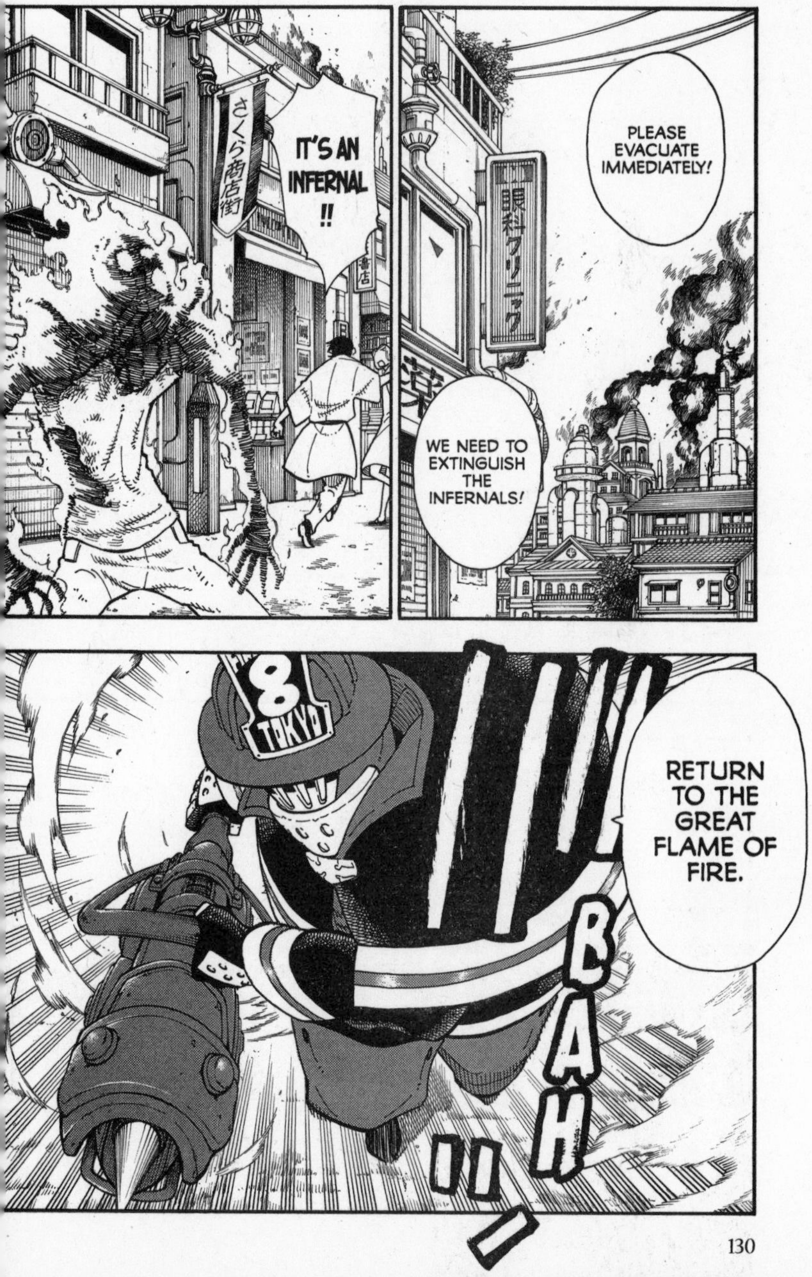
PLEASE EVACUATE IMMEDIATELY!
眼科クリニック
WE NEED TO EXTINGUISH THE INFERNALS!
IT'S AN INFERNAL!!
さくら商店街
書店
RETURN TO THE GREAT FLAME OF FIRE.
8
TOKYO
BAH!!

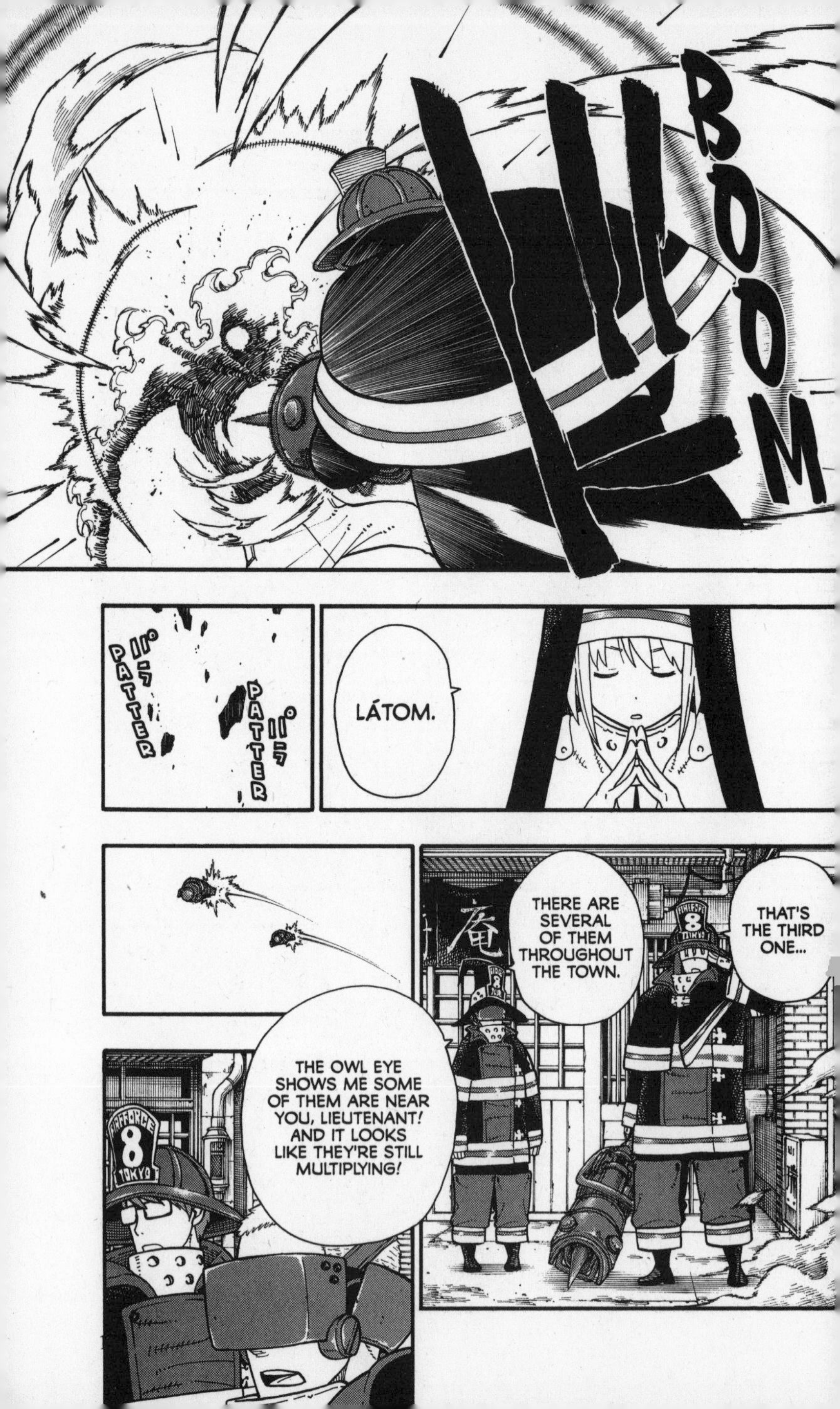
BOOM
LÁTOM.
パラ PATTER
パラ PATTER
THAT'S THE THIRD ONE...
THERE ARE SEVERAL OF THEM THROUGHOUT THE TOWN.
庵
THE OWL EYE SHOWS ME SOME OF THEM ARE NEAR YOU, LIEUTENANT! AND IT LOOKS LIKE THEY'RE STILL MULTIPLYING!

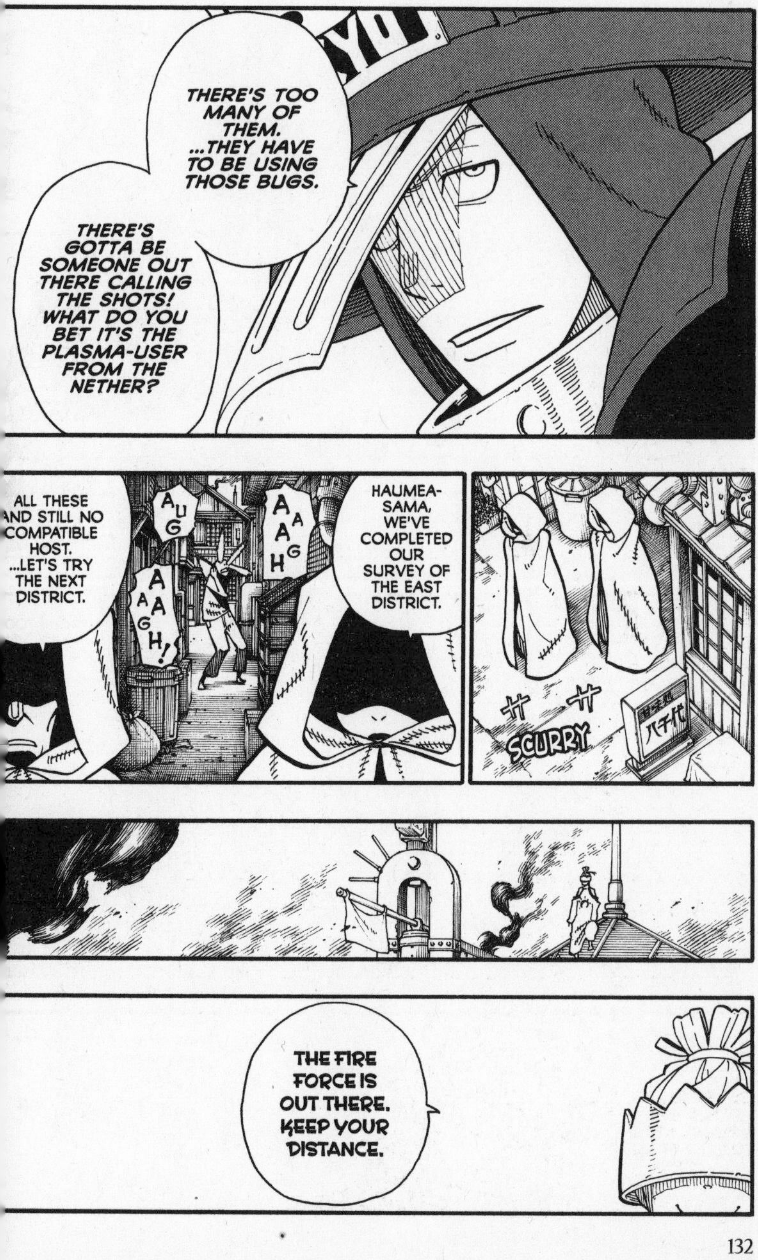
THERE'S TOO MANY OF THEM. ...THEY HAVE TO BE USING THOSE BUGS.
THERE'S GOTTA BE SOMEONE OUT THERE CALLING THE SHOTS! WHAT DO YOU BET IT'S THE PLASMA-USER FROM THE NETHER?
SCURRY
HAUMEA-SAMA, WE'VE COMPLETED OUR SURVEY OF THE EAST DISTRICT.
AAAGH
AUG
AAAGH!
ALL THESE AND STILL NO COMPATIBLE HOST. ...LET'S TRY THE NEXT DISTRICT.
THE FIRE FORCE IS OUT THERE. KEEP YOUR DISTANCE.

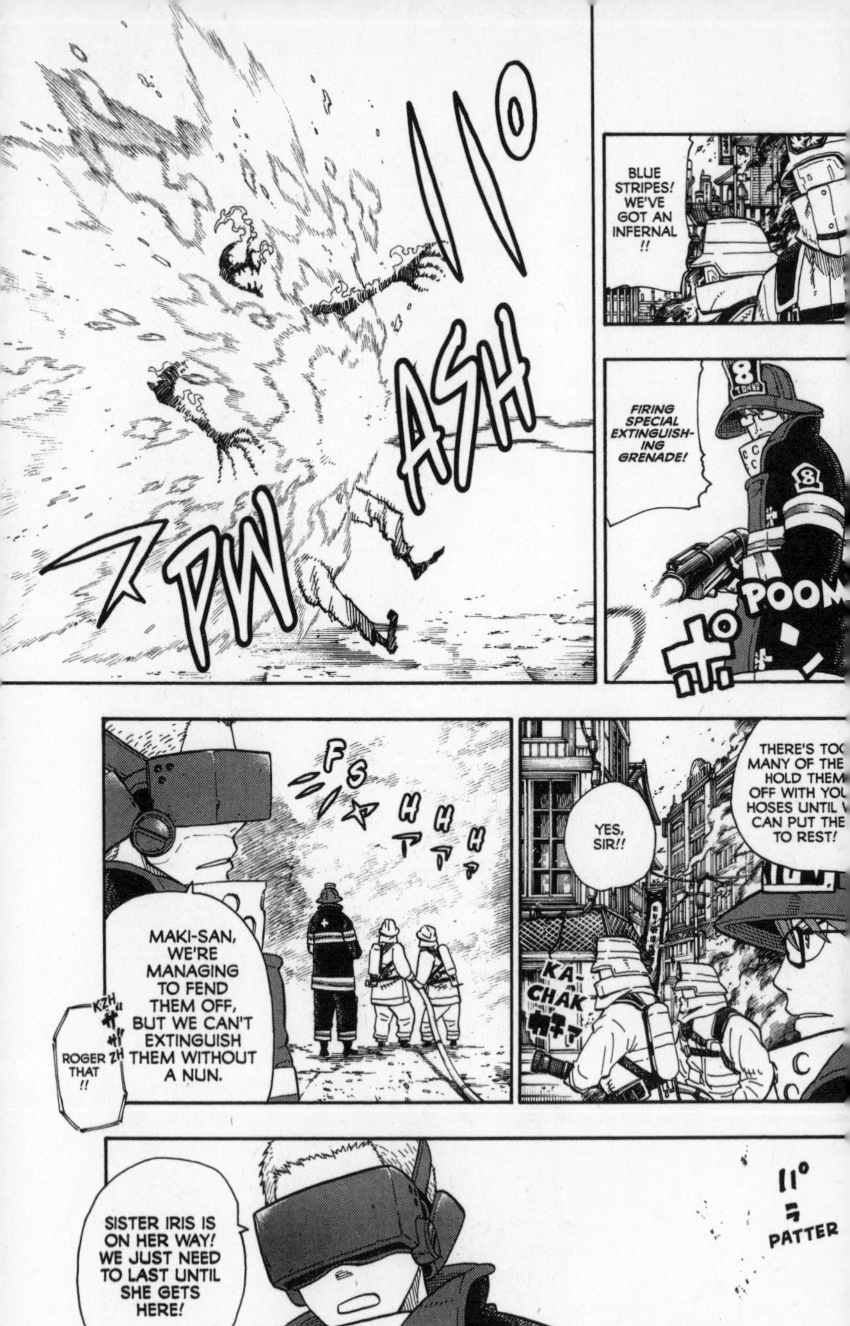
BLUE STRIPES! WE'VE GOT AN INFERNAL !!
FIRING SPECIAL EXTINGUISH-ING GRENADE!
POOM
PWASH
THERE'S TOO MANY OF THE HOLD THEM OFF WITH YOU HOSES UNTIL W CAN PUT THE TO REST!
YES, SIR!!
KA-CHAK
FSHHH
MAKI-SAN, WE'RE MANAGING TO FEND THEM OFF, BUT WE CAN'T EXTINGUISH THEM WITHOUT A NUN.
KZH ZH
ROGER THAT !!
SISTER IRIS IS ON HER WAY! WE JUST NEED TO LAST UNTIL SHE GETS HERE!
PATTER

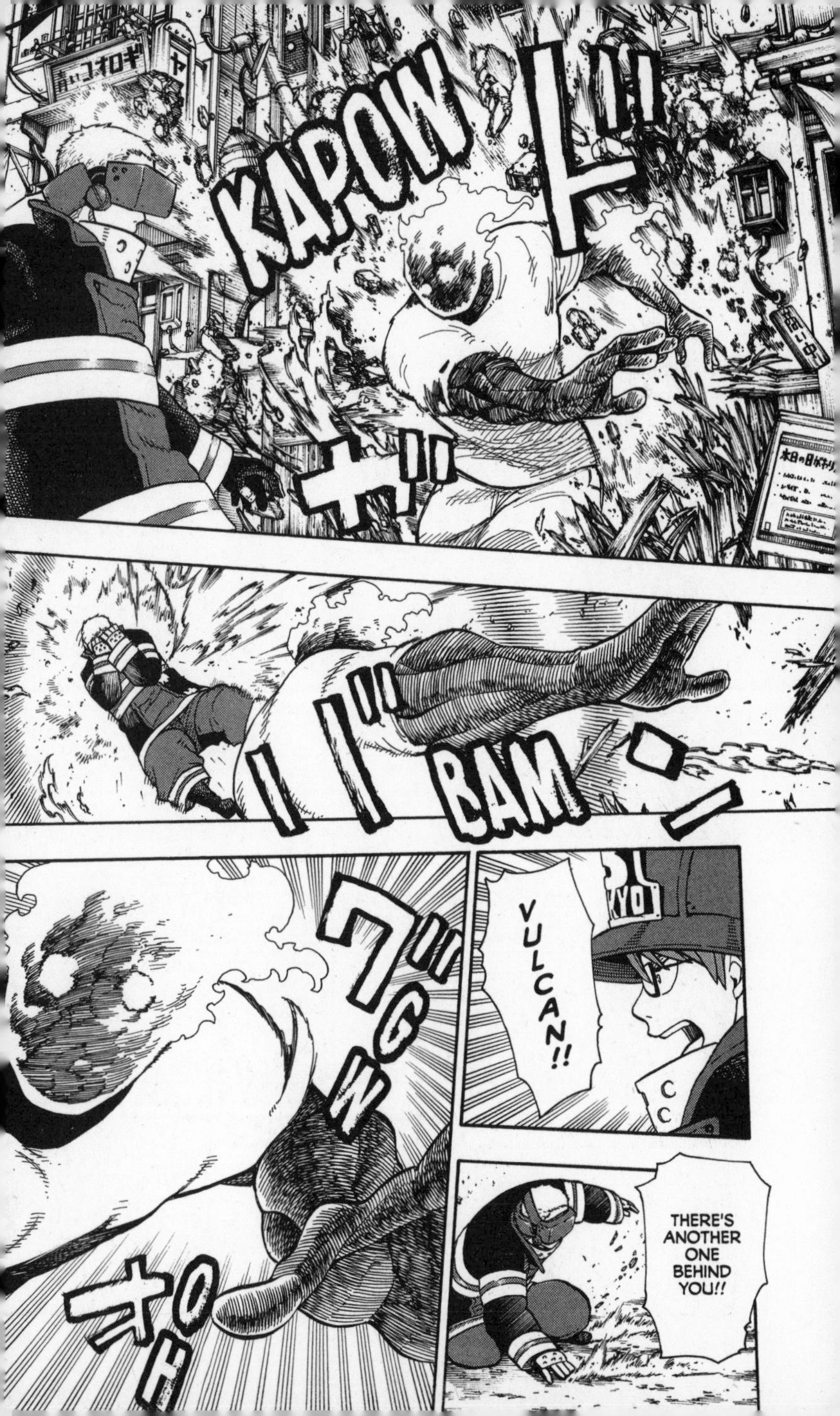

KAPOW
BAM
VULCAN!!
THERE'S ANOTHER ONE BEHIND YOU!!

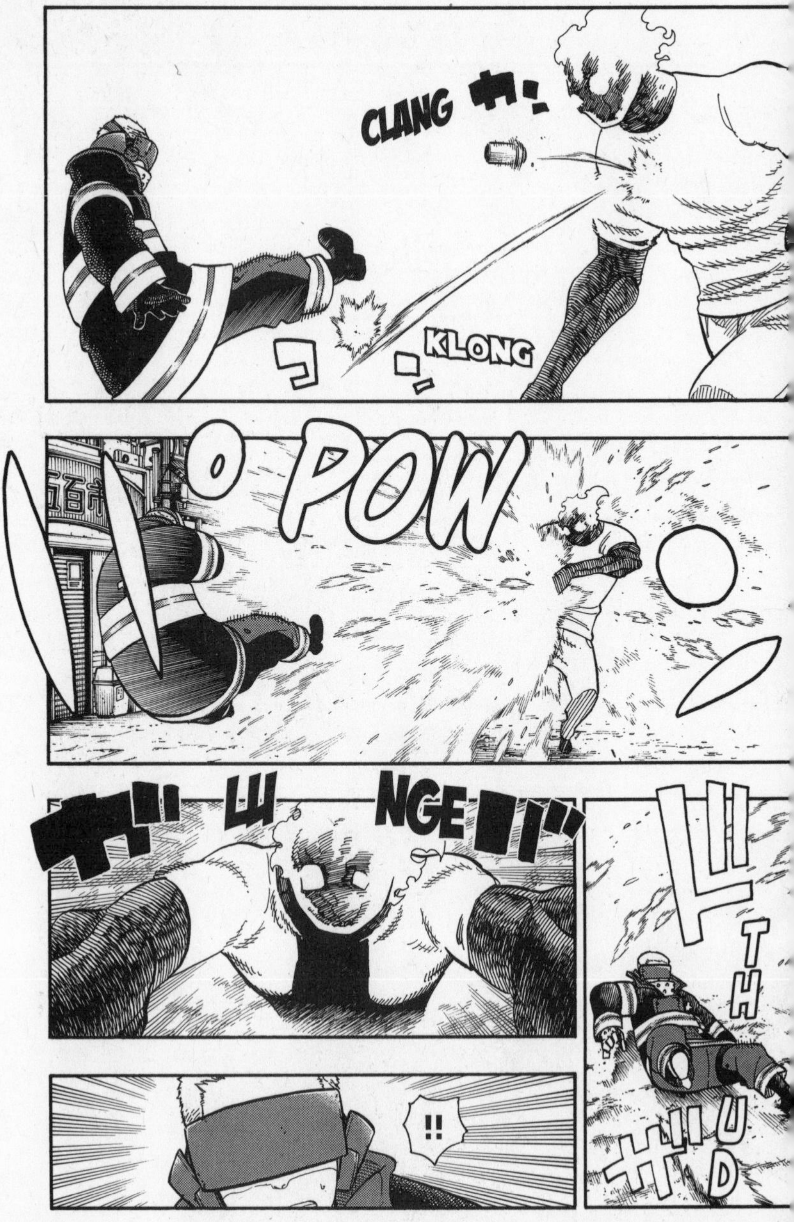
CLANG
KLONG
POW
THUD
LUNGE
!!

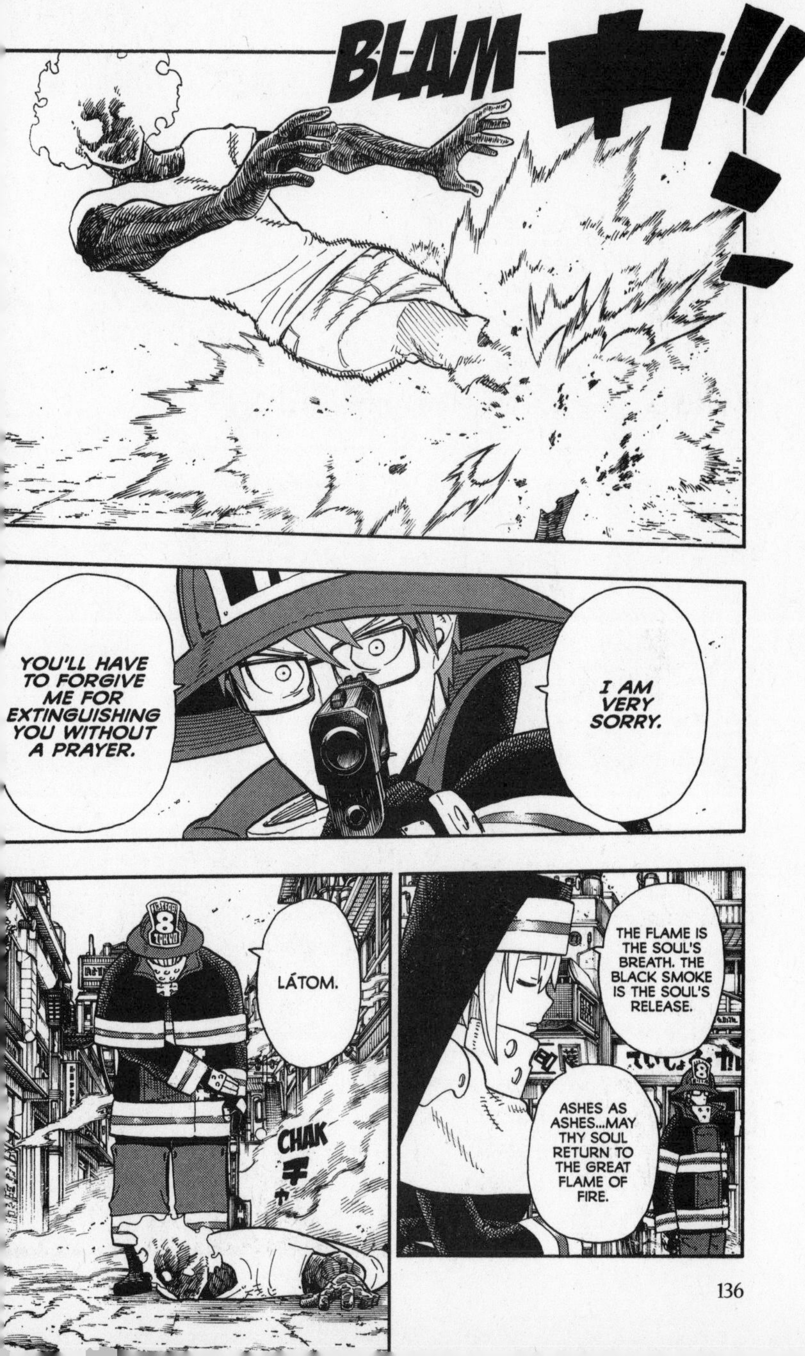
BLAM
I AM VERY SORRY.
YOU'LL HAVE TO FORGIVE ME FOR EXTINGUISHING YOU WITHOUT A PRAYER.
THE FLAME IS THE SOUL'S BREATH. THE BLACK SMOKE IS THE SOUL'S RELEASE.
ASHES AS ASHES...MAY THY SOUL RETURN TO THE GREAT FLAME OF FIRE.
LÁTOM.
CHAK

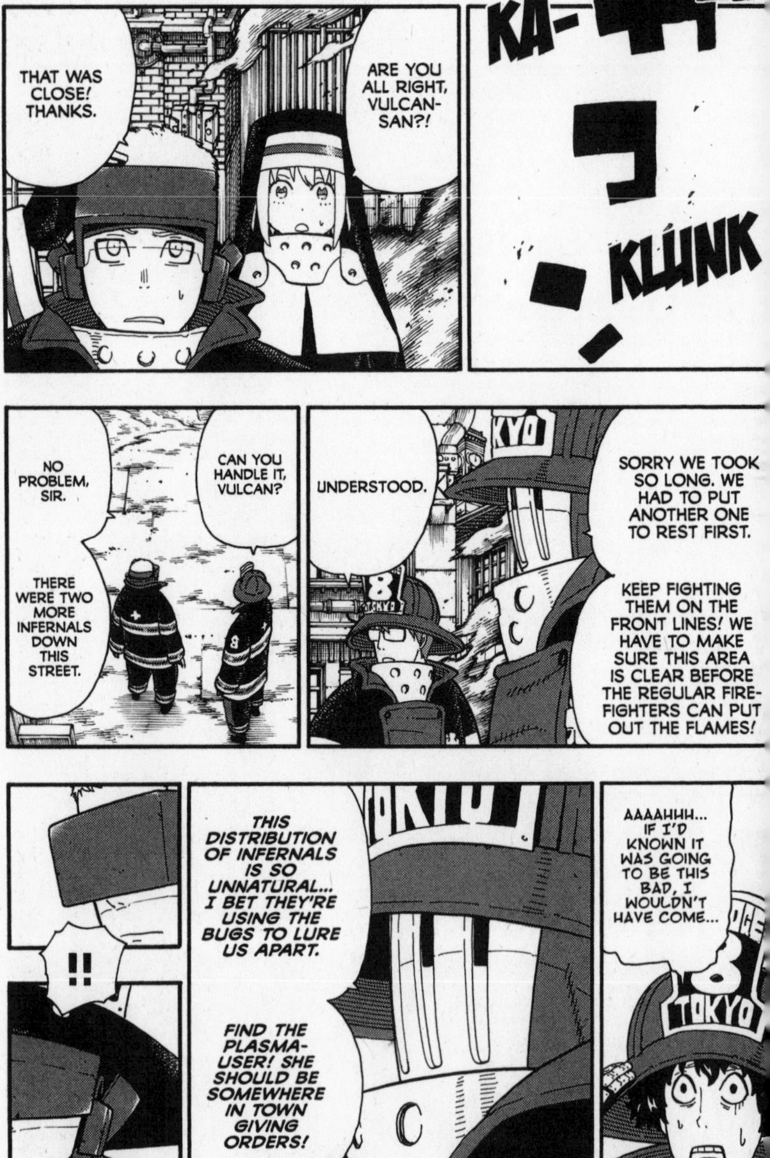
KA-KLUNK
ARE YOU ALL RIGHT, VULCAN-SAN?!
THAT WAS CLOSE! THANKS.
SORRY WE TOOK SO LONG. WE HAD TO PUT ANOTHER ONE TO REST FIRST.
KEEP FIGHTING THEM ON THE FRONT LINES! WE HAVE TO MAKE SURE THIS AREA IS CLEAR BEFORE THE REGULAR FIRE-FIGHTERS CAN PUT OUT THE FLAMES!
UNDERSTOOD.
CAN YOU HANDLE IT, VULCAN?
NO PROBLEM, SIR.
THERE WERE TWO MORE INFERNALS DOWN THIS STREET.
AAAAHHH... IF I'D KNOWN IT WAS GOING TO BE THIS BAD, I WOULDN'T HAVE COME...
THIS DISTRIBUTION OF INFERNALS IS SO UNNATURAL... I BET THEY'RE USING THE BUGS TO LURE US APART.
FIND THE PLASMA-USER! SHE SHOULD BE SOMEWHERE IN TOWN GIVING ORDERS!
!!

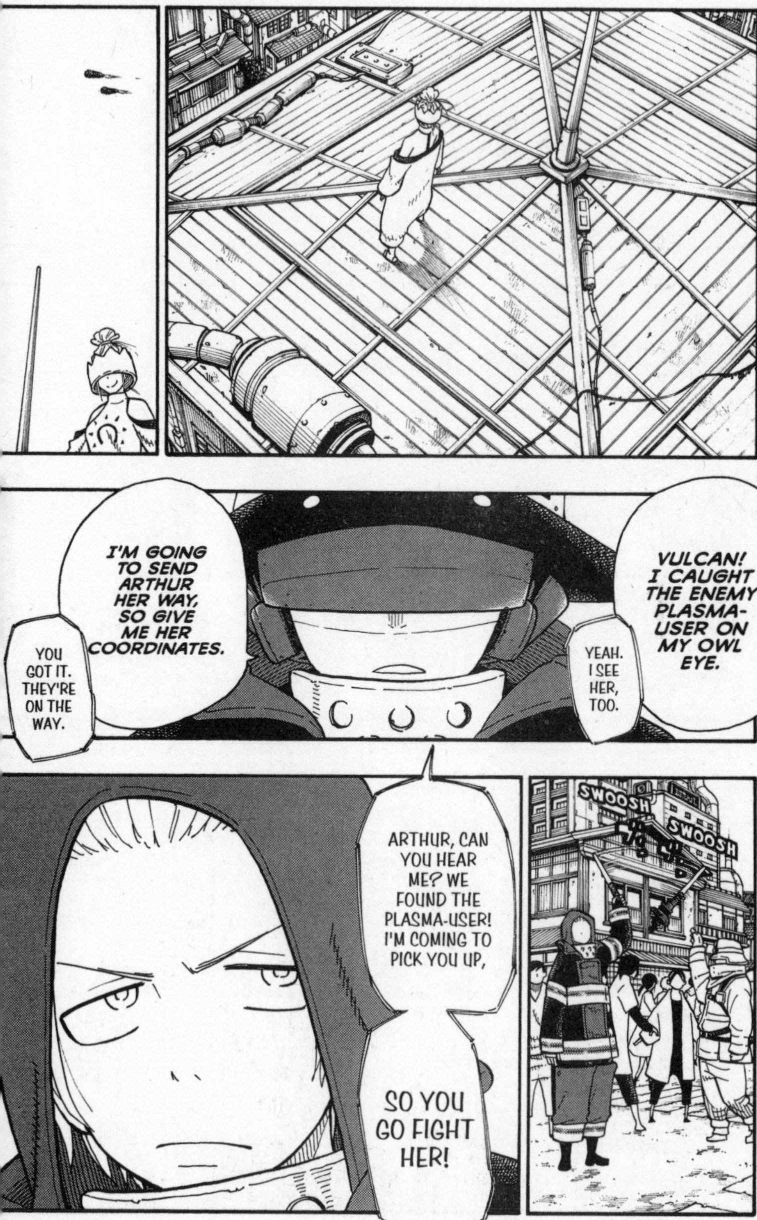
VULCAN! I CAUGHT THE ENEMY PLASMA-USER ON MY OWL EYE.
YEAH. I SEE HER, TOO.
I'M GOING TO SEND ARTHUR HER WAY, SO GIVE ME HER COORDINATES.
YOU GOT IT. THEY'RE ON THE WAY.
SWOOSH
SWOOSH
ARTHUR, CAN YOU HEAR ME? WE FOUND THE PLASMA-USER! I'M COMING TO PICK YOU UP,
SO YOU GO FIGHT HER!

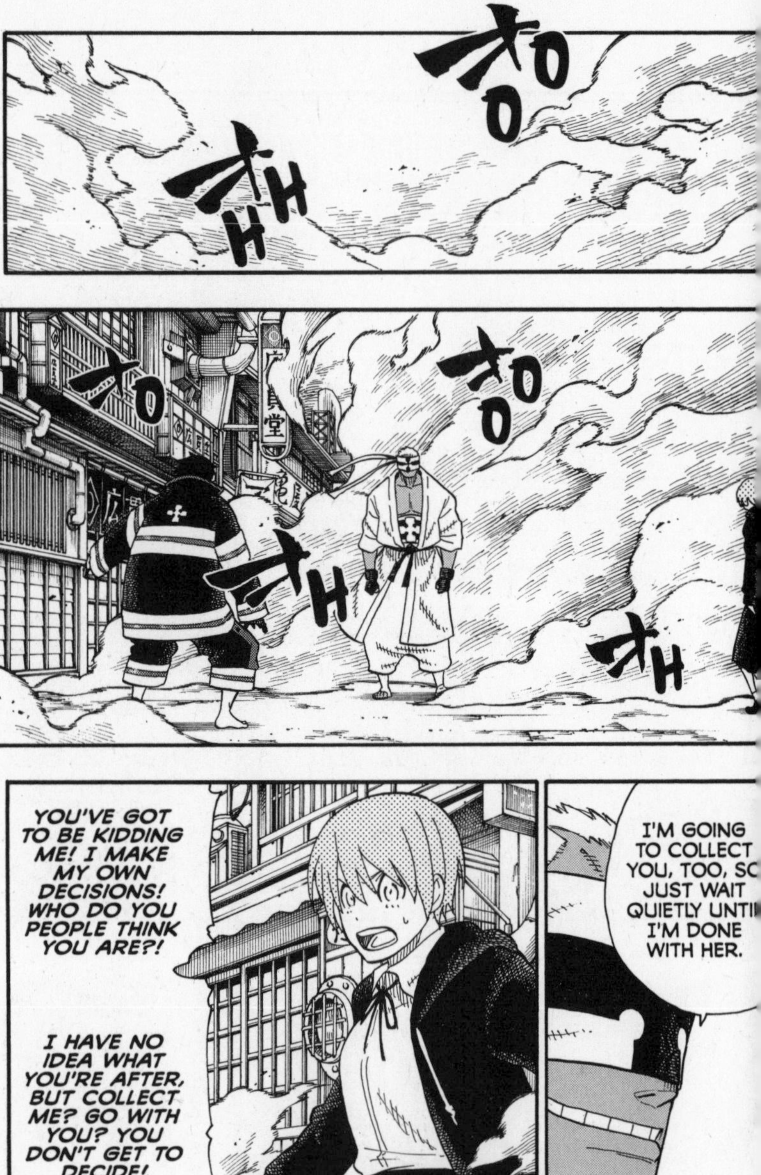

焼鳥
I'M GOING TO COLLECT YOU, TOO, SO JUST WAIT QUIETLY UNTI I'M DONE WITH HER.
YOU'VE GOT TO BE KIDDING ME! I MAKE MY OWN DECISIONS! WHO DO YOU PEOPLE THINK YOU ARE?!
I HAVE NO IDEA WHAT YOU'RE AFTER, BUT COLLECT ME? GO WITH YOU? YOU DON'T GET TO DECIDE!

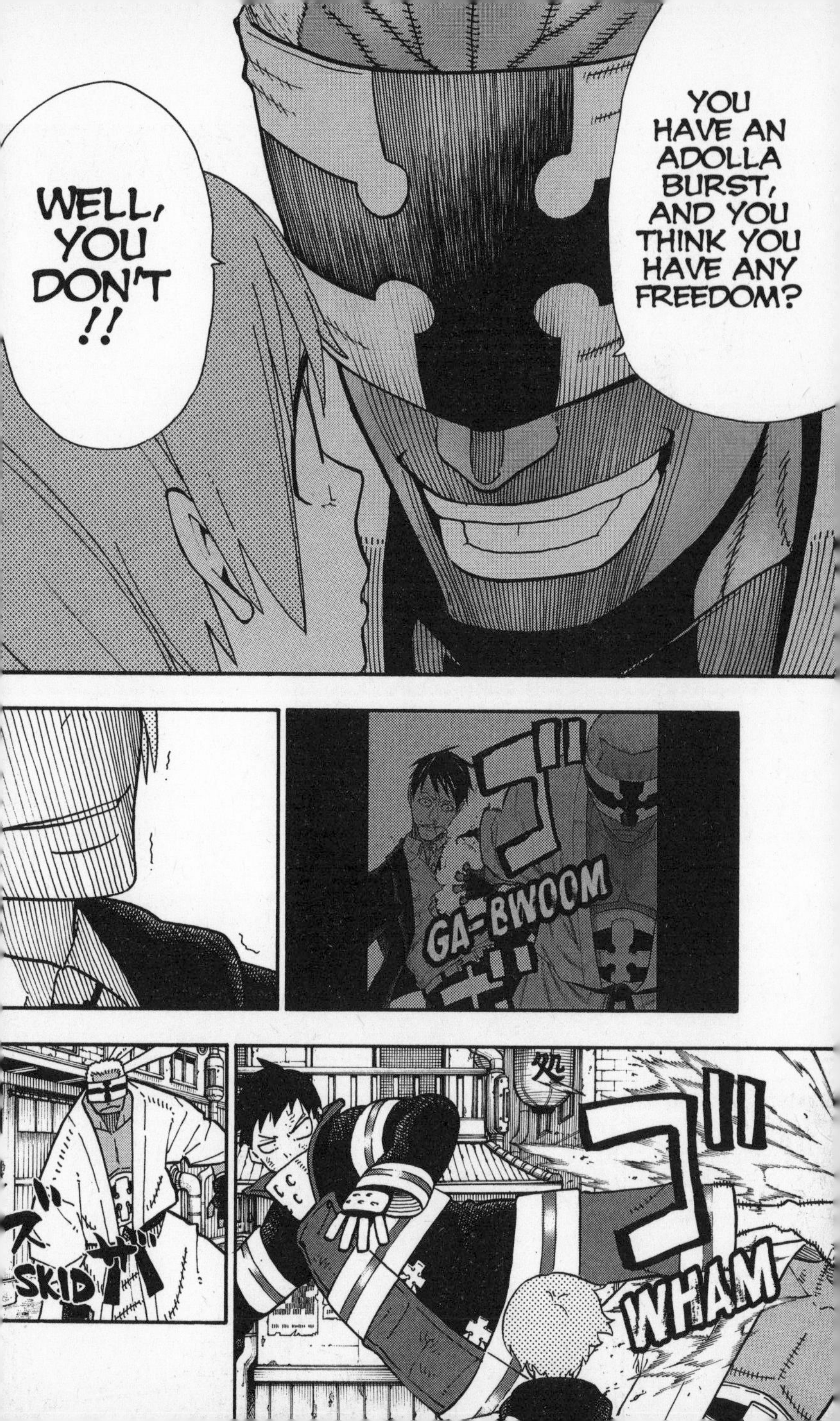
YOU HAVE AN ADOLLA BURST, AND YOU THINK YOU HAVE ANY FREEDOM?
WELL, YOU DON'T !!
GA-BWOOM
WHAM
SKID

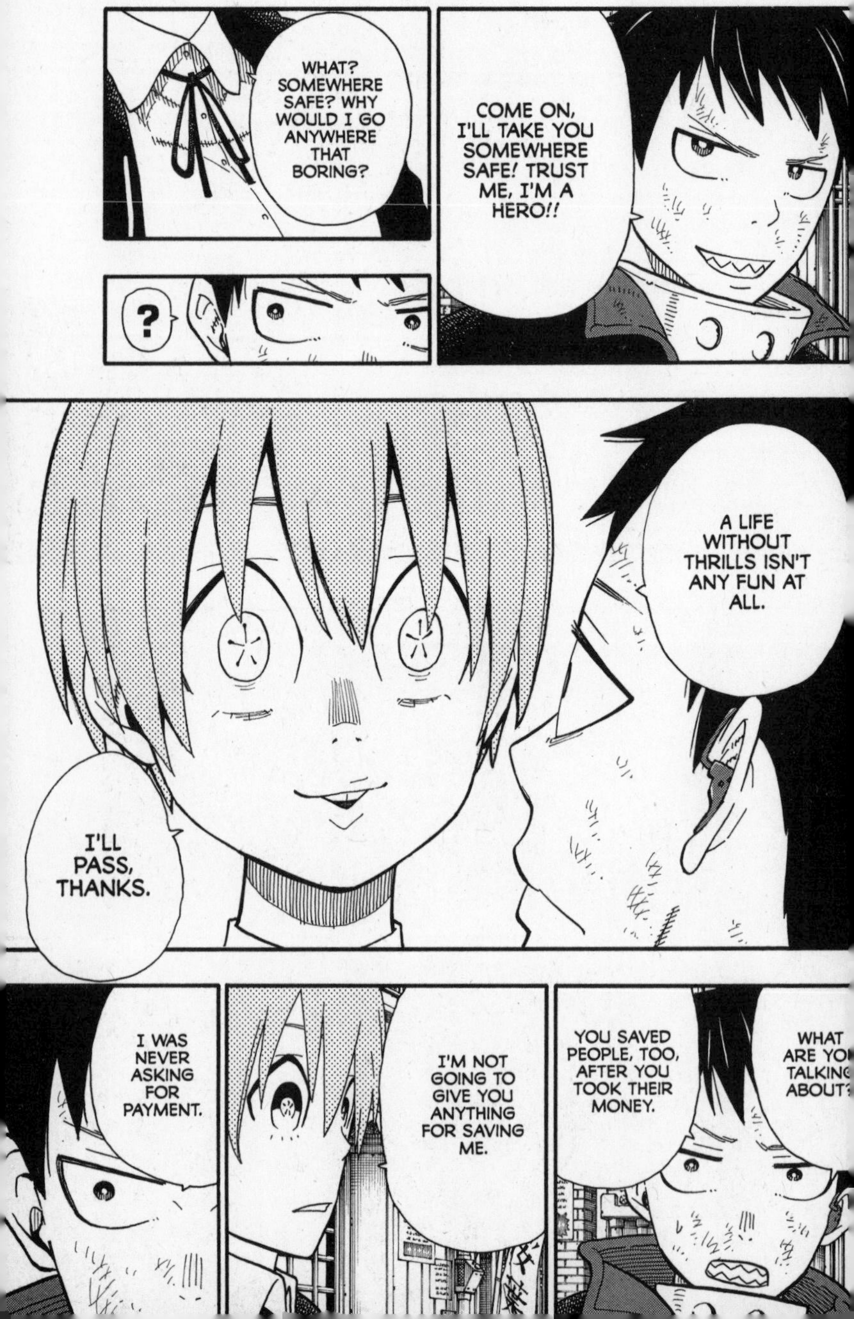
COME ON, I'LL TAKE YOU SOMEWHERE SAFE! TRUST ME, I'M A HERO!!
WHAT? SOMEWHERE SAFE? WHY WOULD I GO ANYWHERE THAT BORING?
?
A LIFE WITHOUT THRILLS ISN'T ANY FUN AT ALL.
I'LL PASS, THANKS.
WHAT ARE YO TALKING ABOUT?
YOU SAVED PEOPLE, TOO, AFTER YOU TOOK THEIR MONEY.
I'M NOT GOING TO GIVE YOU ANYTHING FOR SAVING ME.
I WAS NEVER ASKING FOR PAYMENT.

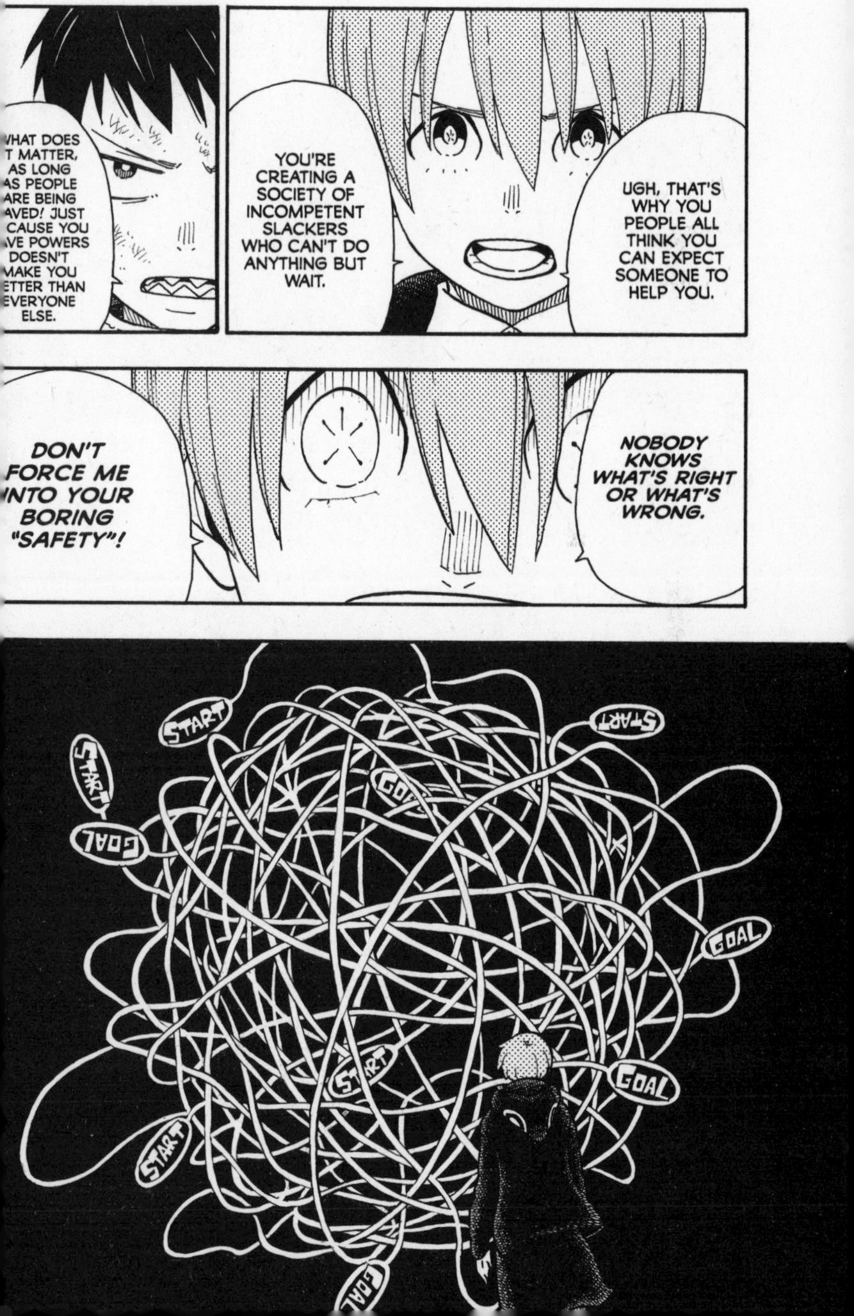
UGH, THAT'S WHY YOU PEOPLE ALL THINK YOU CAN EXPECT SOMEONE TO HELP YOU.
YOU'RE CREATING A SOCIETY OF INCOMPETENT SLACKERS WHO CAN'T DO ANYTHING BUT WAIT.
VHAT DOES T MATTER, AS LONG AS PEOPLE ARE BEING AVED! JUST CAUSE YOU VE POWERS DOESN'T MAKE YOU ETTER THAN EVERYONE ELSE.
NOBODY KNOWS WHAT'S RIGHT OR WHAT'S WRONG.
DON'T FORCE ME NTO YOUR BORING "SAFETY"!
START
START
START
GOAL
GOAL
GOAL
START
GOAL
START
GOAL

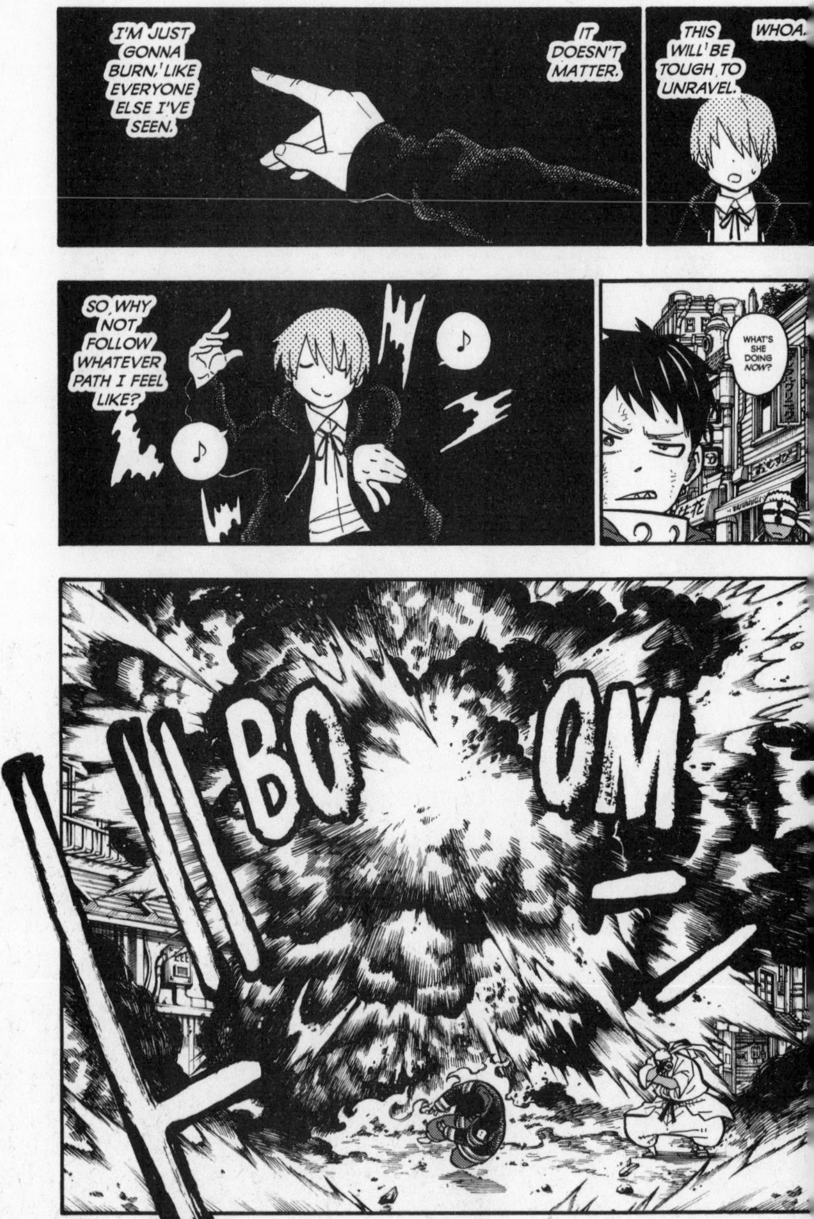
WHOA.
THIS WILL BE TOUGH TO UNRAVEL.
IT DOESN'T MATTER.
I'M JUST GONNA BURN, LIKE EVERYONE ELSE I'VE SEEN.
WHAT'S SHE DOING NOW?
SO, WHY NOT FOLLOW WHATEVER PATH I FEEL LIKE?
♪
♪
BOOM

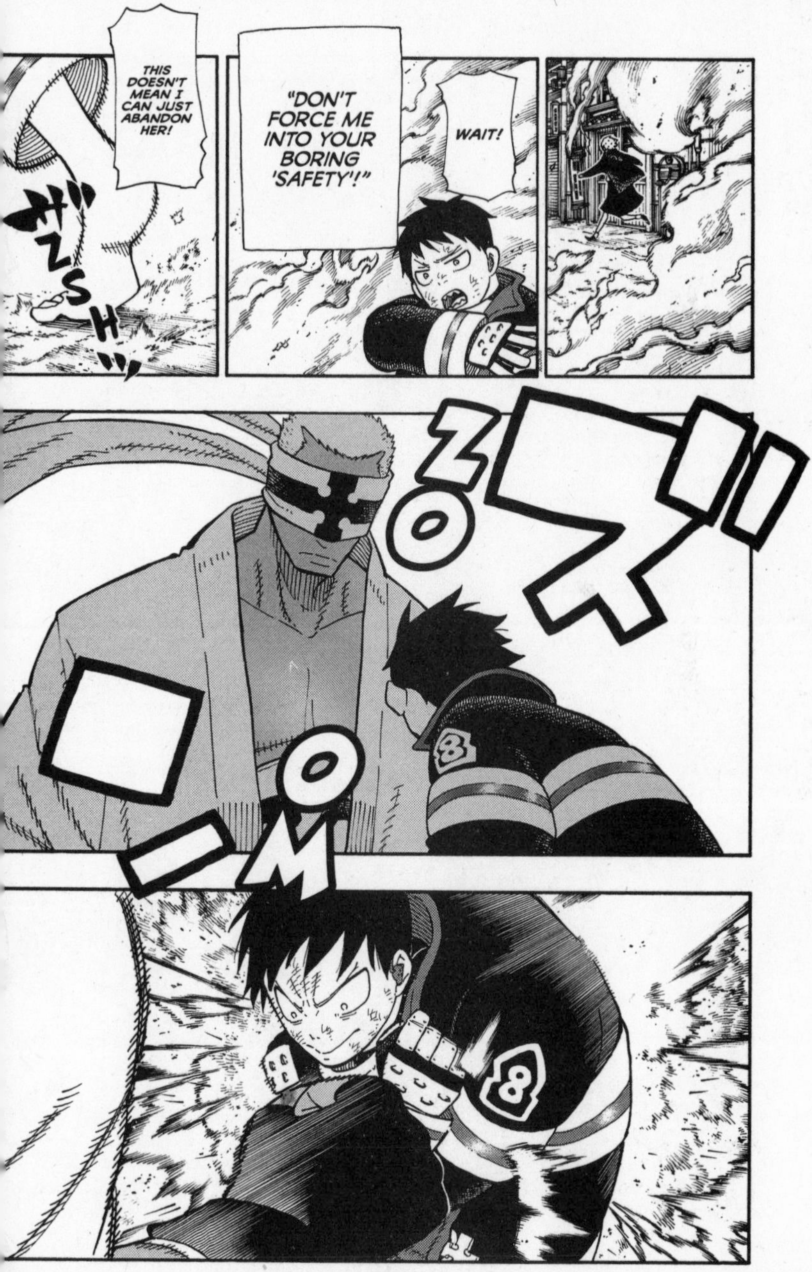
WAIT!
"DON'T FORCE ME INTO YOUR BORING 'SAFETY'!"
THIS DOESN'T MEAN I CAN JUST ABANDON HER!
ZSH
ZOOM

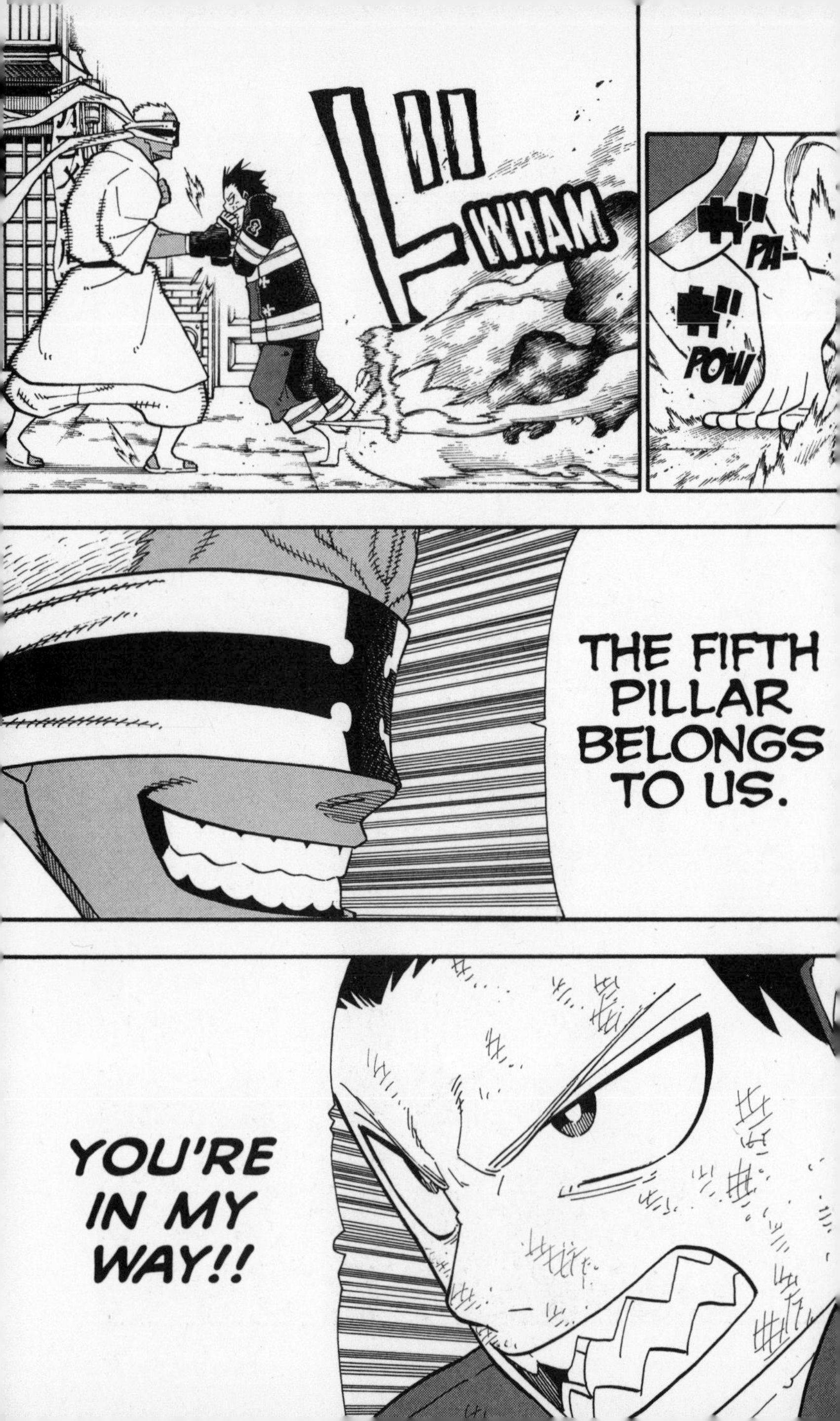
PA-
POW
WHAM
THE FIFTH PILLAR BELONGS TO US.
YOU'RE IN MY WAY!!

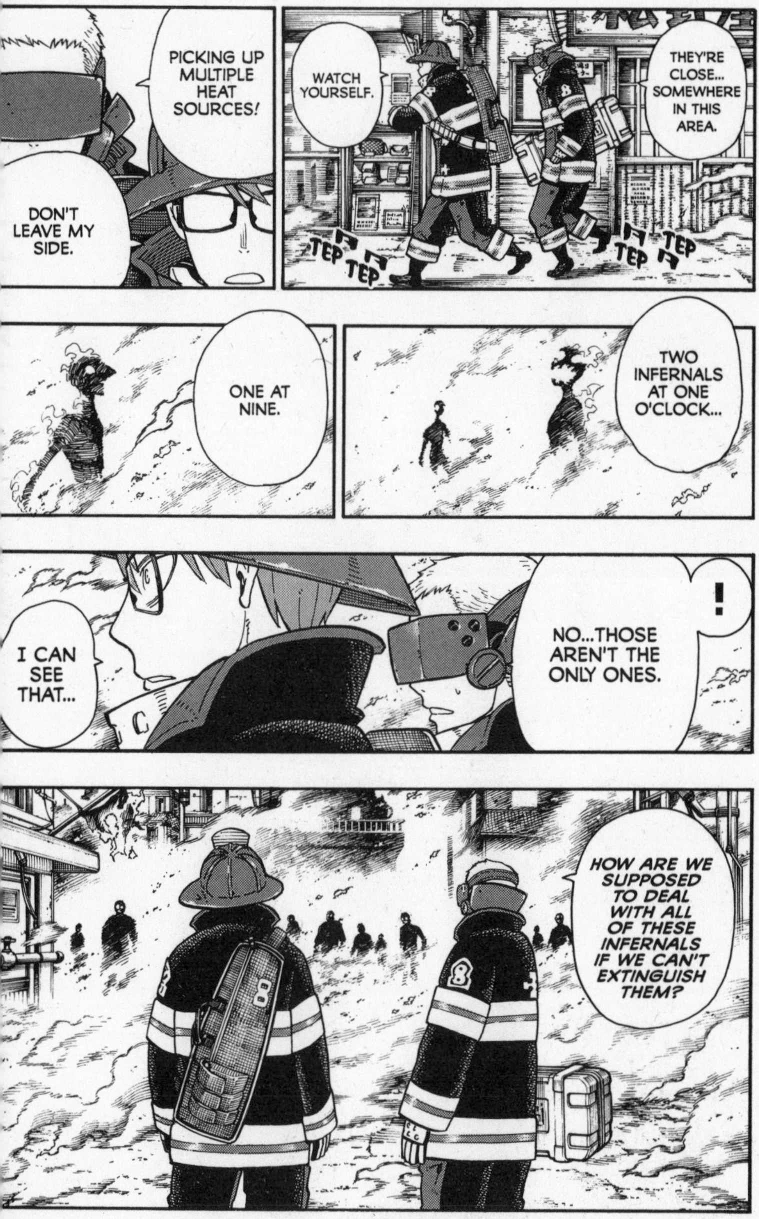
THEY'RE CLOSE... SOMEWHERE IN THIS AREA.
WATCH YOURSELF.
TEP TEP TEP
TEP TEP
PICKING UP MULTIPLE HEAT SOURCES!
DON'T LEAVE MY SIDE.
TWO INFERNALS AT ONE O'CLOCK...
ONE AT NINE.
!
NO...THOSE AREN'T THE ONLY ONES.
I CAN SEE THAT...
HOW ARE WE SUPPOSED TO DEAL WITH ALL OF THESE INFERNALS IF WE CAN'T EXTINGUISH THEM?

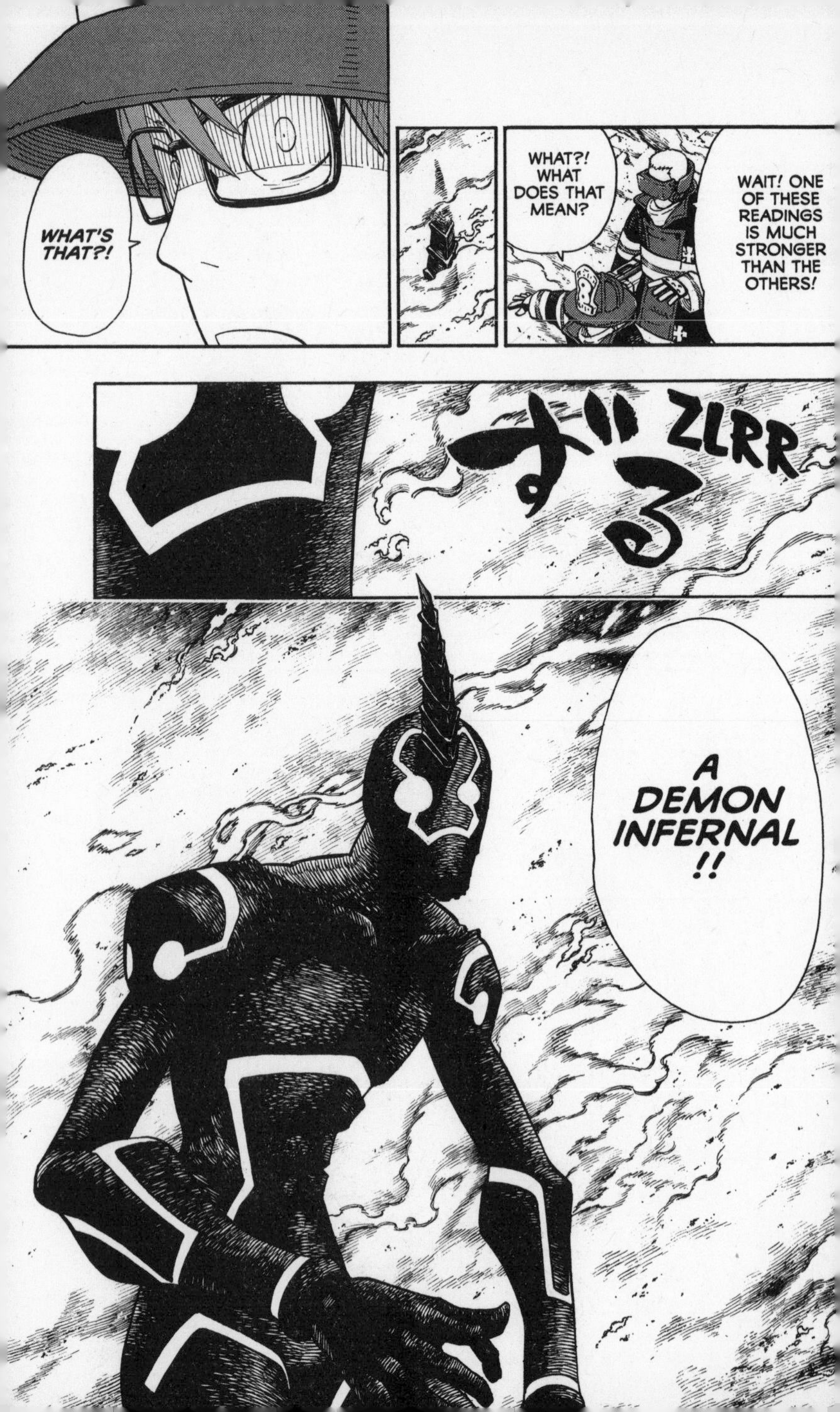
WAIT! ONE OF THESE READINGS IS MUCH STRONGER THAN THE OTHERS!
WHAT?! WHAT DOES THAT MEAN?
WHAT'S THAT?!
ZLRR
A DEMON INFERNAL !!

FIRE FORCE

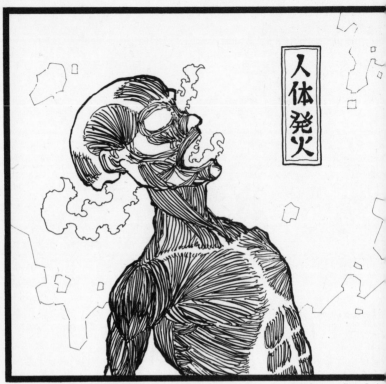

人体発火

Label: Spontaneous Human Combustion

CHAPTER CIV: BONDS OF THE FIREGROUND

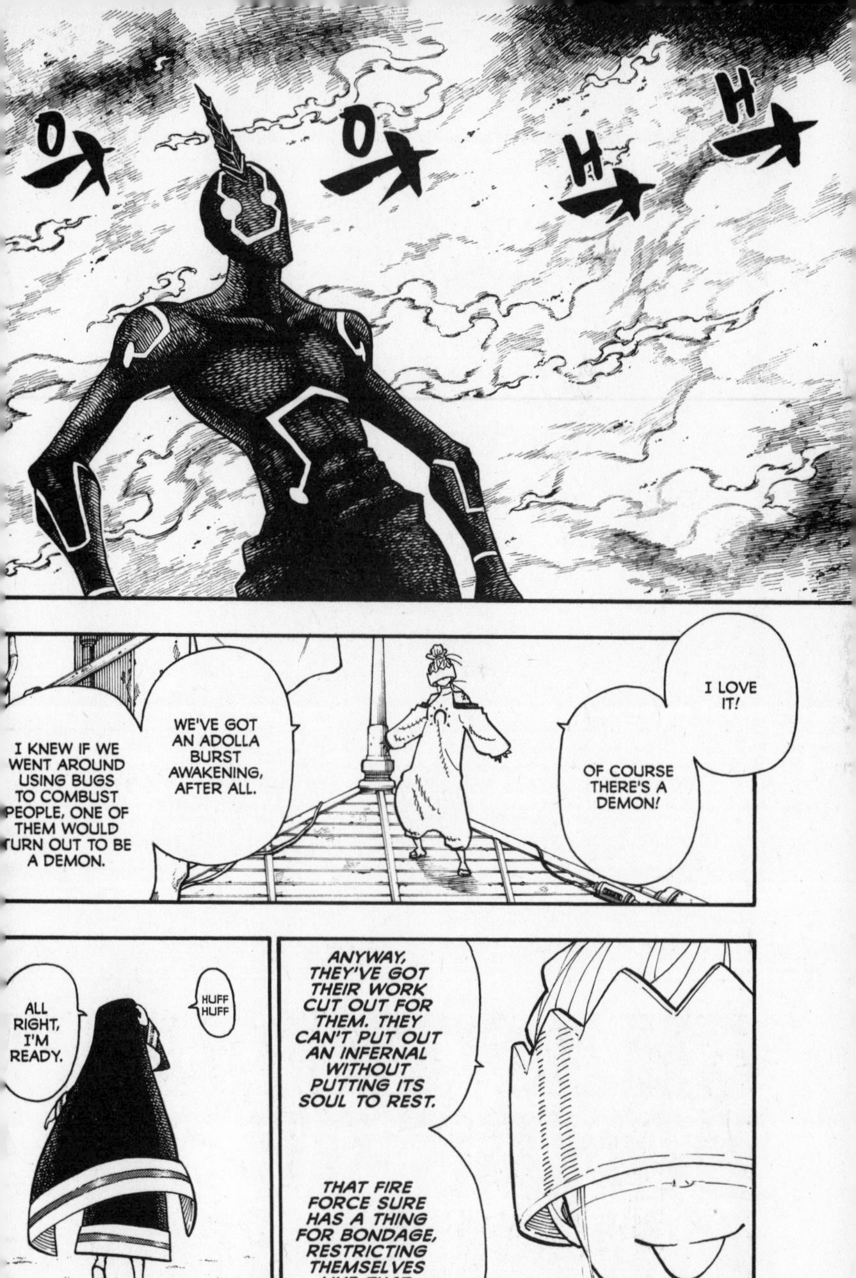
OOHH
I LOVE IT!
OF COURSE THERE'S A DEMON!
WE'VE GOT AN ADOLLA BURST AWAKENING, AFTER ALL.
I KNEW IF WE WENT AROUND USING BUGS TO COMBUST PEOPLE, ONE OF THEM WOULD TURN OUT TO BE A DEMON.
ANYWAY, THEY'VE GOT THEIR WORK CUT OUT FOR THEM. THEY CAN'T PUT OUT AN INFERNAL WITHOUT PUTTING ITS SOUL TO REST.
THAT FIRE FORCE SURE HAS A THING FOR BONDAGE, RESTRICTING THEMSELVES LIKE THAT.
HUFF HUFF
ALL RIGHT, I'M READY.

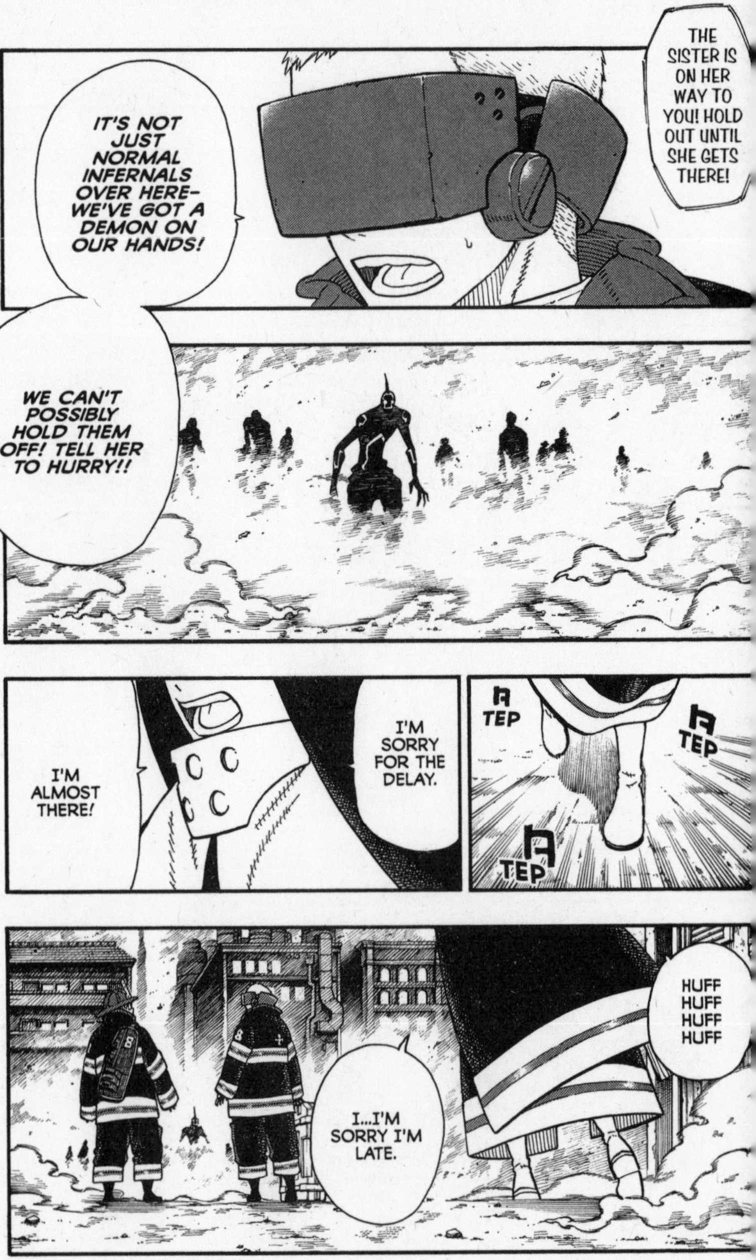
THE SISTER IS ON HER WAY TO YOU! HOLD OUT UNTIL SHE GETS THERE!
IT'S NOT JUST NORMAL INFERNALS OVER HERE- WE'VE GOT A DEMON ON OUR HANDS!
WE CAN'T POSSIBLY HOLD THEM OFF! TELL HER TO HURRY!!
TEP
TEP
TEP
I'M SORRY FOR THE DELAY.
I'M ALMOST THERE!
HUFF HUFF HUFF HUFF
I...I'M SORRY I'M LATE.

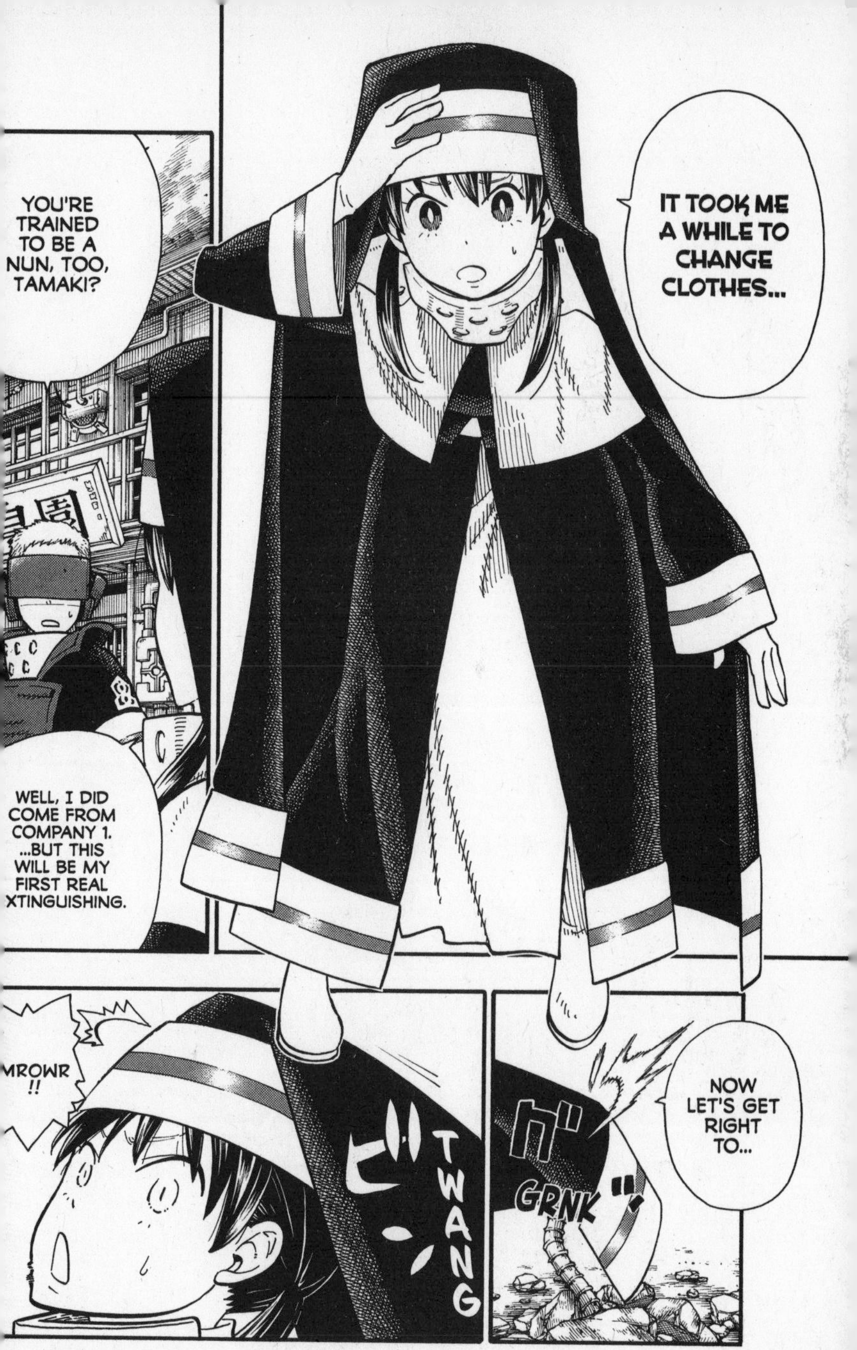

IT TOOK ME A WHILE TO CHANGE CLOTHES...
YOU'RE TRAINED TO BE A NUN, TOO, TAMAKI?
WELL, I DID COME FROM COMPANY 1. ...BUT THIS WILL BE MY FIRST REAL XTINGUISHING.
NOW LET'S GET RIGHT TO...
ガ
GRNK
ビン
TWANG
MROWR !!

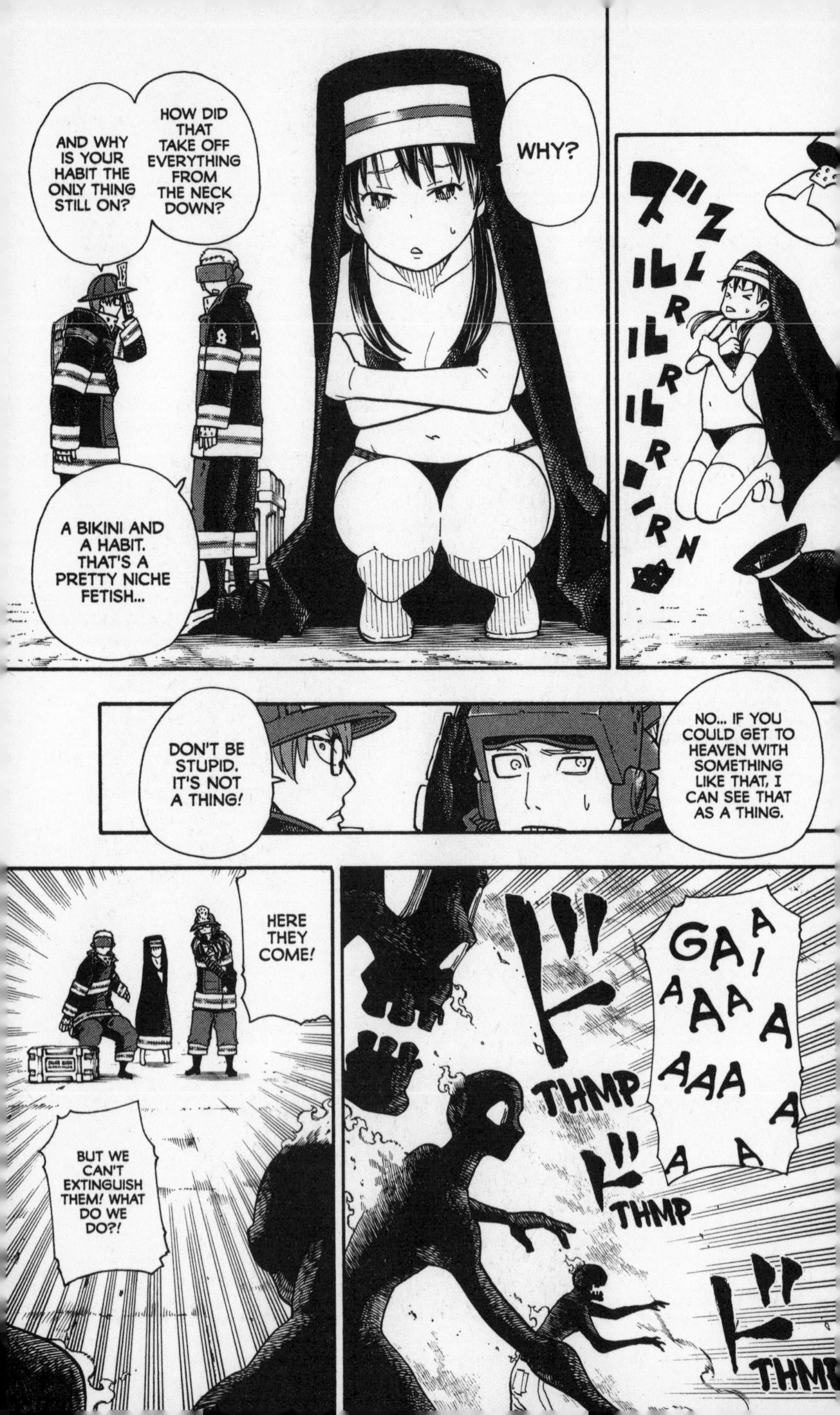
ZLRRRRN
WHY?
HOW DID THAT TAKE OFF EVERYTHING FROM THE NECK DOWN?
AND WHY IS YOUR HABIT THE ONLY THING STILL ON?
A BIKINI AND A HABIT. THAT'S A PRETTY NICHE FETISH...
DON'T BE STUPID. IT'S NOT A THING!
NO... IF YOU COULD GET TO HEAVEN WITH SOMETHING LIKE THAT, I CAN SEE THAT AS A THING.
GAAAAAAAAAAAA
THMP
THMP
THMP
HERE THEY COME!
BUT WE CAN'T EXTINGUISH THEM! WHAT DO WE DO?!

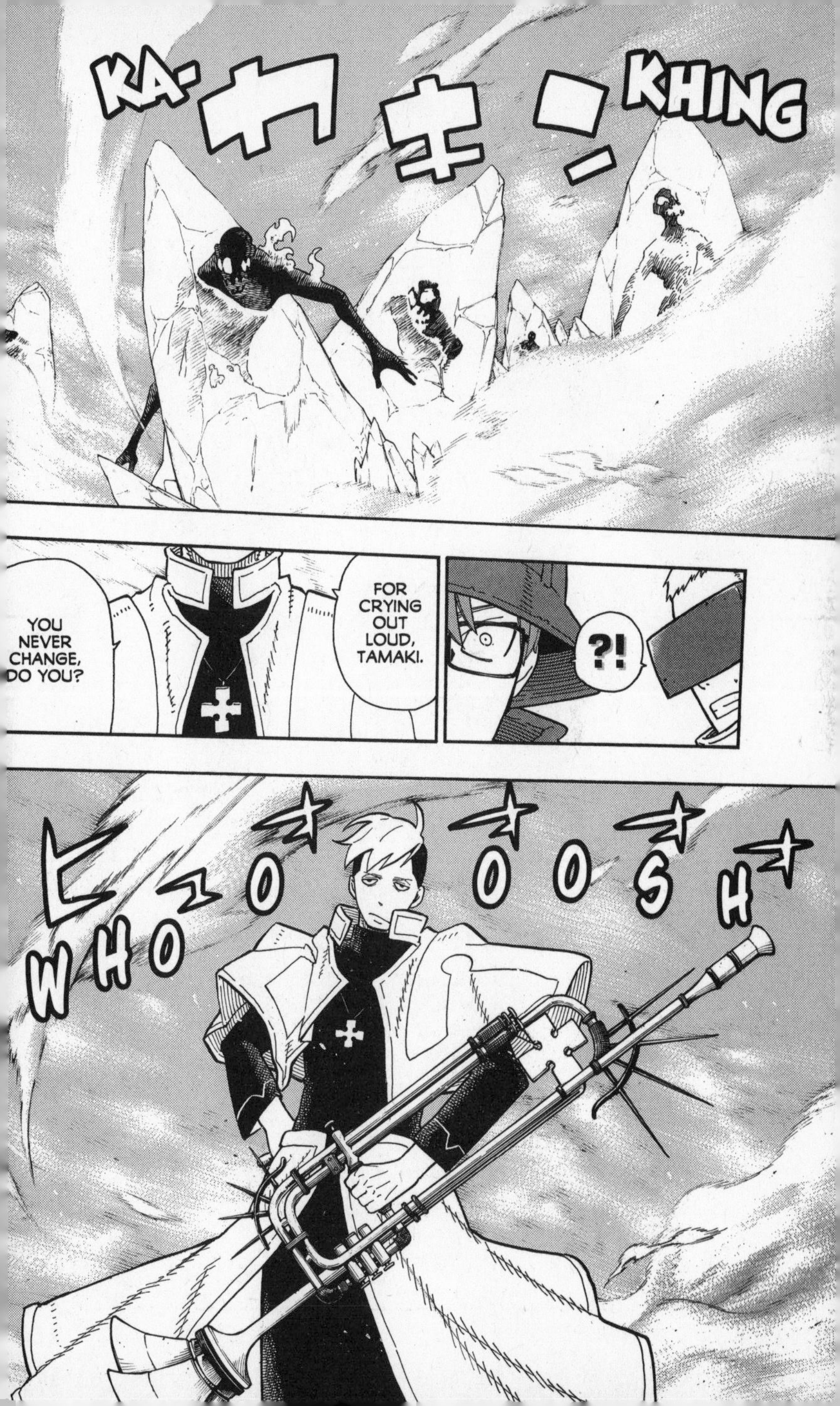
KA-KHING
?!
FOR CRYING OUT LOUD, TAMAKI.
YOU NEVER CHANGE, DO YOU?
WHOOOOSH

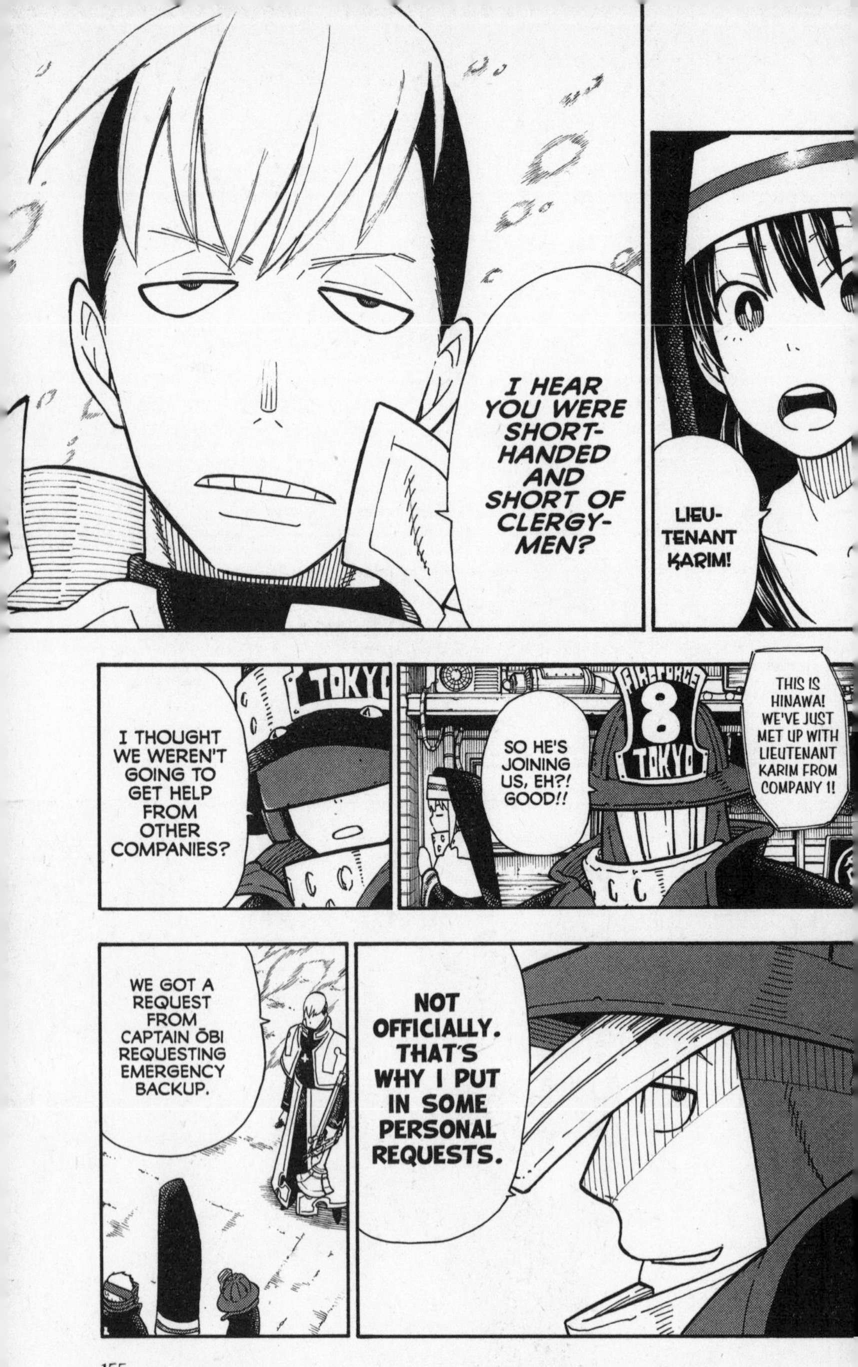
LIEU-TENANT KARIM!
I HEAR YOU WERE SHORT-HANDED AND SHORT OF CLERGY-MEN?
THIS IS HINAWA! WE'VE JUST MET UP WITH LIEUTENANT KARIM FROM COMPANY 1!
SO HE'S JOINING US, EH?! GOOD!!
I THOUGHT WE WEREN'T GOING TO GET HELP FROM OTHER COMPANIES?
NOT OFFICIALLY. THAT'S WHY I PUT IN SOME PERSONAL REQUESTS.
WE GOT A REQUEST FROM CAPTAIN ŌBI REQUESTING EMERGENCY BACKUP.

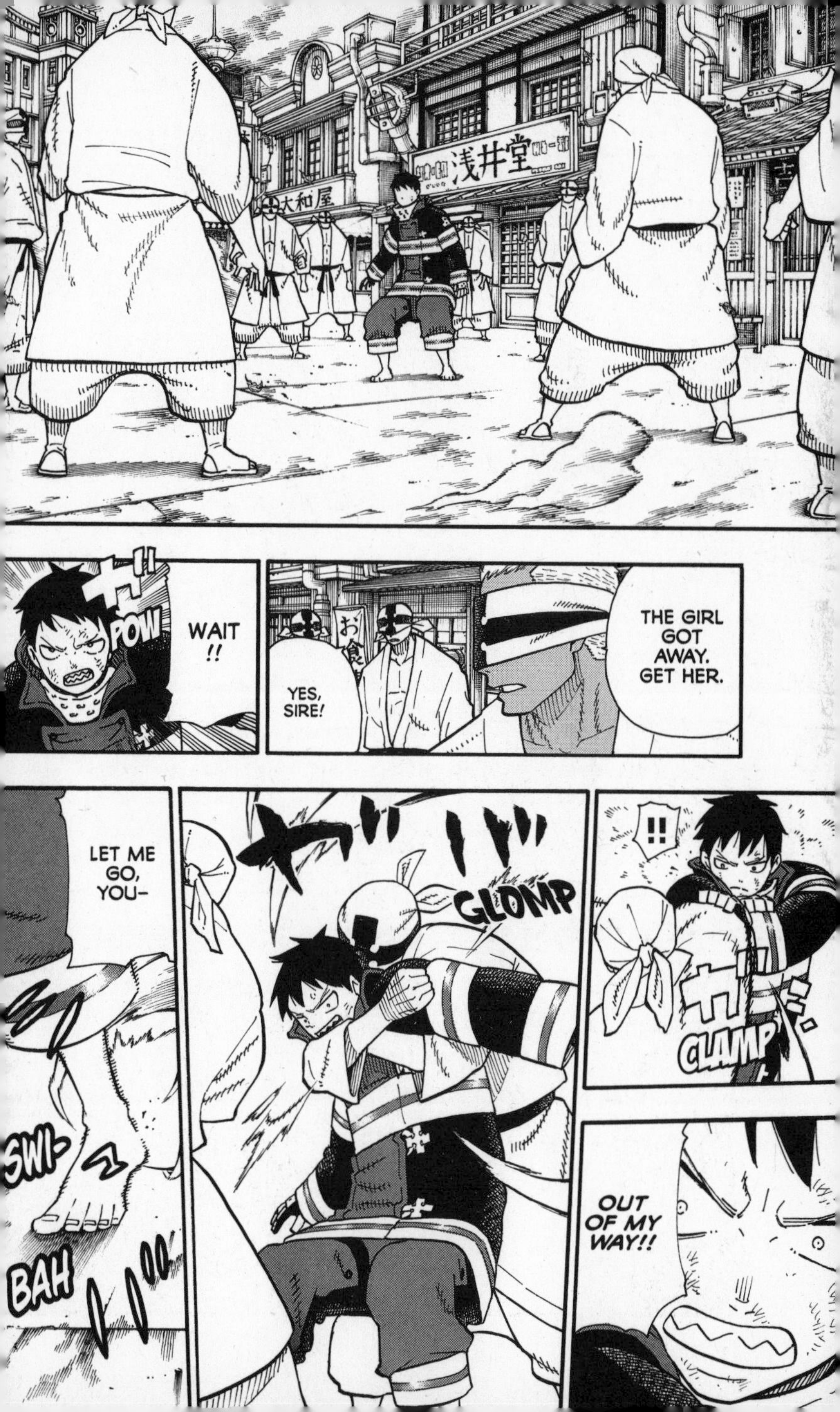
浅井堂
大和屋
THE GIRL GOT AWAY. GET HER.
YES, SIRE!
WAIT!!
POW
!!
CLAMP
OUT OF MY WAY!!
GLOMP
LET ME GO, YOU–
SWI
BAH

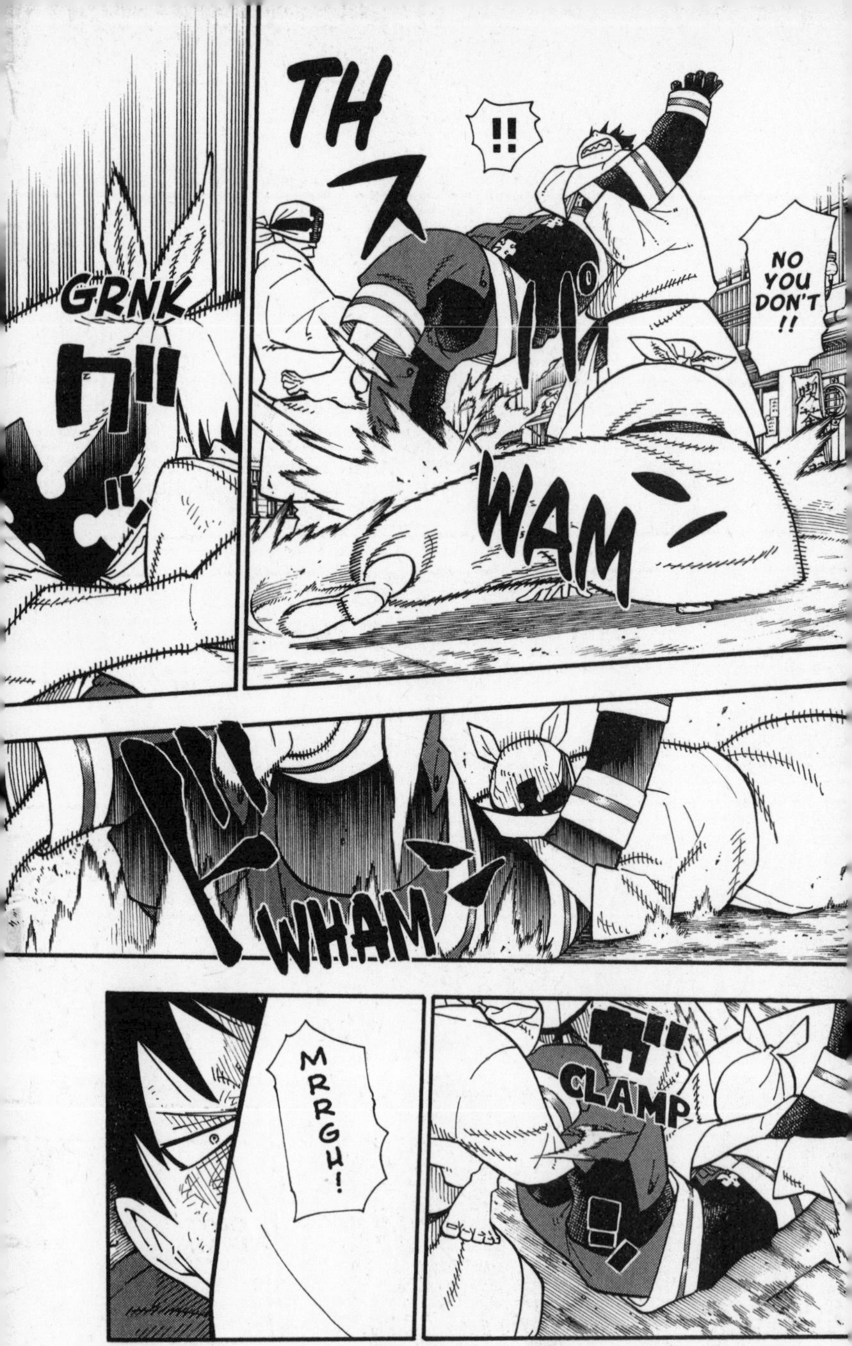
NO YOU DON'T !!
!!
TH
ス
WAM
GRNK
WHAM
CLAMP
!!
MRRGH!

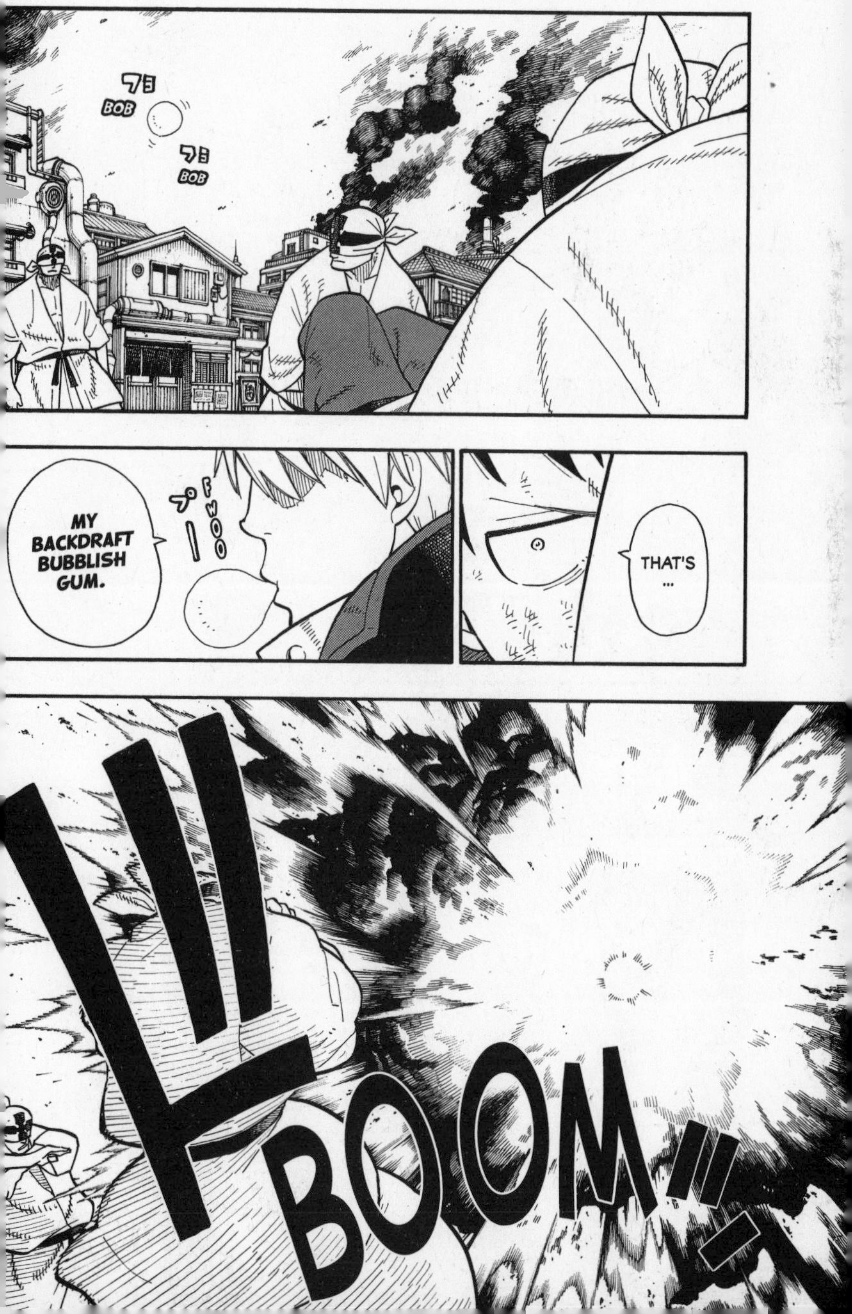
フヨ
BOB
フヨ
BOB
THAT'S ...
MY BACKDRAFT BUBBLISH GUM.
プー
FWOO
BOOM!!

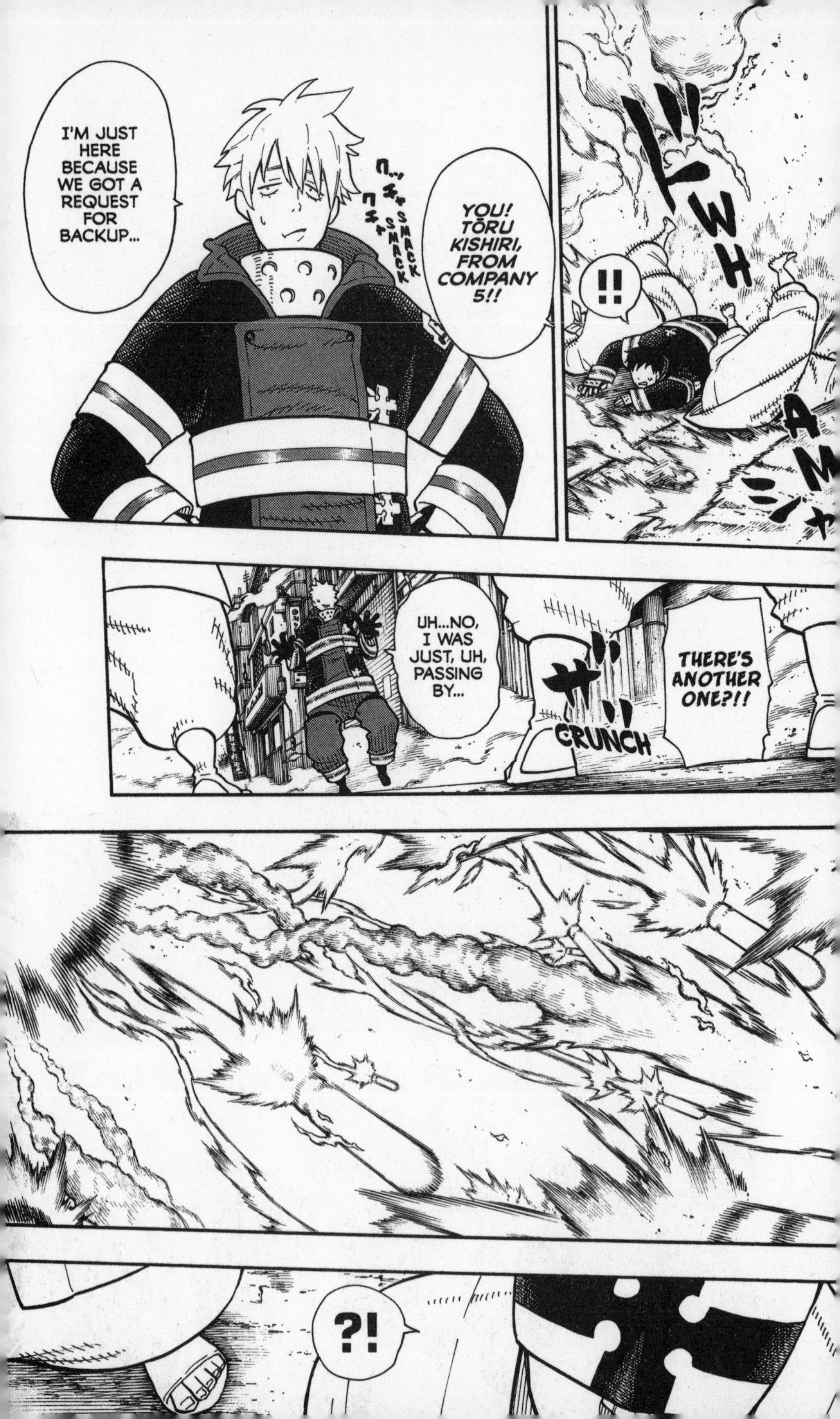
WHAM
!!
YOU! TŌRU KISHIRI, FROM COMPANY 5!!
SMACK SMACK
I'M JUST HERE BECAUSE WE GOT A REQUEST FOR BACKUP...
THERE'S ANOTHER ONE?!!
CRUNCH
UH...NO, I WAS JUST, UH, PASSING BY...
?!

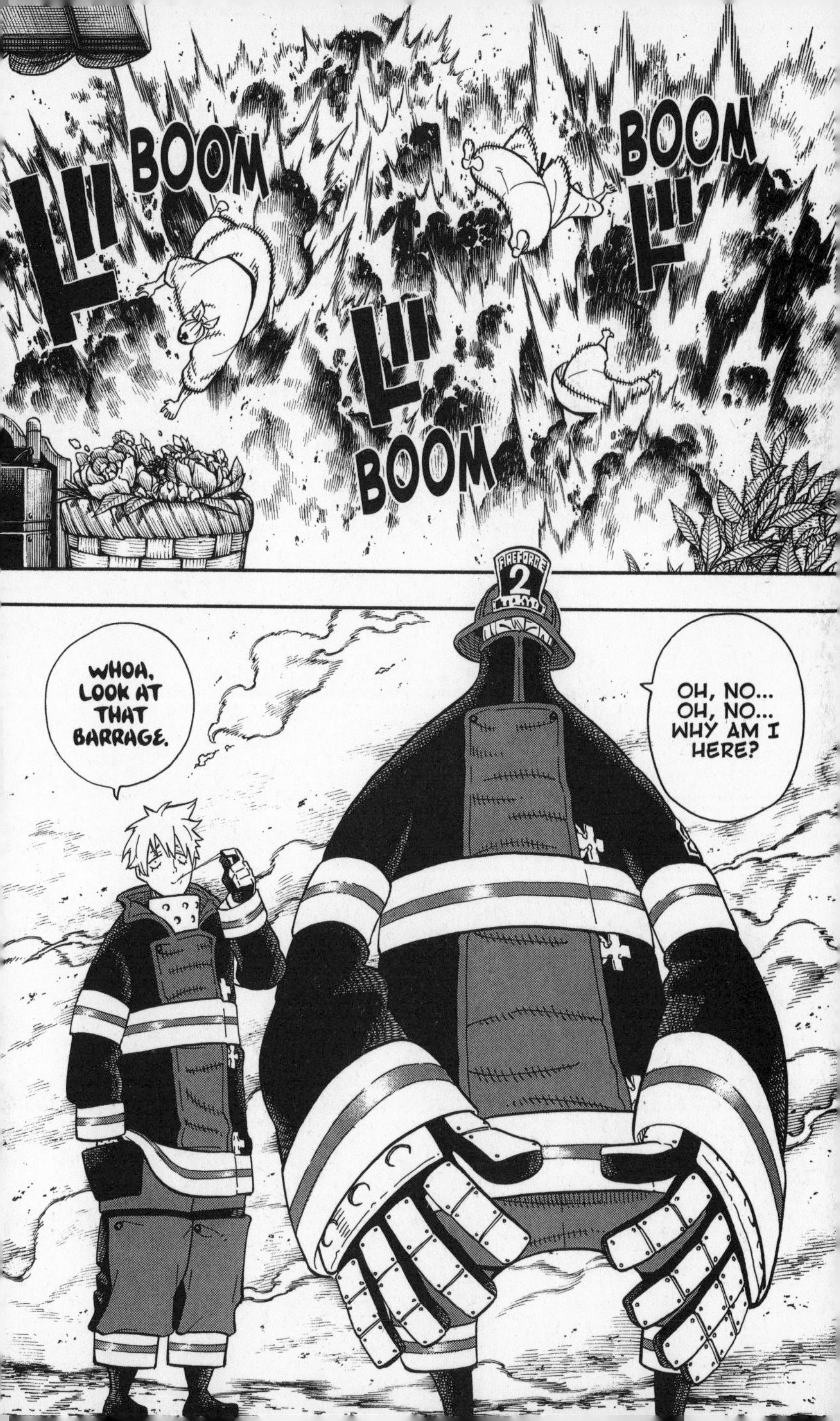
BOOM
BOOM
BOOM
OH, NO... OH, NO... WHY AM I HERE?
WHOA, LOOK AT THAT BARRAGE.

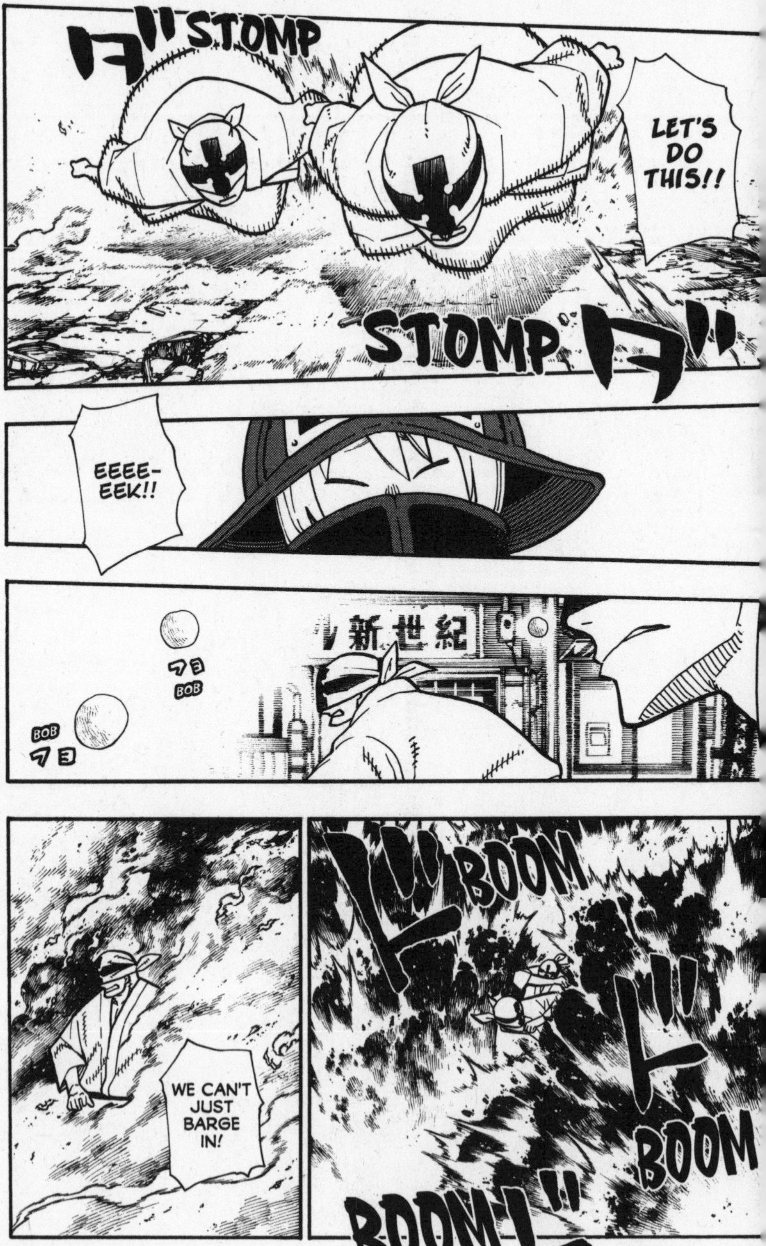

LET'S DO THIS!!
ドッ STOMP
STOMP ドッ
EEEE-EEK!!
新世紀
フヨ BOB
BOB フヨ
ドン BOOM
ドン BOOM
BOOM ドン
WE CAN'T JUST BARGE IN!

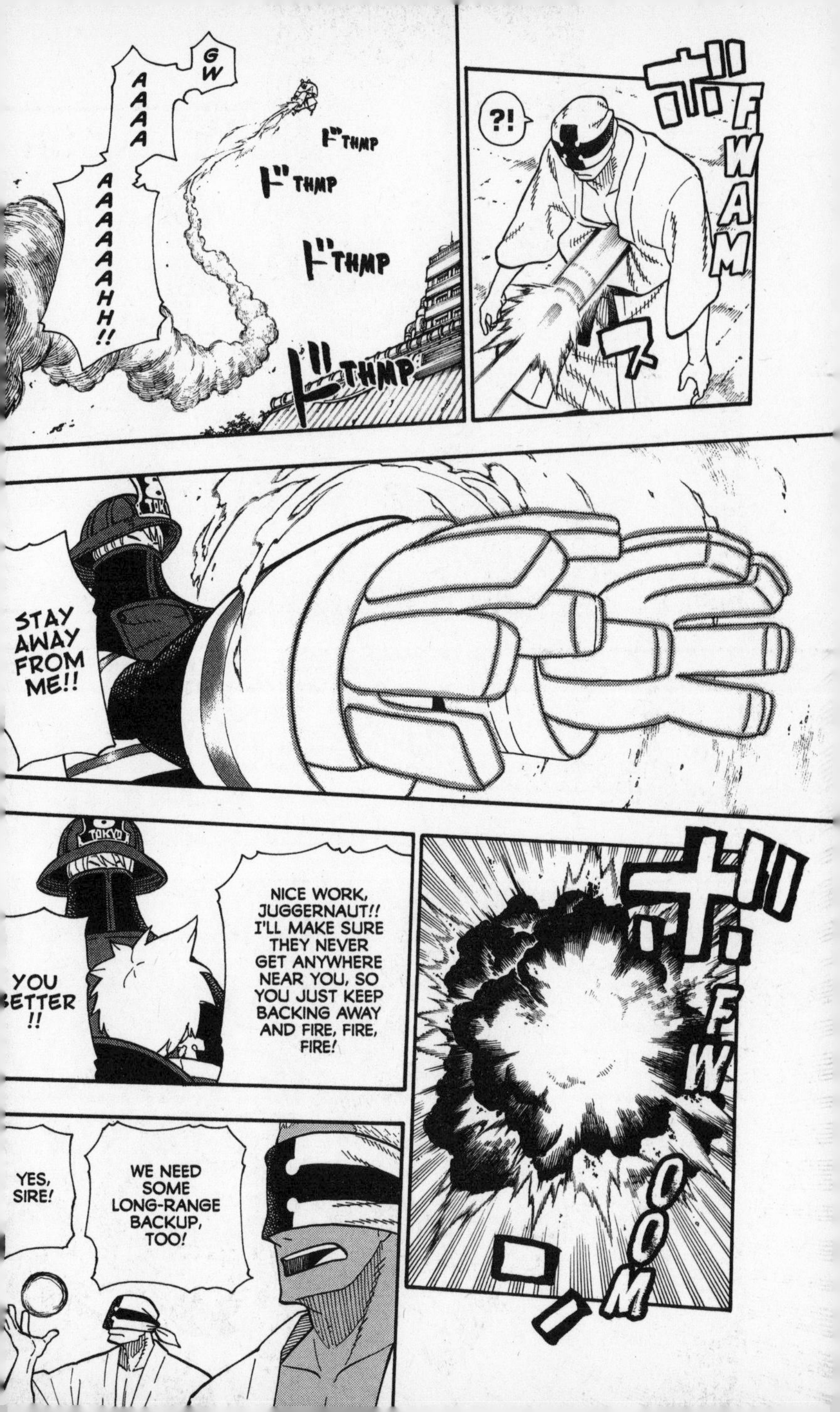
FWAM
?!
GW
AAAA
AAAAAAHH!!
ドTHMP
ドTHMP
ドTHMP
ドTHMP
STAY AWAY FROM ME!!
FWOOOM
NICE WORK, JUGGERNAUT!! I'LL MAKE SURE THEY NEVER GET ANYWHERE NEAR YOU, SO YOU JUST KEEP BACKING AWAY AND FIRE, FIRE, FIRE!
YOU ETTER!!
WE NEED SOME LONG-RANGE BACKUP, TOO!
YES, SIRE!

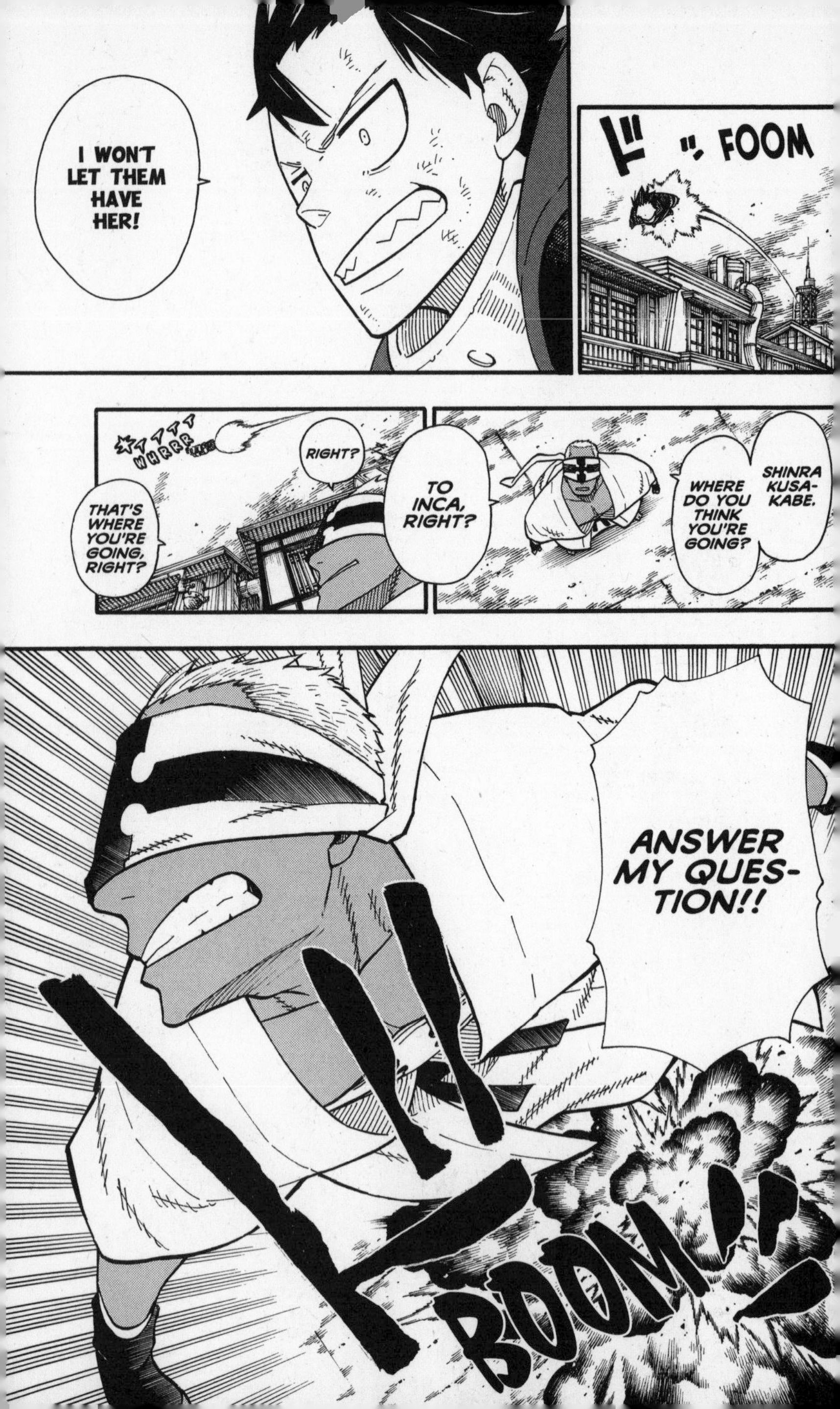
FOOM
I WON'T LET THEM HAVE HER!
SHINRA KUSA-KABE.
WHERE DO YOU THINK YOU'RE GOING?
TO INCA, RIGHT?
RIGHT?
WHRRR
THAT'S WHERE YOU'RE GOING, RIGHT?
ANSWER MY QUES-TION!!
BOOM!!

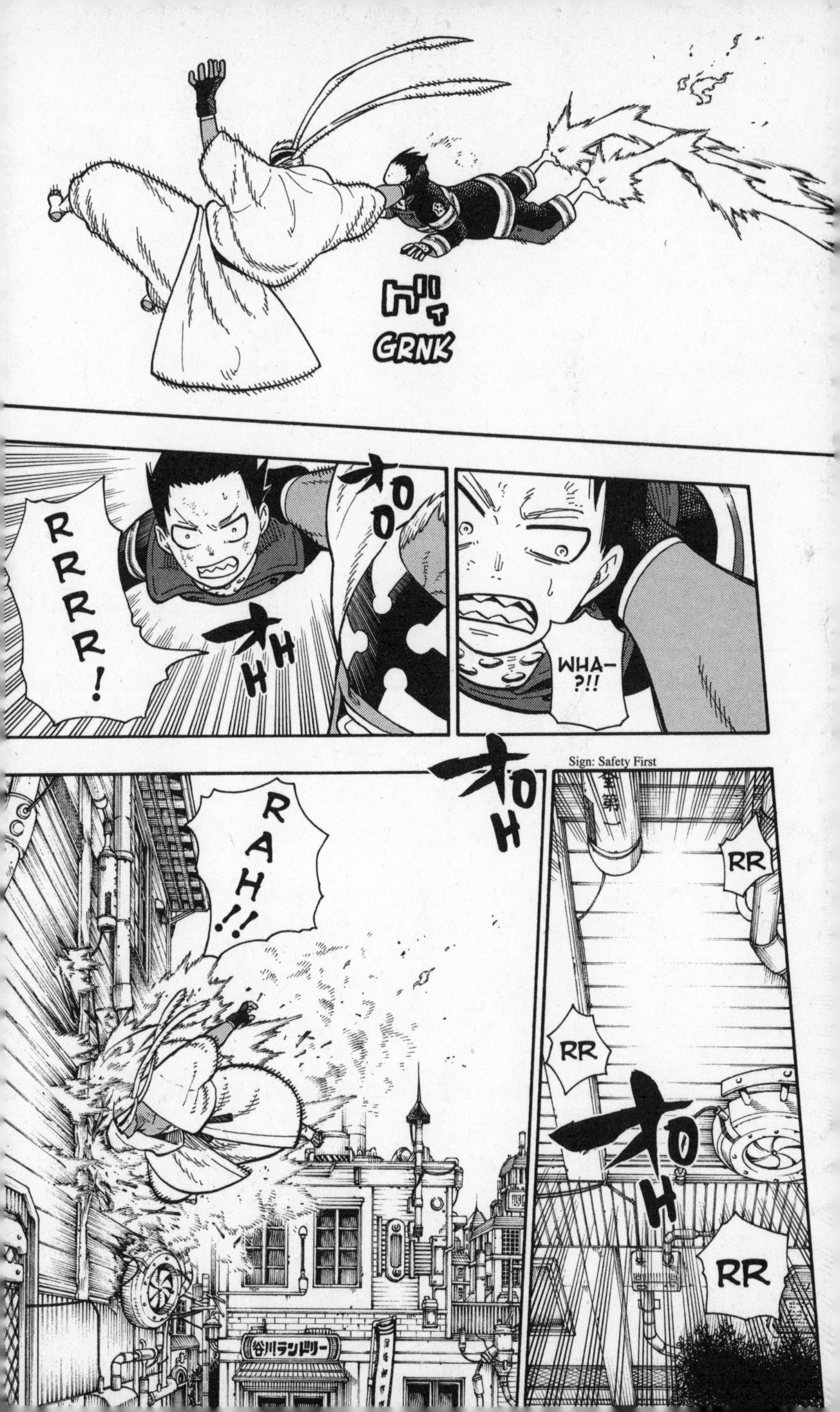

GRNK
WHA-?!!
RRRRR!
Sign: Safety First
RR
RR
RR
RAH!!!

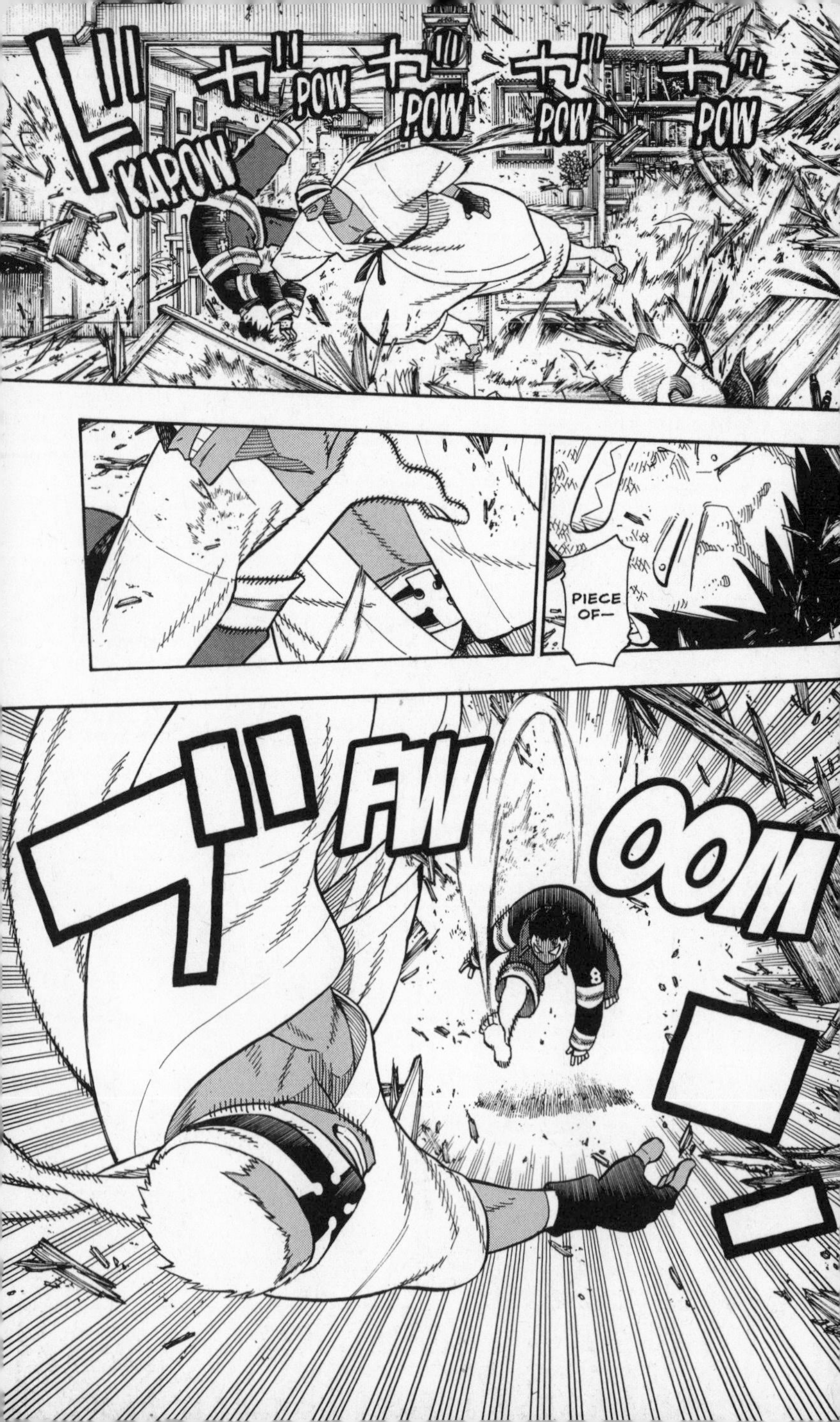
ドガガガガ
KAPOW POW POW POW POW
PIECE OF—
FWOOM

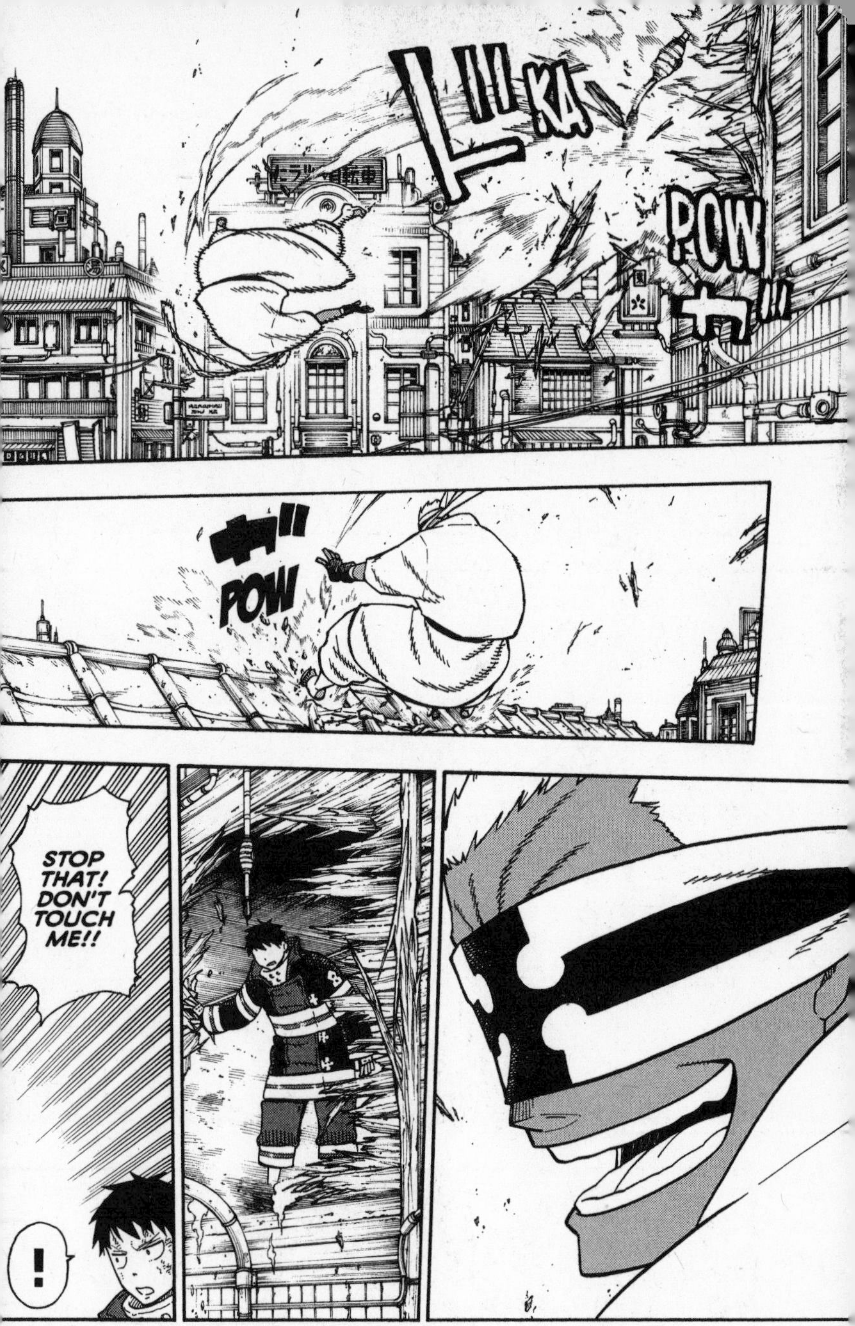
KA
POW
POW
STOP THAT! DON'T TOUCH ME!!
!

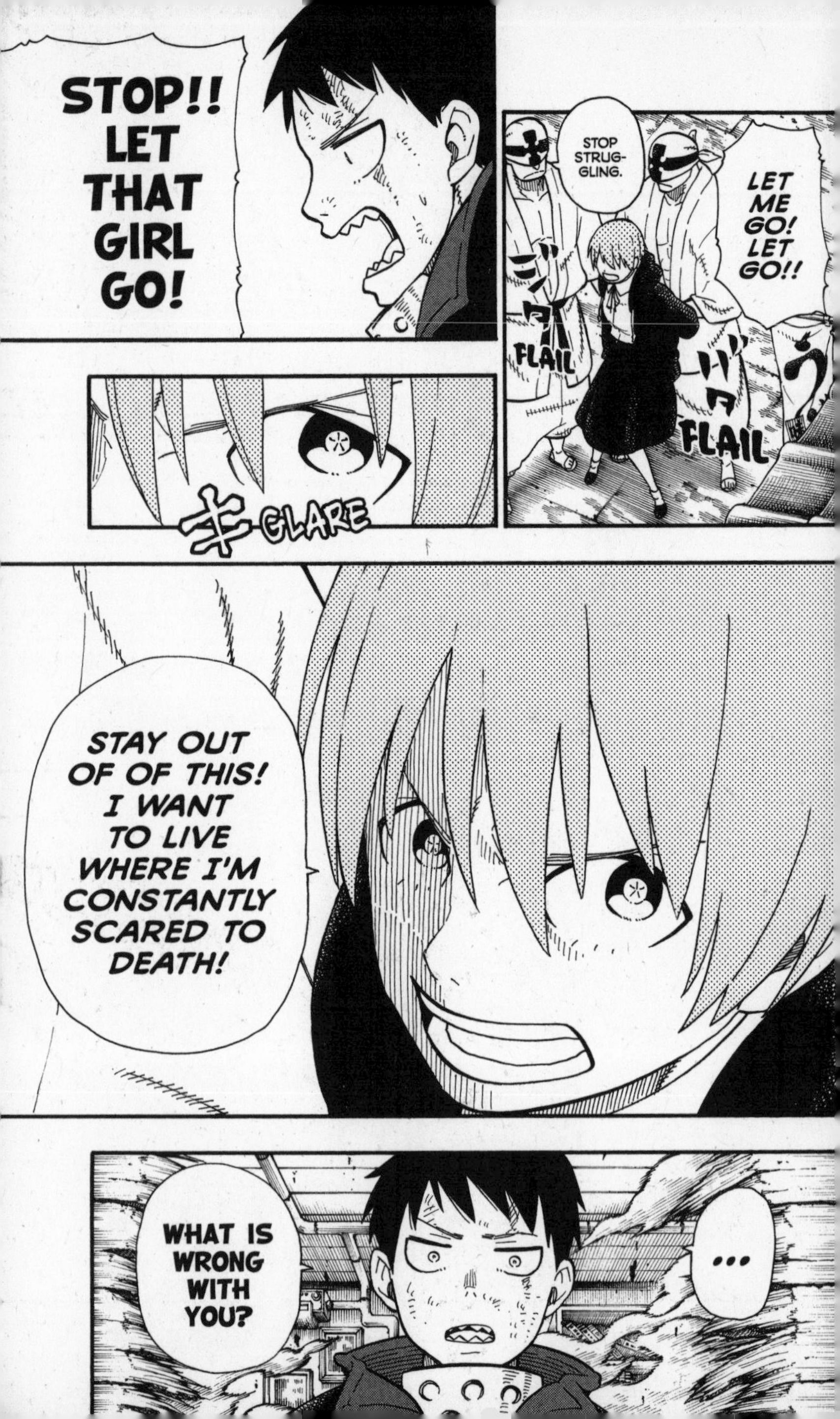
LET ME GO! LET GO!!
STOP STRUG-GLING.
FLAIL
FLAIL
STOP!! LET THAT GIRL GO!
GLARE
STAY OUT OF OF THIS! I WANT TO LIVE WHERE I'M CONSTANTLY SCARED TO DEATH!
...
WHAT IS WRONG WITH YOU?

FIRE FORCE

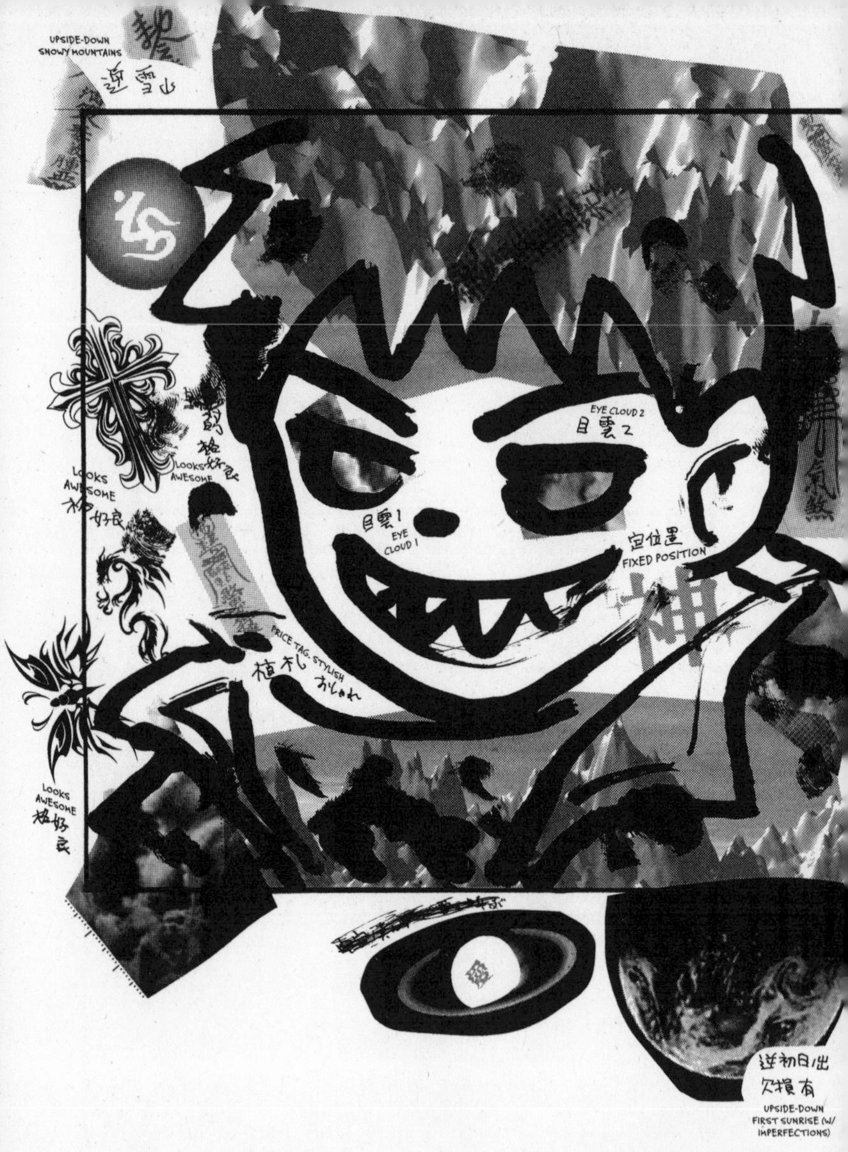
UPSIDE-DOWN SNOWY MOUNTAINS
逆雪山
LOOKS AWESOME
格好良
LOOKS AWESOME
格好良
EYE CLOUD 2
目雲2
目雲1
EYE CLOUD 1
定位置
FIXED POSITION
PRICE TAG, STYLISH
値札 おしゃれ
LOOKS AWESOME
格好良
逆初日出
欠損有
UPSIDE-DOWN FIRST SUNRISE (W/ IMPERFECTIONS)

CHAPTER CV: ASSEMBLE

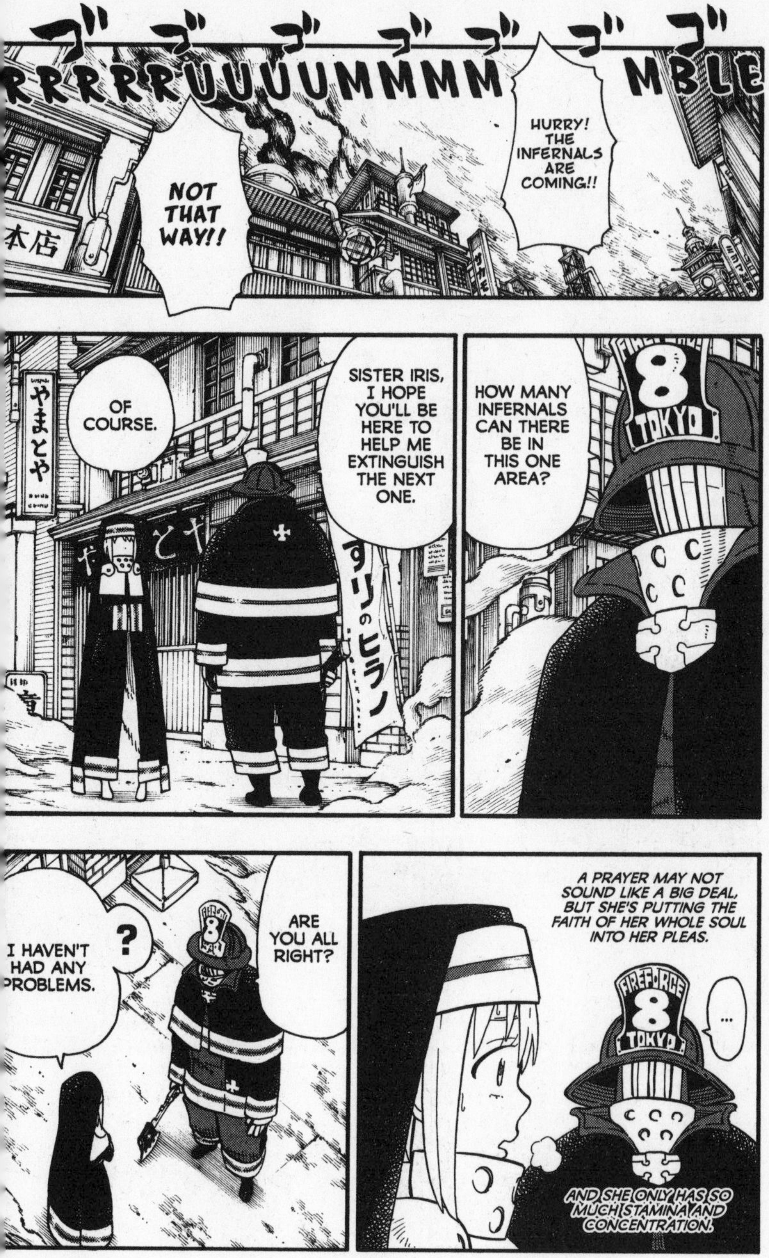
ゴゴゴゴゴゴゴ
RRRRRUUUUMMMM MBLE
HURRY! THE INFERNALS ARE COMING!!
NOT THAT WAY!!
本店
HOW MANY INFERNALS CAN THERE BE IN THIS ONE AREA?
SISTER IRIS, I HOPE YOU'LL BE HERE TO HELP ME EXTINGUISH THE NEXT ONE.
OF COURSE.
やまとや
すりのヒラノ
A PRAYER MAY NOT SOUND LIKE A BIG DEAL, BUT SHE'S PUTTING THE FAITH OF HER WHOLE SOUL INTO HER PLEAS.
...
AND SHE ONLY HAS SO MUCH STAMINA AND CONCENTRATION.
ARE YOU ALL RIGHT?
?
I HAVEN'T HAD ANY PROBLEMS.

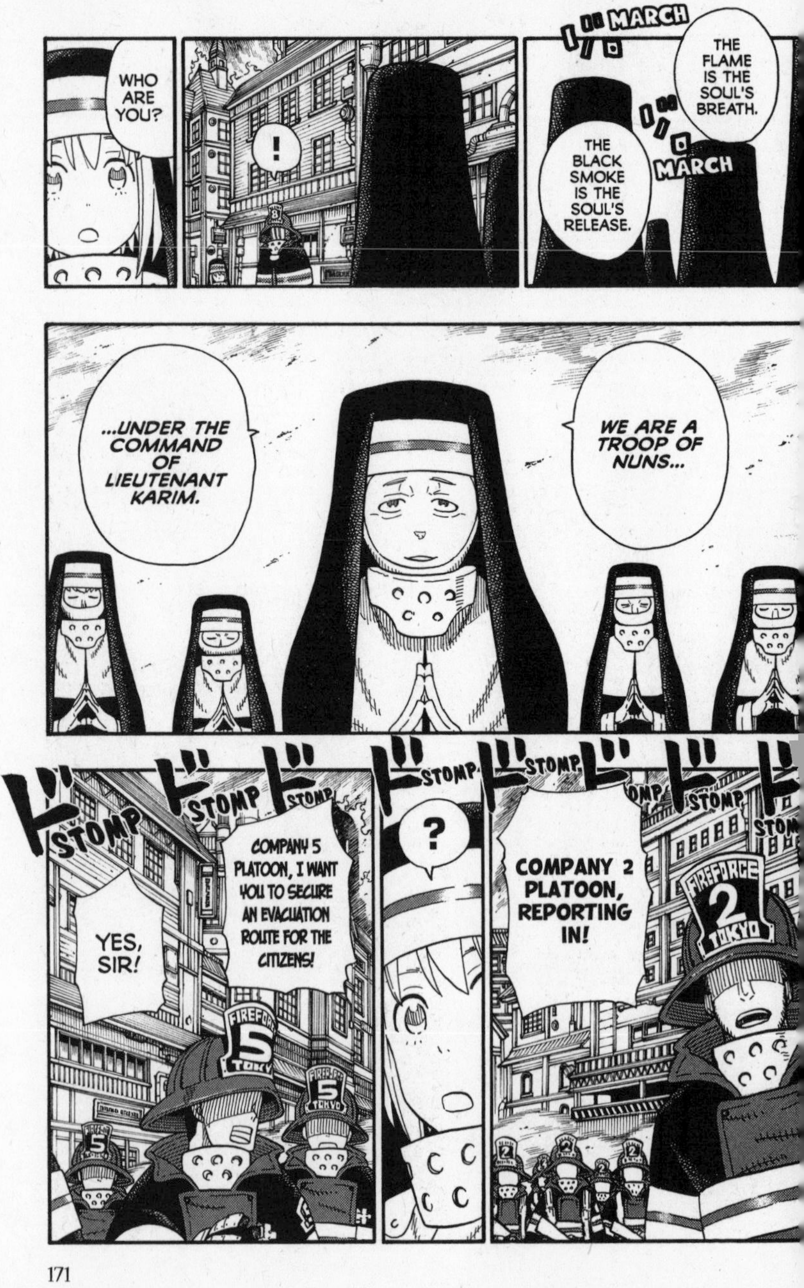
MARCH
THE FLAME IS THE SOUL'S BREATH.
MARCH
THE BLACK SMOKE IS THE SOUL'S RELEASE.
!
WHO ARE YOU?
WE ARE A TROOP OF NUNS...
...UNDER THE COMMAND OF LIEUTENANT KARIM.
STOMP
STOMP
STOMP
COMPANY 2 PLATOON, REPORTING IN!
STOMP
?
STOMP
STOMP
STOMP
COMPANY 5 PLATOON, I WANT YOU TO SECURE AN EVACUATION ROUTE FOR THE CITIZENS!
YES, SIR!

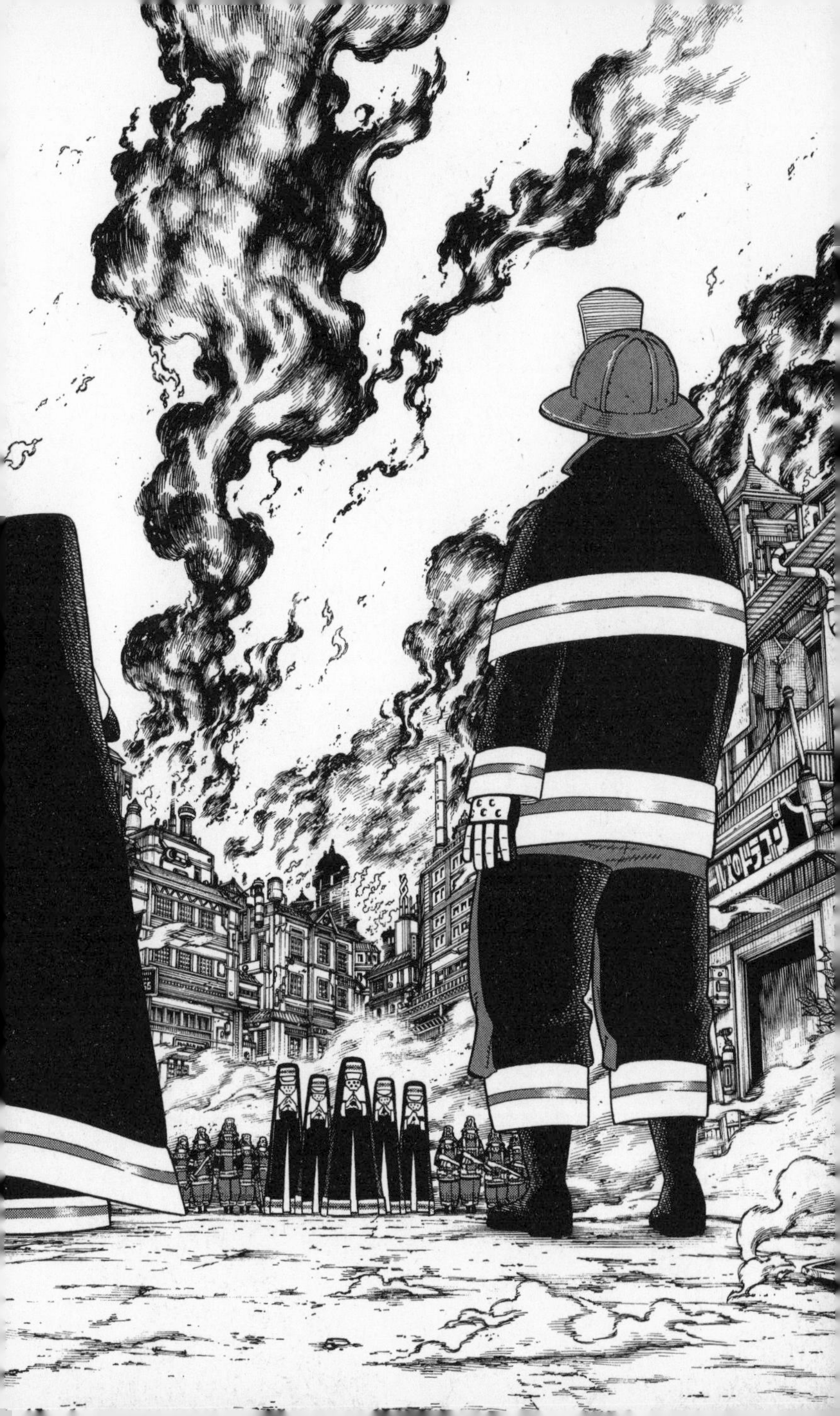
ドラゴン

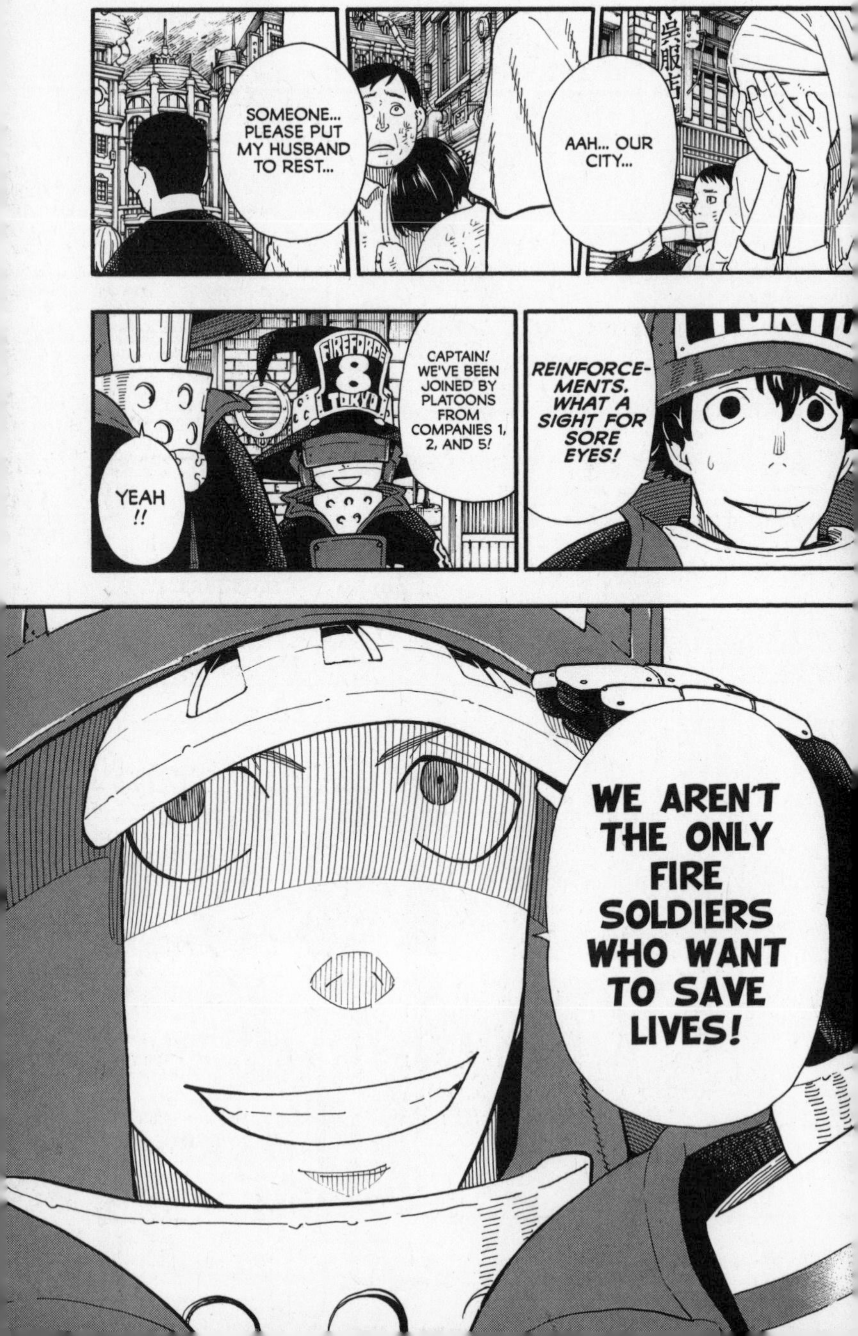
AAH... OUR CITY...
SOMEONE... PLEASE PUT MY HUSBAND TO REST...
REINFORCEMENTS. WHAT A SIGHT FOR SORE EYES!
FIREFORCE 8 TOKYO
CAPTAIN! WE'VE BEEN JOINED BY PLATOONS FROM COMPANIES 1, 2, AND 5!
YEAH !!
WE AREN'T THE ONLY FIRE SOLDIERS WHO WANT TO SAVE LIVES!

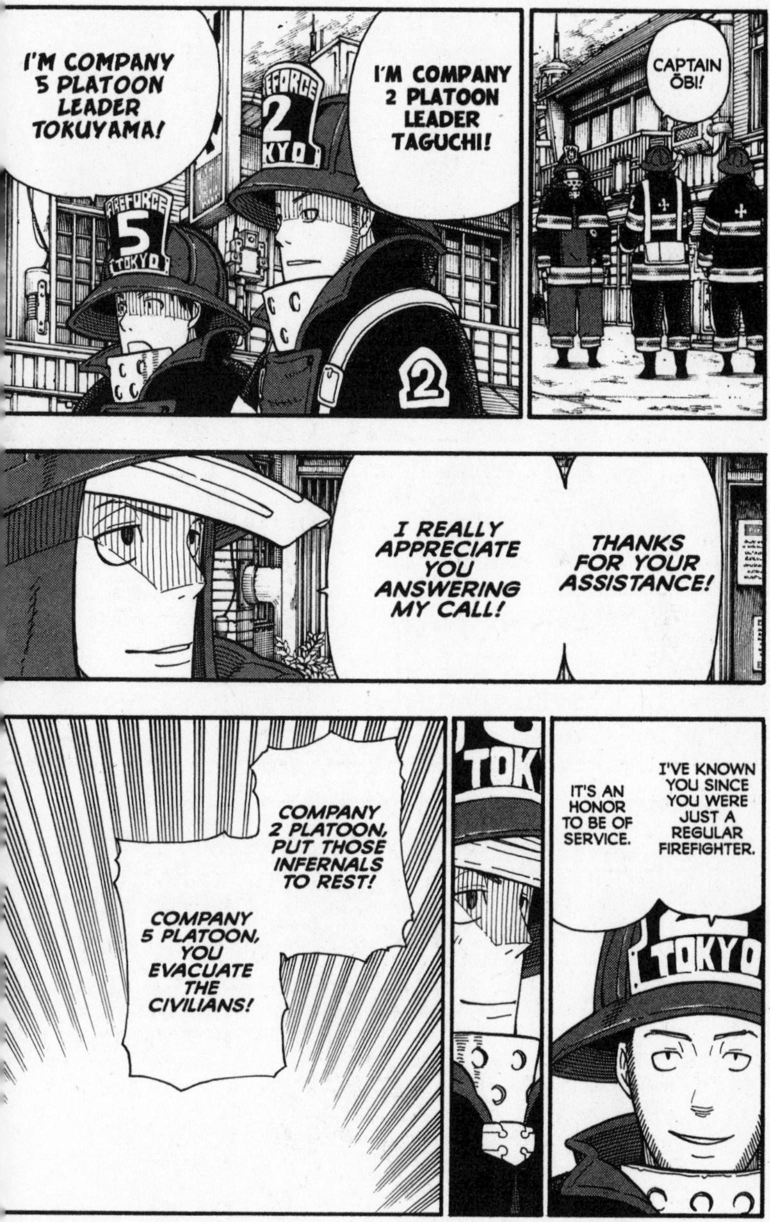
CAPTAIN ŌBI!
I'M COMPANY 2 PLATOON LEADER TAGUCHI!
I'M COMPANY 5 PLATOON LEADER TOKUYAMA!
THANKS FOR YOUR ASSISTANCE!
I REALLY APPRECIATE YOU ANSWERING MY CALL!
I'VE KNOWN YOU SINCE YOU WERE JUST A REGULAR FIREFIGHTER.
IT'S AN HONOR TO BE OF SERVICE.
COMPANY 2 PLATOON, PUT THOSE INFERNALS TO REST!
COMPANY 5 PLATOON, YOU EVACUATE THE CIVILIANS!

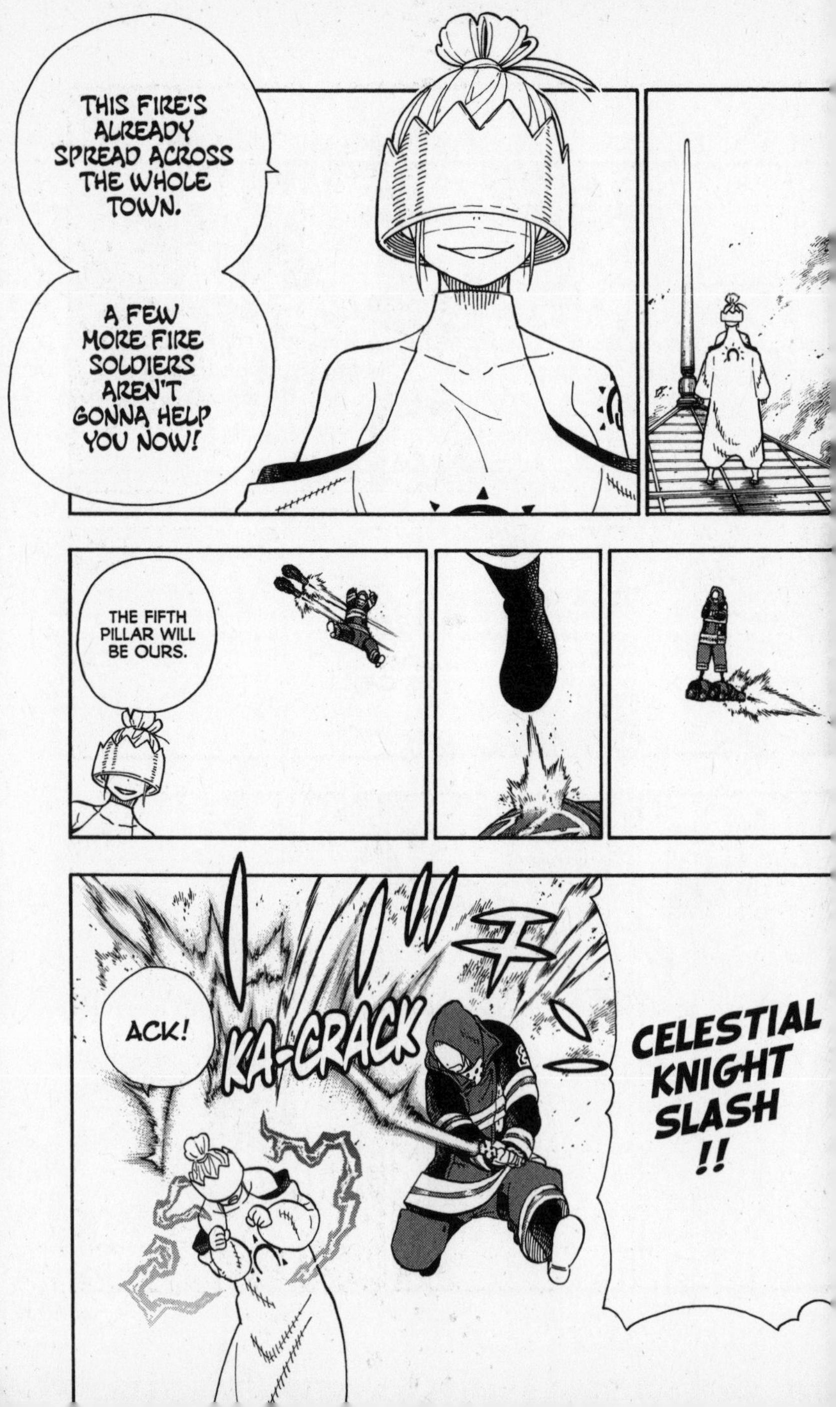
THIS FIRE'S ALREADY SPREAD ACROSS THE WHOLE TOWN.
A FEW MORE FIRE SOLDIERS AREN'T GONNA HELP YOU NOW!
THE FIFTH PILLAR WILL BE OURS.
CELESTIAL KNIGHT SLASH!!
KA-CRACK
ACK!

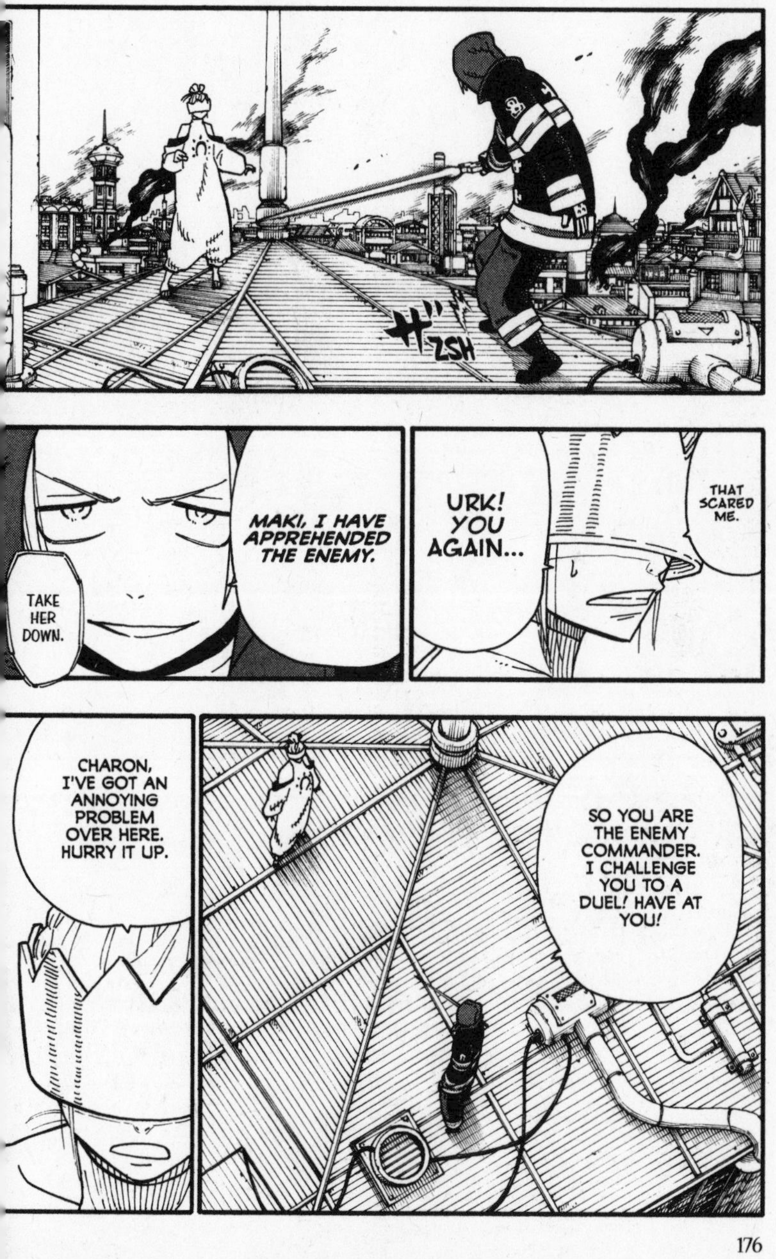
ZSH
THAT SCARED ME.
URK! YOU AGAIN...
MAKI, I HAVE APPREHENDED THE ENEMY.
TAKE HER DOWN.
SO YOU ARE THE ENEMY COMMANDER. I CHALLENGE YOU TO A DUEL! HAVE AT YOU!
CHARON, I'VE GOT AN ANNOYING PROBLEM OVER HERE. HURRY IT UP.

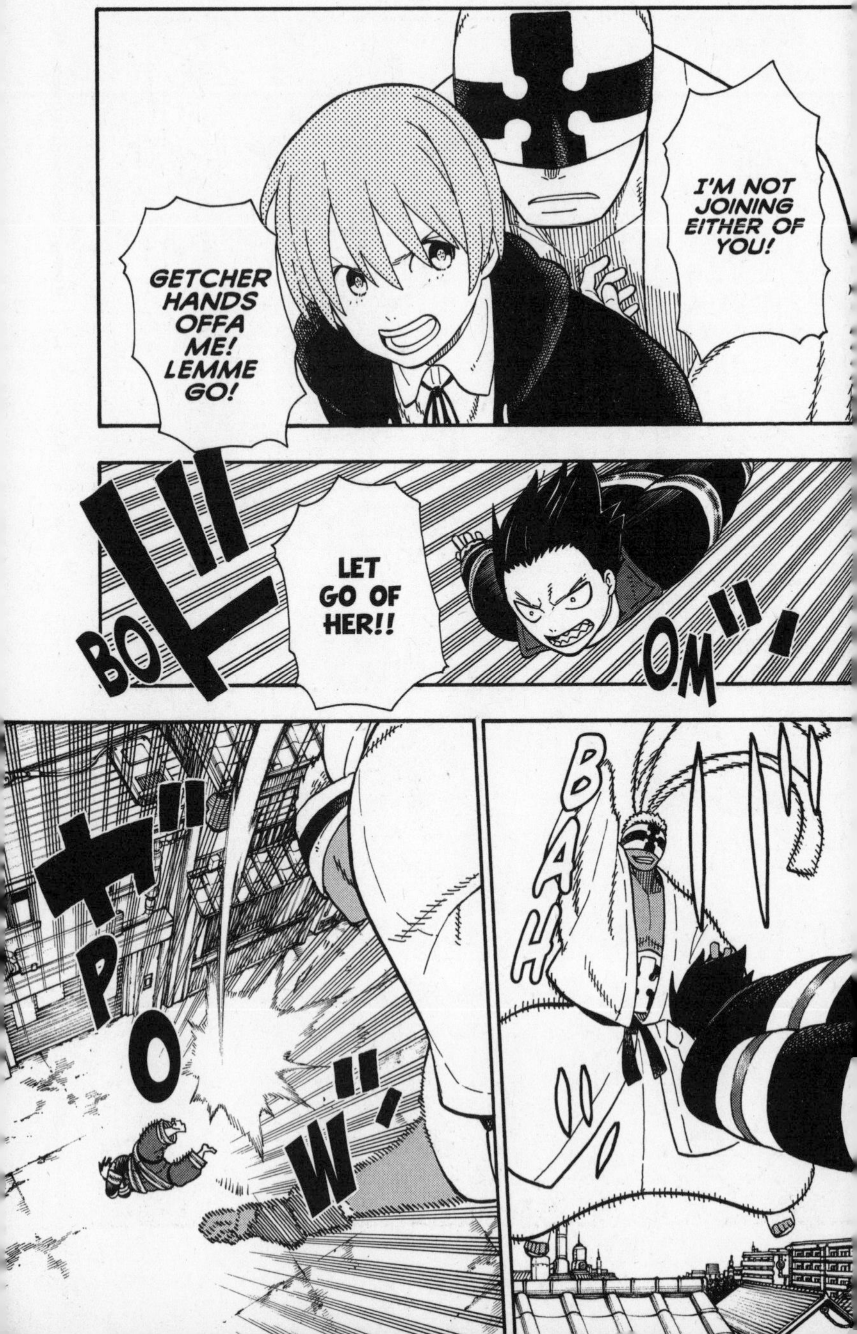
I'M NOT JOINING EITHER OF YOU!
GETCHER HANDS OFFA ME! LEMME GO!
BO
LET GO OF HER!!
OM
BAH
POW

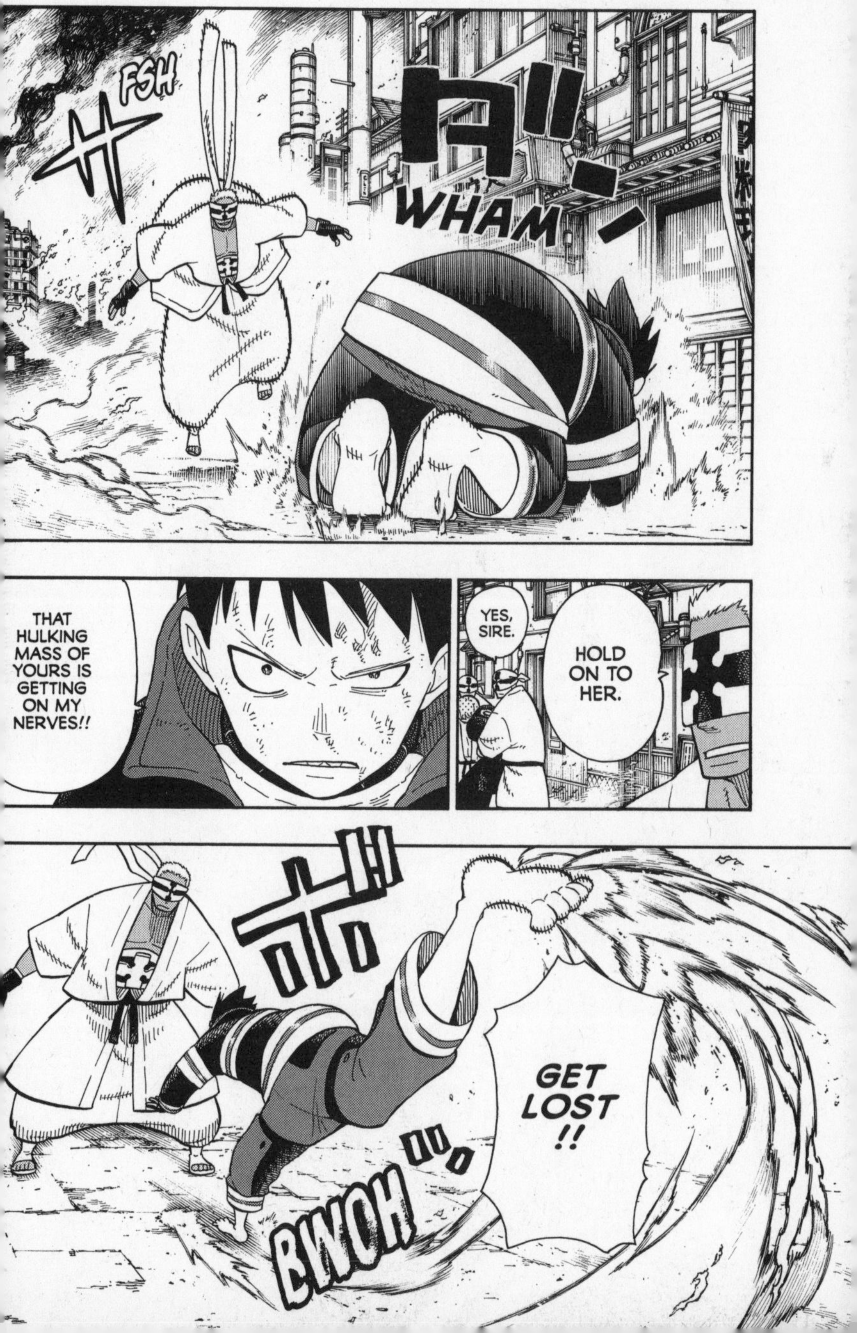
WHAM
FSH
HOLD ON TO HER.
YES, SIRE.
THAT HULKING MASS OF YOURS IS GETTING ON MY NERVES!!
GET LOST!!
BWOH

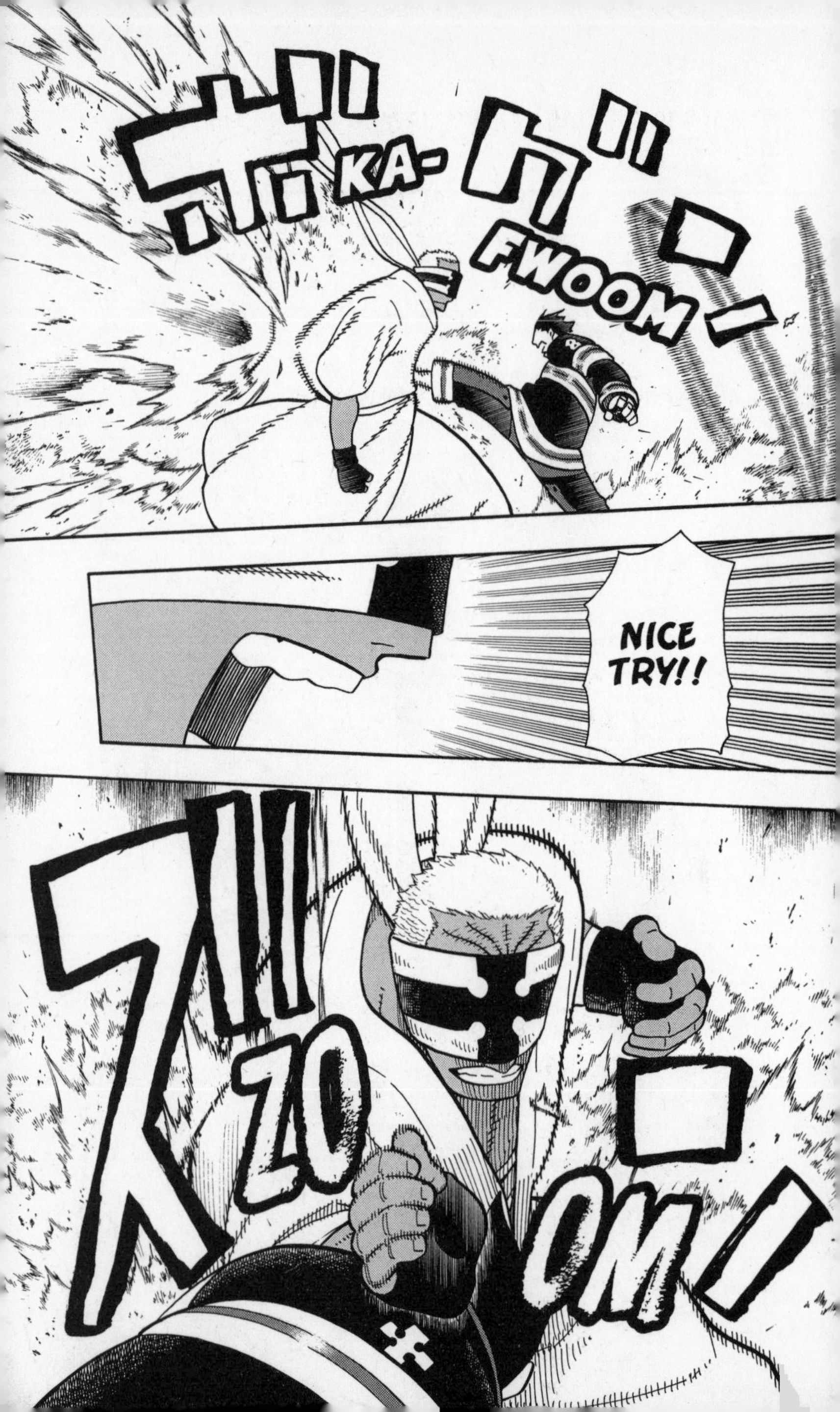
KA-FWOOM!
NICE TRY!!
ZOOM!

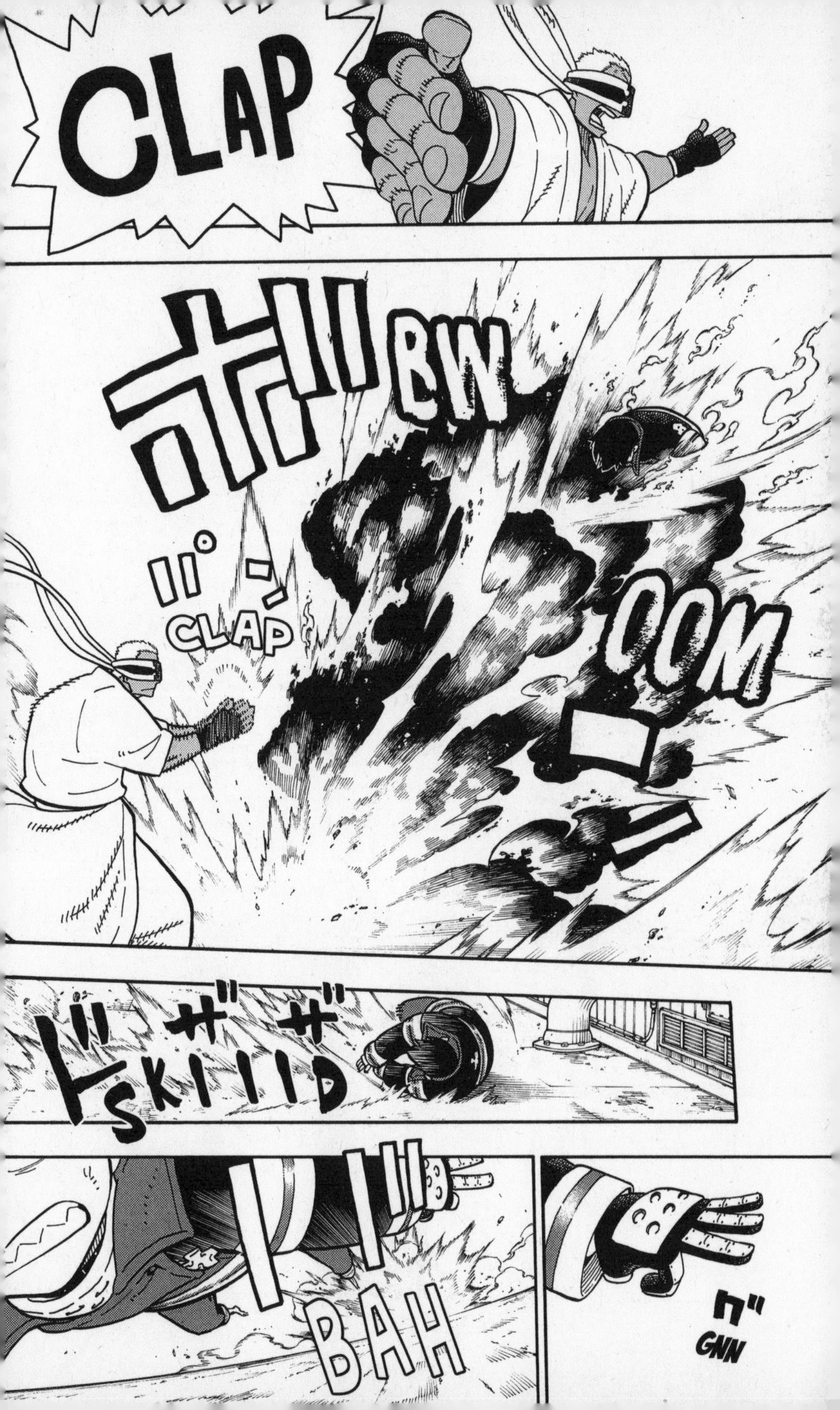
CLAP
BWOOM
CLAP
SKIIID
GNN
BAH

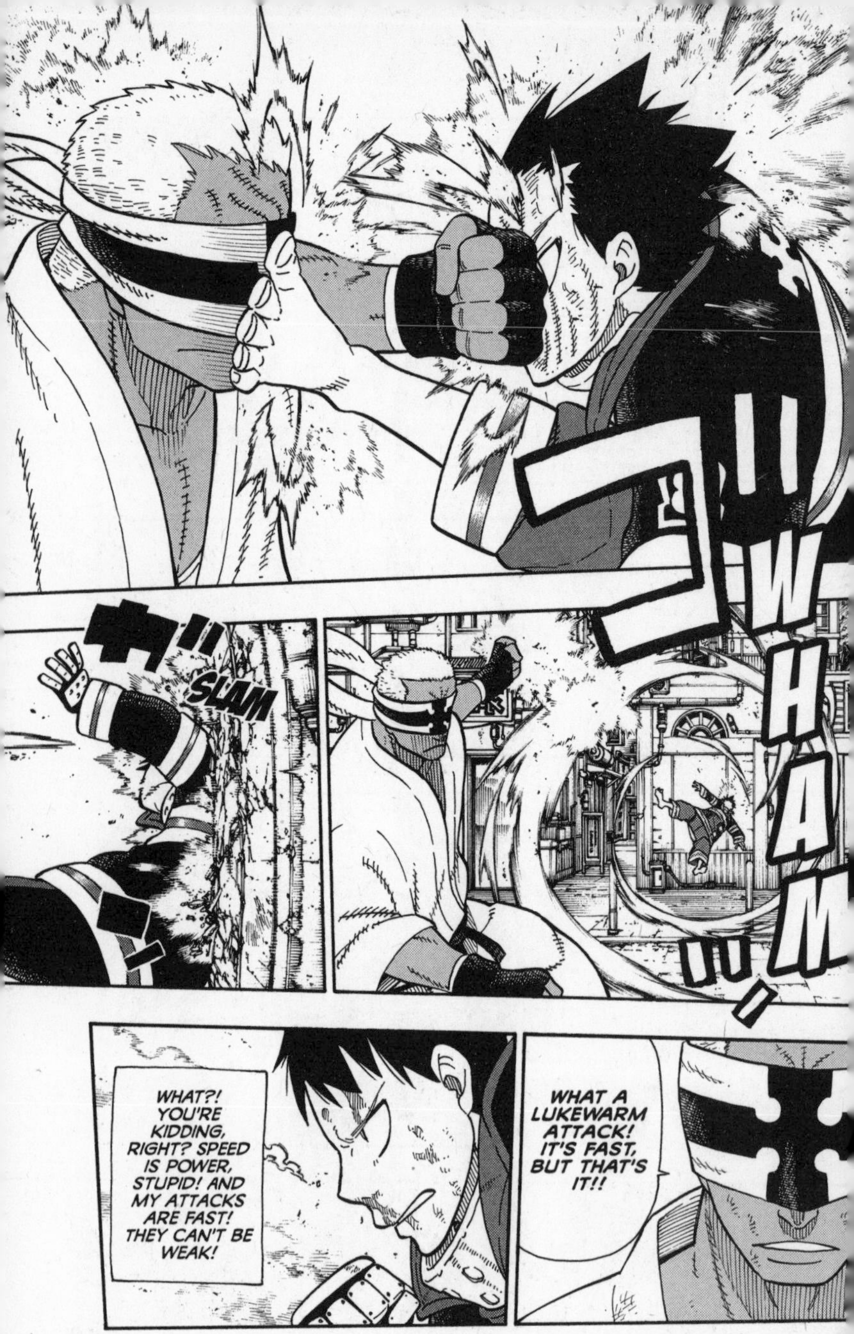
WHAM
SLAM
WHAT A LUKEWARM ATTACK! IT'S FAST, BUT THAT'S IT!!
WHAT?! YOU'RE KIDDING, RIGHT? SPEED IS POWER, STUPID! AND MY ATTACKS ARE FAST! THEY CAN'T BE WEAK!

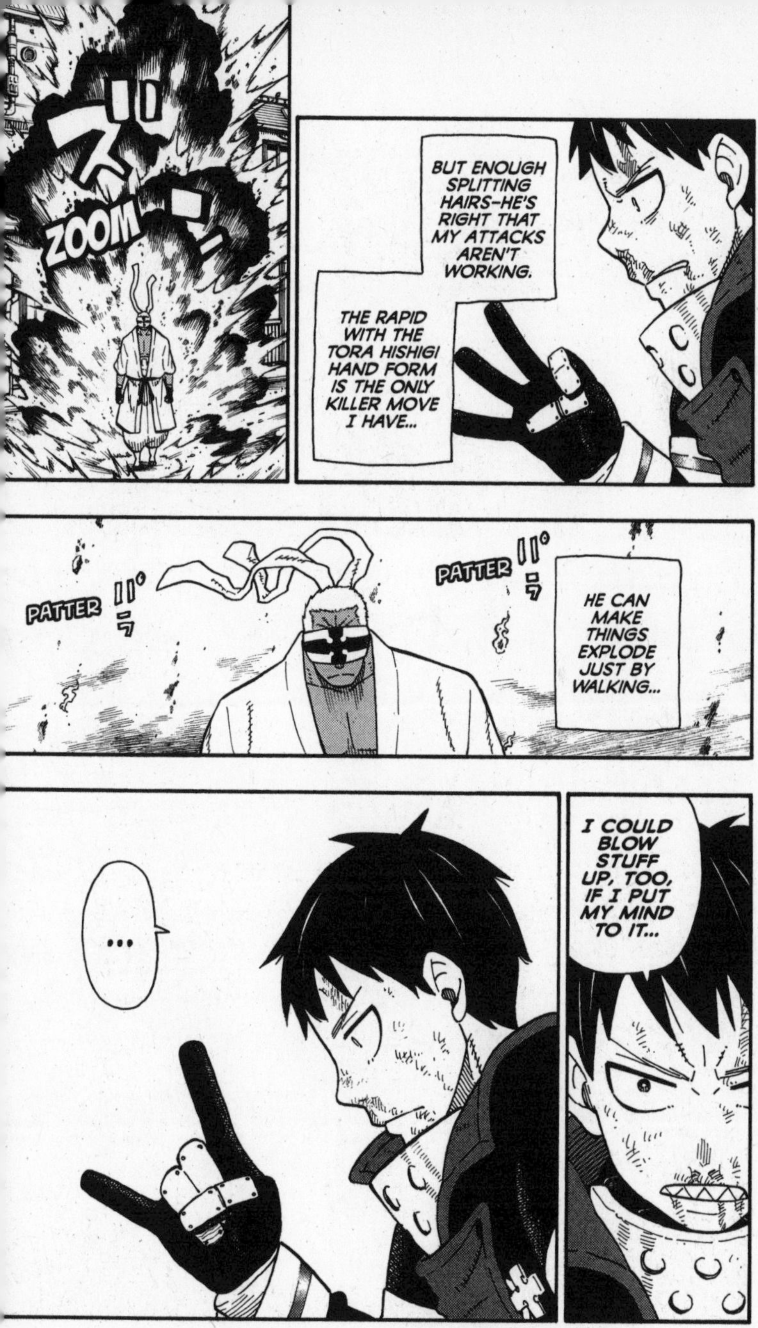
BUT ENOUGH SPLITTING HAIRS—HE'S RIGHT THAT MY ATTACKS AREN'T WORKING.
THE RAPID WITH THE TORA HISHIGI HAND FORM IS THE ONLY KILLER MOVE I HAVE...
ZOOM
HE CAN MAKE THINGS EXPLODE JUST BY WALKING...
PATTER
PATTER
I COULD BLOW STUFF UP, TOO, IF I PUT MY MIND TO IT...
...

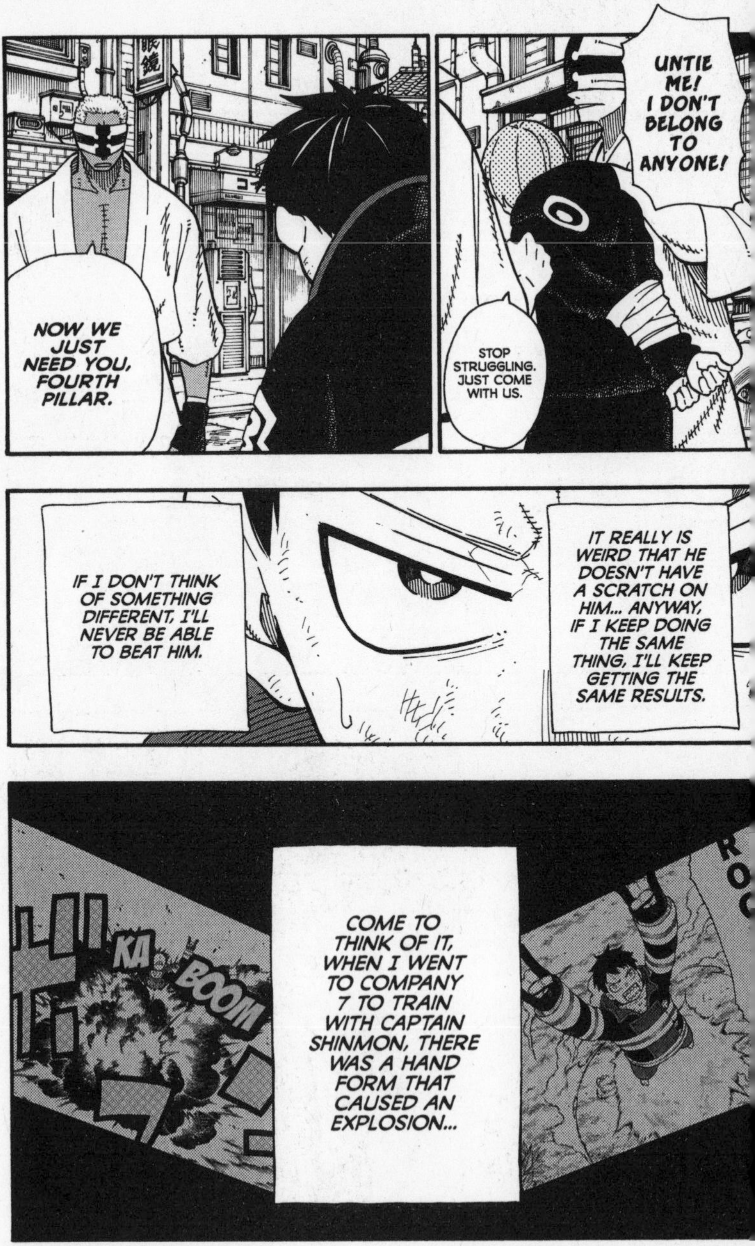
UNTIE ME! I DON'T BELONG TO ANYONE!
STOP STRUGGLING. JUST COME WITH US.
NOW WE JUST NEED YOU, FOURTH PILLAR.
IT REALLY IS WEIRD THAT HE DOESN'T HAVE A SCRATCH ON HIM... ANYWAY, IF I KEEP DOING THE SAME THING, I'LL KEEP GETTING THE SAME RESULTS.
IF I DON'T THINK OF SOMETHING DIFFERENT, I'LL NEVER BE ABLE TO BEAT HIM.
ROO
COME TO THINK OF IT, WHEN I WENT TO COMPANY 7 TO TRAIN WITH CAPTAIN SHINMON, THERE WAS A HAND FORM THAT CAUSED AN EXPLOSION...
KA BOOM

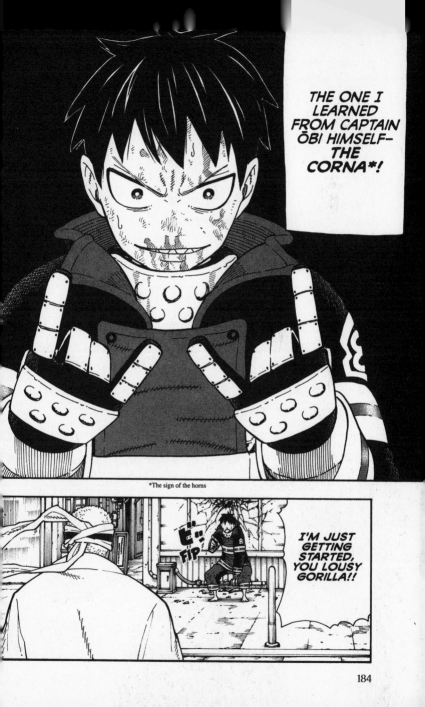

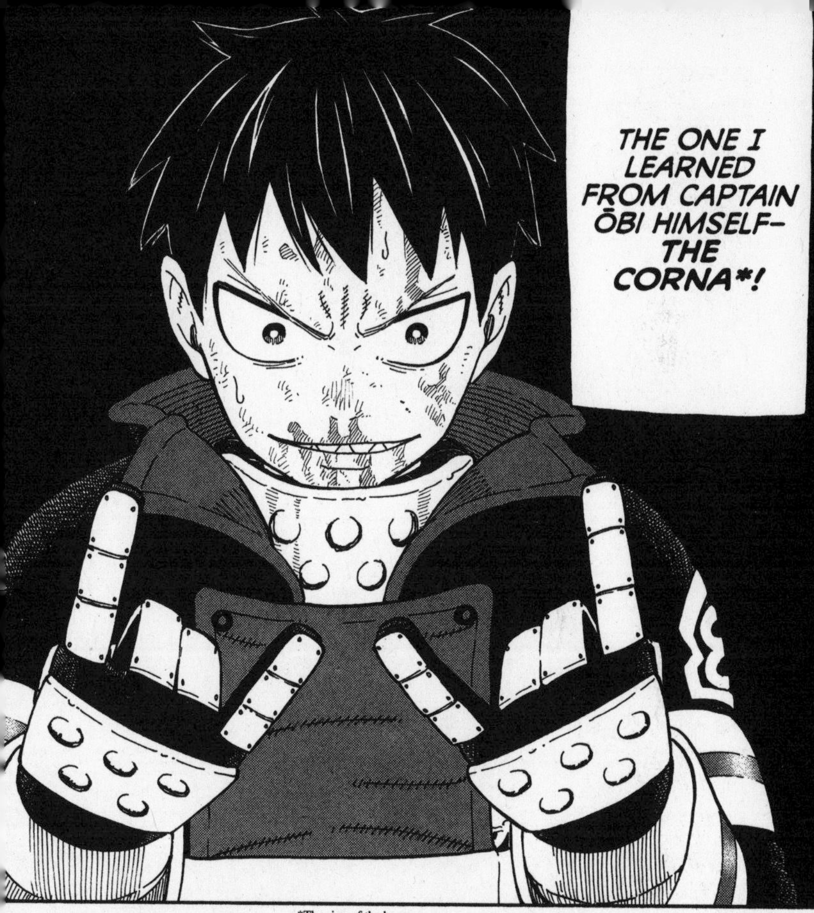
THE ONE I LEARNED FROM CAPTAIN ŌBI HIMSELF–THE CORNA*!

*The sign of the horns

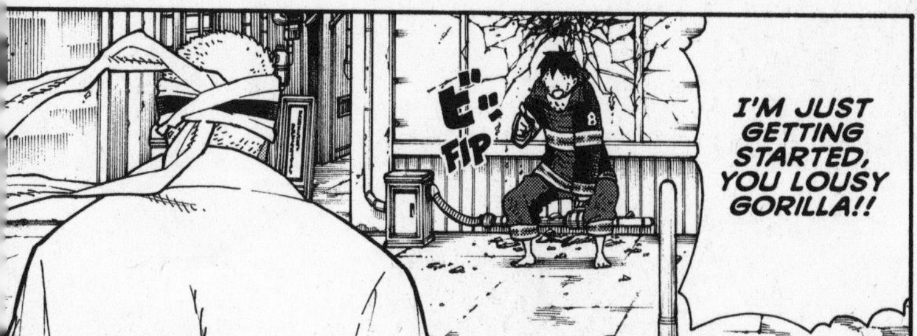
I'M JUST GETTING STARTED, YOU LOUSY GORILLA!!
FIP

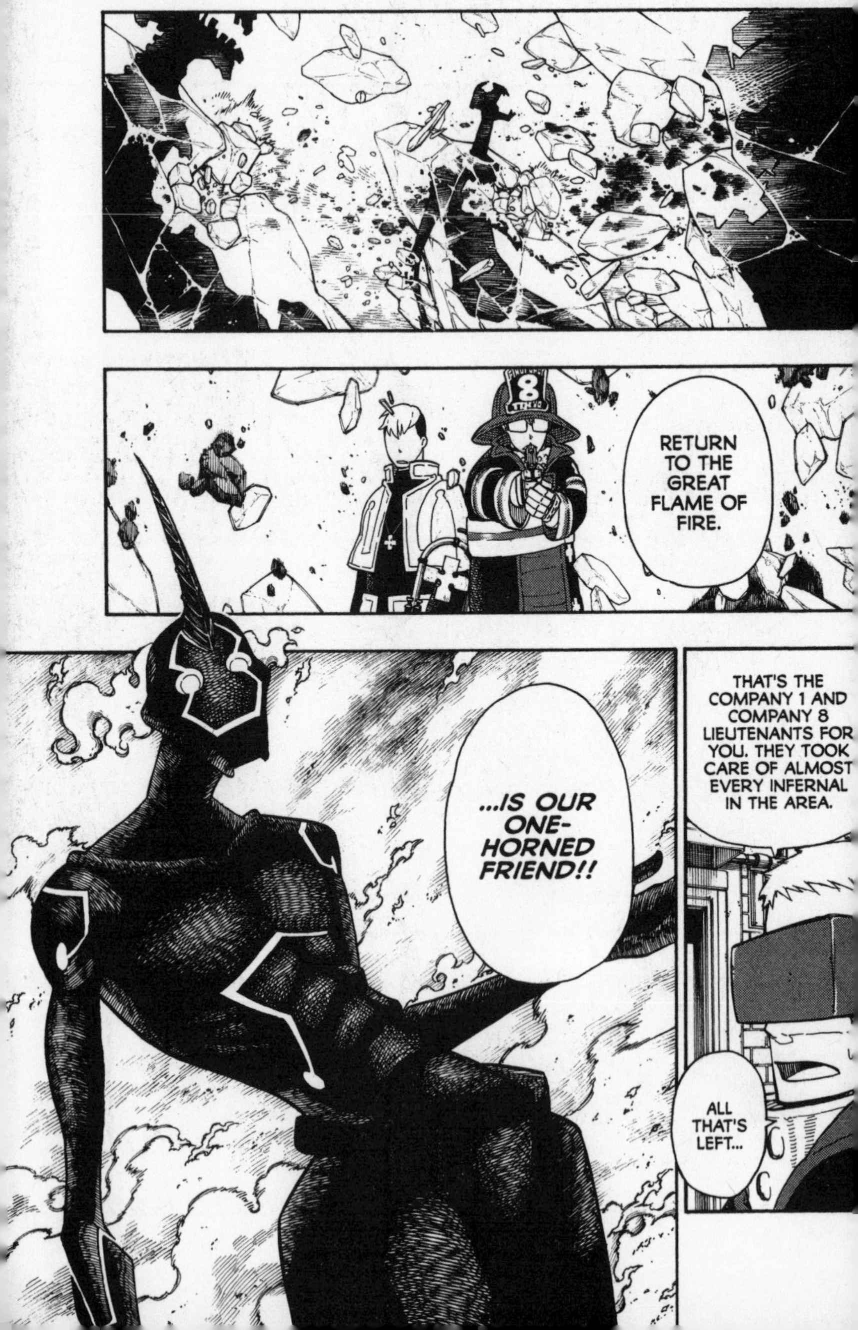
RETURN TO THE GREAT FLAME OF FIRE.
THAT'S THE COMPANY 1 AND COMPANY 8 LIEUTENANTS FOR YOU. THEY TOOK CARE OF ALMOST EVERY INFERNAL IN THE AREA.
ALL THAT'S LEFT...
...IS OUR ONE-HORNED FRIEND!!

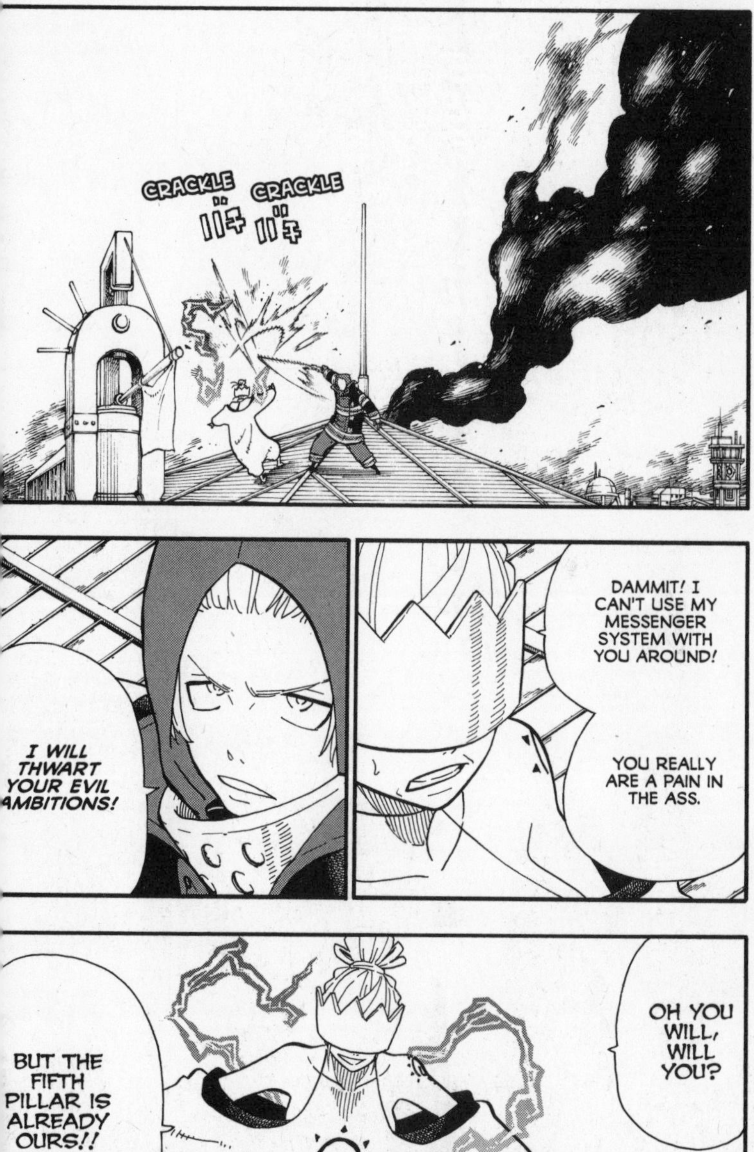

CRACKLE
CRACKLE
バチ
バチ
DAMMIT! I CAN'T USE MY MESSENGER SYSTEM WITH YOU AROUND!
YOU REALLY ARE A PAIN IN THE ASS.
I WILL THWART YOUR EVIL AMBITIONS!
OH YOU WILL, WILL YOU?
BUT THE FIFTH PILLAR IS ALREADY OURS!!

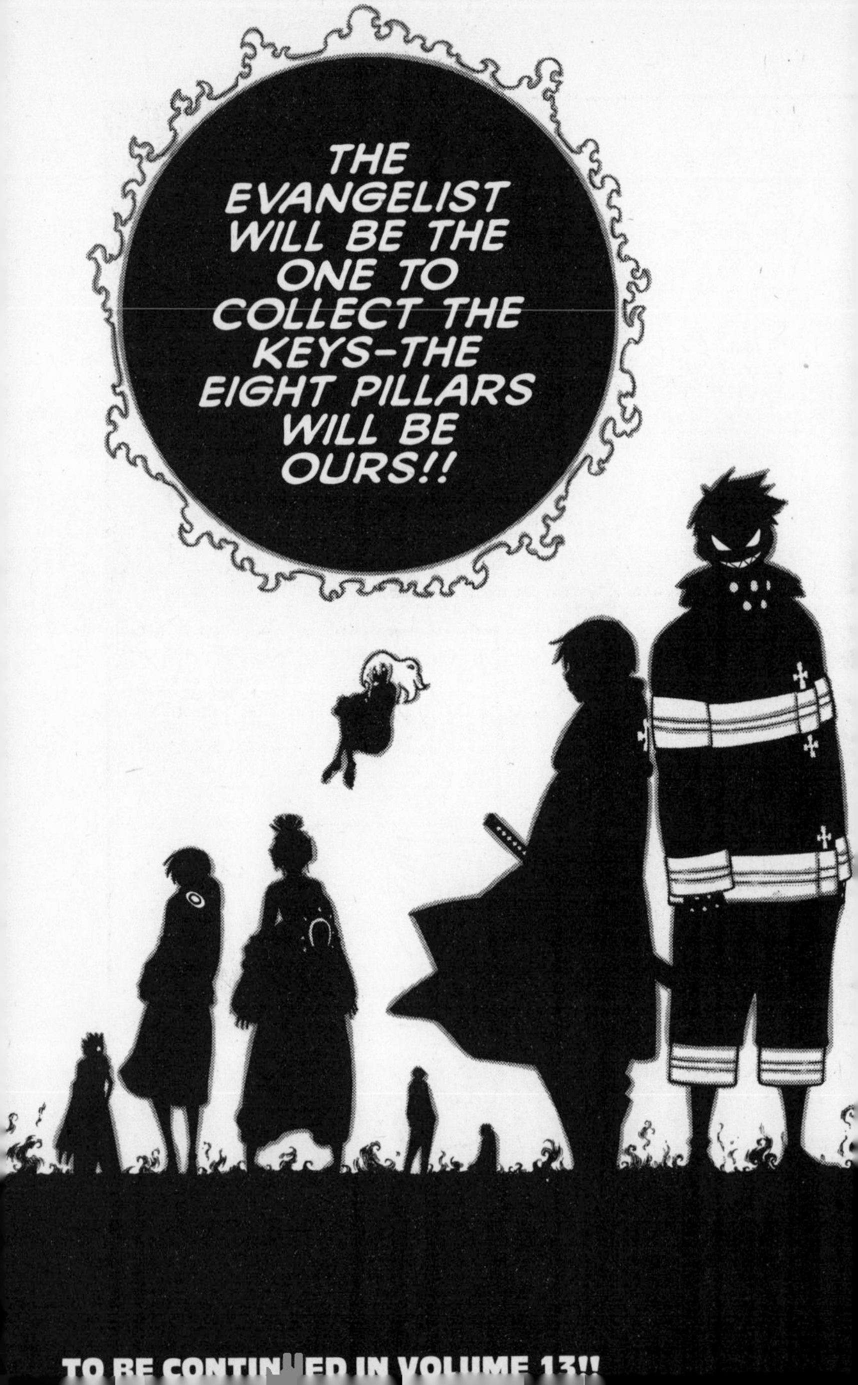
THE EVANGELIST WILL BE THE ONE TO COLLECT THE KEYS-THE EIGHT PILLARS WILL BE OURS!!

TO BE CONTINUED IN VOLUME 13!!

AFTERWORD MANGA: ATSUSHIYA

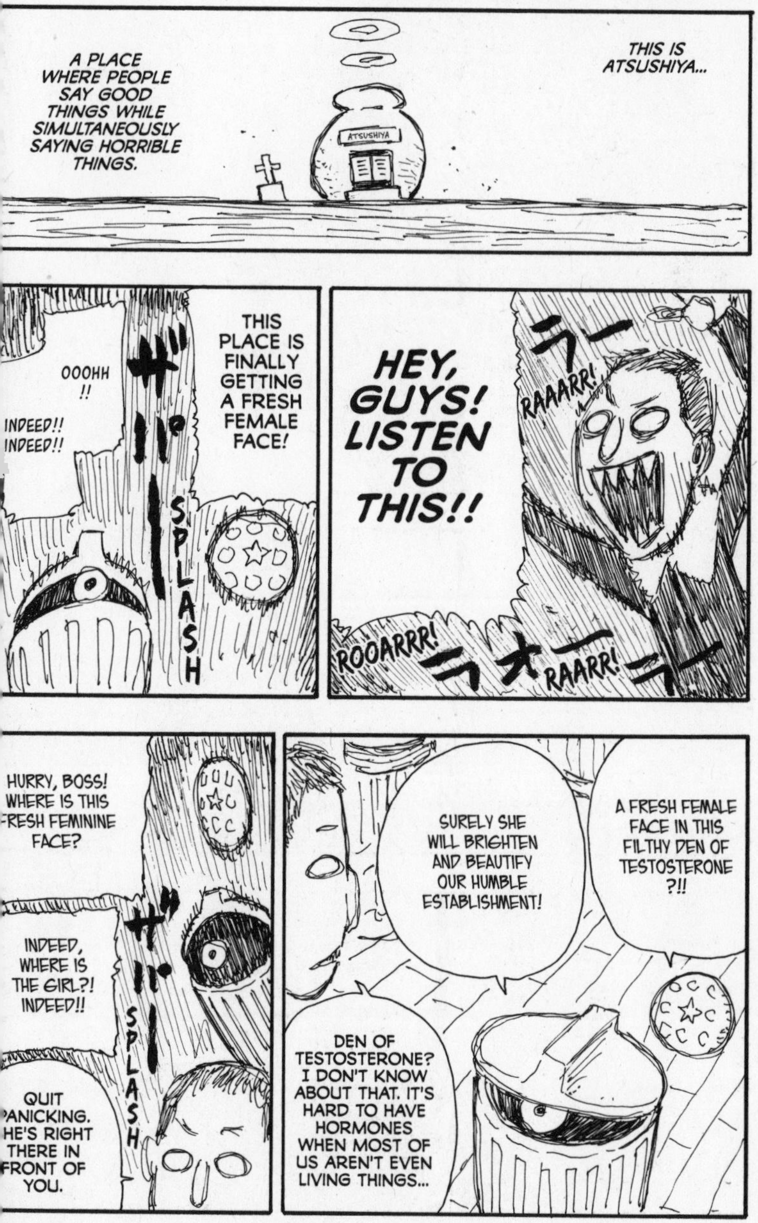
THIS IS ATSUSHIYA...
A PLACE WHERE PEOPLE SAY GOOD THINGS WHILE SIMULTANEOUSLY SAYING HORRIBLE THINGS.
ATSUSHIYA
HEY, GUYS! LISTEN TO THIS!!
RAAARR!
ROOARRR!
RAARR!
THIS PLACE IS FINALLY GETTING A FRESH FEMALE FACE!
SPLASH
OOOHH !!
INDEED!! INDEED!!
A FRESH FEMALE FACE IN THIS FILTHY DEN OF TESTOSTERONE ?!!
SURELY SHE WILL BRIGHTEN AND BEAUTIFY OUR HUMBLE ESTABLISHMENT!
DEN OF TESTOSTERONE? I DON'T KNOW ABOUT THAT. IT'S HARD TO HAVE HORMONES WHEN MOST OF US AREN'T EVEN LIVING THINGS...
HURRY, BOSS! WHERE IS THIS FRESH FEMININE FACE?
INDEED, WHERE IS THE GIRL?! INDEED!!
SPLASH
QUIT PANICKING. HE'S RIGHT THERE IN FRONT OF YOU.

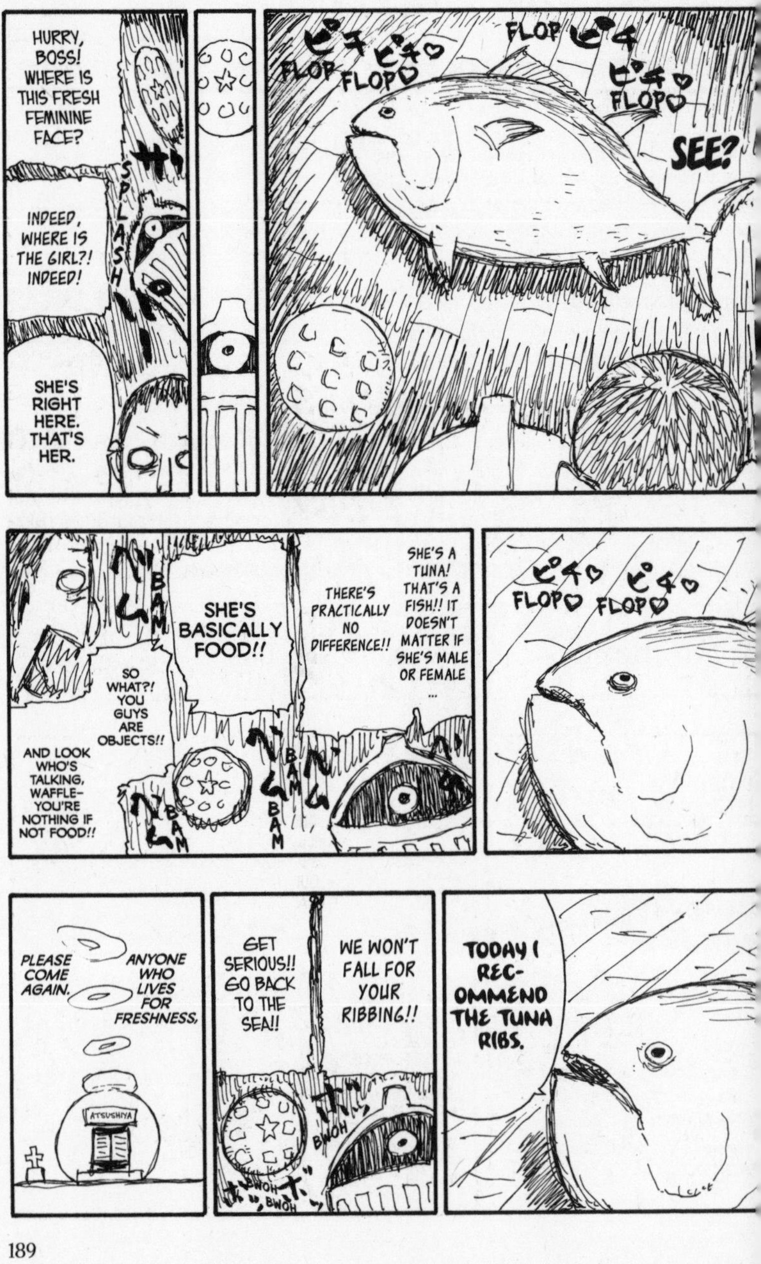
FLOP FLOP FLOP FLOP
SEE?
HURRY, BOSS! WHERE IS THIS FRESH FEMININE FACE?
SPLASH
INDEED, WHERE IS THE GIRL?! INDEED!
SHE'S RIGHT HERE. THAT'S HER.
FLOP FLOP
SHE'S A TUNA! THAT'S A FISH!! IT DOESN'T MATTER IF SHE'S MALE OR FEMALE ...
THERE'S PRACTICALLY NO DIFFERENCE!!
SHE'S BASICALLY FOOD!!
BAM
SO WHAT?! YOU GUYS ARE OBJECTS!!
AND LOOK WHO'S TALKING, WAFFLE- YOU'RE NOTHING IF NOT FOOD!!
BAM BAM BAM
TODAY I REC-OMMEND THE TUNA RIBS.
WE WON'T FALL FOR YOUR RIBBING!!
GET SERIOUS!! GO BACK TO THE SEA!!
BWOH BWOH BWOH
ANYONE WHO LIVES FOR FRESHNESS,
PLEASE COME AGAIN.
ATSUSHIYA

Translation Notes:

Pinched pennies up in smoke, page 13

There is a Japanese term for being in financial straits, *hi no kuruma*, which literally means "fire chariot." It refers to a supernatural creature that is believed to take sinners to the afterlife—in other words, someone is in so much trouble financially that that person is on their way to hell. Here, Arthur says that their fire chariot has burned to ash, meaning what little money his family had left has also disappeared.

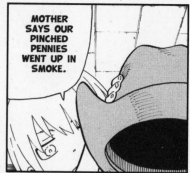

MOTHER SAYS OUR PINCHED PENNIES WENT UP IN SMOKE.

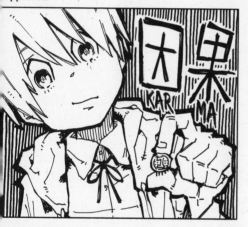

Karma, page 109

The Japanese word used here can also mean "cause and effect," in the sense of "the effects that befall someone are caused by their actions." The word is *inga*, but can be pronounced *inka*.

Big Fire, page 129

This is an homage to a famous woodblock print called *The Great Wave Off Kanagawa* by Katsushika Hokusai. In the original version, a large wave threatens boats in the water, and frames Mt. Fuji, which can be seen far in the distance.

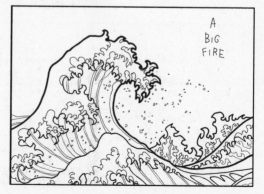

A BIG FIRE

FIRE FORCE

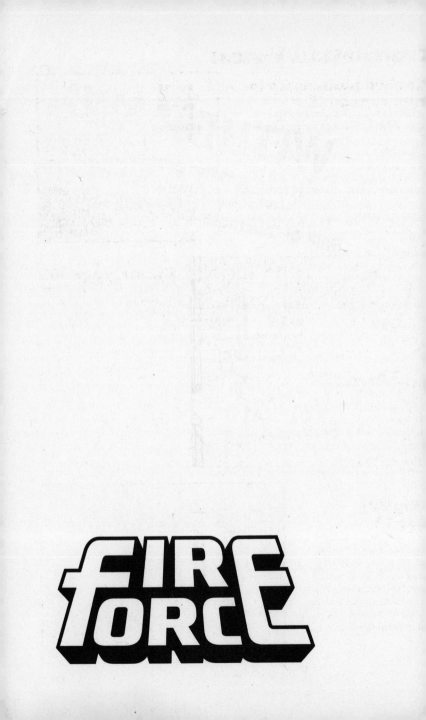

ire Force volume 12 is a work of fiction. Names, characters, places, and incidents are the roducts of the author's imagination or are used fictitiously. Any resemblance to actual vents, locales, or persons, living or dead, is entirely coincidental.

Kodansha Comics Trade Paperback Original.

ublished in the United States by Kodansha Comics, an imprint of Kodansha USA ublishing, LLC, New York.

ublication rights for this English edition arranged through Kodansha Ltd., Tokyo.

rst published in Japan in 2018 by Kodansha Ltd., Tokyo.

BN 978-1-63236-663-4

inted in the United States of America.

ww.kodanshacomics.com

8 7 6 5 4 3 2 1

anslation: Alethea Nibley & Athena Nibley
ettering: AndWorld Design
diting: Lauren Scanlan
odansha Comics edition cover design: Phil Balsman